How to
INTERPRET DREAMS
and
VISIONS

OPENING
THE
GATES
OF
HEAVEN

PERRY STONE

CHARISMA
HOUSE

Most CHARISMA HOUSE BOOK GROUP products are available at special quantity discounts for bulk purchase for sales promotions, premiums, fund-raising, and educational needs. For details, write Charisma House Book Group, 600 Rinehart Road, Lake Mary, Florida 32746, or telephone (407) 333-0600.

HOW TO INTERPRET DREAMS AND VISIONS/OPENING THE GATES OF HEAVEN by Perry Stone
Published by Charisma House
Charisma Media/Charisma House Book Group
600 Rinehart Road
Lake Mary, Florida 32746
www.charismahouse.com

Cover design by Justin Evans

Visit the author's website at www.voe.org.

BOOK I

How to
INTERPRET
DREAMS
and
VISIONS

PERRY STONE

CHARISMA
HOUSE

DEDICATION

I t is only fitting that I dedicate this book to the man who has had the greatest influence upon my life and ministry, my father, Fred Stone. Dad's life and ministry have been of impeccable integrity. He was recognized among his peers as a spiritual, praying man who believed that the Lord still spoke to His children—through the Word of God and through the manifestations of the Holy Spirit. From the time he was a teenager, God visited him in both visions and dreams, many times to warn individuals of coming danger and at other times to bring a word of wisdom in assisting a believer through a time of crisis. Throughout this book I will share some of the remarkable visitations he received to illustrate key points as revealed in Scripture.

On several occasions Dad's dreams have saved the lives of family members as they heeded each warning he gave and were guided by what he said. The same anointing for seeing spiritual warnings in dreams and visions began marking my own life as a young minister. Since the Bible indicates that in the last days God will visit us through dreams and visions, we need a full understanding of this method of receiving revelation from heaven and how to understand the messages from our heavenly Father. May the insight from these pages open a new avenue of knowledge and understanding of how God warns, leads, and guides our steps, and how He reveals His concern about our protection, direction, and spiritual wisdom for daily living.

CONTENTS

INTRODUCTION

In June of 1996 I had a spiritual experience that later proved to be a warning of a future terrorist attack upon America. I was ministering at the Assembly of God in Brooksville, Florida, and was eating dinner at a local member's home on a beautiful Sunday afternoon. After eating, I was suddenly overwhelmed with a feeling of extreme tiredness, so I excused myself from the table to lie down and rest. It was about three o'clock when I lay across the bed, attempting to read my Bible. Within minutes I laid my head on the Bible and immediately went into a very deep sleep.

My very brief sleep was abruptly interrupted by a full-color vision! I was standing at the bottom of a paved road, looking up toward the top of a hill where the road ended at a large concrete wall. There were red-brick, one-story homes on the left and right sides of the road, with sidewalks climbing the hill on either side. Just above the wall in a clear blue sky I saw a black cloud that was a perfect square. I was curious as to what this was, so I began walking up the left sidewalk toward the top of the hill. I noticed I was barefoot, which I later learned was an indication in a dream of not being prepared for what was coming.

I climbed on top of the wall and saw a strange sight. It was a large cornfield with rows of full-grown corn. As I looked from left to right, it appeared endless. However, it was several hundreds yards across in front of me. Directly in the center at the end of the field was a large tower-looking building, the exact form of the World Trade Center in New York. It was shrouded in a solid black cloud from the top to the bottom. The more frightening part was the five grayish, spinning tornadoes that were appearing to form in front of this large tower. The tornadoes were motionless, but suddenly the left one began spinning violently, throwing sparks and other objects out from it. It was as though the second one received its strength from the first one, and soon all five were emitting sparks, spinning with great grayish smoke. I distinctly remember they were not black as normal tornadoes are.

As the left one began spinning, it moved from in front of the tower into the cornfield and began ripping corn out by the roots, leaving an empty straight path. The other four were preparing to move in the same manner—each destroying a line of corn from the back to the front of the corn in the field. That is when I turned, running down the hill yelling, "We must get into the cleft of the rock..." I repeated the same phrase twice.

I suddenly realized I was lying on the bed and my eyes were open. I was so overwhelmed, not knowing what I had witnessed, that I left the room to speak with a fellow minister, Don Channel, who was traveling with me. I told him the vision and said the tower looked like the World Trade Center shrouded in black, but I was uncertain as to what it meant. That night I informed the church what I saw and immediately began sharing the vision with others. The interpretation was unclear—as often happens in a spiritual warning. The understanding either must be prayed about or will be understood as the vision begins to unfold. For several years I told the vision, and in 1999 an artist, J. Michael Leonard, drew a sketch of what I described to him in the vision. He also drew a picture of a second vision I experienced months later, which I felt tied into this one.

THE SECOND VISITATION

Months later I experienced a second vision that involved five gray tornadoes. This time I was in a large city and began to hear people screaming, "The storm is coming; what should we do?" I led them into a downtown church constructed from large grayish stones. I saw three ethnic groups: African American, Hispanic, and Asian men and women all huddled together with their ethnic groups. Some were in shock, and others were in prayer.

Looking through an opening of the church door, I saw five grayish tornadoes, one following another, spinning wildly. This time there were soda cans, computer paper, and all sorts of debris being thrown from the rolling and spinning gray clouds. A total of five tornadoes passed by. When we went outside, there were intact downtown office buildings that were sitting empty, the offices ruined and incapable of conducting business. The entire city was stunned, and outsiders were setting up areas on the streets with food, water, clothes, and even children's toys for those within the city who had experienced some form of destruction from these storms.

I knew these two visions were linked; however, the understanding was uncertain. When I shared these two visions with partners at our main meeting in Pigeon Forge, Tennessee, later that year, I told them I believed there would be a major terrorist attack on the World Trade

Center at some point in the future. After showing the drawings in 1999 during a national prophetic television special and still nothing had happened, I put the sketches in my office closet at work and said nothing further about them—until the morning of September 4, 2001. While cleaning the closet, I pulled the drawings out and told a coworker in our office, Mel Colbeck, "Mel, this is a terror attack coming against the World Trade Center in the future. I don't know when, but it will happen!"

THEN CAME 9/11

On the morning of September 11, 2001, I was working at our ministry center in the *Manna-Fest* order fulfillment room when my secretary ran in and announced, "Someone has flown a plane into the World Trade Center." I was thinking that a small plane had struck the tower when a pilot died in flight. Within a few moments she said, "A second plane was flown into the second tower, and it is believed to be a terrorist attack." That is when the reality of the five-year-old vision hit me! I went home, and on the television screen I saw the black smoke from the first plane pouring upward, forming that black square I saw in the vision. Later, when both towers collapsed, I witnessed the fulfillment of the vision with the *gray smoke* rolling down the street, being described by news commentators as a "tornado," sending multitudes running into buildings for safety. I would later learn from ground zero workers that many people also found refuge in a large church called Trinity Church, seeking safety and praying. It was the exact description of the building and activity occurring within the church I had seen in the second vision.

At that moment, the meaning of five tornadoes was not making sense. I thought there would be five attacks (the Pentagon, the plane crash in Pennsylvania, and perhaps one more making five). However, within forty-eight hours it was clear. Trade centers one and two, the twin towers, were attacked, resulting in the eventual destruction of trade center buildings three, four, five, six, and seven—five other buildings housing thousands of businesses. Other office complexes were ruined by the dust and were closed. Of course there were many relief organizations bringing food, water, and needed resources to both the people in need and the workers at ground zero. What about the cornfield?

In the story of Joseph, the cornfield represented a famine coming to Egypt. The 9/11 attacks did not disrupt food. However, corn in the Old Testament was a staple that was also sold and was a vital part of the economy of the ancient world. In the New Testament parables, the field represents the world, and the corn (wheat) the harvest. Looking back in retrospect, the trade center was the *World* Trade Center with offices representing numerous nations housed within the towers (thus the field—the *world*). Also, corn can represent the economy, and the 9/11 attacks had a devastating impact not only on New York City but also upon the travel industry in general. Thus the corn was *rooted up*, indicating that those in these five buildings would no longer have jobs in those buildings! I later realized that the concrete wall from which I viewed the storms may have been an allusion to *Wall Street*, which was not impacted by the storms in the manner that the other buildings were. Getting in the *cleft of the rock* was a direct reference to Christ, who is the rock of our salvation and a shelter in the time of storm.

WHAT ABOUT YOUR DREAMS OR VISIONS?

Have you ever dreamed a dream that was quite troubling and it remained with you for many days? Have you ever experienced a full-color vision while sleeping—one that is so vivid that you can smell fragrances and feel the cool wind brushing your face? It is possible that your dream has a spiritual connotation and that your vision is definitely some form of a message from the presence of the Almighty.

We humans have difficulty interpreting the meanings of a spiritual dream or vision, as they often contain unique or unusual symbolism. Why does God often use symbolism and not allow us to comprehend a simple, plain meaning for the interpretation? What does the symbolism mean? How can you know if a night encounter seen during your sleep is from the Lord and not just the apparition of a wild imagination? In this book I have detailed biblical insight to assist the reader in understanding the answers to these and many more questions.

It was the Lord Himself who proclaimed in a biblical prophecy that in the last days He would pour out His Spirit upon all flesh, with one major result being that "young men shall see visions...old men shall dream dreams" (Acts 2:17). If the Holy Spirit is going to give to the body of Christ heavenly warnings, divine revelations, and practical instructions through visions or dreams, then believers must be well informed about the methods and meanings of these special and unique manifestations. This is what this book is all about.

All of the best for you and your family,

—PERRY STONE
Founder of Voice of Evangelism and Host of *Manna-Fest*

one

THE LAST DAYS—
TIME TO PIERCE THE VEIL

But their minds were blinded. For until this day the same veil remains unlifted in the reading of the Old Testament, because the veil is taken away in Christ. But even to this day, when Moses is read, a veil lies on their heart. Nevertheless when one turns to the Lord, the veil is taken away. Now the Lord is the Spirit; and where the Spirit of the Lord is, there is liberty.

« 2 Corinthians 3:14–17 »

The spirit world is as real as the air we breathe and the water we drink. The natural realm is a reflection of the spirit world. Earthly things are patterned after heavenly things. (See Hebrews 8:1–5.) Our world consists of trees, rivers, mountains, and cities. The heavenly city, New Jerusalem, has the tree of life, the crystal river of life, and a mountain where God is worshiped called *Mount Zion* (Rev. 22:1–5). These heavenly realities were the original Creation that was reflected on Earth when God created man.

Humanity has struggled to believe in a world that cannot be seen with the eyes, touched with the hands, or smelled when we breathe. To the skeptic, angels are myths, and demonic spirits are the dark imagination of Hollywood scripts. The prevailing attitude is the *Thomas syndrome,* which says, "Unless I can see it and touch it, I will never believe it" (John 20:25, author's paraphrase). The fact is that there is an invisible veil covering both the natural eyes and the spiritual understanding of men and women, and only when the veil is lifted or *pierced* can the realities of the invisible realm become visible. The Bible is a book written by forty different authors over a period of about fifteen hundred years of time that tells the story of men called *prophets* who were inspired of the Lord and who pierced this veil and saw marvelous eternal and heavenly images that brought to mankind the revelation of God.

Paul wrote that there is a veil, similar to scales, over the eyes of our understanding that clouds the light of God's revelation from entering into our minds and enlightening us with life-changing insight. If we live behind this veil, then we will never know or experience God's best for us. This veil, which at times manifests as a lack of interest in spiritual matters, a dullness in our understanding, or a spirit of unbelief toward the idea of Bible-based spiritual manifestations, *must be lifted* to experience the unseen. This ability to see the future was the gift that set apart the biblical prophets from their false counterparts in surrounding idolatrous nations. These Hebrew visionaries had a reputation for knowing the unknown behind closed doors.

One such example can be seen when a Syrian general sent his army to capture one of God's prophets, Elisha. When Elisha's servant saw the army, fear gripped him. However, after Elisha prayed for the eyes of his servant to be opened, the fear turned to faith as the servant saw horses and chariots of fire encamped round about them both, forming a protective hedge. (See 2 Kings 6:8–17.) There is a covering of some sort on our physical eyes, which prevents us from seeing the activity of the spirit world. However, when we sleep, we are still able to *see* images through dreams or visions. In Scripture, men like the apostle John recorded these dreams and visions. John was on an island when he suddenly saw a "door in heaven open," or as we would say, "heaven open," and this opening projected his mind and spirit into another world, a world just as real as the world we live in. (See Revelation 4:1; 19:11.) These two biblical incidents from Revelation indicate two important facts: something occurs on Earth and something occurs in heaven to cause information to be released and the veil removed. On Earth our eyes must be "opened." This happens when our inner vision, which creates the images in our brain at night, receives information from the heavenly realm, which "opens," allowing eternal information to pass from the heavenly realm to the earthly realm.

One question posed by sincere seekers is: "Why would God be concerned about revealing events to us that have not yet occurred?" A simple answer is that He does so to prepare us for something or to cause us to intercede in prayer to prevent or to change a situation. For example, when King Hezekiah was informed by Isaiah to set his house in order because he would soon die, the king began to earnestly pray, and his death was delayed for fifteen years (Isa. 38:1–5).

Another reason God is concerned is because He knows we need to understand certain events in the future.

WHY IS THE SPIRIT WORLD VEILED?

Human eyes cannot see into the spirit world. God is a Spirit (John 4:24). Angels are spirits (Heb. 1:13–14). Satan's kingdom is organized into four levels of spirit rebels (Eph. 6:12), and every man is a tripartite creation of a body, a soul, and a spirit, or, as some teach, a spirit with a soul living in a body (1 Thess. 5:23).

In the time of Adam and Eve, God entered the Garden of Eden and communicated directly with man by walking through the garden in the cool of the day (Gen. 3:8). Adam and Eve could see and hear God clearly. After they fell into sin, "the eyes of both of them were opened," and they saw they were naked and felt shame (Gen. 3:7). Although their eyes were opened, at the same time their eyes were veiled. From that moment forward, angelic visitors appeared in the form of a vision, a dream, or would take upon themselves human form, just as the two angelic messengers did when instructed by the Almighty to investigate the sins of Sodom. (See Genesis 19.) Even the writer of Hebrews wrote to be careful when entertaining a stranger because you might not be aware that it is an angel (Heb. 13:2).

If our eyes could be opened and the veil lifted, we would continually see angels, demonic entities, and other forms of spirit beings. While some may wish to see into the invisible realm, the fact is that when great men of God and Hebrew prophets have pierced this veil and seen, for example, angels in their full glory, the reactions have normally been to fall down and be gripped with an overwhelming feeling of fear. Abraham fell into a deep trance (Gen. 15:12) and fell on his face when God talked to him (Gen. 17:3, 17). Ezekiel describes seeing the Almighty upon His throne, with cherubim and amazing heavenly beings appearing like wheels spinning within wheels (Ezek. 1), and he too fell upon his face (v. 28). In several instances when a vision of God or the angelic realm manifested, the prophet fell down upon his face (Ezek. 9:8; 43:3; 44:4). Daniel described an angelic visitor with brass-colored arms and feet, white hair, a gold belt, and eyes like fire. His reaction was so visibly powerful that even the men with him who did not see the vision became overwhelmed and began "quaking" and fled, hiding themselves (Dan. 10:5–7, KJV). Daniel found himself on his face with no strength remaining in his body (vv. 8–9). When John saw the resurrected Christ in heaven, he "fell at His feet as dead" (Rev. 1:17). Even Balaam's donkey fell down when it saw an angel of the Lord (Num. 22:27)!

When the veil is lifted and a mere mortal taps into not just a vision or dream, but into the actual unseen world of angels, demons, heaven, or hell, the human body is unable to sustain the glory of the heavenly realm without responding in some manner. If we could live with our spiritual eyes continually opened, I suggest we would never get any work done and would be continually disrupted in our sleep.

Scripture instructs believers to "walk by faith, not by sight" (2 Cor. 5:7). I cannot physically see God, but I believe in God because of the Bible's evidence and because I have faith that undergirds my confidence in the Word. With my human eyes I am unable to spot an angel flying through the heavens or a cosmic conflict between warring angels and prince spirits called the "spiritual hosts of wickedness in the heavenly places" (Eph. 6:12). However, because my inner being is also a "spirit," I can at times sense or *feel* the presence of the Lord, the warmth and peace of an angel, or the dark oppressive wicked spirits that are in my earth zone. To pierce the curtain of the unseen, a believer must be *in tune* to that particular realm of spiritual activity.

THERE IS A FUTURE

When my seventy-seven-year-old father was praying for my twenty-year-old son, who was kneeling before him at Dad's small home in Tennessee, with tears in his eyes my father said to Jonathan, "There is a future." He was encouraging his grandson not to just live for the *moment* but to discover, plan, and prevail for his future, which the Lord has already laid out for him and his little sister. At that moment I realized that this is what life is really all about—the future. When God laid out a detailed plan for man's redemption from sin, He prepared the details long before Adam fell. Jesus is called "the Lamb slain from the foundation of the world" (Rev. 13:8). When Christ was praying before His death, He said that God had loved Him from "before the foundation of the world" (John 17:24). *God planned a future for all of mankind before Adam and Eve were created and fell into sin!*

Once man sinned, God Himself released the first prophecy by predicting that the seed of the woman would bruise the head of the serpent (Gen. 3:15). God spoke this about four thousand years before Mary gave birth to the Messiah (Luke 2). After Cain slew his brother, Abel, God wasted no time in replacing Abel with Adam and Eve's new addition to the family, a son named Seth who would initiate a nine-generation lineage of righteous men, leading up to tenth man from Adam, Noah. (See Genesis 5.) *God continually has your future on His mind and in His purpose.*

The Almighty's passion for the future is also witnessed in the fact that God thinks generationally. When God established His covenant through Abraham, He was planning that Abraham's descendants would become a nation. First God promised Abraham a son and to make a "great nation" from Abraham's children (Gen. 12:2). Years later God predicted that Abraham would be "a great and mighty nation" (Gen. 18:18). Years passed, and then God visited Abraham's grandson Jacob, changing his name from *Jacob* to *Israel*. God enlarged His promise by saying to Jacob, "A nation and a company of nations shall proceed from you" (Gen. 35:11). After the nation of Israel expanded from seventy souls to more than six hundred thousand men of war (Exod. 1:5; 12:37), the Lord announced that the nation would be "blessed above all peoples" (Deut. 7:14). From one simple individual, Abraham, to seventy souls who went into Egypt under Joseph, in four hundred years the nation grew to six hundred thousand men marching through the Red Sea and on to the millions of Jewish people now in the world. God was beginning the preparations for one large family called the *children of Israel* when He was making covenant with one man—Abraham! This is why God changed Abram's name (meaning "father") to Abraham, meaning "father of many" (Gen. 17:5). Israel began with a dream and a vision!

PIERCING THE VEIL

Securing confidence and boldness for the future is so significant to the Almighty that He allowed men to enter into the dream dimension and receive vital knowledge for themselves, for their leaders, or for the nations in which they were given authority. A few examples of significant dreams that altered situations, set destinies, or brought prophetic knowledge are:

► God warned King Abimelech with the threat of death if he didn't return Sarah to Abraham (Gen. 20:6–7).

- ► God confirmed in a dream for Jacob to leave Laban, taking his wives and sons to Canaan (Gen. 31).

- ► God prepared Joseph's future by giving him two prophetic dreams when he was a teenager (Gen. 37).

- ► God allowed Joseph to interpret the dreams of the butler and the baker while in prison (Gen. 40).

- ► Joseph interpreted both dreams of Pharaoh and prepared for a seven-year famine (Gen. 41).

- ► It was the "barley cake dream" that gave Gideon confidence to fight the Midianites (Judg. 7).

- ► God appeared to Solomon in a dream, granting his request for the gift of wisdom (1 Kings 3).

- ► Daniel was the only man in Babylon capable of interpreting the dream of the metallic image (Dan. 2).

- ► Daniel later interpreted Nebuchadnezzar's "tree dream," predicting the downfall of the king (Dan. 4).

- ► Daniel experienced a major prophetic dream of world empires symbolized by wild beasts (Dan. 7).

Nearly six thousand years of human history have demonstrated that just because God plans a person's future, it is no guarantee that opposition will not eclipse the light of the revelation. There is a plan by the kingdom of darkness to distract, disrupt, and destroy the future, both God's prophetic plan and your personal destiny. Each person is said to have a "destiny," which is simply *your future according to God.* Just as God revealed to Jeremiah that He foreknew him when he was still in his mother's womb and that He preordained him to be a prophet (Jer. 1:5), God has a predetermined plan for each person. With all of the clutter and clamor and mixed voices speaking into our lives, our minds can become cloudy and our understanding fogged with numerous possibilities from which we must choose. This is why at times God will permit a believer to pierce the world of the natural and enter the realm of a dream or a vision so that secret strategies of the enemy can be exposed and the hidden plans of God can be revealed. Warnings that are perceived and received can help you avoid potholes and pits in your path to destiny, and understanding God's plan will empower you to pursue that purpose.

The disrupting of God's will in our lives can begin at a very early age. During major prophetic cycles and seasons of prophetic fulfillment, children come under severe attack from the adversary. This was seen when Pharaoh ordered the male infants born to the Hebrews to be cast into the Nile River (Exod. 1:22). The time was coming when a deliverer would bring the Hebrews out of Egypt, and the adversary was no doubt attempting to preempt the prophecy by killing the possible male child deliverer before he could become a man! The second assignment of an evil ruler was when Herod commissioned Roman soldiers to encircle the area of Ramah and kill all male children who were under two years of age, attempting to slay the future king of the Jews that the wise men came to worship (Matt. 2).

From a personal perspective, if we survive our birth and live to be teenagers, other battles begin. When he was a teenager (age seventeen), a plot was organized against Joseph by his own brothers (Gen. 37). They were sick of this dreamer, Daddy's favorite little spoiled boy, running around with an expensive coat! Joseph was doing well until he began to confess his dreams of success that would come to him. At that point his brothers conspired against him, and Joseph ended up in a pit, then in a prison, and spent thirteen years in what seemed negative, *dream-killing* circumstances.

I was a young teenager when the Lord began to reveal to me His will and I began planning for it. I encountered various types of verbal persecution from my own spiritual brothers in the same denomination of which I was a member. When David—just a teen—was anointed by Samuel as the next king "in the midst of his brothers," jealousy arose among certain brothers much older who may have felt they deserved the position more than their kid brother (1 Sam. 16:13; 17:28).

When I was a teenager, the Holy Spirit inspired me to organize a ministry called Voice of Evangelism when I had only preached in three states. Ministers said, "Perry isn't the voice of anything, much less of evangelism." They were correct from the natural perspective but wrong in the Spirit. The Lord had a future for me! At age eighteen I formed a "7-Point Outreach Plan" that included a ministry outreach through books, revival meetings, magazines, and other forms of branching out. Then I began overhearing statements like: "Who does he think he is, Billy Graham or Oral Roberts?" Without sounding arrogant, I knew something these other men did not know. I had a small glimpse into the future. I had both heard and seen in my spirit and through dreams and prayer that I would be used of the Lord to one day have a worldwide ministry. *Thus, once you see your future, you can learn how to hold off the adversity and know why there is opposition against your destiny!*

WATCH OUT FOR THAT GIRL

When my father, Fred Stone, was a young, black-haired teenage minister, he met a very attractive girl about his age who was gifted in playing the piano and singing. Of course, the common belief was that if you were a minister, your wife needed to be a singer or musician. The girl took a liking to him. However, Dad had a dream in which he saw this girl coming out of a barn embracing a young man. He realized the girl was having relations with this boy. He heard a voice say, "I have warned you; have nothing to do with that girl." Dad said that after this dream, the girl tried to get close to him in friendship; he would say hello but go no further. Even Dad's uncle, a noted minister, rebuked Dad for not expressing more interest in such a talented young girl. But three months later the girl's father told Dad's uncle he was glad Dad had not formed a relationship with his daughter, because she was pregnant out of wedlock by a fellow she knew.

When I was the same age as my father, a similar situation was repeated in my life. I was eighteen years of age, traveling from church to church conducting weekly revivals. At one location, a family I knew with a daughter about my age wanted me to go out with her to eat. My policy was to only go out with a group of young people and avoid going out alone with the opposite sex. Soon she began to speak to friends that she was serious about me and thought our friendship could lead to eventual marriage. At the same time I dreamed that she was pregnant. In the dream the Lord told me to avoid her. The same week, three noted ministers spoke to me in confidence and said, "You must be careful around this girl. There is something not right about her." I sent word to her through a friend not to have any contact with me again. One month later it was confirmed that she was pregnant, and she married the father of the child shortly thereafter. Years later she and her mother came to hear me minister in a church and asked to speak with me. Her mother, a very godly woman, required her to apologize to me for plotting to pull me into her situation without my knowledge. The girl said, "I was hoping you would suddenly fall in love with me and marry me before anyone knew I was pregnant with this man's baby."

In both cases, more than twenty-six years apart, the same type of snare was laid for Dad and me. By following the same type of dreams and inward warnings, we both avoided missing the will of God and entering into a situation that would have been not only questionable but also embarrassing and detrimental to our early ministries. These illustrations reveal how strategies are set to disrupt God's purposes, but God is concerned about the details of our personal lives because *circumstances* affect our destiny!

Often when we think of a spiritual dream we envision a visitation that warns us of national calamity or an international warning on the same level as what the Old Testament prophets received when warning the priests and the kings of coming calamity. However, God has indicated in Scripture that He is concerned for each individual and not just for the collective population of a nation. Christ revealed that the Father watched a sparrow fall to the ground and saw the lilies in the field grow (Matt. 10:29; Luke 12:28), and if the Almighty is concerned for the smallest in His creation, how much more is His concern manifested toward man, who is made in His image (Gen. 1:26).

THE NEED TO KNOW

The understanding of the Book of Daniel was sealed "until the time of the end," when "knowledge shall increase" (Dan. 12:4). Numerous prophecies are assigned to occur in the "time of the end," a term used in the Book of Daniel five times (Dan. 8:17; 11:35, 40; 12:4, 9). Other predictions will unfold in the "last days," a phrase coined to identify the time frame prior to the return of the Messiah, listed five times in the New Testament (Acts 2:17; 2 Tim. 3:1; Heb. 1:2; James 5:3; 2 Pet. 3:3). The final outpouring of the Holy Spirit will occur in the "last days" (Acts 2:17) and includes sons and daughters prophesying and experiencing visions and dreams. Among this final generation there is a *need-to-know* attitude about their future and destiny.

This *need to know* is obvious when one considers the millions of dollars spent by sincere yet uninformed individuals on fortune-tellers, astrologers, séances, and psychics. According to the Pew Forum for Religion and Public Life, "about 1 in 7 Americans consulted a psychic or fortune teller in 2009."[1] The only reason these false prophets of greed are consulted is to determine the hidden and the unseen and to know in advance the person's future. Why should the body of Christ sit back and refuse to tell this generation to seek God for His direction, when the adversary will provide a horoscope for that purpose? There is a human need to know, and our knowledge for redemption can be found in the Bible—as well as the guide for practical living found in those inspired Scriptures. However, there are times we are uncertain concerning personal and national decisions that can be seen and understood through visions and dreams. However, the invisible veil must be pierced in the mind and in the understanding. This begins with the "dream factor."

THE DREAM FACTOR

Then He said, "Hear now My words: If there is a prophet among you, I, the LORD, make Myself known unto him in a vision; I speak to him in a dream."

« Numbers 12:6 »

It was approximately 2,500 years after the creation of Adam that God came to Moses in the wilderness and revealed the first written record of God's Word to mankind. From Adam to Noah's flood is about ten generations, stretching for 1,658 years. From Noah's son Shem to the arrival of Abraham is another ten generations and a span of several hundred years (Gen. 11:10–26). These years are called by theologians the *dispensation of human government*, as mankind had no written law to turn to and follow. God, however, did not remain silent for 2,500 years. He began revealing His will through dreams, visions, angelic encounters, and even personal visitations from Himself. When a righteous man or a patriarch such as Abraham, Isaac, Jacob, or Joseph dreamed a spiritual dream, there was always a cryptic message encoded in the dream or the symbolism thereof.

In the Bible, dreaming dreams is referred to 115 times, and the word *vision* is used 79 times in the English translation of the Bible. Some suggest that since we have the Bible, there is no longer any need for God to speak through a dream or a vision. However, the Bible itself is clear that as God pours out His Spirit in the last days, the visitations from heaven will be accompanied by both visions and dreams:

> And it shall come to pass in the last days, says God,
> That I will pour out of My Spirit on all flesh;
> Your sons and your daughters shall prophesy,
> Your young men shall see visions,
> Your old men shall dream dreams.
> And on My menservants and on My maidservants
> I will pour out My Spirit in those days;
> And they shall prophesy.
> —Acts 2:17–18

Since dreams and visions are going to be manifested through believers as the Holy Spirit begins flowing throughout the earth in the last days, then we need to be made aware of these two methods of delivering messages, warnings, and instructions and know how to correctly read or interpret the meanings of the dreams and visions.

THE ACT OF DREAMING

There are two types of people: those who dream often and those who seldom dream. I am definitely a nightly dreamer, and my wife seldom, if ever, dreams—or if she does, she doesn't remember the content. At some point all people will experience a dream. Most dreams are a visual mental screen that moves from scene to scene while we sleep. Very few dreams can actually be classified as a spiritual dream, although there have been noted psychologists and researchers who believe every dream may have some type of a hidden meaning through the symbolism.

When believers begin experiencing dreams that hold a cryptic or hidden warning and message, the act of dreaming can be applied to three different categories.

First is the occasional dream that has an important message. As stated, I dream continually throughout the night, but my lovely wife, Pam, seldom dreams. However, if she tells you she had a strange dream, the probability is about nine out of ten that her dream is a message or a particular warning.

The second category relates to dreamers who have a natural gift for seeing future events, which is quite unexplainable. Among the ancient prophetic empires—Egypt, Babylon, Persia, and Greece—when the ruling kings had a troubling dream, they assembled the "wise men" or "seers" from their kingdom to interpret the meaning or give instructions (Gen. 41:8; Dan. 2:2). In most instances these men had a particular gift of wisdom and understanding, even though many if not all were worshipers of strange gods (such as with the case with the magicians of Pharaoh, in Exodus 7:11, and the wise men of Babylon). It is interesting to note that when God gave Pharaoh and Nebuchadnezzar prophetic dreams, not one of the seers, dream interpreters, or wise men in their kingdoms could receive the understanding of the symbolism in the prophetic dream. Only two men filled with the Spirit of the Lord, Joseph and Daniel, could understand the meanings! This fact reveals that God never intends for the so-called "sons of this world" (Luke 16:8) to understand spiritual mysteries. He gives revelation about spiritual mysteries only to men (or women) who have the spirit of wisdom and understanding through the Holy Spirit (Eph. 1:17–18).

The third category of dreamers are those who have received a special gift of revelation and illumination. In Scripture, Jacob, the son of Isaac, was a dreamer of dreams and experienced a dramatic dream of angels ascending and descending from a ladder whose base was upon the earth and whose top was positioned at the gate of heaven (Gen. 28:12–19). Apparently this "dreaming gift" was transferred to Jacob's favorite son, Joseph, who at age seventeen dreamed two distinct dreams indicating that all of his brothers would one day bow before him (Gen. 37:5–10). Joseph irritated his jealous brothers with his exciting revelation, bringing him mockery and eventually landing him in a pit and then leading to his being sold to a group of slave-purchasing nomads! Notice the reaction of his brothers and his father when Joseph shared his dream: "His brothers envied him, but his father kept the matter in mind" (v. 11).

This is the difference between someone who is *carnally* minded and someone who is *spiritually* minded. The brothers had never experienced a dream of their own with any meaning, but their father, Jacob, had on several occasions. No doubt Jacob saw the same type of *anointing* upon his son Joseph, even though one part of Joseph's dream made little sense. Joseph saw the eleven stars, sun, and moon bowing before him. We know there were twelve sons of Jacob if we include Joseph, and there are twelve major constellations in the main circuit that the sun moves through during a solar year. The eleven stars were not eleven single stars somewhere in the heaven, but these eleven stars alluded to the eleven different major star constellations in the heavens. Joseph's father, Jacob, interpreted the dream to mean that the stars were Joseph's brothers, the sun was Jacob, and the moon was Joseph's mother (Gen. 37:10). All eleven brothers and the father were living, but Joseph's mother, Rachel, had died giving birth to Benjamin some years prior (Gen. 35:18–19). Rachel gave birth to only two sons—Joseph and Benjamin. Rachel was Jacob's favorite wife, and these two boys were very special to him. However, Momma was now dead. It would be literally impossible for her to be the symbol of the moon and to bow down to Joseph, and I am certain this is why Jacob did not search out the full interpretation of Joseph's double dream but instead pondered it. Some of the dream—at the time—didn't make sense.

One thing I have learned over many years of ministry as it deals with God sending you an instruction using a dream or vision is that there are times when certain parts of what you see are not completely understood at that moment. What you see in the dream can be explained and is clear and certain, but your *understanding* of the events or what they mean can be fallible within your own interpretation. I almost made this mistake years after seeing the vision of the World Trade Center shrouded in the black cloud. The vision took place in 1996. In 1999, however, when I was showing the drawings of the vision that had been done by an artist who illustrated what appeared to be the World Trade Center shrouded in black (see drawings earlier in this book), a computer mainframe expert said, "Perry, that tall object may be a tall computer mainframe that could be impacted by the Y2K computer glitch that some are saying may occur at midnight of the first day of 2000." I looked at the picture and said, "I always thought it looked like the World Trade Center, but maybe you're right!" In 1999 I hosted a major prophetic special program that was aired on national television, showing the various drawings of the warning vision from 1996. I mentioned it could be a terrorist attack but *added*, "Perhaps it is a computer mainframe." From 1996 to 2001, every day at some time I thought about what I saw but could not put it all together—until the day of September 11, 2001, when it was made clear.

In a strong spiritual visitation in which you see something that is a warning, do not be discouraged or frustrated if you do not always comprehend or understand the events 100 percent. It is written, "It is the glory of God to conceal a matter, but the glory of kings is to search out a matter" (Prov. 25:2). The searching out of something hidden was the process Daniel used when he saw a "thing [that] was revealed unto [him]" but the "time appointed was long" (Dan. 10:1, KJV). Daniel initiated a twenty-one-day fast to receive more insight on the prophetic vision he had seen, which is recorded in chapter 8 (concerning the Tribulation). An angel of God (Gabriel; see Daniel 8:16; 9:21) stood before Daniel and began revealing the most detailed order of future events from Daniel's time in Babylon to the end of the Great Tribulation. (See Daniel chapters 10–12.)

Joseph's dream appeared somewhat contradictory since his mother had died in childbirth. If the moon was a symbol of Rachel and the dream alluded to Jacob and his sons ending up in Egypt, where Joseph would be second in command, then the moon should not have even been in Joseph's dream. However, consider this. The *sun* and all of the *stars* are always visible throughout the year. However, the moon is only full several days out of each month, and there is a brief period when the moon is called a *new moon*, meaning it cannot be seen in the sky from the earth. Darkness appears to fill the night, but the moon is still there nonetheless. Rachel was now dead; however, the prophet Jeremiah, hundreds of years after her death, described her weeping in her grave knowing her children would be taken captive one day:

> A voice was heard in Ramah,
> Lamentation and bitter weeping,
> Rachel weeping for her children,
> Refusing to be comforted for her children,
> Because they are no more.
>
> —JEREMIAH 31:15

How would Rachel know her children were suffering? Perhaps this is a poetic passage symbolizing the sorrow in the heart of a mother of Israel with the loss of her children. Perhaps Rachel's soul and spirit, in the netherworld of departed souls, were made aware that Israel was encountering great sorrow at the time of Jeremiah. The same would be true with the *moon* bowing before Joseph in Egypt. Benjamin, Rachel's only other son, would be present when the dream was fulfilled.

WHEN DREAMS SEEM TO CONTRADICT

This was not the only time that a prophetic vision seemed to contradict itself. In the Old Testament, two major prophets, Jeremiah and Ezekiel, predicted that the Babylonians would destroy Jerusalem in the days of King Zedekiah. Jeremiah predicted that the king of Babylon, Nebuchadnezzar, would "lead Zedekiah to Babylon" (Jer. 32:5), whereas Ezekiel predicted that "he [Zedekiah] shall not see it, though he shall die there" (Ezek. 12:13). The Jewish historian Josephus writes that since these two predictions seemed to contradict—the king would be led to Babylon and yet the king would not see it—it meant that Zedekiah rejected both predictions and refused to believe the words of either prophet.[1]

Here is how both predictions were fulfilled. In 2 Kings 25:6–7, at the final siege of Jerusalem, King Zedekiah was brought before the king of Babylon, where the Babylonians put out the king's eyes, bound him with fetters of brass, and led him into Babylon! He was *led away* but *did not see*. The king should have believed what he heard and not tried so much to figure out how it could occur.

A second example is when Isaiah told King Hezekiah that the day would come when "all that is in your house, and what your fathers have accumulated" would be carried away into Babylon, and nothing would be left (2 Kings 20:16–17). Daniel, who was a young captive in Babylon, wrote in Daniel 1:2, "Some of the articles of the house of God…" were carried to Babylon. Was it *part* or *all* of the treasures from the temple that went to Babylon? Did these two visionaries get their visions of the future crossed? Did one prophet prophesy in the *flesh* and the other in the *Spirit*? The answer lies in the text of 2 Chronicles and in Jeremiah. During the first stage of the invasion, Nebuchadnezzar took only part of the gold vessels. (See Jeremiah 27.) Nebuchadnezzar had appointed Zedekiah's brother, Jehoiakim, the new king of Judah. Jeremiah attempted to exhort Jehoiakim to submit to the Babylonian king. The Judean king refused, and thus we read: "Therefore He brought against them the king of the Chaldeans.…He gave them all into his hand. And all the articles from the house of God, great and small, the treasures of the house of the LORD…all these he took to Babylon" (2 Chron. 36:17–18).

The vision was correct when the entire invasion by the Babylonians was completed.

THE AMAZING PART OF JOSEPH'S DOUBLE DREAM

As stated earlier, Joseph's mother had died in childbirth; it was impossible for her to bow with the father and the other brothers. However, notice in Joseph's sheave dream that there were eleven sheaves bowing. If we omit Joseph, there were eleven sons of Jacob who remained in the family after Joseph was sold to the traveling Ishmaelites as a slave.

Years later, when Joseph interpreted Pharaoh's dream of a coming famine, he set aside seven years of corn to prevent Egypt from starving. When the famine struck, Joseph's brothers traveled to purchase grain in Egypt. We read where Joseph's "ten brothers went down to buy grain in Egypt" (Gen. 42:3). Benjamin was not with them; thus there were not eleven brothers as Joseph saw in his dream. When Joseph saw this, he realized this was not the complete meaning of what he had dreamed twenty-two years earlier when he saw eleven stalks of grain bowing before his sheave. He began manipulating his brothers (without their knowledge), and months later when the eleventh brother, Benjamin, arrived and all eleven bowed before Joseph, he knew this was the complete fulfillment of what he had seen in his dream. That is when he reveled himself to them! This should teach us not to try to force a dream to come to pass or to become impatient, but to exercise care and discretion when following any dream.

DREAMS—SIGNS OF A PROPHET

Prior to the completion of the Torah (first five books of the Old Testament), dreams and visions were two common methods God used to bring revelation, such as establishing covenants, warnings, and divine guidance to individuals and to the nation of Israel. The nations of antiquity, as far back as the Chaldeans in the lands of

Mesopotamia, Egypt, and Babylon, all had men in staff positions in their palaces who were considered to be dream interpreters.

Among the early Hebrews, when a man was gifted to receive dreams and visions, it was a sign that he was a prophet, or one whom God was visiting with divine insight and revelation. When King Abimelech saw Abraham's wife, Sarah, and secretly planned to take her for his wife, God appeared in a dream warning him that he would be a dead man if he so much as touched Sarah. In the dream the Almighty informed the king that Abraham was a prophet and would pray a healing prayer for Abimelech, and God would hear and answer Abraham's prayer (Gen. 20:1–7).

When Samuel was just a young child about twelve years of age, he heard the voice of the Lord calling to him on three occasions. After answering the third time, God revealed to Samuel that He was expelling the high priest Eli and his sons from the future priesthood in Israel. The vision from the Lord to Samuel came to pass. We read that "all Israel from Dan to Beersheba knew that Samuel had been established as a prophet of the LORD" (1 Sam. 3:20).

In Acts 2, on the Day of Pentecost the Holy Spirit descended upon the believers, and they were all filled with the Holy Spirit (Acts 2:1–4). Peter stood among the brethren and began expounding about the prophecies of Christ that were concealed throughout the Old Testament. Peter mentioned a prediction that David gave concerning how God would not leave the Messiah's soul in hell and not allow His holy one to see corruption (v. 31). Peter called David a prophet, since the sweet king of Israel, who had lived a thousand years before Christ, had foreseen the coming of the Messiah.

In each instance these men (and numerous others) received direct knowledge about things to come and were classified as prophets as a result of it! In the last days the Holy Spirit will speak to both young and old men. Some more liberal Christian thinkers and theologians believe that God no longer speaks today to anyone except through Scripture. The fact is, however, that God has always spoken and has never quit speaking; it's just that some people are not listening as well as others. Christ said:

> But when the Comforter is come, whom I will send unto you from the Father, even the Spirit of truth, which proceedeth from the Father, he shall testify of me.
> —JOHN 15:26, KJV

> However, when He, the Spirit of truth, has come, He will guide you into all truth; for He will not speak on His own authority, but whatever He hears He will speak; and He will tell you things to come.
> —JOHN 16:13

The Holy Spirit will speak and will show you things to come. This New Testament promise is still valid today!

three

WHY ARE SOME DREAMS DELAYED IN COMING TO PASS?

He sent a man before them—
Joseph—who was sold as a slave.
They hurt his feet with fetters,
He was laid in irons.
Until the time that his word came to pass,
The word of the LORD tested him.
The king sent and released him,
The ruler of the people let him go free.

« Psalm 105:17–20 »

When the Lord revealed to me the vision that would eventually prove to be the 9/11 attacks, about five years and three months passed before the actual event transpired. During those sixty-three months of seeing nothing that would clarify the meaning of this vision, I can remember becoming somewhat frustrated with the lack of knowing *when* this unusual vision would occur. The night vision of the tragic oil "storm" that impacted Louisiana took about thirty-three months before it was obvious that the result of the fire and collapse of the BP oil rig in the Gulf of Mexico was the clear fulfillment of the details of the night dream/vision in July of 2007.

In July of 2007, I experienced a major night vision involving an oil rig in the Gulf of Mexico. In the vision I was in the city of Baton Rouge, Louisiana, at Christian Life Fellowship with my friend, Pastor Jerry Melilli. The vision began as I was unloading our SUV at the home of a dear couple with whom we stay when we minister in the Baton Rouge area. In the vision, Pastor Melilli asked me if I had any new information or prophetic insight on what was about to occur. As if on cue, we suddenly saw a large black tornado drop from a perfectly clear sky. At that moment the scene changed, and I suddenly found myself inside the back of the *rig* (trailer) of an eighteen-wheeler truck, with one side completely open and covered with a large piece of plastic covering. There was nothing being transported in the truck. The wind struck the truck but did not harm me personally.

After exiting the truck, I heard a voice announce that another storm was forming. Again the scene changed, and I found myself in a mall; the buildings were intact, but the shoppers were missing. Lying on the mall floor were five people, both men and women, who were exposing their hands, arms, and feet and saying, "Help us. This storm has affected us. Look at our wounds." However, their wounds were *plastic* or artificial, and I knew they did not need the help and assistance that others needed. When this thought came to my mind in the vision, I heard a female voice speak and say, "Tell the churches there will be people who will claim to be in need, and they will not be—they are using the system for their benefit. Tell the churches to care for those of the household of faith first." I felt that these individuals wanted some form of money or assistance but were not actually in need as others were.

Immediately the scene changed. As I saw a second tornado was forming, I found myself in a large and rather expensive-looking restaurant filled with customers. As the storm was arriving, I ran into the men's room (a small enclosed room) to escape the violence of the wind. After the building was shaken, I returned to the main dining area, and the entire restaurant was empty. I remember thinking, "How strange for the storm not to physically affect the building, but somehow it is preventing the business from operating."

After this, I then found myself entering a small, square concrete room with a window. It was then that I was joined by two friends: Pastor Dino Rizzo, pastor of Healing Place Church in Baton Rouge, and missionary Rusty Domingue, who at the time of the vision (July 2007) was on staff at a church in Austin, Texas. However, in the vision I saw that Rusty was working with Pastor Dino. (Months later, in 2008, I was amazed when Rusty eventually moved back to Baton Rouge and began working with Dino at the Healing Place. It was just as I had seen at the time when the *storms* broke out.) Looking out the window, I saw the next tornado drop from the sky, and we all covered ourselves with a large covering to prevent any debris from falling on us. When the storm ceased, we arose safely from our secure place. Looking out of an opening in the room, I was able to see a small town's main street with little *mom-and-pop* shops that were all closed. No one was shopping in this particular area. I was again puzzled at why these tornados, which normally tear apart buildings, were not destroying buildings, only stopping people from coming into the areas for business.

Looking out the window, I saw a large fourth tornado forming in the distance. As the fourth storm formed, my entire family joined me in the room. There are several parts of the vision at this point that I have withheld from sharing in public, as they involved a national figure and his parents and some personal family members. Following this fourth storm, I was struggling to understand why these storms were occurring, how they were linked to people from Louisiana, and what the meaning was. It was the fifth and final tornado that answered my questions.

Following the fourth tornado, the scene changed from Baton Rouge to the Gulf of Mexico just off the coast of Louisiana. Pastor Dino Rizzo was standing beside me as we stared at a large oil rig in the Gulf of Mexico off the coast of Louisiana. Suddenly I saw a massive—and I do mean massive—tornado of black oil that began spinning on the gulf waters. As it spun violently, the black oil was being slung across the beautiful waters of the Gulf of Mexico. Suddenly the oil tornado struck an oil rig's platform, and I heard a strange noise, like a popping sound. The top of the tornado began to turn toward me, as though it was bowing down on the top of the water, and as it did, I heard a clicking sound. The top of the tornado became a metal cap that had bolts encircling the top of it. I yelled, "They are going to cap an oil well at an oil rig in the gulf!" I was confused as to why someone would cap a single oil well when there are hundreds of wells and rigs in the Gulf of Mexico. When I awoke, I wrote the details on a piece of paper so I would not forget what I saw. I dated it: *Thursday, July 2007, 12:30 p.m.*

Months later I called Pastor Dino, who was on a foreign trip at the time, and shared the entire incident with him. As a result, he actually made preparations in the event that a *tornado* type of storm or storms struck the area. More than a year later in the fall of 2008, Hurricane Gustav hit Baton Rouge, knocking out electricity in some areas for weeks. Dino later told me, "It happened. We were struck by this storm. Man, it was like the Tribulation down here."

I told Dino, "That is not the big one I saw in the vision. What I saw is yet to come."

Two years and nine months after the vision, on April 20, 2010, the Deepwater Horizon oil rig located in the Gulf of Mexico off the coast of Louisiana exploded. At first the explosion and its repercussions didn't *click* with me, until I began receiving numerous calls from partners of the ministry who remembered when I shared the *black oil tornado* vision with them at our Partner's Conference. When the platform collapsed and the underwater camera began to capture the oil pouring from the opening in the pipe, I was stunned—the oil looked like a miniature tornado spinning underwater! The black, unrefined oil was pouring into the waters of the Gulf of Mexico and slowly creeping toward the marshes of Louisiana.

On the forty-first day, the BP underwater camera announced that the pipe had been cut, and the camera caught a picture of the round, steel pipe with large bolts encircling it. This was where the oil was gushing into the water! I literally yelled and began calling my office workers upstairs to view the flat-screen television on the wall. "There it is," I said. "That's what I told you I saw at the top of the black oil tornado in the vision. There it is—the oil is spinning out of the top!" Then I said, "They will cap this well!"

THE MEANING OF THE FIVE STORMS

Now that I understand the meaning of the vision, why did I see four tornadoes prior to the final large one? Consider the impact of the oil on the coasts of Louisiana. There were countless trucks that delivered

Louisiana seafood to restaurants throughout the nation that were unable to deliver because of the damage to the seafood industry from the leaking oil. This resulted in thousands of personal fishing trips being canceled, which impacted the small shops in the towns along the coast that depend on those who enjoy sports fishing in the inlands and the gulf region of Louisiana to supply the shops with seafood. According to some, smaller restaurants in some towns went out of business or saw an 80 percent decline in customers during the crisis. All fishing was halted for months, and other forms of shopping in the area were also affected. Financial help was available for those whose businesses had been impacted from the crisis. However, just as in the vision, there were some individuals who sought financial assistance who didn't need direct help but were taking advantage of the situation for their personal gain. According to reports in October 2010, the fishing industry in Louisiana could suffer a loss of $115 million to $172 million as a result of the oil spill during the years of 2011 to 2013. Job losses linked to the industry number between 2,650 to 3,975, with an earnings loss of $68 to $103 million.[1] Recent reports indicate that the fishing industry in Louisiana may be impacted for several years before it fully recovers.[2]

Just as with the 9/11 vision, when a dream or vision is linked to a national warning, the understanding of the vision or dream may not always be completely understood at the time. It may take days, weeks, months, or even years before the fulfillment of the event comes to pass. However, if the dream or vision is a national warning, unless repentance can alter the outcome, the events will eventually transpire.

This was one of the challenges that even the famous Old Testament prophets had when relating prophetic warnings to their generation. Isaiah informed King Hezekiah that the Babylonians in the future would enter Jerusalem and lay siege to the city, destroying the temple and carrying the priceless gold temple treasures back to Babylon. This invasion would be restrained in the king's lifetime, but the descendants from Hezekiah's own bloodline would suffer when the moment came (2 Kings 20:16–21). The prophecy did come to pass, however, many years after Isaiah spoke it. Both Isaiah and Hezekiah were dead by then.

The prophet Jeremiah began to bring warnings of Jerusalem's coming destruction to the elders and priests at the temple in Jerusalem. He was predicting massive destruction by the Babylonians, and he even nailed the exact number of years—seventy—that the Jews would be taken captive into Babylon (Jer. 25:11–12). The priests and religious seers at the temple became so angry at Jeremiah's prophetic vision that they rose up against him and threatened to kill him for his negative warnings. In fact, Pashhur, a man who was the son of the priest and chief governor over the temple, locked Jeremiah in stocks in a dungeon to silence him (Jer. 20:1–3). Jeremiah became so discouraged at the temple leaders' and priests' unbelief and lack of concern for the danger and trouble that was coming that he determined not to speak anymore. However, when he tried to remain silent, he said it was like a "fire shut up in his bones."

> Then I said, "I will not make mention of Him,
> Nor speak anymore in His name."
> But His word was in my heart like a burning fire
> Shut up in my bones;
> I was weary of holding it back,
> And I could not.
> —JEREMIAH 20:9

Jeremiah was so certain his predictions were true that he purchased the field of his uncle's son for seventeen shekels of silver and took both a sealed and opened title deed, burying them in the ground in a clay (earthen) jar as a sign that the Jews would one day return to the land and rebuild on the property that would lay dormant during the captivity. (See Jeremiah 32.) The assault by the Babylonians did occur years later, as predicted, and Jeremiah chapters 51 and 52 give a detailed summary of all of the vessels and sacred pieces of furniture carried away to ancient Babylon, the city on the Tigris. The priests didn't believe Jeremiah's prediction, but the old prophet believed the word the Lord had given him.

Imagine the stress these godly men experienced in their day when warning dreams and visions from the God of Israel, Jerusalem, and the Jews came to them, and they were commissioned by God to speak aloud what was being revealed in their prayer closets. Many times their dreams and visions would not come to pass in their own lifetimes. For example, both Daniel and John saw the final prophetic empire identified as a beast with ten horns, and these predictions, which will unfold in the last day, have not yet occurred. God instructed Daniel to "seal the book until the time of the end" (Dan. 12:4), knowing these latter-day visions were a long way off. Some warnings are so advanced in their visual presentation that their fulfillment may not occur during the lifetime of the visionary. This is also true with warnings and even dreams or visions that reveal good things to come, such as the future binding of Satan, Christ's one-thousand-year reign on Earth, and the New Jerusalem coming down to Earth as seen in John's vision in the Apocalypse (Rev. 21; 22).

We also may experience a unique or encouraging dream, and we may anticipate that it should come to pass immediately. However, the Lord revealed to Abraham at age seventy-five that he would be a father of a nation (Gen. 12:1–4), but the promised son was not born until Abraham was one hundred (Gen. 17:1; 17:21). It took twenty-five years for the promise to occur. When Abraham was about eighty-five, his wife, Sarah, offered her handmaid, Hagar, to Abraham as a second wife to give a child to Abraham (Gen. 16:1–4). After ten years of waiting, Sarah knew she was barren and was attempting to *help God* fulfill her husband's promise of a son. The reason God waited until Sarah was ninety to allow her to become pregnant with Isaac is because by age ninety, Sarah had "passed the age of child-bearing" (Gen. 18:11), meaning she went through menopause, making it impossible for her to conceive. The birth of Isaac, when Abraham was one hundred and Sarah was ninety, made Isaac's conception and birth a miracle.

Joseph was seventeen when he was sold as a slave (Gen. 37:2) and thirty years old when he left a prison and became second in command over Egyptian affairs (Gen. 41:46). He had seven years to prepare for the famine (v. 53) and was two years into the famine (Gen. 45:6) when he revealed himself to his eleven brothers. Thus, twenty-two years had passed before both of Joseph's dreams were fulfilled! The entire episode was a test of God's Word in Joseph's life (Ps. 105:16–21).

In a dream of a ladder stretching upward with angels ascending and descending, Jacob was promised that he too would be blessed and would inherit the land of Abraham. After Jacob deceived his brother, Esau, his mother ordered him to get out of town and head to her brother's estate in Syria. When Rebekah sent him to Syria, she thought Jacob would just be there a "few days," until Esau cooled off (Gen. 27:44). However, Jacob spent twenty years at his uncle Laban's ranch in Syria. God eventually appeared to Jacob in a dream and instructed him to return to the Promised Land (Gen. 31:11–18). Jacob's early life was directed by dreams, but there was, and always is, a time element involved in waiting for any dream to come to pass.

I have learned by experience that an encouraging dream that reveals God's will or purpose for you may take years to come to pass, but it is given to you in advance to *undergird your faith*, helping you to continue holding on to God's promise for you. In 1988 I had a very clear dream of seeing a beautiful little girl with straight hair that appeared to be about five years of age. She was full of personality and very animated when she spoke. I asked her, "Whose little girl are you?"

She replied, "My name is Amanda, and I am the little girl you are going to have!" This little girl appeared to me in two different dreams months apart! We found out a short time later that my wife was pregnant. We both assumed the child she was carrying was a girl because of the dream. We talked about painting the baby's room pink, and our closest friends began purchasing frilly little dresses for the baby to wear. On December 23, 1989, at six o'clock in the morning, my wife gave birth to a wonderful son we named Jonathan Gabriel Stone. I was very happy since there is a blessing upon a mother when her firstborn is a male child (Exod. 13:2–15). For years we didn't think any more about the dream as we were enjoying our son so much, and he was such a trooper in traveling. After Jonathan grew up, Pam and I discussed having another child, but our travel schedule, the homeschooling of Jonathan, and other responsibilities were very time consuming.

In the year 2000, I returned home from a foreign trip. I was lying on our bed in the upstairs master bedroom, my eyes closed and very tired, when I literally felt what was the *invisible* hand of a child on my left ankle. I was so startled by it I sat up. Pam entered the room at the same time, and I told her what had happened. She asked, "What does it mean?"

I said, "I sense we are supposed to have another child!" That same year Pam became pregnant, but in the month of October, while attending our main Fall Conference, she had a miscarriage at seven weeks. After this tragedy, she felt she could not emotionally or physically carry another child. We began praying, and she became pregnant in December. I told her, "You will carry this baby, and it is the little girl I saw in the dream in 1988!"

Months later, by ultrasound, the child was confirmed to be a girl! However, in the seventh month, the OB-GYN saw an ultrasound and said to Pam, "Your embryonic fluid is low, and it is possible your child will have Down syndrome."

Pam returned home somewhat troubled. I encouraged her, "I saw a very healthy girl in that dream, and this child will NOT be sick and will NOT have an infirmity in the name of the Lord!" My wife followed the doctor's orders and went on bed rest for an entire month. At eight months into the pregnancy, on August 2, 2001, the little girl I saw *thirteen years before* in the dream was born. We named her Amanda, as this was the name she gave me in the dream. She is full of personality and is exactly like the girl in the dream. While we didn't discuss it much, during those years the dream was always in the back of my mind. Perhaps this is why it is written:

> Then the LORD answered me and said:
>
> "Write the vision
> And make it plain on tablets,
> That he may run who reads it.
> For the vision is yet for an appointed time;
> But at the end it will speak, and it will not lie.
> Though it tarries, wait for it;
> Because it will surely come,
> It will not tarry."
> —HABAKKUK 2:2–3

An hour after Amanda's birth I wrote this poem for her:

> Deep in sleep in the middle of the night
> A vision, a dream, such a wonderful sight

A dark-haired girl who calls me Dad
I awoke—just a dream—oh, so sad.

Days turn to years, then again you appear
Late in the night, in a dream you are there
Your name is Amanda, meaning worthy of love
I awoke and prayed to the Lord up above

That in His time make this dream come true.
Years passed, we waited for the time we'd see you.
A hand on my ankle—what is this strange sign?
An inner voice tells me, "Now is the time."

Late in October sudden tears fill our eyes
But the winter soon passes and our spirits now rise
A heartbeat is heard and an image is seen
It's a girl in the womb, "It's Amanda," we sing.

August the second, excited we wait
The time soon arrived, but the labor was great
But pain turned to joy when we all saw your face
Dark hair, it is you, in pink ribbons and lace.

Your mommy and brother and I are here
To love and protect you from danger and fear
To teach you about the place you came from
Heaven, the angels, and the land from above.

Watching you grow will be my life's joy
Until you are married with your own girl or boy
I'll be there for you till my journey is through
And when you arrive there, I'll be waiting for you.

—WRITTEN BY YOUR DADDY IN YOUR MOMMY'S ROOM
THE DAY YOU WERE BORN, AUGUST 2, 2001

There is a difference in the vision or dream *tarrying* and you being the one doing the tarrying or delaying the dream. A *tarrying dream* is one that you do not see come to pass for an extended, rather long period of time. However, at times you can delay what God is ready to perform in your life because you are fearful of failure, short of the needed provisions to fulfill it, or uncertain of the timing. You may not always receive insight of God's purpose into the future through a night dream. Your inspired dream may manifest in a strong inward pull that you sense in your spirit to take a journey, change jobs, or make a decision that could impact you or your family for years to come. At times the only way to test a *dream* or a strong inner impulse that continually throbs in your spirit is by actually stepping out in faith.

For example, I have known of individuals who were burdened to assist the poor or minister in a foreign nation through a mission project. When they saw the suffering children and the heartbreaking poverty, their hearts would reach out, but their feet never left their hometown. A year or two would pass, and the desire to travel remained, but the excuses for not going outweighed the obedience of going. There was not enough time, not enough money, and not an open door. However, *the only way to soothe the throb is to do the job* and take a journey, even if it is only one week out of a year, and minister to those faces you continually see in your *dream imagination.*

GOD GIVES YOU THE DESIRES

> Delight yourself also in the Lord, and He shall give you
> the desires of your heart.
> —Psalm 37:4

This word *delight* in Hebrew can allude to being *pliable,* or to enjoying something. When we begin to enjoy our relationship with

God, He will give us the desires of our hearts. There are two ways this passage can be understood. The primary meaning is the word *desires*, which in Hebrew simply means "the request or the petition of our hearts." The simple meaning is that our prayers and petitions will be answered. A second, implied meaning is that God gives us our desires—in the manner of what we feel and sense in our heart and spirit was put there by the Lord.

In 1980, when I was ministering in a four-week revival in Northport, Alabama, I saw a beautiful seventeen-year-old girl named Pam standing in a group of about eighty youth who were worshiping as the choir was singing. I can still see her in my mind. I heard an inner voice say, "That is the girl you will marry." At first I tried to ignore the voice, as this was in the middle of a church service! However, the voice repeated the words twice. At that very moment she was placed in my heart—and I hadn't taken her on the first date! *She was God's desire for me, and He placed inside of me His desire.* However, His desire became my desire. We would say, "She was God's will for my life," but the will of God can only be revealed through desire. The desire I am speaking of is the other common Hebrew word for desire, *ta'avah*, meaning "to long for or delight in something." This word is found in the following passages:

> The fear of the wicked, it shall come upon him: but the desire of the righteous shall be granted.
> —Proverbs 10:24, KJV

> The desire of the righteous is only good: but the expectation of the wicked is wrath.
> —Proverbs 11:23, KJV

> Hope deferred maketh the heart sick: but when the desire cometh, it is a tree of life.
> —Proverbs 13:12, KJV

> The desire accomplished is sweet to the soul: but it is
> abomination to fools to depart from evil.
> —PROVERBS 13:19, KJV

A positive dream or vision can actually motivate and stir up the desire to see the thing come to pass. It may, however, require a season of patience and careful guarding of our hearts to prevent the dream from dying within us. If you think about it, the one place where more dreams have died is at the local cemetery. So many individuals have passed on having never fulfilled those desires that were forged in their minds or birthed in their spirits. Perhaps they said, "Maybe one day when I get more time," or "When I get the money," or "When the door opens," yet they never pursued their desires.

A DELAY IS NOT A DEFEAT

Never read a delay as a defeat, just as you should never think that because you have prayed and the Lord has not answered that He is giving you a final no. The *no* may be a temporary no and not a permanent no. When Moses cried out for God to heal Miriam of leprosy, the Lord immediately said no—not at that moment, but she was healed seven days later in order to follow a pattern of the law and teach the outspoken sister of the prophet Moses to henceforth restrain herself from making careless comments. (See Numbers 12.)

Some delays are actually seasons of preparation to get the junk out of us so the Lord can get His direction in us! We are not always ready to enact God's will when we think we are. One of the greatest dangers in ministry is when a minister or even a church thinks they have *arrived* and have all of the answers. As long as the fruit on a tree is green, it will grow, but if it keeps hanging on after it matures, it can eventually turn rotten. If we maintain a teachable spirit in the process of moving toward the favor of God, we will always learn and step up to the next level of revelation for God's kingdom. Once we think that we have arrived, we can stagnate.

When Bathsheba and David's illegitimate son was born, he was stricken with a sickness. David spent seven days with his face on the ground in intercession asking God to heal the child. After seven days the child passed away. God did not heal the child, but that's not the end of the story. Bathsheba became pregnant with a second son of David's, who was named *Solomon*, meaning "peaceful" and "loved of the Lord" (2 Sam. 12:24). The sorrow of one son's early death was replaced by the joy of another son's birth. Solomon would become one of the Bible's wisest men and the builder of the most magnificent temple in Israel's history!

Not every road is straight. There will be potholes, roadblocks, and detours on the journey. This is because you must deal with people when you pursue your dream. Always remember that people will never understand what you are sensing in the same way that you do. When our ministry began to grow and I hired many wonderful workers, it took years for me to realize that they will not have the burden for the *baby* (ministry) that I birthed and carried in just the same way I will. A babysitter may love the infant he or she is watching, but once the sitter walks out the door, his or her burden and sense of responsibility is over—until the next time that sitter enters the child's home.

As a young teenage minister, I attended ministers' meetings with many wonderful pastors and evangelists of the same denomination. Many times I was returning from an extended revival—four to eleven weeks in one church, where hundreds were converted to Christ. I entered the room like a little whirlwind, excited about the Lord's blessing and the spiritual results. Imagine one revival going eleven weeks with more than five hundred converts to Christ! Most of the time I couldn't refrain from telling what happened, and all

I would get in response was a smile and a look like, "OK, let's talk about something else." It seemed the other brethren were not as excited—in reality they weren't. They would have been more thrilled if the revival had been in their church and not someone else's!

IT WILL HAPPEN QUICKLY

Most scholars believe that the famed vision in the Book of Revelation was penned about A.D. 95. For those who believe that chapters 4–22 are futuristic in their interpretation, imagine writing about the future, and more than nineteen hundred years have passed and the events still have not unfolded! This may be one reason why some suggest that the book has been fulfilled throughout history, which is called the *historic interpretation*. Within the Book of Revelation there are several revealing passages that indicate when the time will arrive for the fulfillment of the prophecies.

They shall come to pass very quickly:

> The Revelation of Jesus Christ, which God gave him to show His servants—things which must shortly take place.
> —REVELATION 1:1

> "These words are faithful and true." And the Lord God of the holy prophets sent His angel to show His servants the things which must shortly take place.
> —REVELATION 22:6

In both verses the word "shortly" does not mean it will occur in the very near future (or shortly after John's death). Both Greek words mean "rapidly, quickly and swiftly." Christ was indicating that when the time comes, these events will begin happening in succession very quickly, one after the other.

A delay in a dream or vision will cause a person to exercise patience in waiting for the event to occur. In the Bible, faith and patience are the two power twins that keep a believer from becoming weary and faint in his or her spirit while anticipating the prayer to be answered or the event to come to pass. As it is written:

> And we desire that each one of you show the same diligence to the full assurance of hope until the end, that you do not become sluggish, but imitate those who through faith and patience inherit the promises.
>
> —Hebrews 6:11–12

> Therefore do not cast away your confidence, which has great reward. For you have need of endurance, so that after you have done the will of God, you may receive the promise.
>
> —Hebrews 10:35–36

Remember, a delay is not a defeat. Being patient (having long endurance) is a part of the faith walk. In the end, what God has revealed will come to pass, and usually it happens very quickly.

four

NIGHTMARES AND DIRTY DREAMING

*When I say, "My bed will comfort me, my couch
will ease my complaint," then You scare me
with dreams and terrify me with visions.*

« Job 7:13–14 »

Many years ago in the days of cassette tapes, I taught a two-tape series simply called, "The Lust of the Flesh." My wife would tell me, "When people are at the resource table, looking over the cassette tape albums, you should see how they react to that album. When purchasing it, they turn it over so no one can see the title! It's like they are embarrassed for someone near them to think, 'Wow, are they having trouble with the lust of the flesh?'" The same is true when it comes to nightmares and dirty dreams. A person may tell you about a nightmare or a dream with frightening imagery, but there are some types of dreams no one wants to talk about. People need instruction about that, something I call *dirty dreaming*.

At times a person will experience dreams that would be considered *vile* or *violent*. In a dream a person may see a violent attacker, a thief, or a dangerous character who is attempting to harm him or a family member. These negative nightly apparitions have that individual participating in them like an actor on a stage, causing his blood pressure to rise and heart rate to increase while he is sleeping. Some people awaken and are breathing heavy. Such a dream is often called a *nightmare*, although the word has nothing to do with a female horse called a *mare*. It is said to have originated in the 1300s as *nigt-mare*, a female spirit that attempted to afflict a sleeper with the feeling of suffocating at night. The word was also used throughout parts of Europe and was eventually linked with an *incubus spirit*, which caused people to have bad dreams. By the year 1829, it became a common word to describe a bad dream.[1]

There are also rare occasions in the life of a believer when a person experiences a dream that he or she prefers not to talk about because the scenes in the dream were very lewd, vile, or seductive. It may involve the dreamer in an act of adultery, in a compromising position, or acting in a manner that the believer would never participate in. These troubling, unclean dreams can simply be called *dirty dreams.*

From a Jewish rabbinical point of view, nightmares and unclean dreams can be the result of a demonic spirit (called a *lilin* or a night spirit) that is in the room of the person attempting to sleep or in the process of sleep.[2] In the New Testament there are several terms used for wicked spirits, including: evil spirits (Luke 8:2), foul spirits (Mark 9:25, KJV), unclean spirits (Mark 1:27), spirits of infirmity (Luke 13:11), and seducing spirits (1 Tim. 4:1, KJV). These spirits are types of what Christians call demons. The word *demon* is the Greek word *daimon,* meaning "a spirit or something with divine power." In the New Testament, such as in Matthew 8:31 (KJV), the word "devils" is the Greek word *daimon.* In the Old Testament, demons were associated with idolatry and led people into worshiping idols, as indicated in Deuteronomy 32:17; Isaiah 13:21; 34:14; 65:3.[3] If an evil spirit in the atmosphere can send fiery darts (Eph. 6:16) into the mind of a believer sleeping at night, then it is no fault of a believer if they dream some strange and bizarre dream. For many years I have said that believers are certainly responsible when they are awake for what they see and hear, but they actually have no control over their sleep and any dream they may have.

Normally, if a person does not watch violent or vile movies before going to bed and has not eaten a huge meal that is causing the body to work hard to digest while the person is sleeping, he or she normally will have a regular cycle of dreams and sleep quite well. In this setting, it will be rare to have a nightmare or a dirty dream. However, there are times when you have kept your mind clean and you still have a very nasty dream. While this may happen rarely, it causes a person to feel unclean when he or she awakes. The images of the nightmare or seductive dream will remain with that person throughout the day. This is one reason why praying before going to bed and after rising up is very important. In the time of the temples, the Lord instructed the priest to place a lamb on the altar in the morning and in the evening (Exod. 29:39–42). In the morning you begin your workday, and in the evening you are preparing to rest. Prayer can renew your mind in the morning when you begin your day and in the evening as you conclude your day. We no longer apply the physical blood of a slain animal, but through our faith and confession we can apply the blood of Christ, the Lamb of God, and this is how believers overcome Satan (Rev. 12:11).

THE SOURCE OF NIGHTMARES

There is no direct Scripture passage or, to my knowledge, church tradition as to why at times sweet dreams turn sour. After many years of a full-time traveling ministry, I have several suggestions from the library of personal experience.

The atmosphere surrounding you

If you travel much, you soon learn that all hotels and motels have their own *atmosphere*. The *spiritual air* has little or nothing to do with the type of bed, the colors in the room, or the pictures on the wall. Early in my ministry, our local church revivals would often continue for an average of two weeks, some lasting as long as eleven weeks each night—without a break. Pam and I, and later Jonathan, our son, would live in a small motel room with a bed, a round table, and two chairs for weeks on end. In the early days, few churches could afford to provide a suite or a large living space, and the smaller towns did not have contemporary facilities. Believe me, after about two weeks, *cabin fever* hit us, and we had to get out for brief periods to prevent the four walls from driving us a little batty! I recall in the early 1980s that there was one hotel in Calhoun, Georgia, where we camped out in one small room for three weeks. My wife and I experienced extreme difficulty sleeping, were restless the entire time, and felt uneasiness with the entire place. It took me several years to realize that in a motel/hotel setting, there were other people sleeping in the room before we arrived who may have had their own unclean spirits controlling their lives, and individuals possessed with unclean spirits may be sleeping in a room next door!

These individuals are often not Christians and may spend their evening watching pornography, violence, or horror movies on the hotel cable or pay channels. At times, some folks would be in their rooms high on drugs, and you could occasionally hear men through the walls mumbling in a loud tone under the influence of alcohol. The lesser-priced hotel rooms attracted more of these types of individuals. We have actually heard couples fighting behind closed doors or groups of young people partying in their rooms until three in the morning, knowing we had to be up at seven for an early Sunday morning service at the church. There were times I felt like getting up, opening the door, and just yelling, "Praise God," at the top of my lungs in retaliation to the beer guzzlers who disrupted my sleep all night!

The atmosphere in the more family-oriented hotel chains did not permit these types of disruptions, and thus sleep came easier and naturally. After years of pondering why some rooms seemed more restful than others, I realized that when a person sleeps (in a room near me), if that person is under the influence of an unclean spirit, that spirit does not sleep when the person is sleeping, because the spirit world does not require sleep as we humans do (Ps. 121:4). Thus when a person is sleeping, the evil spirit is free to enter and exit the person's body at will (Matt. 12:43). At times I could sense a troubling presence in my room and knew it was not something I had invited to join me!

An example in the Bible is when King Saul was troubled by an evil spirit, and as David played the harp, the evil spirit departed from Saul, and he was "refreshed and well" (1 Sam. 16:23). At a later time, the same spirit returned to Saul, and he attempted to kill David with a javelin (1 Sam. 18:10–11). Only when David ministered to Saul through anointed music was the nervous king relieved from his mental oppression. Just as this evil spirit could enter and exit at times, when Pam and I would stay in certain areas, our sleep could be disrupted, I believe, by evil entities that were roaming in the night. This uneasy presence in the atmosphere may be the result of who was previously in the room or who is staying in nearby rooms.

The spirits ruling over the region

During our extensive evangelistic traveling ministry, there were two major cities in which I could sense a very dark, almost depressing or oppressive spiritual presence. The first was Savannah, Georgia, and the other was Tampa, Florida. My first experience in Savannah was shortly after I was married in the early 1980s. We were staying in the home of the pastor of a large church where I was ministering nightly. Both my wife and I were very restless and unable to get any complete sleep. Our dreams were very troubling and left us tired when we arose. After extended prayer I sensed there was some form of *occult spirit* in the area. When I told the pastor, he revealed this to the church, as Reverend Lester Sumrall had recently stated that he sensed a very strong occult spirit over the city. The pastor stood before the church and said that it was confirmed that there was a spirit of the occult over the area. That night we also learned of a group of six witches who lived across the street from the pastor's house. Thus our own spirits were sensitive to the very atmosphere in the area.

In the late 1980s we began ministering in the Tampa area. The area we were ministering in and staying in was located in South Tampa. At the time this was perhaps the darkest and most oppressive atmosphere I had ever encountered. Our son was still an infant, and each night at exactly twelve thirty he would awake, screaming and shaking. This went on the entire time we were in the city and ceased when we departed. I soon discovered that the Tampa area was noted for being a very seductive area, with one man in particular in charge of numerous adult strip clubs and other forms of pornography that surrounded us in every direction. It was a city where certain types of people came out at night to party, drink, take drugs, and pack out the strip clubs. It was also rumored that the Mafia had moved their center to Tampa because of the drugs being run through Florida.

It appears that often the atmosphere in major cities can be traced to the types of sins, iniquities, and carnal pleasures that dominate or control those living in those particular areas. Sin is more than a three-letter word. It involves carnal thoughts that lead to actions that impact the person and alter the person's personality, which in return alters the spiritual atmosphere. When there are numerous believers influencing the morals and laws of a community, there will follow a spirit of peace and tranquility throughout the region. When drugs are being sold on street corners, gangs roam like hungry wolves, bars are filled with drunken men, and seducing spirits capture the imagination of the youth, then a covering of spiritual evil can be felt when a person is awake and asleep. As it is written, "When the righteous are in authority, the people rejoice; but when a wicked man rules, the people groan" (Prov. 29:2).

The signs and sounds stuck in your head

The third possible reason for the type of dream is related to what a person may see or hear prior to going to bed. Years ago in Ohio, I was concluding a message when a man jumped to his feet shouting, "My boy... please help my boy; something is wrong with him!" I asked the church to stretch their hand toward the lad, who appeared to be having a seizure. We began to pray, and I did as Christ would—I began rebuking the spirit that was attacking the eleven-year-old. Immediately the shaking stopped and his eyes were back to normal. The father was weeping and the church rejoicing.

Afterward I asked the father if his son was an epileptic, and he responded, "No." He then said, "This has never happened before." I was in shock and could not understand why this had happened to the lad. Then the father confessed, "I allowed him to watch the movie *The Exorcist* on a movie channel. Do you think this opened a door?"

My jaw dropped, and I just stared at him for a moment. I knew the Bible told of a young child that a spirit had controlled, often throwing him into the water and fire to destroy him (Mark 9:20–23). I also recalled where the father informed Christ that a spirit had come upon his son from the time he had been a child (v. 21). Spirits can physically attack children, but it is important not to allow any form of visual or verbal activities that emphasize the occult, demonic activity, or seductive sexual innuendos from planting seeds in their minds. Such seed planted can actually open a door to a tormenting or oppressive spirit. It may have been fear of what the lad saw that opened the door for a physical attack to come.

If you enjoy bloodthirsty horror movies with vampires chewing human flesh and coloring their fangs with human blood, then never question why you are having terrible dreams at night. If you spend your free time feeding your spirit violent programs, movies, or reading the latest "kill them and bury them" magazines, then when you begin dreaming that you are carrying a shotgun shooting up the innocents in the town, you have sights and sounds stuck in your head during the day whose wrong *seeds* are producing bad *fruit* in the night.

Many men are drawn to a secret addiction—Internet pornography. In the past, full nudity was only available to purchase under the counter at certain stores or purchased as pay-per-view movies. The technology has now moved to the personal laptop, with thousands of images available with the click of the button. The male mind can be easily pulled into the cyber world of pornography, cementing images on the brain that will never be removed. Men will then go to bed with their wives, uninterested in her love and affection, having become rooted in an emotional affair with a lifeless, full-color image of a female stranger. Peaceful sleep will turn into a tormenting nightmare or a *dirty dream*, which will leave even a loving husband restless in the morning from a night journey in the world of the subconscious. Many homes are being wrecked because a man or woman became connected to a total stranger on the World Wide Web. Perhaps the word *web* describes well what can happen when you log on to the wrong sites.

HOW TO STOP NIGHTMARES AND DIRTY DREAMING

Set the atmosphere in the room.

I have discovered by experience some practical insights on how you can change the atmosphere. Years ago a Christian musician, Phil Driscoll, shared how music alters any atmosphere. He told that when he checked into a hotel, he took a tape player with praise and worship cassettes. When he went out for a meal, he left the music playing to *purge the atmosphere* in the room. After hearing this, I decided to try this, and did—and it became a routine, not just on one occasion, but continually during my extended revivals. The Word and worship coming from the cassette tapes (now CDs) filled the atmosphere. When I would forget the tapes, I would keep the television channel on a Christian television program.

You can experience this *shifting* in a church service. The atmosphere begins to change, similar to when clouds bring a cool rain in the summer heat. The Bible is God's written Word, but it must be spoken to become a life-changing force. There is no difference between someone speaking (or singing) in person and speaking or singing on a DVD or audio CD, as there is power and authority in the spoken Word (Heb. 4:12).

Set the atmosphere in the room where you are going to sleep, including your own personal bedroom. If it is not with worship music, then let it be through prayer and personal worship prior to sleeping. Worship brings heaven down to the earth, and evil spirits are unable to remain in the same room where the worshipers are exalting Christ. In Mark 5 there was one man possessed by a legion of evil spirits. However, when Christ stepped off the boat, the possessed man "ran and worshiped him" (Mark 5:6). Not even a legion of spirits could prevent this man from worshiping the Lord!

Purge the mind by the renewal of the spirit.

There is a simple but powerful passage in 2 Corinthians 4:16: "Therefore we do not lose heart. Even though our outward man is perishing, yet the inward man is being renewed day by day." The same thought is repeated in Colossians 3:10: "...and have put on the new man who is renewed in knowledge according to the image of Him who created him." The Greek word for *renewed* in these passages comes from two words: *ana*, meaning "back again," and *kainos*, meaning "made different." It means to make different again.[4] It is a continual process of making it new and helping you to think differently. The renewing of the mind is a daily process. Throughout a common day, there is much clutter and excessive baggage that distracts and fills our thoughts. To remove this means to clear the channels through the "washing of water by the word" (Eph. 5:26).

I have never been able to explain this, but every time I have opened my Bible and began to read it, there is a peace and a renewal that I sense. There are wisdom books such as Psalms and Proverbs that give practical instructions and inspire a person's spirit. After reading and meditating on the Scriptures, my mind feels clean and refreshed. It can be compared to the mind being washed in water!

Claim the promises of rest.

There are two beautiful passages believers can read, speak aloud, and receive for their personal benefit prior to going to bed at night:

> I will both lie down in peace, and sleep; for You alone, O LORD, make me dwell in safety.
> —PSALM 4:8

> When you lie down, you will not be afraid; yes, you will lie down and your sleep will be sweet.
> —PROVERBS 3:24

One of my staff workers, Andrea Anderson, shared during a Friday morning staff devotional how when she was a little girl she would have nightmares continually. Her father, a dedicated believer, would go into her room and pray for her to have a good night's sleep. She commented, "Every time my dad prayed, I would go right to sleep and never have a scary dream or nightmare. However, if for some reason he was not able to pray, it seemed on those nights I did not sleep as well and would have disturbing dreams."

Having two children, my wife and I have both discovered the significance of praying with our children prior to their going to sleep each night. We have taught our children never to go to sleep without first praying. Our daughter is read a story each night, and she prays a special prayer from her heart. She sleeps very well and always gets up alert and ready to go. (I wish I could bottle that energy!) I can recall our son, Jonathan, as a young child lying beside me in the bed, and we would talk about how there were angels assigned to protect children. At times, just before he went to sleep he would say, "Dad, raise your hands and see if you can feel an angel in the room!" He nicknamed my right arm the "angel detector"! We had so much fun, and he too rested well and seldom (that I can recall) awoke with any form of troubling dream.

During Christ's earthly ministry, parents would present their children to Christ requesting Him to lay His hands upon them and bless them. In my book *Breaking the Jewish Code*, under the chapter that deals with how Jewish parents raise their children according to life cycles, I wrote about the importance of parents blessing their children:

> The Torah reveals the importance of verbally blessing your children. Isaac spoke blessings over Jacob and Esau (Gen. 27), and Jacob blessed the two sons of Joseph (Gen. 48), later passing blessings to his sons (Gen. 49). Before Moses's death, he pronounced a prophetic blessing on the tribes of Israel (Deut. 33). Devout Jewish parents and grandparents continually offer blessings over their children and grandchildren, believing in God's ability to transfer His favor through their prayers.
>
> Blessings are preformed on Sabbath days, feast days, and various special occasions. It is important to begin the prayers of blessing when the children are young, tenderhearted, and more receptive, as they tend to feel more awkward as they enter their late teens.
>
> The pattern for blessing children is narrated in Genesis 48:2, when Jacob blessed Ephraim and Manasseh. Jacob sat on the edge of his bed when blessing his grandsons. The writer to the Hebrews wrote that Jacob blessed his own sons, "…leaning on the top of his staff" (Heb. 11:21). Today, those performing the blessing on their children prefer to stand up in respect to approaching God's throne. When preparing for a blessing, ask the children

to bow their heads, teaching them reverence to God, and tell them the blessing was practiced by their ancestors as in Genesis 24:48 and in Exodus 12:17, when Israel was departing from Egypt.

In Hebrew, the word *smicha* means, "laying on of hands." In the temple, the priest would lay hands upon animals, symbolizing the transfer of sins. On the Day of Atonement, a goat was used, which became the scapegoat. Jacob blessed the sons of Joseph, Ephraim and Manasseh by laying hands upon their heads (Gen. 48:14). Before his death, Moses transferred his wisdom and authority to Joshua by the laying on of hands (Deut. 34:9).

Prior to the blessing, lay both hands upon the head of the child or one hand on the head of each child if there are two children. A general Jewish blessing that is prayed every Sabbath by the father over his a son is: "May God make you as Ephraim and Manasseh." A general blessing spoken over a daughter is: "May God make you as Sarah, Leah, Rebekah, and Rachel." A favorite blessing that can be pronounced is the same words Jacob spoke over Ephraim and Manasseh:

The Angel who has redeemed me from all evil,
Bless the lads;
Let my name be named upon them,
And the name of my fathers Abraham and Isaac;
And let them grow into a multitude in the midst of the
    earth.
—GENESIS 48:16

One ancient blessing that was prayed over the people by the high priest is the special blessing the priest prayed over the people in the time of Moses and at both Jewish temples.

The LORD bless you and keep you;
The LORD make His face shine up you,
And be gracious to you;
The LORD lift up His countenance upon you,
And give you peace.

—NUMBERS 6:24–26[5]

Another important comment from the book reads:

Christ's disciples said, "Teach us how to pray" (Luke 11:1). They knew Christ engaged in early morning prayer (Mark 1:35) and witnessed miracles resulting from His prayer life. The best way of teaching your children how to pray is to be an example and pray yourself!

As a child in the 1960s, I can recall my father praying in his upstairs church office with the windows opened. I just knew they could hear him across the river at the county jail. Many times in the evening I could hear Dad's prayers filtering up through the air vents in my bedroom floor as he interceded in the basement of our house. When I was sick or in difficulty, I believed God would hear Dad's prayers. His prayer life was an example and a pattern for me to understand *how* to pray. Let your children see and hear you pray at home, and not just in church.

The simplest *beginner* prayers are praying at bedtime. In bedtime prayer, Orthodox Jews mention four archangels, two which are mentioned in the Bible (Michael and Gabriel) and two found in Apocryphal (nonbiblical) sources. They pray, "In the name of the Lord, the God of Israel: Michael on my right, Gabriel on my left, Uriel before me, Raphael behind me, and above my head the Shekinah [presence] of God." Raphael was traditionally an angel of healing, and Uriel was believed to be the guiding light of the Holy Scriptures.[6] Children should learn a bedtime prayer as soon as they can speak.

Before sending a child off to school, a parent should pray with them. Using the scripture "So Abraham rose early in the morning" (Gen. 22:3), the *Shacharit,* meaning "early morning hour," prayers were the first of three daily prayers. The moment a devout Jew awakes, he prays, "I gratefully thank You, O living and eternal King, for You have returned my soul within me with compassion— abundant is Your faithfulness."[7] We know Christ prayed a great while before sunrise (Mark 1:35), and at the temple morning prayers were offered as the sun rose, beginning a new day. As a parent, speak a protective prayer over your children before they depart from the security of your dwelling.[8]

Perhaps you are a single parent and are very busy working and raising your children. It is important for you to use those special moments at night prior to your child (or children) going to bed to share a devotional and for you to personally pray over your children, asking the loving heavenly Father to give them "sweet sleep" (Prov. 3:24). If you are troubled with your own ability to properly rest at night, then consider the following promise from the Word of God:

> You will keep him in perfect peace, whose mind is stayed on You, because he trusts in You.
> —Isaiah 26:3

> You will guard him and keep him in perfect and constant peace whose mind [both its inclination and its character] is stayed on You, because he commits himself to You, leans on You, and hopes confidently in You.
> —Isaiah 26:3, AMP

In the 1611 King James translation the verse says "perfect peace." In Hebrew, the original language of Isaiah, it reads that God will preserve you in "shalom, shalom." The Hebrew word *shalom* means "to be at peace, to be complete and whole." It is used among Jews as a greeting similar to saying "good morning" or "hello" and is often used when saying good-bye.

If the English translators had translated this literally, it would read: "that God will guard you in 'peace, peace...'" In English the repetition of a word back to back would appear to be a grammatical error. In English you would never say, "God loves, loves you," or "You look good, good," but you would say, "God has *great* love for you," or "You look exceptionally well." It appears that when the Bible translators saw the words "peace, peace," they translated the two words for peace as "perfect peace." Years ago as I was meditating on this double peace reference, I recalled that the human brain consists of two different hemispheres, the left and right, with each hemisphere being the command center for different parts of the body. This double peace, to me, can allude to peace covering both the left and right hemisphere in the human brain! In other words, God will keep (guard) and secure all parts and sections of your mind in His peace!

God believes in rest. He set a pattern for us all when He rested on the seventh day of Creation (Gen. 2:2) and established a day of rest each week for us to enjoy (Exod. 16:26–29). He also desires that you sleep well and that your dreams be peaceful, not troubling, and that you be instructed by the Word and the Holy Spirit to discern between a carnal nightmare and a true spiritual warning from the Lord.

five

FALSE PROPHETS AND FALSE DREAMS

*I have heard what the prophets have said who
prophesy lies in My name, saying, "I have dreamed,
I have dreamed!" How long will this be in the
heart of the prophets who prophesy lies? Indeed
they are prophets of the deceit of their own heart,
who try to make My people forget My name by
their dreams which everyone tells his neighbor,
as their fathers forgot My name for Baal.*

« Jeremiah 23:25–27 »

When writing about the significance of spiritual dreams, I want to be perfectly clear that a person is not to live their life by dreams but by the Word of God. A true dream or vision will always be in agreement with the written Scriptures and will complement the will of God in a person's life. The Scriptures make it clear that some self-acclaimed prophets can and will attempt to manipulate the hearts of innocent and sincere individuals with a false word and false dream.

From the time of Moses and throughout the generations of the biblical prophets, one of the major thorns in the flesh of true prophets was the number of false prophets who often challenged the prophets of the Lord. In the time of King Ahab, a battle strategy was being planned in the war room, and King Jehoshaphat had aligned himself with the wicked leader Ahab. King Ahab marched his procession of *prophetic puppets* before his throne, all of them sounding like a broken record—predicting that if Ahab would go to battle, he would win! King Jehoshaphat sensed the hollow sound of these predictions, which sounded like a parrot repeating the same words. He demanded to hear from one true prophet of the Hebrew God. The only man of God capable of bringing a true word was being held in the dungeon to prevent his *negative* predictions from mixing with the *positive* prophets and possibly confusing someone! The *real* prophet, Micaiah, was released long enough to give a word, only he was placed on a verbal restriction from the prison guard to only speak a smooth, positive word that agreed with the false prophets. He played the game, until Ahab demanded him to speak the truth.

That's when the wicked king got an earful! Micaiah saw a vision in which the angels of heaven were gathered on the left and right side of God's throne. The prophet saw where God was going to set up Ahab to be slain in the battle by permitting a "lying spirit" to deceive all of the palace's false prophets and set up Ahab to believe their lying prediction of victory (2 Chron. 18:1–27). I call this *the battle of the dueling prophets.* One alleged prophet, Zedekiah, slapped Micaiah on the face and demanded to know, "Which way did the spirit from the Lord go from me to speak to you?" (v. 23). One man was predicting a great victory and the other was predicting death. One was going to be correct and the other proven a liar. God's prophet won the duel!

PERSONAL PROPHECY

Today there is a real hunger among multitudes to experience a genuine, life-changing spiritual encounter and to hear a clear word from the Lord. Any individual who has an inner craving for knowledge, understanding, and wisdom must begin feeding himself or herself with what is called the "milk of the word" (1 Pet. 2:2). It is written in Hebrews 5:13 that those who use milk are babes in Christ and are not skilled in the word of righteousness. That is, they do not yet understand the deeper things of God. The spiritual meat (v. 14) is for the strong and mature believer. For example, a new convert to Christ should not attempt to tackle the prophetic teachings in the Book of Revelation! He or she should begin with the simple yet profound doctrines of salvation, sanctification, and the Holy Spirit baptism. Most ministers suggest that babes in Christ study the Gospel of John first. Also, new converts need knowledge in baptism in water and how to live and walk by faith. Once the foundations of faith have been laid, then a believer can move on to the deeper truths in the Scripture. The writer of Hebrews wrote:

> But solid food [meat] belongs to those who are of full age,
> that is, those who by reason of use have their senses exercised to discern both good and evil.
> —Hebrews 5:14

As believers read, study, and feed from the Word of God, their spiritual hunger and thirst will be satisfied. The Word of God is "quick, and powerful" (Heb. 4:12, KJV). These two words mean "alive and energized." I have more than fifty thousand hours of Bible study, research, and reading of thousands of books; I have often said that some people need a drug to get them high, but my *high* comes from receiving a nugget or insight from God's Word that I was unaware of! The answers on how to believe, how to pray, how to treat others, and how to give and be a blessing are all found in the Bible. The new covenant is established on promises, and you can live a victorious life when you plant the seed of the Word in you and allow it to mature and bring forth fruit of righteousness.

Many believers, however, have never learned to hear that still small voice within and to follow those little nudges and sudden inner urges. The Holy Spirit directs and leads us from inside our spirit. Because baby believers may struggle with understanding and hunger to hear from the Lord, they can easily become caught up with a person who allegedly is giving out *personal prophecies*. A personal prophecy is usually spoken by someone who has labeled himself or herself as a *prophet* or a *prophetess*.

I am a fourth-generation minister and have a very solid heritage in the truth of the Word, and I have seen about every type of spiritual *fruit and nut* that has ever popped out of the Christian garden. I have heard from deluded individuals who claimed they were Elijah or one of the two witnesses of Revelation 11. I have read the letters of self-acclaimed prophets who said if I did not send them money, I would be under a curse. I have heard of deceivers who would manipulate the masses or use their alleged prophetic gifts to draw in income for their own selfish greed. One-self acclaimed prophet came to a church in Georgia to *preach*, claiming he was gifted with a special anointing to increase your blessing under one condition: if you gave an offering to his ministry. The only *catch* was that the length and type of prayers he was *anointed* to pray for a person were based upon the amount of money that person gave to him in the offering. The man organized four different lines: the $50, $500, $1,000, and $5,000 lines. Those giving $50 got a slap on the head and a "God bless you." The $500 folks got a longer prophecy with more *benefits* guaranteed for their obedience. The one woman who gave $5,000 received a long *word*, a long prayer, the personal address of the self-acclaimed prophet, and his private phone number.

The sad aspect is that Christians sitting under this shyster's ministry believed he had some hotline to heaven that could release God's special favor. For some reason, many of these self-acclaimed prophets and prophetesses link their ability to be a blessing to you on the amount of money that comes from you. Can you imagine the apostle Peter's reaction today if he was a false prophet and Simon the sorcerer from Samaria came to him and said, "I'll give you money, if you will give me the gift of laying hands upon people to receive the Holy Spirit"? (See Acts 8:18–19.) Some of today's so-called prophets would grab Simon, bring him to the platform, and shout, "Folks, God is moving! This man is a sorcerer, but he has felt impressed to plant a large seed in the ministry. You know God can bless a man even if he's not all right at this time, so raise your hands this way and let's pray a blessing on him!"

However, Peter was a true prophet, and instead of taking the magician's money, Peter rebuked Simon and said, "Your money perish with you, because you thought that the gift of God could be purchased with money!" (Acts 8:20). Peter discerned the sorcerer was "poisoned by bitterness and bound by iniquity" (v. 23).

While some may disagree with what I am going to say, when it comes to the area of personal prophecy, I cannot find in the Scriptures where any apostle or prophet had a ministry of continually giving individuals a *word from the Lord.* At times they received a word of wisdom or a word of knowledge (1 Cor. 12:7–10), but no believers stood in a long line to *get a word;* instead they sat and heard the preaching of God's Word and then allowed the Holy Spirit to confirm that word through signs, wonders, and the gifts of the Holy Spirit (Heb. 2:4). I once had a worker who was constantly saying, "The Lord told me this, and He told me that." The problem arose when little of what she said came to pass! I told my wife, "This girl seems to receive more words from God than the prophets of the Bible received."

Most of the personal prophetic utterances in the New Testament were words of *warning*—not *blessings* or *guarantees of prosperity.* (See Acts 11:28; 21:10–11.) In fact, in the Book of Acts, the disciples in Jerusalem were selling their property and dividing the money among other believers. The main reason was that Christ had already predicted that Jerusalem would be destroyed within one generation. If the city was doomed, then why continue living there? These followers of Christ *got out while the getting was good!* The message they heard was not, "Yea, I say I am going to bring thee out and prosper thy business with great money for the kingdom." It was, "Not one stone shall be left upon another....When you see Jerusalem surrounded by armies...flee to the mountains....Let him who is on the housetop not go down to take anything out of his house" (Matt. 24:2; Luke 21:20–21; Matt. 24:17). A real prophet would not just pronounce a prosperity blessing on the unsanctified, but he would chastise the ungodly and rebuke the believer who was living contrary to the Word of God.

I feel about this issue the way the great minister named Lester Sumrall did. I once heard him teach and say that he believed that under the new covenant, if you prayed and lived close to the Lord in the way you should, the Lord would speak directly to you, and you would not need a second party to bring the message to you!

Any *word* from a second party would only confirm what you already knew in your heart. This is the reason why anyone giving a prophecy is required to be judged by others (1 Cor. 14:29). Some believers remind me, "But Paul talked about the gift of prophecy and said all could prophesy." We must understand that the word *prophesy* does not hold just one meaning—to reveal the future. Paul said that "you can all prophesy…that all may learn and all may be encouraged" (v. 31). A *prophetic word* in the church comes from a person who speaks under divine inspiration to edify, exhort, and comfort believers through the revelation of the Word and the Spirit (v. 3). A prophetic word may contain a warning of coming danger.

As believers mature in the Word and in their spiritual walk, they will discover that God begins to direct them inwardly. Then the Almighty will release words of wisdom and knowledge, and eventually He will permit insight to be revealed through dreams and visions. You must exercise discernment, however, when any individual begins to relate a dream in which *you* were in the dream. You should have knowledge of that person's spiritual life, his or her integrity in the Word, and if past dreams have had true meanings and have come to pass. Otherwise, some may either ignorantly or willingly manipulate a person's plans or decisions by a dream that is misinterpreted.

In the late 1980s I was hosting a tour to Israel with more than two hundred fifty believers joining me. A woman who was not going on the trip was washing dishes when suddenly she dropped a glass, and it broke. She said that suddenly she had a vision in her mind and heard a voice say, "Those going to Israel will come back broken like this glass!" She immediately called her friends and encouraged them to cancel their trip or they would return broken or injured. People planning to travel on the tour began calling me, concerned for their safety.

That is when I shared with them that years ago the Lord gave me a solid, faith-building word about any time I would travel to the Holy Land, saying, "The LORD your God is with you wherever you go" (Josh. 1:9). Since receiving that word in 1986, I have never hesitated to make the journey each year.

At that time, some fearful travelers canceled and others went. We returned, and no one was hurt or injured. The woman totally misread what she *felt*.

Often when a person *misses their prediction*, they will attempt to cover their mistake. This was witnessed with a man who wrote a book titled *88 Reasons Why the Rapture Will Be in 1988*. The book caught on like a brush fire, with millions of Christians waiting until that set day in September to see if indeed the day and hour had arrived. When the date passed, the author wrote a new book, stating he had missed the fact that there is no zero year between 1 B.C. and A.D. 1. Thus he suggested the calculation was off by one year. The new date was the fall of 1989. After that date passed, we never heard back from the fellow.

The false prophets of the Old Testament had no ability to "read the times" in the same manner the righteous prophets could. One tribe of Israel was given a gift of *knowing* where things were *going*:

> ...of the sons of Issachar who had understanding of the times, to know what Israel ought to do...
>
> —1 CHRONICLES 12:32

"I WILL MARRY PERRY"

Many years ago I was preaching a three-week revival in Montgomery, Alabama. At the time I was a twenty-two-year-old single preacher who was engaged to be married the following Friday after the revival closed. After I stood to announce that I was leaving Montgomery to get married in Northport, I received a call the following morning from a woman from the church. She said that she had a dream that I was missing the will of God and should not be getting married at that time. She was very adamant and said she heard from the Lord a lot, and I should take heed to her warning. Herein was the *clash* between the *dueling revelations*. This woman said she was hearing from the Lord. However, the Holy Spirit had spoken to me in a four-week revival three years earlier at the same church in Northport, Alabama, telling me that I would marry a beautiful girl named Pam Taylor. For more than two and one-half years we *dated* by phone. I was certain I was in the will of God and had perfect peace (which I discovered is the key to knowing you are in the will of God). I found out later that the woman who called had a teenage daughter who had a *crush* on me during the revival. This woman was obviously speaking out of her own spirit, since I have been happily married for more than thirty years!

The point is that when a second-party person brings you warnings, you must "recognize those who labor among you, and are over you in the Lord and admonish you" (1 Thess. 5:12) in order to determine the level of trust you can safely place in their words. Just as the Bible teaches, "Do not lay hands on anyone hastily" (1 Tim. 5:22), we must exercise caution in receiving a *personal word*. It is very possible that the Lord can and will use another person to speak a warning or an encouragement into your life, as this is one way the body of Christ can "bear one another's burdens" (Gal. 6:2). However, the *word* must be judged. I know of one man who claims a major *prophetic gift* and continually makes predictions that are all marked as a *word from the Lord*. His reputation is in doubt because of his level of *accuracy*, as more than 50 percent of the time what he predicts never happens (he often places dates and times upon events). I don't know about you, but this is not the type of person I want giving me a *word*, for how would I know if it was from the Lord or if he was just speaking out of his own intellect?

It reminds me of the story of a minister who called a woman from the audience and announced, "God said you are called to go to China." She began weeping. He called a man out and said, "The Lord says you are called to be a missionary in India." He began crying, and he grabbed the woman, and they both were arm in arm crying. The minister said, "Do you know each other?"

The woman said, "Yes, we are husband and wife!" In an attempt to get out of the dilemma, the minister cried out, "I see it now—you are both called to Indochina!" Of course he was off target, but the couple lived in fear that they were out of God's will. One of my ministry partners, who has a successful personal business, called me concerned and said, "A man came to our church who said he was a prophet. He called me up, telling me I was to prepare to travel full-time overseas, preaching and singing the gospel. First, I can't sing. Second, I don't feel called, but now I am totally confused!"

I replied, "God is not the author of confusion (1 Cor. 14:33), and if you don't bear witness with the prophetic word he gave, then pay no attention to it, as it must be judged before it is received anyway (1 Cor. 14:29). You are a praying man, and you can hear from God for yourself!" This is one reason why we are to "know them which labour among you" (1 Thess. 5:12, KJV).

The Lord instructed Moses, "It there arises among you a prophet or a dreamer of dreams, and he gives you a sign or a wonder, and the sign or the wonder comes to pass, of which he spoke to you, saying, 'Let us go after other gods'—which you have not known...you shall not listen to the words of that prophet or that dreamer of dreams" (Deut. 13:1–3). That person would be a false prophet.

JUDGING THE DREAM

It seems odd that we must *judge* a dream or vision, but this is true, since there are dreams that come from the flesh, dreams that come from the Spirit of God, and fiery mental darts (Eph. 6:16) that can create a dream from the presence of some unclean spirit, which may shoot an arrow in a believer's mind while he is asleep. How do we judge a dream?

Judge it by the Word of God.

As we have and will continue to discuss in this book, there are established methods we can use to determine if a dream is from the Lord. The greatest confirmation comes directly from the Word of God. If the dream instructs or implies that you are to act, speak, or live in a way contrary to God's Word, then it is not from the Lord. One married man said he had a dream that he was to leave his wife and marry another woman in the church, who was also married, thus breaking up two marriages to *fulfill God's purpose*. This is a seducing dream and definitely not from the Lord. According to Ephesians 5:25, husbands are to love their wives as Christ loved the church, and a "bishop then must be...the husband of one wife" (1 Tim. 3:2). If it's not right, it won't stand the test in the "light" (Ps. 119:105).

Judge it by the reputation of the dreamer.

The Bible is clear; there are occasional false teachers and false prophets. The apostle John wrote that there was a woman, identified as Jezebel, who "calls herself a prophetess" and who was sexually seducing men in the church (Rev. 2:20). She had a reputation on Earth as a prophetess, but in heaven she was a seducer. We need to begin to see people as *heaven sees* them, not as people *perceive them.* I have known of believers who truly loved God, but they followed ministries whose leaders were morally repugnant in their private lives, beating their companion, cursing, sleeping with numerous women, getting drunk, and still trying to reveal the mysteries of God in prophetic words. The reputation of the minister and the credibility of what he has spoken in the "name of the Lord" must always be considered before accepting any alleged word that God is sending you through a person.

For a moment I must boast about my precious father, who is a very humble individual. He can hardly talk about the Lord without weeping, and when he relates the old stories, he breaks down every time and cries. I cannot tell you the number of times Dad has experienced a warning dream or a vision, and it came to pass in great detail. In fact, I cannot think of one time when he was warned about something when the dream or vision did not come to pass. This is the test of a true prophetic person who is sensitive to the Holy Spirit.

One of the most bizarre accounts occurred years ago when we were praying in a house together. Dad began to "pray in the Spirit" (1 Cor. 14:15) and soon saw a mental vision. He said, "The Lord told me that great darkness is coming out of Lebanon. He also said that there would be confusion created between Yasser Arafat's group and Hamas." Within a few months Lebanon began stirring, and eventually Israel had a major summer war with Hezbollah in Lebanon. I was stunned when the PLO and Hamas in Gaza began killing each other during a power struggle. Dad used the word *Hezbos* and said the Lord would eventually judge "Hezbos."

I said, "Dad, it is Hezbollah."

He said, "I heard the word *Hezbos*."

I decided to go to the Internet and look up this word. It was actually a derogatory abbreviation and name for Hezbollah in Lebanon! The Lord was speaking down on this terror group! The word *Hezbos* is the plural form of *Hezbo*, which is often an abbreviated word for the name of the Hezbollah. In some instances the name *Hezbos* is used in a negative manner or even derogatory manner when speaking about Hezbollah, the noted terror network headquartered in Lebanon. How odd that Dad heard the name *Hezbos*, which indicated to me the Holy Spirit was mocking this group.

Paul taught that we should judge prophetic words (1 Cor. 14:29), and yet Christ taught in Matthew 7:1, "Do not judge, or you too will be judged" (NIV). Is this a contradiction? Paul was instructing believers not just to accept any word as from the Lord, but to weigh it as a group to ensure that the group judging the statement all bore witness to the accuracy of the statement. In Christ's warning not to judge, He was speaking about judging another person's personal life or spirituality, which was a common error among the Pharisees who always were criticizing others for the same sins they themselves were committing and trying to hide.

The closer the body of Christ moves toward the time of the end, the more important the ability to discern will be, for there will not only be false prophets with false words, but also there will arise a higher level of spiritual wickedness that causes a spiritual clash like that between Elijah and the false prophets of Baal!

six

THE PSYCHIC VOICES VERSUS
THE PROPHETIC VISIONS

*Give no regard to mediums and familiar
spirits; do not seek after them, to be defiled
by them: I am the LORD your God.*

« Leviticus 19:31 »

When empires are under spiritual and economic stress and nations flirt with iniquity while playing on the brink of an abyss called *judgment*, there always comes a clash between two kingdoms: the kingdom of God and the kingdom of Satan. It is more than a struggle between political parties called the conservatives and liberals, or divisions caused by two opposite moral views. This clash includes angelic messengers and demonic beings that are assigned in both camps to plot and plan against the opposing side. (See Daniel 10.) We see this battle when two Egyptian magicians, Jannes and Jambres, withstood Moses and duplicated Moses's miracle by turning the rods into serpents (Exod. 7:11–12; 2 Tim. 3:8). Centuries later, Elijah began preaching on Mount Carmel as 850 false prophets failed to pray down fire in the name of the weather god, Baal (1 Kings 18). These "prophets of Baal" were men motivated by compromise who had freely eaten at Queen Jezebel's table and were more concerned with a full belly in a famine than having the fullness of God during the crisis.

Most secular people view spiritual manifestations differently than a believer does. A secularist who hears that a believer was healed by prayer will call the process a *faith healing* and equate the results with some guru living in a hut on foreign soil who claims his followers believed and saw miraculous results. When a secular American with no biblical background hears of a minister of the gospel revealing a detailed word of wisdom or knowledge that comes to pass, the unbeliever will classify the minister as *just another psychic*. Once when I was ministering, a man who was cynical of spiritual manifestations said, "So what is the difference between a psychic telling someone correct information about himself and some preacher telling someone God's future plans?"

I replied, "The difference is that an alleged psychic will tell you what's on your mind, but a man of God will tell you what is on God's mind!"

Years ago a fad was spun that was quite expensive for those people caught in its web. There were alleged psychic phone networks that connected anyone in America with self-acclaimed psychics who were gifted to reveal your most intimate secrets and predict your future. The only stipulation was that it required your credit card to be charged between $3.95 to as high as $4.95 a minute to speak to this *professional* fortune-teller. There were individuals who ran up credit card bills as high as $30,000 after being hooked on their personal psychic. One woman said, "It was amazing. The psychic knew I was going through some emotional problems and that I was struggling with relationships and was having family difficulties." This poor, deceived soul was paying nearly five bucks a minute to have some unknown voice tell her *what she already knew*! It doesn't take a so-called psychic to tell you, "I see some difficulty you are experiencing, and you've had some broken relationships in your past," when about 99.99 percent of the people living have gone through difficulty and broken relationships.

These networks eventually went out of business. One in particular owed more than twenty million dollars for advertising and eventually filed for bankruptcy.[1] I would be quite upset with my *team of psychics* if this was my psychic network. With their ability to predict what was coming, why didn't at least one foresee the future and say, "I see in the future we are going bankrupt...get out of debt!" This is about as ludicrous as a story I heard in the mid-1990s while I was preaching in Modesto, California, about a self-acclaimed psychic who sued a hospital for millions of dollars, alleging that the hospital did an MRI on her brain and she lost her ability to see into the future.[2] If I had been the hospital's attorney, I would have placed the psychic on the stand and asked, "So you can prove you could reveal the future before the MRI?" If she replied yes, then I would ask, "If you were a real revealer of the future, why didn't you know that you would lose your power after you had the MRI?" Case closed!

Most of these networks were actually staffed by men or women operators on the other end who claimed gifts they did not have and who read from scripts while attempting to hold the caller on the line and collect as much money as possible. However, while the majority of these phony psychics could be arrested for false impersonation, there are some individuals who appear to have some form of an ability to *read a person's mind* or to reveal detailed information that is not normally known.

THE RISE OF FAMILIAR SPIRITS

In the early days of nations and empires, and in the infant stage of the nation of Israel, it was common for kings to inquire of men concerning the future. These included astrologers who claimed to read the positioning of the stars, including lunar and solar eclipses, meteorites, and comets. Ancient history could fill volumes with accounts of superstitious leaders who looked to the creation instead of the Creator. Pharaoh had magicians in his court. Nebuchadnezzar was teamed with his astrologers, magicians, and fortune-tellers. These kings believed these fortune-tellers were capable of interpreting dreams, omens, and signs in the sky.

There were, and still are today, times when a psychic, fortune-teller, or a *mind reader* is actually operating with what Scripture calls a "familiar spirit." In the days of Saul, the rebellious king had grieved the Holy Spirit, and God refused to answer Saul's prayer requests. In desperation the king sought out a witch who was operating through the force of a familiar spirit (1 Sam. 28:7, KJV). The witch conducted what is called a *séance*, attempting to bring the spirit of a departed righteous man, Samuel, from the underworld. An aged-looking spirit suddenly appeared to the witch, coming up from below the ground, and Saul *assumed* it was Samuel (1 Sam. 28:7–14). There are disagreements among theologians as to whether this was literally the spirit of Samuel or a familiar spirit imitating Samuel. Most believe the witch saw an apparition of some familiar spirit and the king did not, but the king "perceived that it was Samuel" (v. 14).

The reason for suggesting the spirit was a familiar spirit is because God had refused to answer Saul through known biblical methods such as dreams, prophetic words, or by the Urim (v. 6).

The Law of God forbade contact with witches:

> There shall not be found among you anyone who makes his son or his daughter pass through the fire, or one who practices witchcraft, or a soothsayer, or one who interprets omens, or a sorcerer.
> —Deuteronomy 18:10

Alleged contact with the dead is called *necromancy*. This was practiced among the heathen nations and empires of antiquity, but it was also forbidden by the Lord in the Law:

> Regard not them that have familiar spirits, neither seek after wizards, to be defiled by them: I am the Lord your God.
> —Leviticus 19:31, KJV

> There shall not be found among you any one that maketh his son or his daughter to pass through the fire, or that useth divination, or an observer of times, or an enchanter, or a witch. Or a charmer, or a consulter with familiar spirits, or a wizard, or a necromancer.
> —Deuteronomy 18:10–11, KJV

The English word *necromancer* is supposed to indicate the practice of consulting the dead for the reason of predicting the future.

The pagan tribes were very much into worshiping the dead, as was indicated in God's warnings to the Hebrew people. The Almighty told His chosen not to put any "cuttings in your flesh for the dead" (Lev. 19:28, KJV); neither should they make any "baldness between your eyes for the dead" (Deut. 14:1, KJV).

The false notion held among some ancients was that once a person's spirit departed his or her body and entered the next life, that person would be privy to information that was being discussed in the spirit realm, which was not known among those living on the earth. Thus the spirit of the departed was conjured up, and, using the voice of the *medium*, the spirit would speak through the medium and reveal the future. Kings could know if they would win or lose a war (this is the answer Saul was searching for). The biblical truth is that once a person's spirit has departed from the body at death, the spirit of the righteous enters the third heaven in a place called *paradise*, where it waits for the resurrection of the righteous (2 Cor. 12:1–4). If the soul and spirit are from a person who was unrighteous or wicked, when they departed the body, they were carried into a permanent chamber under the earth, where they are separated from God but will be raised to be judged in heaven at the Great White Throne judgment (Rev. 20:11–14). (See my book *Secrets Beyond the Grave* for detailed insight on the subject of life after death.)

How was it possible for a witch or a wizard to divine up information that was accurate and yet not known to the witch or fortune-teller? Some suggest it is a psychic gift. However, the answer is that it is accomplished through a *familiar spirit*. Those in the world of the occult incorrectly believe that a familiar spirit is actually the spirit of a departed loved one who is bringing information from the next world to those friends and family members living. However, this form of alleged spirit contact is forbidden according to the

Scripture (Lev. 19:31; 20:6, 27). In Scripture, the Hebrew word for *familiar* is *owb* and is used to describe a hollow sound, such as the sound produced when a person blows into the opening of an old water skin (an animal skin sewed together that held water). It is the same action as when a ventriloquist *throws his voice*, creating the illusion that the puppet on his lap is speaking. This is the same concept for how a person (called a medium) channels a familiar spirit. As the demonic presence enters the room, the medium, sometimes called a *channeler*, opens his or her mouth to speak, and instead of it being that person's normal voice, the pitch changes into a male or female voice. This is because the familiar spirit is "possessing," or taking control of, the physical body in order to communicate the message.

The reason a familiar spirit is called a *familiar* spirit is because it is familiar with the region from which it operates as well as the people and the circumstances that have existed in that region for centuries. We must remember that both angels and demons have existed from the earliest days of mankind. In Revelation we read of Michael the archangel battling Satan and casting the accuser from the second heaven to the earth during the final tribulation (Rev. 12:7–9). Yet we also read where the same angel, Michael, in centuries past, battled Satan for the body of Moses upon the death of the prophet (Jude 9). These two wars were with the same angels, yet more than thirty-five hundred years apart. The angel Gabriel brought heavenly understanding to Daniel, and hundreds of years later appeared to Zacharias and Mary (Dan. 9:21; Luke 1:19–35).

Since both angels and demons are spirit beings, and spirits never age and continually exist from generation to generation, they are familiar with the location, people, and circumstances in the region where they have dwelt and have had rulership for centuries. This may be why when Christ commanded the evil spirits to depart from the possessed man in Mark 5, the spirits requested that Christ would not send them out of the country (the region where they were, Mark 5:10) and that He would not confine them, at that moment, in the "deep," which is "the abyss" or bottomless pit in the Greek (Luke 8:31, KJV). These evil spirits were aware that Christ was the Son of God (Matt. 3:17). This was known from the time of His conception (Luke 1:31–35) to the time of His presentation in the temple (Luke 2:22–38) and during the season of His forty-day temptation prior to His public ministry (Luke 4:1–14). The first prophecy in the Bible was given by God Himself after Adam and Eve sinned in the Garden of Eden. God predicted, "I will put enmity between thee and the woman, and between thy seed and her seed; it shall bruise thy head" (Gen. 3:15, KJV). Thus, the demons knew who Jesus was from the beginning!

When the chief spirit in the possessed man asked Christ not to send them into the "pit" (abyss), how did these spirits know this would be their final place of confinement? After all, it would be more than sixty years later when the apostle John would actually see and record the obituary of Satan and his angels as they were cast into the abyss (the King James Version says "bottomless pit," Rev. 20:1). One Old Testament prophet, Isaiah, predicted that Lucifer would be "brought down...to the lowest depths of the Pit" (Isa. 14:15). We know from the temptation of Christ that Satan is familiar with the Bible, as he quoted a passage in Christ's presence that is found in Psalm 91:10–12. The adversary is also aware that when he is eventually cast out of heaven, he "has a short time" remaining (Rev. 12:12).

This information undergirds my point: the familiar spirits are familiar with information from the past and are able to relate it through the voice of a person who opens himself or herself up to being controlled or possessed by these spirits. In what is called the

New Age movement, individuals connect to spirits by *channeling* them in their bodies. Some claim these are *ascended masters* from the past whose spirits roam through the cosmos and bring supernatural or divine insight into the cosmic mysteries linked with life. I have read occasional stories of some who claim that ancient Indians have given them insights from the past, and the information revealed later proved accurate through detailed historical research. This allegedly *proves* that these spirits are the spirits of ancient men and women. In reality, it *proves* no such thing when you understand the operation of a familiar spirit.

However, these incidents do prove that the spirit world is real. These manifestations are not the spirits of the departed; they are demonic entities that have existed since the fall of Satan. Any *past information* can be revealed to a medium who channels the evil spirit. The deception comes, for example, when a family member who lost a loved one through death consults a medium who claims to be able to make contact with the departed soul of that person's loved one. Once the process begins, the spirit begins to speak about an event in the person's life or accurately names several family members. The family member is overwhelmed with joy to know that he or she can contact the loved one. At times the family member will even be told certain things to do to make this *spirit* happy or at peace.

For several years a famed psychic hosted a popular television program during which he claimed to make contact with the dead. Sometimes I would watch how he manipulated a question to get a certain response or would *hit and miss* until he could finally put together a story line that the family agreed was a message from the next world.

In the Bible we do read where Moses (who had died) and Elijah (who was translated) appeared to Christ (Matt. 17:1–4). This was a rare instance and was under the supervision of God Himself. Christ did not conjure up these men, but God sent them to reveal information to Christ. However, the law of God in Scripture totally forbids the use of mediums, soothsayers, fortune-tellers, and witchcraft in any and all forms.

Witchcraft is nothing to play with and is a very dangerous spiritual bridge over dark waters that a believer should never cross. A believer must rely upon biblical methods to receive spiritual insight, direction, and the path for the future.

We can all be assured that Christ will return (1 Thess. 4:16–17). The righteous dead will be raised at the resurrection (1 Cor. 15:52). Heaven does exist, and we will see the New Jerusalem (Rev. 22). And we will rule and reign with Christ for a thousand years if we are faithful (Rev. 20:1–4).

In those areas where a personal prayer requires an answer, we must rely upon the promises of God's Word and understand that He can reveal Himself to us—primarily through the Scriptures and, at various times and seasons, through His Holy Spirit's gifts (1 Cor. 12:7–10) or through a dream or a vision.

THE *REAL* PROPHETIC

Turning our attention from the false to the real, it is important for believers to understand that God can and will reveal truth to His children. Paul wrote in 1 Corinthians 14 that believers can speak by "revelation" (vv. 6, 26). This word in Greek is *apokalupsis* and alludes to something hidden that is disclosed and made known. Prior to Christ's suffering, resurrection, and ascension, He encouraged His disciples by predicting that when He departed from them, He would send "another Comforter," which is the Holy Spirit (John 14:16, KJV; 16:7, KJV). The Holy Spirit would "teach them all things, and bring to your remembrance all things that I said to you" (John 14:26), and He would "tell you things to come" (John 16:13). It is very contradictory that although many mainline churches believe the Holy Spirit is the Comforter and the Teacher who assists in your ability to recall the Scriptures, using passages from John's Gospel to prove their point, yet the part about "telling you things to come" is omitted at times. It is only used to exclaim that He reveals the correct interpretation of Bible prophecy to you. All of this is correct, but the Holy Spirit also provides believers with warnings and instruction through the inward leading of the Spirit and as we pray with understanding or in the Spirit (Rom. 8:26–28; 1 Cor. 14:14–15).

The Book of Acts is called *the Acts of the Apostles*. However, it is actually the Acts of the Holy Spirit! Without the power of the Holy Spirit, there would be few acts of the apostles! The nine gifts mentioned in 1 Corinthians 12 are not the *gifts of the apostles* but the "gifts of the Holy Spirit," and they will continue until the return of the Lord (1 Cor. 1:7). The Almighty began His story with man by walking with Adam in the Garden of Eden, and there was never a time in the four thousand years from Adam to Christ that God was not revealing Himself or His truth to a people. The Bible is the final written revelation from God, and there are no *new truths* beyond the revelation of Scripture; but there is fresh insight from old truth. Christ taught:

> Then He said to them, "Therefore every scribe instructed concerning the kingdom of heaven is like a householder who brings out of his treasure things new and old."
>
> —MATTHEW 13:52

The revelation the Holy Spirit brings forth involves situations occurring now or in the future. At times you enter a season where you are uncertain of the will of God or of how to handle a difficult circumstance. Wisdom can be given by a revelation through the gift of the word of wisdom or the word of knowledge (1 Cor. 12:8). When a believer needs a word of encouragement or comfort, a prophetic word for "edification and exhortation and comfort" can be received—sometimes through preaching, or through a song, or through an individual (1 Cor. 14:3).

Believers should never seek the counterfeit methods of men working through familiar spirits but must look to the Word of God and the operation of the Holy Spirit for insight into God's will and purpose. Throughout the New Testament, warnings were given in advance to prepare believers for what was coming. A prophet named Agabus warned the church that a severe drought was coming and the saints should prepare to send relief to those in need (Acts 11:28–29). The same man revealed by the Holy Spirit that if Paul went to the temple in Jerusalem, he would be arrested and delivered into the hands of the Gentiles (Acts 21:10–12). On another occasion Paul was being sent by ship to Rome. He was warned in his spirit that if the ship loosed from the dock, there would be severe consequences (Acts 27:9–10). Later the ship hit a storm, and the lives of the entire crew were in danger. After fourteen days of no sun or stars, Paul received a vision of an angel that predicted the ship would be torn apart, but the entire crew of 276 men would survive the shipwreck (vv. 22–44).

The entire Bible is a book of revelation. The Hebrew nation was formed as a result of angelic visitations, dreams, and visions.

AMAZING ANCIENT DREAMS

Joseph, the son of Jacob, was sold by his brothers to the Ishmaelites and then later sold to an Egyptian to be his personal slave. By interpreting two warning dreams, Joseph was exalted by Pharaoh as second in command over the land of Egypt. Joseph eventually married the daughter of an Egyptian priest named Asenath (Gen. 41:45).

Scripture says that Joseph had a silver cup used to "practice divination" or to reveal the future (Gen. 44:2, 15). Pharaoh most likely gave this cup to Joseph for Joseph's interpretation of his dream. There is no record that it was ever used or needed, since Joseph was directed by the Spirit of God.

A believer should never consult a secular source for words of instruction, as God only works through His Word and the Holy Spirit. Even the ancient wise men, soothsayers, and astrologers of biblical history were helpless to interpret the dreams and visions given to Pharaoh, Nebuchadnezzar, and other men (Gen. 41:8; Dan. 2:10). Only the Holy Spirit can interpret the revelations given from the heavenly Father (John 16:13). When Nebuchadnezzar had the troubling dream of the metallic image and could not recall what he had dreamed, his own wise men said, "There is no other who can tell it to the king except the gods, whose dwelling is not with flesh" (Dan. 2:11). Thus, it took Daniel, a man full of the Holy Spirit and wisdom, to interpret the dream. The same is true today!

In the days of Sesostris II (1906–1887 B.C.), the priest of Heilopolis had a vision he recorded. The words appear to be a prediction:

> He sees the ideal ruler for whose advent he longs.... "He brings cooling to the flame. It is said he is the shepherd of all men. There is no evil in his heart.... Where is he to-day?...Behold his might is not seen."[3]

The Hebrews were shepherds, and Egyptians hated shepherds (Gen. 46:34). When Joseph requested that his estranged brothers meet Pharaoh, he instructed them that when the king asked about their occupations, they reply, "We raise cattle." The brothers instead chose to reveal they were shepherds. Joseph may have been fearful that Pharaoh would restrict his family from living in Egypt, since the predicted future leader was called a "shepherd."

There was also an ancient prediction from a dream concerning a lamb that would defeat Egypt. This account comes from Adam Clarke's commentary:

> Jonathan ben Uzziel gives us a curious reason for the command given by Pharaoh to the Egyptian women: "Pharaoh slept, and saw in his sleep a balance, and behold the whole land of Egypt stood in one scale, and a lamb in the other; and the scale in which the lamb was outweighed that in which was the land of Egypt. Immediately he sent and called all the chief magicians, and told them his dream. And Janes [*sic*] and Jambres, (see 2 Tim. 3:8) who were chief of the magicians, opened their mouths and said to Pharaoh, 'A child is shortly to be born in the congregation of the Israelites, whose hand shall destroy the whole land of Egypt.' Therefore Pharaoh spake to the midwives, etc."[4]

The Jewish historian Josephus wrote this:

> One of those sacred scribes [said to be Jannes or Jambres in the Targum of Jonathan], who are very sagacious in foretelling future events truly, told the king, that about this time there would a child be born to the Israelites, who, if he were reared, would bring Egyptian dominion low, and would raise the Israelites; that he would excel all men in virtue, and obtain a glory that would be remembered though all ages. Which thing was so feared by the king, that, according to this man's opinion, he commanded that they should cast every male child, which was born to the Israelites, into the river, and destroy it...that if any parents should disobey him and venture to save their male children alive, they and their families should be destroyed.[5]

It would truly be a lamb that would defeat the entire empire of Egypt. This lamb was the Passover lamb offered at each house prior to the Exodus (Exod. 12). The lamb's blood was placed in the left, right, and top outer parts of the door to prevent the destroyer from taking the life of the firstborn sons (v. 7). The lamb was then roasted and eaten, bringing healing to the entire Hebrew nation all in one night (Ps. 105:37). That night all of the Egyptians' firstborn among the people, the animals, and the captives died (Exod. 12:29).

A VISION BEFORE MOSES'S BIRTH

The Jewish historian Josephus records that Moses's father, Amram, had a lengthy dream (vision) in which God appeared to him and exhorted him not to despair concerning the future. In the vision, God previewed Hebrew history from Abraham, Isaac, and Jacob and informed Amram that He was with these men in all their ways. He predicted that Amram's child (Moses) would deliver the Hebrew nation and would be concealed from danger. His memory would be famous while the world would last. The vision revealed that this child would also have a brother who would obtain a God-ordained priesthood, and his posterity would have it after him to the end of the world.[6] Thus, the birth of one of the world's greatest deliverers was preceded by a prophetic dream.

Three years before the birth of Moses, there was a conjunction of Jupiter and Saturn, which occurred in the constellation Pisces (the fish). Pisces has always been considered to be a sign of the nation of the Hebrews (Israel). This was interpreted as a sign that a great person was born among the Jews. Some rabbis suggest this was the motive for Pharaoh instructing the midwives to kill male children by throwing them into the Nile River (Exod. 1:22). The alligator was one of the gods of Egypt, and slaying the Hebrew infants could serve as an offering to another Egyptian god. God had the final word. About eighty years later, the Egyptian army was drowned in the Red Sea (Exod. 14).

Julius Caesar was the first emperor of imperial Rome. He passed laws that caused people to move from one location to another. One such group was colonists from Capua. While constructing buildings they came across ancient graves and found vessels and began searching them. In the tomb of Capys, the founder of Capua, was a brass tablet with a prediction recorded in Greek which read:

> Whenever the bones of Capys come to be discovered, a descendant of Iulus will be slain by the hands of his kinsmen, and his death revenged by fearful disasters throughout Italy.[7]

Julius Caesar's wife, Calpurnia, had a troubling *dream* that their home fell apart and warned her husband not to go to the Senate. He ignored the warning and was stabbed twenty-three times, dying at age fifty-six in 44 B.C.[8] Thus the strange prediction, made years before, came to pass. The fellow should have heeded his wife's warning.

Never doubt God's ability to speak today and to bring the insight needed for your protection, direction, and inspiration, and never follow counterfeit men and methods that offer deception.

seven

CAN A WARNING DREAM BE ALTERED THROUGH PRAYER?

So I sought for a man among them who would make a wall, and stand in the gap before Me on behalf of the land, that I should not destroy it; but I found no one.

« Ezekiel 22:30 »

There have been countless believers who have experienced a dream with a warning of coming danger, a threat to their life, or a satanic attack that was being plotted against them. One of the most common and most important questions asked is: "When you receive a warning of coming danger through a dream (or a vision), is it possible to alter the situation and prevent it from occurring?"

Let's begin by considering prophetic warnings in the Scripture. When Moses was given the Torah (the Bible's first five books), the prophet told the people of Israel that if they disobeyed the commandments and laws of God, they would be given the opportunity to repent and prevent judgment from overtaking them. However, he warned them that if they persisted in their sins and continued their rejection of God's divine instructions, they would be taken captive by their enemies, drought would destroy their crops, their animals would suffer, and they would see the consequences of their disobedience. (See Deuteronomy 28; Leviticus 26.)

In Israel's history, God did not immediately move His hand from mercy to judgment. There was always a gap of time that gave the people opportunity to turn or repent. Christ warned the church at Thyatira that a self-acclaimed female "prophetess" was seducing God's servants. She and the entire church were given "time to repent," and if they refused, a "great tribulation" would come upon them (Rev. 2:21–22). Year after year, generation after generation, Israel continued its rejection of God's commandments, and so the Almighty predicted that the nation would be taken into captivity in Babylon for seventy years (Jer. 25:11). Once the time frame for this judgment had been set, it eventually came to pass.

When Christ predicted that the temple (Matt. 24:1–2) and Jerusalem would be destroyed within one generation (Matt 23:34–36), He also revealed that He would have often gathered the city and the people together as a hen gathers her chicks under her wings, but the people refused (v. 37). Once the sands in the hourglass of grace reached their end, the glass was shattered along with the sand. It was while the nation was still under great prosperity that Isaiah and Jeremiah both predicted the Babylonian captivity. Eventually the prosperity ceased, and Jerusalem was left in smoldering ruins. Some false prophets were predicting that God loved Jerusalem too much to allow its demise. The deceitful dreams of these false dreamers also went up in smoke.

Warnings and mercy always precede judgment. In Scripture, the warnings came through angelic visitations (Gen. 19), dreams, and visions, or they were pronounced by a prophet. Many of the warnings we receive in a dream (or vision) are not geared to an international, national, or city judgment, but they are usually warnings for individuals, their families, or their churches. Many warning dreams deal with future spiritual, emotional, physical, or economic difficulties. In these cases intense prayer can possibly prevent the attack or alter the circumstances.

I SAW HIM—THEN HE DIED

There is also a danger of accepting what you see with a rather "whatever will be will be" attitude and not standing in the gap through prayer. Shortly after my wife and I were married, I was ministering for Pastor Tony Scott in Sylvania, Ohio (Toledo area). Pam and I were staying at Pastor Scott's home. During those early days, I would stay up until two or three in the morning, studying and at times praying. On this night I went to bed around 2:00 a.m., and shortly after lying down and attempting to sleep, I saw a very brief, full-color scene of a man standing before me. He wore a plaid shirt, old blue jeans, and brown leather boots. He was clearly staring at me. I was so stunned that I sat up and said to my wife, "I just saw a man who attends your home church!" When I described him to her, she knew whom I was talking about, but neither of us could recall his name. I spent about fifteen minutes trying to remember his name. Finally I lay down, and for the *second time* I saw an exact repeat of the same image. There he was, looking at me wearing the same clothes.

Again, I woke up and said, "I just saw him again! What is all this about?" I did not see anything or anyone else. I never prayed for him or asked the Lord why I saw him so clearly in this vision (it was not a dream).

The following afternoon, my wife spoke to her sister in Northport, Alabama, my wife's hometown. Her sister Shelia said, "Pam, did anyone call you and tell you about Bill Ward?"

"No," Pam responded, "who is that?" When Shelia described him, Pam replied, "Oh my, that's his name. That's the man the Lord touched in Perry's four-week revival at the church!"

Shelia proceeded to tell us that early that morning (a few hours after I saw him), Bill was returning from work when he lost control of his truck, was thrown out, and was killed! We were both in shock. It was months later when I spoke with his widow and described the clothes he wore in the vision—which she confirmed he was wearing the morning of his death.

At the time I did not know the spiritual law of the "double dream," or how in a double dream the event is established and will came to pass. Time and experience are valuable twins that teach us truth and how to discern events and how to pray. When Israel sinned with the golden calf, it was the intent of God to destroy the entire nation of Israel and leave one man alive—Moses (Exod. 32:8–10), thus raising up a nation through this faithful prophet. Moses immediately reminded the Lord of His covenant with Abraham, Isaac, and Jacob, and how the heathen nations would mock God's name and accuse Him of bringing Israel out of Egypt to slay them in the desert (vv. 11–13). After being reminded of His promise to Abraham to bring his children out of Egypt and back to the Promised Land, the Bible says, "The LORD repented of the evil which he thought to do unto his people" (Exod. 32:14, KJV). God was not *repenting of sin* but was simply changing His mind concerning His plans. The prayer of Moses changed the direction of God!

When the Almighty informed Abraham that He was planning on destroying the cities of the plain, including Sodom and Gomorrah, God's covenant man Abraham began a deep discussion with the Lord to negotiate for the safety of the righteous who may be living among the unrighteous in the city. Abraham began with fifty people, and God promised to preserve the wicked city if He could find just fifty in the city. Soon the number dropped to ten, and God agreed to stop the destruction if ten righteous people were found in Sodom (Gen. 18:23–33). This action taken by Abraham is called *intercession.* The act of interceding is when one person stands in place for another to prevent the other person from experiencing judgment, danger, or destruction. For example, Christ is now in the heavenly temple, standing to represent us as our eternal High Priest, and He "always lives to make intercession for them" (Heb. 7:25). An intercessor is one who makes a petition on behalf of another. In our case, when we sin we need a person who serves as a *lawyer* (called an *advocate* in 1 John 2:1) to represent us in heaven, because Satan, the "accuser of the brethren," much like a prosecutor in a courtroom, is continually hurling accusations before the eternal throne against us (Rev. 12:10).

We have an intercessor in heaven, Jesus Christ, and a Comforter on the earth, the Holy Spirit (John 14:16, 26). My precious father had taught me for years that a warning dream does not always mean that what you see is set to happen and cannot be prevented. But the dream can be given so that the person receiving it can *pray to prevent the event from coming to pass.*

eight

LEARNING TO LISTEN TO YOUR WIFE'S WARNING DREAMS

While he was sitting on the judgment seat, his wife sent to him, saying, "Have nothing to do with that just Man, for I have suffered many things today in a dream because of Him."

« Matthew 27:19 »

One of the most interesting, yet often overlooked, warning dreams in the Bible involved a wife who gave a warning to her husband about his treatment of Jesus. During the public trial of Christ, a raging mob of religious zealots was demanding Christ's execution. The biblical narrative begins with Pilate, a man appointed by Rome to be the governor in the region of Judea. Before any death penalty could be enacted, Pilate would need to condemn Christ. Just as Pilate was preparing to judge Christ and condemn Him to be put to death, Pilate's wife sent a message saying that she had a troubling dream of Christ that showed Him to be an innocent man.

No detail is given in the Scripture as to what she dreamed or why she "suffered many things." The *suffering* was not a physical pain but was a mental or an emotional stress that she experienced as a result of her dream. In Scripture she is simply called "Pilate's wife," but church tradition says that she was a believer in Christ and was later named as Saint Procula, or, as some suggest, Saint Claudia. The early father Origen, in his *Homilies on Matthew*, suggests that she became a Christian. There is a suggestion that in Paul's last letter to Timothy (2 Tim. 4:21), the Claudia he alludes to may refer to Pilate's wife, who became a believer. The Eastern Orthodox and Ethiopian Orthodox churches celebrate her in the church each year. Hundreds of years later, a letter written in Latin says that she actually sought out Christ to heal her son Pilo's crippled foot.[1]

Did Pilate pay attention to his wife's warning? Apparently something moved him not to condemn Jesus. In fact, Pilate publicly said that Christ was "just" (Matt. 27:24). When the raging crowd demanded that Christ be crucified, Pilate offered to release a prisoner to them. I suggest that Pilate was hoping they would release Jesus. However, they demanded instead that Barabbas, a thief, be released (vv. 16–21). Christ was later crucified between two thieves. Barabbas, who was scheduled for execution with his two cohorts, was to hang on the third cross on Mount Calvary, but instead, the middle cross was prepared for Christ!

Pilate then asked for a basin of water and washed his hands—attempting to free himself of the guilt of innocent blood (v. 24). This was a procedure known to the religious Jews, based upon instruction in Deuteronomy, requiring that when a corpse is discovered near a city, the elders living closest to that city are to take a heifer, cut off its head, and wash their hands in water over the slain heifer while declaring that they are innocent of the blood of the slain corpse (Deut. 21:3–6). Pilate did not ask for a heifer, but he did wash his hands, and the Jewish religious authorities knew what he was doing. He was declaring himself free from the blood of Christ, which was about to be shed. It was at that moment that the religious Jews said, "His blood be on us and on our children" (Matt. 27:25). According to the Law of Moses, this brought a curse upon the city of Jerusalem and the land of Israel, as Christ indicated was possible when there was a continual shedding of the blood of innocents and the righteous (Matt. 23:34–36).

Clearly, something emboldened Pilate not to agree with the death sentence that the multitude was screaming out should be placed upon Christ. I believe he was moved by his wife's warning dream.

THE INSTINCT OF A WOMAN

Married couples often make jokes about the fact that a wife has a certain type of *inner instinct* that seems to be missing in the average husband. This *inner radar* (as some call it) is unique when considering that Eve was seduced by the serpent in the garden (2 Cor. 11:3). The adversary's crafty, smooth words inspired the woman to eat from a forbidden tree (Gen. 3:1–7). This may be the one weakness in the female nature. Normally a woman is not moved so much by the physical appearance of a man as she is by the care, compassion, affection, and *kind words* he expresses. I have often said that if the serpent had been a female, Eve would have chased the snake from the garden while beating it on the head with a stick and screaming, "Get out of here, you lying woman—you're just trying to steal my man!"

Men (husbands) can be very rational in their thinking process and often lack the discernment that a wife can sense in her spirit. I have a side hobby, of which the inspiration for it often comes and goes. I enjoy writing songs and have been blessed to have had more than forty songs published and sung on numerous CDs. Many years ago my wife and I were friends with a young married couple who were traveling ministers. The man was a dynamic preacher, and his wife accompanied him, often singing in the meetings. She asked me if I would like to work with her on her new musical CD project, using some of my songs. Of course I was thrilled with the prospect of getting my songs out, and even creating more music that would bless many people.

I approached my wife, and she said it was fine, that we could work at the ministry office on the project.

However, late that night my wife had a very troubling dream. It was actually a twofold warning. In the first dream, she saw this very woman in a very compromising situation and saw me in the distance. Pam felt this woman was, as we used to say, "scoping me out" in a seductive manner. She then dreamed of a large tarantula that was approaching an area where Pam was standing near a high fence. Pam took a small dagger and drove it into the heart of this large spider. The next morning she related the dream to me, and we researched this type of spider to see if there was some *spiritual understanding* as to why she saw a tarantula. We discovered that this kind of spider slowly weaves its web to capture its prey and leads its prey into a slow death.

Pam felt this was linked to the woman, and she said, "I don't feel good about the idea of her working around you. I think she is going to try to weave a slow web and pull you in." Because my wife seldom dreams, and when she does it usually contains a meaning, I immediately told the woman that it would not work out to assist her, but I could recommend some individuals who could help with her project. Both Pam and I felt we made a wise decision.

A few months later it was discovered that this woman was actually having numerous affairs. Imagine the shock when we received a phone call from a close pastor friend who shared with us a terrible encounter that had occurred between this woman and a male member of his church while this woman's husband was ministering in their church. God spared me from perhaps a moral disaster or, at the least, a possible emotional attack with this dream.

PAY ATTENTION, FELLOWS

The female radar is very effective in pinpointing the hidden motives of other women. My wife has often said, "No one knows a woman like another woman." As a man, this female instinct amazes me, especially in understanding how this *gift* is possible and how it works. However, in every instance when my wife (who is a very spiritual and praying woman) has given me a warning, it was later proven to be accurate. Ministers will often mention numerous women in the Bible who were masters of seduction, such as Delilah, who gave Samson the world's most destructive haircut, or Jezebel, who was a seducer of men in the early church (Judges 16; Rev. 2:20). However, women like Anna, Mary, and her cousin Elizabeth were all sensitive to the leading of the Holy Spirit. Anna was the first female prophetess to see the infant Christ, as Simeon the rabbi announced that Jesus was the anticipated Jewish Messiah (Luke 2:36–38). Mary was receptive to the angel who announced that she, as a virgin, would conceive a child (Luke 1:30–35), and Elizabeth, the aged, barren wife of a priest, became pregnant through a super-natural visitation (vv. 1–25). These were all women of great faith whose names are memorialized in the Bible and in the history of the Christian church.

MY MOTHER'S DREAM

My mother, Juanita Stone, was blessed with three children—Diana, myself, and Phillip—and at age thirty-nine she became pregnant with her fourth child. Because she had a C-section when delivering each of her previous three children, when her doctor discovered she was six weeks pregnant, he immediately suggested three options to her: she should have a test to help determine the health of the child, or she should abort the *fetus* because there was a high risk that the child may have severe physical or mental birth defects, plus the great danger there was to her with the pregnancy, or, a third choice, she could take a chance and continue the pregnancy. My mother informed the doctor that aborting the child—although she was *only six weeks pregnant*, was not an option. The doctor said she would need to make a decision before the third month of pregnancy.

Mother meant it when she said, "Abortion is not an option." She also knew that there were numerous physical and medical indicators that leaned toward this being a high-risk pregnancy with a high possibility that the child would be born mentally challenged. Mom began to pray, knowing that God foreknew she would become pregnant and that He knew she would be forty when the child was born. Yet He permitted the conception to occur. During her time of seeking the Lord, it was a *dream* that confirmed her confession of faith.

She dreamed that she saw a child, a beautiful girl with curly hair. She knew this was the child in her womb. In the dream the child was not sick, feeble, or deformed but was in perfect health. When Mom returned to the doctor, she told him the Lord showed her she would have a healthy baby girl with curly hair. Of course you can imagine his skepticism. He viewed her as an overly zealous Christian woman who was denying the medical facts that were now facing her.

The pregnancy—near death

Mom carried the child full term. When the time came for delivery, it was discovered she had a severe blockage in her intestines, and the doctors wanted to perform emergency surgery. But mother's strength was gone. She began to bleed profusely in the delivery room, and it came to a point where the doctor felt he was *losing her*. Mom actually experienced an *out-of-body experience* in which her soul (or spirit) came out of her body. She was hovering above, looking down upon the doctor and nurses working on her to stop the bleeding. This occurred on a Sunday. I was a teenager at the time. A call came to Dad's church (he was a pastor) to pray for Mom. I didn't know at the time that I almost lost my mother. However, Mother lived and gave birth to that little curly-headed girl, Melanie Dawn Stone. My mother, now in her seventies, still works part-time at my office, and my *little* sister, now in her thirties, is one of our data-entry personnel. God used this dream to remove fear and confirm Mom's faith. When things became difficult, she would remind the Lord of the promise He gave her.

ANOTHER PREGNANCY DREAM

One of the most dramatic demonstrations of the power of a woman's dream that my wife and I still occasionally discuss occurred many years ago and involved a very dear and well-known minister and his wife. I had been on an overseas trip and was returning to

Atlanta Hartsfield Airport, where my wife was waiting at the baggage claim. When we were driving out of the airport, she said, "I had a dream. I believe the Lord wants us to go visit this couple in their service tonight." In the dream, Pam saw this pastor's wife crying as she sat in a restroom. She was troubled because she had learned she was pregnant. She was saying, "I can't go through with this." Pam saw that the woman was very distressed, and a heavy depression had overwhelmed her. Pam commented, "I think she's pregnant, and I must go and tell her this dream and tell her it will be all right." Without the couple's knowledge that we were coming, we drove for quite some time and arrived just after the Wednesday night service had begun. The pastor saw us in the audience and welcomed us to the service. His wife was not in her normal seat. Pam said, "I don't think she is here, but her mother is. I'll speak with her after service."

After service Pam spoke to the woman's mother, who said, "Pam, guess what... she is pregnant again!" Pam turned pale and replied, "I must tell you this dream," which she proceeded to do. The mother began weeping, saying, "You must go see her. She is so depressed, she didn't come to church tonight. The Lord sent you to her!" After telling the pastor the dream, he began to cry and said, "You both have no idea what we have been through the past several weeks. I have almost quit pastoring because of the stress I've been under."

That night we arrived at their house to the surprise of the wife! We sat down with her and her husband, and Pam related in detail the dream and began to share from her heart. What Pam saw had literally occurred the night she dreamed it! My wife is a very quiet and a behind-the-scenes person, yet I was so proud of her for obeying the Lord. Not only did the Holy Spirit touch the couple that night, but also the pregnancy went great. That infant is now a beautiful young woman who is wholly dedicated to the Lord!

What if Pam had *ignored the dream* and said, "I had a really stupid dream the other night," or was not sensitive to discern the warning of the Holy Spirit? It is possible that the stress upon the couple could have moved them out of the perfect will of God.

Women tend to be more spiritually minded and sensitive than most men. This is witnessed in the two visitations of the angel Gabriel: one to a male priest named Zacharias, and the other to the Virgin Mary. When Gabriel stood at the temple's golden altar announcing that Zacharias's barren wife would conceive a son, Zacharias required a *sign* that the event would happen! His sign for his unbelief was that he was unable to speak during his wife's pregnancy—for nine months (Luke 1:1-20). Mary was also informed that she would become pregnant with a son, and her attitude was, "Let it be to me according to your word" (Luke 1:38). The *preacher* was skeptical of an angelic messenger, and the simple handmaiden from Nazareth was ready to believe what seemed impossible! When Christ was crucified, the disciples ran for their lives (with the exception of John); however, the women stuck with Him until the end (Mark 15:40-41). At the tomb, it was three women who were plotting to remove a massive stone to anoint the body (Mark 16:1-4), since no men were among them, as the disciples were hiding behind closed doors in fear. Some of the chief financial supporters of Christ's ministry were women:

> …and certain women who had been healed of evil spirits and infirmities—Mary called Magdalene, out of whom had come seven demons, and Joanna the wife of Chuza, Herod's steward, and Susanna, and many others who provided for Him from their substance.
>
> —LUKE 8:2-3

Men tend to think in the realm of logic, and in Western culture, men are often taught from the time they are boys not to express their emotions, especially in the form of crying or being overly humble. This tends to make men uncomfortable with religious expression, especially if it involves holding another guy's hand in a church service when *agreeing in prayer* or expressing their emotions through tears. Women, on the other hand, are created with the ability to show more empathy, compassion, and intuition because they are more closely in touch with their emotions. Most have no difficulty flowing with soothing words, hugs, kisses, tenderness, and crying when the occasion deems necessary. Religion may come across as formal and dry in its approach, but an experience with God brings an encounter with righteousness, peace, and joy in the Holy Spirit (Rom. 14:17). If a husband is married to a dedicated, praying, believing woman, then he should learn to pay attention to her inner senses, her nudges, and those dreams from time to time, as well as those feelings she may seem to bug you about.

If a husband was to ask himself, "Why doesn't the Lord show me what He is showing my wife?" the answer might be, "Your spiritual antenna is not up the way hers is."

DON'T ABUSE THE GIFT

It is very important that every Christian woman understands and guards this unique ability and never abuses it, especially in the area of attempting to *control* your companion. You must never allow fleshly jealousy to be interpreted as some *feeling* you have toward someone, when in reality you are jealous of the other person's favor or blessings. In the Book of Judges, a woman named Delilah was paid to gain secret information from a man named Samson. Knowing that a seductive woman could make a fellow do things that they would normally never do, Delilah continually pressed Samson with her words: "Tell me your secret...tell me where your strength comes from...tell me or you don't love me...you really don't love me if you don't give me what I want." (See Judges 16.) Samson had killed a lion and destroyed a thousand Philistines, but he couldn't handle the continual verbal wearing down he received from his forbidden Philistine girlfriend who owned the local beauty salon in Gaza.

One of the great dangers that have existed for centuries in the Christian church is the abuse of spiritual gifts. Church history is replete with individuals who claimed to be prophets and led people astray with some alleged prophetic inspiration or warning. In my book *Unusual Prophecies Being Fulfilled*, book number 7, I wrote:

> It was in the late sixteenth century. Along the rivers and lakes in Austria and Germany, they were building arks. They were mostly simply farmers using hammer, nails, and hewn trees, building large boats to protect their families from another "global flood," similar to the flood of Noah's day. The people were following the prophetic instructions of an astrologer and self-acclaimed prophet, Johann Stoffler. According to the irrefutable calculations of Stoffler, another massive flood was about to strike all of Europe, and the only survivors of this deadly deluge were those following his instruction to prepare arks for the saving of their families.
>
> The date arrived and went without any storms, floods, or destruction. In retrospect, if the commoners had possessed Bibles and could have read God's promise to Noah every time they saw a rainbow draping the sky, they would have known that God made a covenant never to destroy the earth by water again (Gen. 9:13–16). People began looking for answers, and another astronomer entered the scene, another alleged prophet from Vienna, Austria, named Georg Tannenstetter, and disproved the

calculation of Stoffler and declared no flood would come. Oh well, so much for the houseboats.[2]

If an individual has been gifted to hear from the Lord, then he or she must guard against using this gift in the wrong manner or even participating in merchandising of the gift for personal gain, which is forbidden in Scripture:

> And many will follow their destructive ways, because of whom the way of truth will be blasphemed. By covetousness they will exploit you with deceptive words; for a long time their judgment has not been idle, and their destruction does not slumber.
>
> —2 PETER 2:2–3

There are so-called *prophets* who ask for payment (*offerings*) in exchange for a word from the Lord. I heard of one person who allegedly interprets dreams, charging the person for the interpretation. Legitimate ministries and churches that operate on tithes and offerings according to this *charging* are simply merchandising God, and this is displeasing to God!

One reason to express this warning is because there have been women in the past who became so *spiritual* in their own eyes that they left their children and husbands for their own *ministry*. They began believing that their families were interfering with the *gift* God had given them for the world. May I suggest this, ladies: do not be getting on a bus that is heading to Washington DC to *bind the evil spirits over our nation* when you cannot deal with the little spirits affecting your home or your own personal life. Women, if you are married with children, then your first priority is to be a mother to your children and a wife to your husband. I want to strongly say that God does not need *your gift* badly enough for you to leave your children without a mother and hit the road for the kingdom. (See 1 Corinthians 7.)

Whatever form of gift God has imparted to you, follow the Lord with all meekness and humility, seeking to be a blessing to others, and always give God glory for all He performs through you.

nine

WHAT IT MEANS WHEN DREAMING
OF A DEPARTED LOVED ONE

We are confident, yes, well pleased rather to be absent from the body and to be present with the Lord.

« 2 Corinthians 5:8 »

The death of a close friend or a loved one is a sorrowful and often traumatic experience. The emptiness that prevails and the loneliness that is felt, caused by their absence, can be emotionally overwhelming. Many people long to hear that familiar voice, that warm laughter, or the departed speak to them again. At times the grieving person will receive comfort from a dream in which the departed person appears to be speaking with them. There have been many questions sent to me about what it means when an individual sees a departed loved one in a dream.

My grandfather John Bava was a minister, songwriter, book publisher, and multigifted man whom I admired greatly. He went to be with Christ in 1998. Since that time, seldom a week goes by that I don't have a dream that he is in. At times we are at the old home place in West Virginia. Other times I see him with Grandmother, and we are on a farm, sitting with the family eating or just hearing him laugh. After a loved one, especially a believer, passes away, it is quite common for a close family member to dream about that person. Part of this is because the individual is locked forever in your memory vault and a permanent image is imprinted in your heart. Anyone who has been an active part of your life remains in the seat of your spirit, whether they are living or deceased. In fact, there are times when it seems as though my grandfather and grandmother are still with us, although we know their spirits are in the presence of the Lord (2 Cor. 5:8).

Out of the many times I have seen Granddad, they were simply a dream. There was no particular meaning to the dream, and I was rather joyful when I awoke to remember him as a part of my life. Oddly, however, there have been occasions when the Lord would allow a person who has departed to appear in a dream to a loved one, at times to bring comfort. One of the most dramatic incidents that I know occurred years ago in Tuscumbia, Alabama. I was ministering in a local church, and an elderly woman told me of this personal incident. She and her husband had been believers for many years. He suddenly and unexpectedly passed away. She came to a point where she needed some additional income to pay bills. When living, her husband told her he had hidden some money in the house in the event of an emergency, but the fellow never told her where the money was hidden. She had looked in drawers, in the cupboard, and other areas and found nothing. She cried out to the Lord to help her and to reveal—if there was money in the house—where it was hidden. One night she awoke and saw her husband standing near the foot of her bed. She was stunned! He said nothing but walked toward the bedroom closet and pointed to a stack of blankets. He turned and pointed to the bottom blanket several times, smiled, and then vanished. She came to herself and didn't know if she had dreamed this or if it was a vision.

To *test this spirit* to see if it was from the Lord (1 John 4:1), she arose and went to the closet. She pulled down a stack of blankets on the top shelf. As she laid them on the bed and began opening them, she opened the bottom blanket, and there were thousands of dollars folded in the blanket! Obviously the Lord was concerned for this precious widow, and He knew where the money was. The Lord used a dream-vision to bring her what she requested. Notice that she did not ask to see her husband, but she asked for God to reveal the location of the money. However, God used this event to encourage and bless her.

DAD'S SUPERNATURAL CALL INTO THE MINISTRY

The most dramatic encounter I know of as it relates to the Lord allowing someone to see the spirit of a departed loved one was my own father. For many years Dad has retold the story over and over of the day when he was called into the ministry as a teenager.

Dad was converted at age seventeen and began hosting prayer meetings with other young men his age. One fellow, Al Collins, became Dad's prayer partner, and they attended church, studied, and prayed continually. One night Al had a dream in which he and Dad were on a large, solid rock surrounded by murky waters. He and Dad were fending off snakes by using a large rod in their hands. Suddenly Al's feet began slipping, and he said to Dad, "Fred, I left you on that rock to fight the battle. I went into the water and was taken under!" They both knew this was a warning of an impending satanic attack, but little did they realize that Al would be diagnosed with a brain tumor that months later would take his life.

After Al's death, Dad was sorrowful and was praying about entering the Korean War. He was alone, praying outside of a small one-roomed shack that the fellows had built for study and prayer. Leaning his chair back against the outside wall, Dad felt a hand grab his right shoulder through the wall! He suddenly slumped over and instantly felt his spirit depart his body, moving faster than the speed of light upward into the universe. He thought perhaps he had died of a heart attack. Dad described how he eventually stopped somewhere out in the universe and was surrounded by the most beautiful sapphire blue heaven. He was standing on nothing, but he felt no fear.

Suddenly he observed a silver ball of light approaching him in the far distance. To his amazement, Al Collins stepped from this light, raised his right hand, and said, "Fred, God has called you to preach." He lowered his hand, then lifting it a second time, he spoke, "Fred, God told me to tell you that you must preach." Without any warning, Al stepped back into the light and appeared to travel into the beautiful blue open space and disappear. Dad suddenly felt his spirit moving at a high speed as it reentered his body. (See 2 Corinthians 12:1–4.) When he came to himself in the chair, the hair on Dad's body was standing straight up. The energy he felt from the experience was *electrifying*! Dad gave his name to the draft board, but he was never called into the military!

There are some who do not believe the Lord could or would allow such an amazing incident to occur. However, consider the supernatural calling of Saul of Tarsus into the ministry. Saul was traveling to Damascus, Syria, with legal papers to arrest key Christian church leaders. Saul's journey was suddenly interrupted by a heavenly light, as Christ Himself spoke to Saul from heaven (Acts 9:3–5). The light was so brilliant that Saul became blind and had to be led into the city of Damascus (Acts 22:11). The calling from God came directly out of heaven and was verbally given by Christ Himself, who had died, been raised from the dead, and was positioned in heaven when He spoke to Saul and announced that Saul was a chosen vessel. While my father was certainly no Saul of Tarsus, his call into the ministry was dramatic and necessary, as he was preparing to enter the Korean War, which would have completely *disrupted the destiny of his future family.* In all likelihood, had he entered the Korean War, he would not have married my mother, and she would not have given birth to four children—including their preaching son who is writing this book!

In using this illustration, remember that according to the Scriptures, when we are absent from the body we are present with the Lord (2 Cor. 5:8), and our spirit departs our body at death (Matt. 27:50; Acts 5:5; 12:23). A righteous spirit will enter the third heaven in a dwelling place called *paradise* (2 Cor. 12:1–4). Thus, the righteous are not actually dead; their eternal spirits are very much alive and living in another realm.

I believe my father had an *out-of-body experience* similar to what

Paul described when he saw the third heaven (2 Cor. 12:1–4). God allowed Dad to see his close friend, who confirmed to him that God's will was for Dad to preach. Please note: Dad did not ask or pray to see Al, but God permitted it in His sovereignty.

DYING SAINTS SEE DEAD SAINTS

Prior to the death of Christ, God sent two Old Testament prophets to speak with Him on the Mount of Transfiguration. These two great leaders, Elijah and Moses, appeared and discussed with Christ the events that would surround His death in Jerusalem (Luke 9:28–33). I cannot tell you the number of times that family members have told of their precious mother, dad, or grandparents who, just prior to death, began to see the family members who had gone on to be with the Lord. Many times a dying person will be physically weak with his or her eyes shut and suddenly will become fully alert and aware of all of the surroundings. Then, in a weak voice that person will say, "Let those young men through; they are coming for me," or ask, "Can't you see the angels in this room?" When a person in a hospital or at home who is expected to die begins seeing loved ones who have passed, it usually indicates that the person will shortly go to be with the Lord. When Stephen, the first martyr in the early church, was being stoned to death by the religious fanatics of his day, he said, "I see the heavens opened and the Son of man standing at the right hand of God!" (Acts 7:56). Stephen saw into the spirit world moments before he called upon the Lord to "receive [his] spirit" (v. 59). Moments before departing, his eyes were opened to see into the next dimension.

I have personally spoken with individuals who survived major surgery and saw (in a clear vision) loved ones who had passed on. What I am going to share now is very important. In every instance the only people to appear were those who were solid, praying people who loved the Lord. At times the person in the hospital would question where other family members were, but they never appeared. In each instance a believer never saw a person who died without Christ! In other words, in such situations those who died lost have never appeared to anyone to warn them about the land of lost souls. Why is this?

In Luke 16:19–31 Christ revealed a true story of a poor man who begged for food and a rich man who refused to feed him. Both men died. The poor man went to paradise, and the selfish rich man found his spirit in hell. The rich man begged that the poor man would come back from the dead and warn his five brothers not to come to this forbidden place. The answer to this tormented man's request was, "They have Moses and the prophets; let them hear [believe] them.…If they do not hear [believe] Moses and the prophets, neither will they be persuaded though one rise from the dead" (vv. 29–31). The reason for this comment is that someone who believes in the Bible should also believe in the supernatural and the afterlife, which are taught about through the Scriptures. Sinners, agnostics, or unbelievers would never believe if they actually saw someone from the dead. They would tag it as a hallucination, a wild imagination, or a result of some medication they were on. This happens now when a believer tells the average doctor that he or she saw the afterlife or a loved one who had passed. An unbeliever is an unbeliever, and seeing a departed loved one will not change that.

Christ had to stop Saul on the road to Damascus, blind him in a light, show him a vision, and speak in an audible voice before this rebellious and stubborn Pharisee of Pharisees would pay any attention (Acts 9:1–8). Saul later revealed that those traveling with him that day saw the "light" but never heard the "voice" (Acts 22:9). Saul, whose name was later changed to Paul, called this incident a "heavenly vision" (Acts 26:19). Some saw a light and heard nothing. What

God allows you to see and hear can be based upon your personal level of spiritual commitment to Him.

One of my staff workers, Sherree Fister, recently lost her stepfather, Rev. Eugene Nicola, because of cancer. Days before he passed, he became quite weak. However, he also became very alert to the spirit world. He began telling the family, "I have seen the colors of heaven." He also said he could hear the music of heaven. After several unusual encounters when his eyes were opened to the next life, he told his family gathered near his bed, "I want to go on home because it's too carnal here!"

WHY GOD LETS YOU SEE A DEPARTED LOVED ONE

At times when a person dreams about a departed loved one, it *can be* a dream from the Lord. When seeing a vision, a person appears very clear and in a three-dimensional form. A vision can be so *real* that the person may seem to have returned from paradise to *literally* appear before you. In Stephen's vision Christ appeared and was standing in heaven. In John's apocalyptic vision, the seer was on the island of Patmos but was caught up "in the Spirit" to the heavenly temple (Rev. 1:10). The entire Book of Revelation is a vision of things to come.

Seeing a departed loved one appear to you on Earth may not necessarily indicate that person has actually left the paradise of the righteous souls in heaven and returned to Earth. God can permit a soul that is now in heaven to appear in a vision in the same manner Christ appeared to Saul on the road to Damascus. The question is this: Why would the Lord allow a person to see someone in a dream or a vision who has gone home to be with Him? I believe there are four possible reasons.

1. At times to bring you comfort

There are times when a person departs and the family members are uncertain of the spiritual condition of the departed. Perhaps they were raised in a church, confessed Christ at one point, but had not been as active for the kingdom as they should. On several occasions in the Bible the Lord allowed people who had died to appear and tell their family members that they were all right and not to worry about them. This does not mean that in every case we can ask for some type of confirmation and experience a dream or a vision of a person. For this to occur it must be the sovereign purpose of God, which is something none of us can manipulate or control.

2. To bring back positive memories

When a wonderful person who brought you joy is taken from you, it leaves you with only memories. These memories are like precious pictures that capture a moment in time on photo paper. From time to time we pull out numerous albums and laugh when we see how much we changed over the years. My wife always tells me I am much better-looking now, so needless to say, I love pulling those pictures out to remind her how blessed she is (bear with me in my folly)!

God can see when we are sad, lonely, or despondent. At times we may see a husband, wife, or a child in a dream who is now with Christ, and the wonderful memories resurface, bringing us joy and recharging all of the fun family memories that we keep hidden in our spirits.

3. To give you hope for the resurrection

One of the greatest comforts for a believer in Christ is the hope of the resurrection. This is the exciting hope that a believer has that when the dead in Christ are raised, we will be reunited with our dear friends and loved ones. This is perhaps the reason why, after many years, it seems as though my precious grandparents are still living—because they are in the paradise of God in heaven, where their spirits are waiting for the resurrection of the dead!

When we see them in a dream, we are reminded that one day the dream will become a reality at the return of Christ. We will see them again. Martha understood this when she reminded Christ that at the resurrection she would see her brother, Lazarus, again (John 11).

4. To give you a premonition of death

I want to be very careful in expressing and explaining this fourth reason, as it would be easy for someone to misunderstand a simple dream that may occur with a departed loved one in the dream. However, there have been times when an older saint would see godly family members appear in a dream to tell them it was getting time for them to come home. I remember that several months before my grandfather passed on, he called me and said, "I had an unusual dream. I fell asleep in my easy chair and saw my dad, my mother, and my little brother Tony, who died in the 1930s."

I asked him what he saw. He said, "They were telling me, 'Johnny, it's about time for you to come home.'" He had also seen a large mansion-like building in a dream that was located somewhere in heaven. He felt he was given a warning that he would soon pass away. He was in very good health for his age except for some minor heart problems.

My father and I were both given dreams about the same time involving Granddad. I dreamed I was standing in the bathroom of the old home place. Suddenly three of the four walls collapsed near the toilet. I was uncertain of what it meant, but it was the restroom Granddad always used that was next to his and my grandmother's bedroom. Dad then dreamed that Granddad was working in the attic and became twisted in wires. He fell among the wires and died.

Weeks later Granddad was taken to the Elkins Hospital for surgery on his intestines. After the surgery he had three strokes, affecting his brain, and he became like a vegetable, lying in the intensive care unit. It seemed as if wires were connected to every part of his body. This is where he passed away. The restroom and the toilet in my dream indicated the intestinal problem, and the three walls that fell were the three strokes he had that collapsed his body. The house with the attic was his body, and the attic his mind. He was hooked up to machines with various wires to monitor the heart, breathing, and brain activity, and he died hooked up to the equipment. The two dreams were actually the same from a slightly different perspective.

Please understand that a dream of a departed loved one does not mean you or anyone else near you is going to die. There can be numerous reasons, including no specific reason at all, why you have a dream.

DREAMING OF YOUR OWN DEATH

As parents, we are all concerned about our children, and often in our subconscious we find our minds musing on the numerous possibilities of what could bring harm to them, especially when they are infants or children too weak to defend themselves. We all know there are promises of angelic protection for our children (Matt. 18:10). This subconscious concern can lead to silent worry, which, in return, causes tormenting dreams that something terrible will happen to them.

Because my mother became pregnant at age forty, she was very protective of her little girl Melanie, as any mother would be. Mom said she would have tormenting dreams of something bad happening, but she realized this was the adversary causing her to fret. The same occurred after my son was born. I dreamed several times that he died as a child. Pam and I prayed each day (and continue to pray) that an angel of the Lord would protect our son and our daughter. When Jonathan was about four, we were staying in a hotel in Maryland. His mother was downstairs doing laundry, and I was in a room beside him where he was watching television. Pam came in and said, "Where's Jonathan?"

I relied, "He's in the next room." She walked through the door adjoining the rooms, and he was not there. We panicked! We went down the hall, listening to hear a child crying, and ended up at the elevator. We pressed the button, and there he was, all by himself. He said, "I want Mommy." He did not know the button to press inside the elevator. Anyone could have snatched him and left without us ever seeing him again.

As he grew, I knew we must trust the Lord to protect the family at home and in our journeys. The adversary will lay additional weight on your heart if fear is present. Then you will have tormenting dreams that haunt you throughout the day. Dreaming of a death of a child should cause you to check if there is a fear that needs to be dealt with or if it is a warning. Pray for protection and peace—both of which are promised in the Scriptures.

What if you dream of your own death? Secular dream researchers tell us that this may indicate a new beginning of a marriage or job. However, it can also be an indication of a fear of death. On rare occasions it may be a warning that you should pray, as prayer can change circumstances. Hezekiah was told he was going to die, but his crying and prayer reached God, and his life was extended fifteen additional years (2 Kings 20:6).

I was friends with a well-known Jewish rabbi from Jerusalem named Getz. The rabbi would go to his office every day in the late evening to pray, often until the early hours of the morning. He told his wife that the Lord came to him and told him that he was going to pass in two weeks. It happened exactly as he said.

It is noted that President Abraham Lincoln was given two dreams about his death. The first occurred before his 1860 election. In it he saw he saw two images of his own face in a mirror. One was very pale and disappeared when he looked at it.[1] Many believed it was a sign he would not survive his second term.

Abraham Lincoln wrote about a strange dream he had in March or April of 1865:

> I retired very late. I had been up waiting for important dispatches from the front. I could not have been long in bed when I fell into a slumber, for I was weary. I soon began to dream. There seemed to be death-like stillness about me. Then I heard subdued sobs, as if a number of people were weeping. I thought I left my bedroom and wandered downstairs. There the silence was broken by the same pitiful sobbing, but the mourners were invisible. I went from room to room; no living person was in sight, but the same mournful sounds of distress met me as I passed along. It was light in all of the rooms; every object was familiar to me; but where were all the people who were grieving as if their hearts would break? I was puzzled and alarmed. What could be the meaning of all of this? Determined to find the cause of a state of things so mysterious and so shocking, I kept on until I arrived at the East Room, which I entered. There I met with a sickening surprise. Before me was a catafalque, on which rested a corpse wrapped in funeral vestments. Around it were stationed soldiers who were acting as guards; and there was a throng of people, some gazing mournfully upon the corpse, whose face was covered, others weeping pitifully. "Who is dead in the White House?" I demanded of one of the soldiers. "The President," was his answer; "he was killed by an assassin!" Then came a loud burst of grief from the crowd, which awoke me from my dream.[2]

Two weeks later, on April 14, Lincoln was assassinated at Ford's Theatre by John Wilkes Booth. His casket was laid in the East Room, guarded by soldiers as seen in his dream!

It is reported that the very night before his assassination Lincoln informed a member of his cabinet about this dream. On the morning before his assassination, Lincoln told his bodyguard, W. H. Crook, about his dream, saying he had dreamed about the event three times. Crook begged the president not to go to the theatre that evening. Crook noted that before they left for the theatre, Lincoln, who normally said, "Good night," said to Crook, "Good-bye."[3]

This is a strong example of a well-known person dreaming (according to Crook) three times that he would die.

THE PREMONITION OF DEATH

People often speak of having a *premonition* of a future event, or a foreboding that something is going to happen. A *premonition* is an advance warning of something that is going to happen. This occurred when Elijah and the sons of the prophets were given a forewarning that the prophet Elijah was to be taken alive to heaven. Elisha was following Elijah to the towns of the sons of the prophets, who all knew Elijah was going to heaven that day:

> Now the sons of the prophets who were at Bethel came out to Elisha, and said to him, "Do you know that the LORD will take away your master from over you today?" And he said, "Yes, I know; keep silent!"
>
> —2 KINGS 2:3

At two locations, Bethel and Jericho, "sons of the prophets" were forewarned about the departure of the great prophet to occur on that day (2 Kings 2:1–6). The text indicates that Elijah was the first to know he would be taken in a whirlwind that day (v. 1). What is interesting is that Elijah was actually taken up in a *chariot with horses of fire*, which Elisha saw (vv. 11–12), but the sons of the prophets at Jericho only saw the physical *wind* and later requested a search party to look three days for Elijah's body (vv. 16–18). The men at Jericho saw the whirlwind, but Elisha saw the chariot of fire, which, to the natural eye, was invisible (v. 17). One man saw the invisible chariot and others saw only the wind. This indicates that godly people may be at different levels of spiritual perception. Some have greater spiritual insight and vision than others, and much of it comes through generational blessings (Elisha received a double portion of Elijah's anointing) and also through continual personal prayer.

I can count seven different occasions when I came under a very heavy burden—a strong foreboding that someone would soon pass. The inner weight I felt was a burden unlike any other I have experienced. I always inform my wife and my closest associates at work when this overwhelming sense of loss comes. At times the spiritual pressure in my heart becomes so strong I leave work and go home to meditate and pray. I am unable to enjoy anything or be around anyone, only with the Lord. Always, when this happens, a very close relative or friend passes away unexpectedly within seven days. I confess that when this gut-wrenching feeling suddenly overwhelms me, I do not treat it lightly. This is simply the Holy Spirit preparing me for the loss.

When you either dream of a death, including your own, or have a premonition that something is rising over the horizon, the single most significant act for you to engage in is intercessory prayer. When you are uncertain what or for whom to pray, the Holy Spirit "makes intercession for [you]"; He is sent to assist you in your personal prayer life (Rom. 8:26–28). As you pray, you may have a strong impression of a certain person, and your spiritual focus becomes that individual. This *can be* an indication of death for the one you are praying for, and your prayers could prevent a premature departure (Eccles. 7:17). On several occasions my father saw in a mental vision that something bad was going to happen. Each time he would enter his prayer room to intercede. Usually within twenty-four to forty-eight hours, we would know what his burden was about.

In my book *Angels on Assignment* I share a very dramatic incident in the life of my father and his brother Morgan. This illustrates the power of prayer to prevent a premature *death*.

> In the mid 1980s, Dad was in deep prayer and saw a vision of an accident. He clearly saw a coal truck hitting a vehicle head-on, and he saw that the person sitting on the passenger side had been decapitated. He sensed it was a warning for his brother Morgan, who lived in West Virginia. Dad went to the phone and attempted to call Morgan several times but to no avail. He told Mom, "I am going to the church to pray, and don't let anyone bother me under any circumstance." Dad described to me that he interceded under such a heavy prayer burden that his stomach muscles began to hurt. He was pleading with God to spare his brother's life.
>
> After one hour, he heard the Holy Spirit tell him, "Son, you are asking Me to spare the life of one who has known Me but willfully has chosen to turn from Me. He is not walking in covenant with Me." This caused Dad to pray even more intently for another thirty minutes, asking God to extend his mercy to Morgan. It was then that Dad heard the Holy Spirit speak to him again, saying, "When you pastored in Northern Virginia, I showed you an angel that would be with you when you needed him. If you will ask the Father to send your angel to protect your brother, He will do so." Dad began to ask the Lord to send a protective angel to wherever Morgan was at that time.

It was later that evening when Dad got Morgan on the phone and told him that he had prayed for him to be spared from death. Morgan related this story to Dad: That morning he and a friend had gone to town and were returning home in his truck. Morgan felt a strange urge to stop at a small restaurant and get a soda. Morgan's neighbors, who lived across the street, were following them in a car and passed them as Morgan's truck turned into the restaurant parking lot. A few minutes later, both men were on the road heading home. To their shock, as they rounded a curve a mile up the road, they discovered that a large coal truck had struck the car with the neighbors, killing them both and decapitating the woman passenger. Dad said, "Morgan, that was intended for you, but the Lord sent His angel to have you stop for a few minutes so you would not be on the path of that huge coal truck!" This incident brought Morgan into a restored relationship with the Lord.[4]

Whether you experience a vision, a dream, or a premonition, prayer is the key to understanding what is planned and, at times, to prevent a tragedy! The only way to know if a warning is changeable is by seeking the face of the Lord and asking Him to alter and change a dangerous situation or to protect those you have seen in the dream or vision from harm and danger. Again, I have witnessed this so many times in the life of my father, as he was warned about family members, church members, or other individuals and would spend hours in prayer petitioning God to prevent a tragedy or alter a situation.

ten

THE LAW OF THE DOUBLE DREAM

And the dream was repeated to Pharaoh twice because the thing is established by God, and God will shortly bring it to pass.

« Genesis 41:32 »

This one passage found in the story of Joseph interpreting Pharaoh's dream presents a special nugget to the reader. The king of Egypt had dreamed two dreams the same night. We read:

> Then Pharaoh said to Joseph: "Behold, in my dream I stood on the bank of the river. Suddenly seven cows came up out of the river, fine looking and fat; and they fed in the meadow. Then behold, seven other cows came up after them, poor and very ugly and gaunt, such ugliness as I have never seen in all the land of Egypt. And the gaunt and ugly cows ate up the first seven, the fat cows. When they had eaten them up, no one would have known that they had eaten them, for they were just as ugly as at the beginning. So I awoke. Also I saw in my dream, and suddenly seven heads came up on one stalk, full and good. Then behold, seven heads, withered, thin, and blighted by the east wind, sprang up after them. And the thin heads devoured the seven good heads."
> —Genesis 41:17–24

These two dreams were dreamed back to back on the same night, with the king waking up for a brief time between the first and the second dream. It is clear that the skinny cattle and the thin stalks of grain devouring the good cows and grain both deal with the same event—a famine. However, one truth about a spiritual dream that Joseph revealed should be noted: dreaming the same dream twice the same night can be an indicator that the dream is certain and will come to pass (Gen. 41:25, 32).

There is another *double* principle in the Scripture—when God calls a person's name twice. Normally we read, "And the Lord said to Abraham..." (Gen. 18:13), or "The Lord spoke to Moses..." (Exod. 6:10), or "The Lord said to Solomon..." (1 Kings 11:11). When addressing or appearing before a person in most references, the

Scripture indicates that the Lord spoke their name *once*. However, there are several occasions in which the Almighty spoke the person's name *twice*. We read:

> But the Angel of the LORD called to him from heaven and said, "Abraham, Abraham!" So he said, "Here I am."
>
> —GENESIS 22:11

> Now the LORD came and stood and called as at other times, "Samuel, Samuel!" And Samuel answered, "Speak, for Your servant hears."
>
> —1 SAMUEL 3:10

> And the Lord said, "Simon, Simon! Indeed, Satan has asked for you, that he may sift you as wheat."
>
> —LUKE 22:31

> Then he fell to the ground, and heard a voice saying to him, "Saul, Saul, why are you persecuting Me?"
>
> —ACTS 9:4

God called these names twice to seize the attention of the individual. The purpose was to indicate to that person that a major *transition* or *change* was in the process. God called Abraham's name twice to prevent him from offering his son on the altar. With Samuel, he was a young boy, and God was preparing to transfer the office of the priesthood in Israel from Eli's house to Samuel. The lad would become the future spiritual adviser for Israel's first and second kings, Saul and David. Simon's name had been changed to Peter by Christ Himself (Matt. 16:17–18). However, in Luke 22:13, Christ used his former name, Simon, and spoke it twice. The Lord warned Peter that Satan was setting a strategy against him, determining to shake Peter's faith. The fourth example where God said, "Saul, Saul," is where the proud Pharisee from Jerusalem was, at that very moment, receiving a heavenly visitation from Christ, which led to his conversion while on the road to Damascus. Saul's name was then changed to Paul (Acts 13:9).

Just as the *double name* caught the attention of the person addressed, so a double dream on the same night is an indicator that the dream is established from the Lord and will come to pass in a short time. Many years ago in my earlier ministry I had a very troubling dream involving serpents. During the first dream the symbolism indicated that some form of difficulty (actually a spiritual attack) would follow a revival at a local church. This dream was immediately followed up by a second dream about a serpent in which the snake bit my feet and then rose up and bit my forehead. I knew the feet represented carrying the gospel (Rom. 10:15), and my head represented my thought life. Needless to say, I was very concerned about these two warnings, as serpents in a dream always represent great difficulty in the form of a trial.

Several months later, the very symbolism I saw in those dreams, which indicated a sudden trial, actually unfolded at a local church. The repercussion of that event was so intense at that season that I fought one of the most difficult mental battles of my ministry. One part I remembered in the first dream helped to sustain me through the entire trial. In the dream, when the serpent bit me in the feet and the head, I heard an audible voice say, "The serpent will bite you, but it will not kill you!" In the midst of the fiery trial, these words continually echoed in my mind. Somehow I would survive and even defeat the attack in the end. That is exactly what occurred.

WHY DOUBLE?

Many believers have experienced a dream that later came to pass, and yet they did not dream the same images twice. Just because you have a spiritual visitation and it does not occur twice does not mean the single dream is not from the Lord or that it will not come to pass. However, there may be a deeper reason as to why a dream is doubled.

There is a biblical principle concerning the power of agreement that is linked with the number two. Christ selected twelve disciples (Luke 9:1). However, He divided a team of seventy ministers into thirty-five teams of two each and commissioned them to teach and pray for the needs of the sick in every community (Luke 10:1). There has been speculation as to the purpose of having two disciples on each team. The writer in Ecclesiastes gave insight when he wrote:

> Two are better than one,
> Because they have a good reward for their labor.
> For if they fall, one will lift up his companion.
> But woe to him who is alone when he falls,
> For he has no one to help him up.
> Again, if two lie down together, they will keep warm;
> But how can one be warm alone?
> Though one may be overpowered by another, two can
>   withstand him.
> And a threefold cord is not quickly broken.
> —ECCLESIASTES 4:9–12

There is a certain level of strength that multiplies when one person joins with another. Spiritual authority is increased when two join together in agreement. Christ said:

> Assuredly, I say to you, whatever you bind on earth will
> be bound in heaven, and whatever you loose on earth will
> be loosed in heaven. Again I say to you that if two of you
> agree on earth concerning anything that they ask, it will
> be done for them by My Father in heaven. For where two
> or three are gathered together in My name, I am there in
> the midst of them.
> —MATTHEW 18:18–20

This authority is not released just because two people are in the same room. They must *agree* as to what they believe God for. The Greek word for "agree" is *sumphoneo*, and it means to be in harmony, or, in this instance, to say the same thing. For example: When a church is informed that a fellow member is in critical condition in the hospital, and they are asked to pray, some may stand and petition the Lord with this prayer: "Father, may Your will be done..." A second group may be praying, "Lord, help him somehow..." The third group may sense faith and request, "Lord, enter that room and raise him from his deathbed..." A final circle of saints may be actually praying, "God, he's lived a long life. Don't let him suffer, and take him on if You see fit..." This is what I call a *hit-or-miss* prayer, or a *shooting-from-the-lip* prayer! There is only unity when the group is asking for the same thing. In this illustration there are four different types of prayers being offered, with no single *agreement* among the whole congregation. Perhaps this is why there is a lack of seeing congregational prayers answered; there are too many arrows being shot in different directions, and none are hitting their mark!

The authority is released when two people agree. The same is true with the manifest presence of the Lord. When two or three are "gathered together," Christ is in their midst. Throughout the world, on any given occasion there may be two or three believers in the same room—and no particular presence of Christ can be felt. So is this verse untrue? No, because the key is in the words "gathered together," which is more than just meeting in one place; it alludes to being *led* to the same place. When you are led by the Holy Spirit as you gather, then the Lord is in your midst. All it takes is at least two to agree or be led together in one place!

Just as revealed by Christ, the law of God established the need for two witnesses in any judicial case involving manslaughter. One witness alone could not condemn a person, for it is written, "Whoever kills a person, the murderer shall be put to death on the testimony of witnesses; but one witness is not sufficient testimony against a person for the death penalty" (Num 35:30). We read, "Whoever is deserving of death shall be put to death on the testimony of two or three witnesses; he shall not be put to death on the testimony of one witness" (Deut. 17:6). Moses taught the people that in the mouth of two or three witnesses every word would be established (Deut. 19:15).

The necessity of at least two verbal statements to establish a fact comes into play when we understand that Pharaoh had the dream, but a second person, Joseph, interpreted the meaning. Thus there were two men led together in an inspired moment that would save Egypt and set the destiny for the nation of Israel. The double dream is similar to two witnesses who can establish a fact. When a dream is doubled, it means it is confirmed to come to pass.

Personally, I don't recall speaking to many believers who have dreamed the same dream twice. It is certainly a rare occurrence, but a person should give heed to the dream and understand there is a spiritual precedent about dreaming twice.

eleven

ANGEL APPEARANCES IN DREAMS

Then he dreamed, and behold, a ladder was set up on the earth, and its top reached to heaven; and there the angels of God were ascending and descending upon it.

« Genesis 28:12 »

What visual impression do you experience when a person says "an angel of the Lord"? As a child, I would visualize a tall supernatural being that looked somewhat like a man with huge golden wings connected to his shoulders and blond hair the color of gold. His face was glowing and radiating like the noonday sun. Throughout the Scriptures, there were numerous appearances of angels. However, there are very few references that give a detailed description as to what their appearance is like. In many instances the appearance is based upon the type of angel each scripture is speaking of.

For example, the prophet Daniel was fasting for three weeks to receive the understanding of a very complicated vision he had experienced. After twenty-one days, an angel of the Lord appeared to him and gave him a lengthy, detailed interpretation, revealing many events linked to the time of the end. (See Daniel 10–12.) Here is the description of the "man" Daniel saw:

> Now on the twenty-fourth day of the first month, as I was by the side of the great river, that is, the Tigris, I lifted my eyes and looked, and behold, a certain man clothed in linen, whose waist was girded with gold of Uphaz! His body was like beryl, his face like the appearance of lightning, his eyes like torches of fire, his arms and feet like burnished bronze in color, and the sound of his words like the voice of a multitude. And I, Daniel, alone saw the vision, for the men who were with me did not see the vision; but a great terror fell upon them, so that they fled to hide themselves.
>
> —DANIEL 10:4–7

This male being, an angel, was clothed in linen, which is the same material worn by the seven angels in the Book of Revelation (Rev. 15:6), and is the same white cloth remnant worn by the saints at the marriage supper of the Lamb in Revelation 19:8. The white linen represents "righteousness" (Rev. 19:8). This angel wore a golden belt, which is similar in description to the golden belt (girdle) worn by Christ Himself in John's vision (Rev. 1:13). The description of this angel's body is interesting; it was identified as appearing like beryl. Pure beryl is colorless, but beryl with impurities can appear with a greenish, greenish-blue, or yellow color. The greenish-colored beryl is similar to that of an emerald. The streets in heaven are gold, but transparent gold (Rev. 21:21). Even twenty-four-karat gold is not transparent. The gold in heaven must have a level of purity that is unknown on Earth. If pure beryl is colorless and has the appearance of a crystal, then this angel may have had a translucent, glassy-like color, almost like a hologram, with some slight form of color that reminded Daniel of a beryl stone—a greenish-yellow gold type of appearance. This is significant, since angels are *spirits*, and spirits cannot be seen with the natural eyes.

The face of this angel was shining as the sun, which is also the same imagery painted by John when he saw Christ in the vision recorded in Revelation 1:16. The eyes of the angel were like "torches of fire." In ancient times, oil lamps were used to bring light into a building at night. When burning, an oil lamp forms a flame that can be similar to the shape of human eyes. Christ is also identified in Revelation with "eyes like a flame of fire" (v. 14). The body, arms, and feet of the angel in Daniel's vision were similar to polished brass. The same words are used to identify Christ, when John wrote that "His feet were like fine brass, as if refined in a furnace" (v. 15). When brass is taken from the earth, it has a mix of copper and zinc; thus it only becomes a bright yellow-gold color after being refined in fire. The imagery here is that the angel had a very reflective, yellow-gold appearance. When the angel spoke, his voice sounded like a multitude of voices combined at once. Once again, John used similar words to describe Christ when he wrote, "And His voice as the sound of many waters" (v. 15).

Theologians have noted the similarities between this unnamed angel in Daniel and the appearance of Christ to John in Revelation 1. They identify the Daniel vision as a *theophany*, which is a Greek word meaning "appearance of God." In Christian and Jewish thought, a theophany is "any direct, visual manifestation of the presence of God." It would include the occasions in the Bible when God manifested Himself to men. Some theologians believe the angel in Daniel's vision was actually Christ Himself appearing to Daniel. The difficulty with this theory is that a demonic prince of Persia restrained this angel of the Lord for twenty-one days, and God assigned a mighty archangel named Michael to assist this angel, providing him the ability to be released from his warfare and appear to Daniel. I cannot see the preincarnate Christ as being hindered by any demonic spirit! However, angels do battle in the heavens with evil forces. (See Daniel 10 and Revelation 12:7–10.) This is only one description of an angel.

We know that angelic beings can appear in the form of light and fire. On two occasions the prophet Elisha saw "horses and chariots of fire." The first encounter was when his teacher, Elijah, was transported into heaven on a chariot of fire, driven by spirit horses that also manifested in the form of fire (2 Kings 2). When the Assyrian army was preparing to capture him, Elisha also saw a circle of protection around him and his servant. Elisha saw "horses and chariots of fire" (2 Kings 6:17).

When men like Ezekiel, Daniel, and John saw visions of heaven, they identified numerous types of angels, such as cherubim, seraphim, and living creatures. (See Ezekiel 1; Isaiah 6:1–3; Revelation 5.) These angels are beings that minister before the throne of God on a consistent and eternal basis, and their description of color of brass, many wings and many eyes, and the appearance of an eagle, lion, and man are both amazing and almost difficult to comprehend. However, when ministering angels appear in dreams, visions, or on Earth with a warning or instruction, they seldom appear in these higher-level forms.

ANGELS AS MEN IN DREAMS

Throughout especially the Old Testament, angels would appear to the patriarchs and the prophets in the form of men. These appearances were at times in visible human form and at other times in dreams or visions. In the time of Abraham, the Lord and two angels paid a visit to the tent of Abraham, where they ate with him and the Lord entered into a negotiation with Abraham concerning the city of Sodom. After the final agreement was sealed, the two angels traveled to Sodom and were mistaken for two men. Obviously they were not wearing white linen and did not have two golden wings. They had a flesh tone very similar to that of human men. In the Book of Hebrews, the writer informs the reader that we should be careful when entertaining strangers, for we may be unaware that they are angels (Heb. 13:2).

In a spiritual dream, an angel can appear in the form of a man. In one major experience in 1988, which remains with me to this day, I was given a direct instruction in a dream related to the future of my ministry. I was preaching in a tent in Leeds, Alabama, in a revival that had extended into its fourth week. Early in the morning, while in a deep sleep, I entered into a dream/night vision, which was very clear and vivid. I walked up a hill, crossed a paved road, and saw a set of concrete steps. I observed television towers with satellite dishes attached, and a man with an olive complexion and beautiful white hair, who stood about six feet four inches and was dressed in a black suit, was standing beside the television tower. He said

to me, "Son, if you obey the Lord, God is going to give you this."
Then he proceeded to give me three direct instructions from the
Lord that required my obedience if I was to receive the fullness of
God's blessing and minister to the world on television. At the time
I did not own a television camera, did not have a studio, and knew
nothing about a television ministry.

When I came out from under the influence of this dream/night
vision, I was fully alert and awake and recalled every detail of what
I saw. I told my wife and the head of my board of directors, Richard
Towe. Rick replied, "The Lord has already spoken to my spirit that
you will have a major television program in the future!" This was a
confirmation.

When I told my father of this marvelous experience, I asked him,
"Dad, who do you think the man was who was speaking to me?"

He replied, "That's obvious." He continued, "First, he called
you 'son.' I am your earthly father, but God calls all men who are
believers His sons. Because this man brought you a direct message
from the Lord, he was a divine messenger, or an angel of the Lord."

I said, "I always thought that if an angel appeared in a dream, he
would be in a white robe, with a gold tone, and maybe with a few
wings." Dad reminded me of the angels that came to Sodom and the
angel that wrestled with Jacob, who was described as: "a Man wrestled with him..." However, this "man" was actually an angel (Gen.
32:24–30). In fact, afterward, Jacob confessed that he had "seen God
face to face" and lived through the experience (v. 30)!

Dad also noted that throughout his ministry, when the Lord gave
him a spiritual dream or a vision, whenever the man in the dream
would address him as "My son" or as "son" or "My servant," that the
person in the dream/vision was a messenger from the Lord or an
angel of the Lord.

This significant *nugget* from my wise father, Fred Stone, has been a great help to me over the years when I dream and see a man that may appear as just another person, but the dream or vision has biblical symbolism and imagery and the person is bringing a message from the Lord.

The Book of Ezekiel is a major prophetic book with warnings and apocalyptic overtones throughout the book. Ezekiel witnessed the heavens open and saw four living creatures carrying the throne of God throughout the earth (Ezek. 1). He experienced the vision of the dry bones (Ezek. 37), the war of Gog and Magog (Ezek. 38–39), and the future millennial temple in Jerusalem (Ezek. 40–48). The Lord appeared to Ezekiel and called him "son of man" ninety-three times in the Book of Ezekiel!

Under the redemptive covenant, believers are called "sons of God" (John 1:12, KJV; 1 John 3:2, KJV).

I truly believe that one of the reasons that the Lord allows an angel to appear in the form of a normal-looking man in a dream is because the mental, physical, and spiritual responses we would encounter if the Lord showed us the full glory of the cherubim, seraphim, or the living creatures would be too overwhelming for us to handle. When men saw angels in their fullness in the Bible, they fell to the ground! In Daniel 10, when Daniel saw the angel, he was on his face toward the ground. The other men with him saw nothing, but they also began trembling and fled from the scene (Dan. 10:7–9). Abraham fell on his face when he heard the voice of God (Gen. 17:3). Joshua fell down when he saw the "Commander of the army of the LORD" near Jericho (Josh. 5:14). Even the donkey of Balaam fell down at the presence of an angel (Num. 22:27). During John's vision of the resurrected Christ, he "fell at His feet as dead" (Rev. 1:17).

Seeing any angel in a full-color, three-dimensional vision causes trembling, fear, and a physical response. I have experienced *nightmares* where I woke up feeling like my heart was beating out of my chest. If the Lord allowed us to see the full glory of an angel in an open or night vision, many of us could not take it! We would suffer from a heart attack! This is why I suggest that God will send an angel in human form to prevent the *shock* the human mind and body could experience if we were to see the full manifestation and the total glory of the realm of heaven and the world of spirits.

ANGELS WITH NEW REVELATIONS

If you experience a dream in which the Lord calls you a son or daughter and an *angel* brings you a message from the Lord, always remember that messages from heaven will always agree with the Holy Scriptures. I am an avid reader of all types of books, news articles, and commentaries. I recall reading a lengthy article months ago in which a noted *Christian seer* was claiming visitations from an angel that was giving her important information from varied "heavenly sources." There was a major problem, however, because her "messages" indicated that there were other sources of redemption outside of Jesus Christ. She was actually preaching the traditions that can be found among some who claim that there is a secondary source of intercession and forgiveness of sins besides Christ. At this point, any alleged messenger is not from the Lord. This is why Paul wrote:

> But even if we, or an angel from heaven, preach any other gospel to you than what we have preached to you, let him be accursed. As we have said before, so now I say again, if anyone preaches any other gospel to you than what you have received, let him be accursed.
>
> —GALATIANS 1:8–9

There are two well-known and quite popular religions that are based upon the founder allegedly receiving messages and revelations from angels, including the angel Gabriel. I have studied both of these religions and their beliefs, and the alleged angel totally contradicted the inspired Word of God. In one case the founder reported that Gabriel revealed to him that God has no son and that Jesus is not the Son of God. Of course we read in Luke's account that Gabriel told the Virgin Mary that the child in her womb would be "called the Son of God" (Luke 1:35). Therefore, the real Gabriel is not going to change his mind and bring a new revelation more than six hundred years after the conception of Christ! The woman *seer* and others like her are claiming to channel angel spirits. Those unfamiliar or ignorant of the Scriptures could fall prey to a false doctrine—and even dangerous heresy—by believing there are other sources of redemption, including even *co-redeemers* outside of Christ. The Bible is clear: "Nor is there salvation in any other, for there is no other name under heaven given among men by which we must be saved" (Acts 4:12).

In a dream or vision an angel of the Lord can bring you certain instructions or directions, but a true heavenly visitor will never contradict the revelation of Scripture. If the message causes divisions, turns men from Christ, and introduces other forms of redemption, it is a counterfeit angel of light. Paul warns against such a thing in 2 Corinthians 11:13–15:

> For such are false apostles, deceitful workers, transforming themselves into apostles of Christ. And no wonder! For Satan himself transforms himself into an angel of light. Therefore it is no great thing if his ministers also transform themselves into ministers of righteousness, whose end will be according to their works.

CAN ANGELS APPEAR
AS WOMEN IN DREAMS?

On several occasions there have been very godly and biblically sound believers who have testified to receiving an important, personal word from the Lord in a dream in which the person was an angel of the Lord but appeared more in the form of a female than a male. In the past I would question why this was so or think that the person perhaps misread what he or she saw. However, after searching the Bible, I was quite amazed to read a unique passage written by the prophet Zechariah describing angels with female appearance:

> Then I raised my eyes and looked, and there were two women, coming with the wind in their wings; for they had wings like the wings of a stork, and they lifted up the basket between earth and heaven.
> —ZECHARIAH 5:9

When reading this, I first examined the word *women,* which does appear in the Hebrew text. The word is *ishshah*, a feminine word used for a woman or a female. The prophet indicated that these two "women" had wings like a stork. Some commentators mention that the stork is an unclean bird (Lev. 11:19), thus these two angelic-like figures are actually symbols of evil in the land of Shinar. I suggest that the prophet is simply attempting to identify how the wings looked when he saw these two lift up the lead basket and carry it into the land of Shinar. A stork has long wings attached to its back. This is the imagery the prophet is painting. These two women also have the wind in their wings. While some suggest this phrase is a metaphor, we do know from the Bible that during the Tribulation angels are seen "holding the four winds of the earth" (Rev. 7:1).

When suggesting that there are possibly angels in heaven that have the appearance of women, the first reaction is remembering that when Christ was asked about the resurrection of the dead and marriage in heaven, He replied, "For when they rise from the dead, they neither marry nor are given in marriage, but are like angels in heaven" (Mark 12:25–26). When studying the Bible, there are scriptures that reveal a direct and clear truth, and there are other times when certain truths can be *deduced* from the verse and the implications of what was being said. For example, when the Bible says that everyone will "receive a mark on their right hand or on their foreheads, and that no one may buy or sell except one who has the mark" (Rev. 13:16–17), this passage does not tell you what the mark is or how it can impact the ability of the entire world's population to purchase and sell. However, with computers and identification technology, we can see how this verse could come to pass.

When asked about marriage in heaven, why didn't Christ say, "Of course there is no marriage in heaven, as all of the angels are male, and therefore there are no females to marry." Instead He said, "They are like the angels, neither marrying or being given in marriage." The verse is silent, yet the *implication* is that there is a possibility of both male and female angelic beings in heaven. However, there is no marriage among the angels in heaven.

If these two women carrying the basket are female in gender, and the Hebrew word indicates they are, and they are *wicked spirits* and not angels of the Lord, then this would indicate female spirits in the satanic realm. If Satan's kingdom consists of fallen angels, and these two women are fallen angels, then their appearance would be like that of the angels before the wicked angels were cast out of heaven with Satan.

Perhaps the least controversial manner of interpreting this, according to some scholars, is to say that they appeared to the prophet to look like women but were not women. This is similar to the strange demonic locusts that come from the abyss during the

Tribulation and had "faces of men" and "hair like women's hair" (Rev. 9:7–8). In ancient cultures, women grew very long hair. Thus John described either the hairlike appearance or the headdress on these creatures as the appearance of women's hair. If these women simply had long hair and feminine-looking faces, then the argument is that all angels in Scripture are masculine in *appearance* except these two.

However, in most spiritual dreams and visions the messenger will appear in a masculine form. It is possible that God could permit an angel to appear as a woman in a dream, but this is certainly a very rare instance. Perhaps the controversy is better settled when we get to heaven!

It is certainly possible that a believer can experience a dream or vision in which the angel of the Lord appears in bright clothing and in a glorified form. At times, prior to a believer's departure from this life, some will speak of seeing either departed loved ones or a heavenly, angelic-like being just prior to their death. This is not uncommon, as Scripture indicates that angels are assigned to help a believer depart from their physical body at death. In Luke 16, when the poor beggar died, he was carried by the angels into the paradise of God, known in that time as "Abraham's bosom" (Luke 16:22). In these instances the appearance of an angel is often described as a glowing being in a white garment, standing in a room or near the bed. Whether the dying soul is actually seeing the angel or is having a true *open vision* is known only to the Lord. The fact is, angels have appeared and do appear in dreams, as indicated in both Testaments!

In summary:

▸ God can allow an angelic messenger to appear in a dream or a vision.

► The angel will more often appear in the form of a man and rarely, but occasionally, a woman.

► The angel will often address you as a son or daughter when speaking.

► The angel will inform you that the message has come for you from the Lord.

► The message will also agree with the Word of God.

I wish to make it clear that biblically we are not to be involved in angel worship or seeking angels. God's angelic messengers are commissioned into ministry activity by the voice of God Himself, and they respond only to the Word of God (Ps. 103:20). Any appearance of an angelic-type visitor in a dream, vision, or possible appearance in *human form* is completely controlled by the sovereignty of the Almighty and based upon the covenant of His Word.

twelve

WHY THE SYMBOLISM—
CAN'T GOD MAKE IT PLAIN?

*Pharaoh had a dream; and behold, he stood
by the river. Suddenly there came up out of the
river seven cows, fine looking and fat; and they
fed in the meadow. Then behold, seven other
cows came up out of the river, ugly and gaunt,
and stood by the other cows on the bank of the
river. And the ugly and gaunt cows ate up the
fine looking and fat cows. So Pharaoh awoke.*

« Genesis 41:1–4 »

One aspect of my ministry is the teaching of biblical prophecy. Today, more and more people are becoming aware of the ancient dreams and visions of the biblical prophets and are poring over the pages of the Holy Bible to unlock the cryptic codes and strange passages that have stumped scholars in previous generations. When I ask why a believer does not study or even read the apocalyptic books of the Scriptures, there always seems to be one main answer: "I don't understand all of the symbolism used, so I don't study it." The same is true with a real spiritual dream.

Oddly, most spiritual dreams that have instruction, warning, or important insight are often slightly veiled in symbolism. Many people who have experienced a spiritual dream may write the event off as some type of weird result of eating too much pizza before retiring for the night. Just as some folks can be slightly spiritually lazy when it comes to digging through the prophetic symbols to discover the dynamic insights, some believers have the attitude, "Well, if God wants to show me something, He can just show me!" This brings up a good point: Why can't the Lord just show you what is going to happen without using all of the strange symbolism often accompanying a spiritual dream? I believe I have found an answer.

First, most people dream throughout the night. In most dreams we are with friends or family and others we know, perhaps on a journey, in a church service, or on vacation, and it's just a *normal dream.* Then one night you have a dream that is quite different from the others. In this dream you see dark clouds slowly crawling in the sky toward your house. As you approach the door, there is a large snake lying in the entrance, looking for a way to get in. You see a sword and attack the serpent until he is dead, and then you enter. When you wake up, you know this was not a normal dream. You realize that in the Bible a serpent is Satan (or an enemy), and the door is the entrance to your home. A sword in Scripture is the "word of God" (Heb. 4:12), and you took a sword (the Word) to attack an enemy trying to get into your home! Thus, the symbolism was interpreted by using the Bible, and the dream is a warning of someone or something trying to get through the entrance of your home. You will need to fight it by the spoken Word of God!

The point is, without the symbolism it would be difficult to know if your dreams were just dreams or a dream from God! When Pharaoh dreamed, he saw seven good cows and seven lean cows, and seven good ears of corn and seven bad ears of corn near the Nile River. Cows eat grain and need water. Without grain and water, the cows become lean or die. The grain needs water to grow; without water, the grain will wither. The interpretation is clear; there was coming a lack of rain, leading to a famine. Grain was planted on a yearly cycle, thus seven stalks is a seven-year cycle. Joseph understood this to be a famine with a seven-year cycle. How else would God warn the king? The symbolism troubled Pharaoh and caused him to search out a man capable of the interpretation. Had it been just a simple dream, Pharaoh's own wise men could have revealed the meaning, and Joseph would had stayed in prison!

The same was true with Daniel. King Nebuchadnezzar dreamed of a metallic image that looked like a man. The head was gold, the chest and arms were of silver, the thighs were brass, the two legs were iron, and the two feet and ten toes were a mixture of iron and clay. (See Daniel 2.) The king was so troubled that he could not remember the dream. Daniel was called, and he not only revealed the dream, but he also gave the meaning, revealing that the various metals were different empires that would rule in succession of one another. How did Daniel know this was the meaning?

In Daniel's time, there was a belief among the Persians (Babylon's next-door neighbors) that the world empires were similar to a man with seven different kinds of metals. Although he did not understand the meaning of his dream, Nebuchadnezzar would also have been aware of this Persian belief. Babylon (the head of gold) had amassed huge amounts of gold, including the gold from the temple in Jerusalem. The Persians (represented by the silver chest and arms) raised tax money in silver coinage. Some even had silver harnesses for their horses. Since Greece and Rome were in the future, it would have been impossible for Daniel to give the meaning without the inspiration of the Lord upon him!

In the apocalyptic visions recorded in the Book of Daniel, even animals are used and identified with certain empires. I often wonder why certain animals were chosen to represent various empires. However, in my study I came to a conclusion that these were images that were already in existence and known among the ancients. For example, the ancient and modern empires all have animal-like symbols that are used to represent their particular empires, which are the same images found in the heavens. Daniel chapters 7 and 8 speak of a lion, a ram, and a goat.

Emblem	Empire	Heavenly Symbol	Parallel Emblem
Lion	Babylon	Lion emblem in heaven	Leo
Ram	Media-Persia	Ram emblem in heaven	Aries
Goat	Greece	Goat emblem in heaven	Capricorn
Eagle	Rome/America/Russia	Eagle emblem in heaven	Aquila
Dragon	China	Dragon emblem in heaven	Draco
Bear	Modern Russia	Bear emblem in heaven	Ursa Major

SIMPLE DREAM—
COMPLICATED DREAMS

Some significant dreams are very plain, and others are veiled in symbolism. When my father was a teenager, the Korean War had broken out, and many young men from West Virginia were inducted into the army. The military had reported that two young men from the area of Bartley, West Virginia—namely, C. N. Morgan and Dale Smith—were missing and assumed killed in battle. The army was willing to pay death benefits to the parents. The mother of one soldier was a strong Christian and a faithful member of the church Dad was attending in Atwell, West Virginia. She requested prayer one evening, saying, "I don't believe my son is dead, and I want the saints to agree with me that God will find him and bring him home to me!" Some believers suggested that she was in denial, while others stood in faith with her.

Shortly thereafter Dad had a dream in which he saw both young men in very poor conditions, imprisoned in a North Korean prison camp. He saw Dale Smith standing deep in mud, holding onto a section of barbed wire. In the dream Smith spoke and said, "Brother Fred, please tell my mother that I am alive and being held as a prisoner in this camp. If she and the saints will pray, God is going to release us and bring us home safe." Dad immediately contacted the mother, informing her that both soldiers were alive, but that prayer was needed to bring about their releases! Some of the older believers felt that Dad was giving the mother false hope and that the dream was a smoke screen for a vivid and hopeful imagination. Others received the word and began continual intercession for their release.

Six months later Dad returned home from preaching a revival. When he stepped off the bus, his eye caught the local newspaper with the headlines, "Two Men Exchanged in Panmunjom Prisoner

Swap." The writer reported that there had been a prisoner exchange between the United States and North Korea, and these two missing West Virginia men were being released as part of the exchange. Needless to say, there was, as old-timers used to say, a *high time in Zion* when the news spread throughout the church!

This dream was a simple dream with a clear meaning. The men were missing but held in a camp. If the believers prayed, they would be released. There was no symbolism, simply a message with a meaning.

Many years later Dad was in his early thirties when his youngest brother, Lewis Stone, was ordered to Vietnam. I can remember hearing Dad pray for Lewis, and he always had him in his heart. One night in the month of December, Dad lay down in the bedroom to sleep. As he was dozing off, he was suddenly awakened by light coming into the room through a window located on the side of the driveway. He assumed that a car was turning around, when instantly he heard a voice say, "Lie down, I want to show you something." As he obeyed the voice, he immediately experienced a full-color vision. He was taken either in his mind or in the spirit to Vietnam. There he saw a group of marines digging a trench for the evening. In front of them was a field with tall grass. At the edge of the field were several trees. Dad saw three serpents crawling on the ground with rifles strapped to their backs; two had knives in their mouths. They were slowly crawling toward the marines, and Dad knew this was an unseen ambush. Dad marked the surroundings and suddenly came out of the vision with his heart pounding.

Not knowing what to do with the information, he sat down and penned a letter to Lewis, giving him the details of the planned ambush, including the site information, the three trees, and all other details he could remember. Dad sent the letter, praying that God would allow Lewis to get it in time. Many weeks later Dad heard back from Lewis, and the opening words were, "Fred...your dream was a true one..." He went on to describe the day they were digging in, how an ambush was set, and that the point man was shot to death. Out of eight hundred men who went into Vietnam with Lewis's company, only eight returned—Lewis Stone was one of those eight.

Other dreams or visions are veiled in symbolism. Years ago while touring Rome, Italy, I pondered as to why the Book of Revelation was written with so much symbolism. It occurred to me that chapters 17 and 18 speak of mystery Babylon's destruction—the city ruling over the kings of the earth. This is believed by many scholars to be a cryptic reference to the city of Rome, which was the headquarters of the Roman Empire in John's day. If John was predicting the total destruction of Rome and using the symbolism of Babylon to conceal the meaning, then it is clear why God chose the symbol of a woman riding a beast. If John would have clearly stated that the great city of Rome would be judged and destroyed in the future, then the Roman government, which had confined him to the desolate island of Patmos (Rev. 1:9), would have refused to allow John to bring the apocalyptic scroll with him when he was released from his captivity. John's prophecy of Rome's demise would have been considered to be anti-Roman propaganda. The Book of Revelation would have been confiscated and destroyed, never to be read in any church.

Imagine when John's Roman captors asked to see his writing, and they read of a flying red dragon, a women with a crown of twelve stars who was giving birth in heaven, and a woman hanging on to a ten-horned beast. Perhaps they would have thought, "This old man has been in the cave too long and needs some fresh air!" The bizarre symbolism may have actually provided protection for the actual scroll, allowing it to be copied and read throughout the first-century church.

While at times it may be challenging to the average believer to know if a dream is a natural or spiritual dream, there are several important guidelines to determine this difference that I have used during years of ministry. First, many *natural* or carnal dreams have no particular order and jump from scene to scene, person to person, or circumstance to circumstance. On the other hand, a spiritual dream usually has some form of order or progression to it. A spiritual dream will also have symbolism, which was also used in both the Old and New Testaments. As one example, a serpent throughout the Scriptures is a reference to Satan or an adversary of some form.

BIBLICAL SYMBOLISM AND PATTERNS

In the principles of biblical interpretation there is what is termed the "law of first mention." This hermeneutical principle states that when an object, number, color, or symbol is first mentioned in Scripture, then that sets the pattern for that object, number, color, or symbol throughout the Bible. Let's begin with certain biblical numbers.

The number four appears in Genesis when God created the sun, moon, and stars on the fourth day (Gen. 1:16–19). Afterward, it is mentioned when Moses wrote that there were four rivers that encompassed the Garden of Eden (Gen. 2:10). We later discover there are four directions on the earth: north, south, east, and west. Thus, from the onset of Scripture, the number four is an earthly number. Four Gospels reveal the earthly ministry of Jesus. The four living creatures around the throne reveal the four mighty powers on the earth: the ox, the mightiest of the four-footed domestic animals; the eagle, the king among the fowls of the air; the lion, the king of the beast; and man, who was given dominion over all creation.

Man was created on the sixth day, and the number six has always been considered in biblical numbers as the number of man or mankind. When David fought Goliath, the giant was six cubits tall (1 Sam. 17:4). The Hebrew children were commanded to bow to the image in Babylon when six different types of instruments were played in unison (Dan. 3:5, KJV). The future mark of the beast is 666 (Rev. 13:18).

The number seven is alluded to in Genesis 2. When God completed His creative work, "He rested on the seventh day" (Gen. 2:2). This imagery of the number seven alludes to a cycle of rest, completion, or perfection. The *rest* cycles are: each seventh day is a Shabbat (rest); followed by each seventh year, called a Sabbatical cycle; followed by seven years of seven sabbatical cycles (forty-nine years). In each cycle of seven days, seven years, or seven cycles of seven years, the people, animals, and the land rested (Lev. 25:1–7).

The use of seven in representing completion or perfection can be seen in the seven seals, seven trumpets, and seven vial judgments in Revelation (chapters 5, 8, 15). Jesus spoke seven sayings from the cross before completing His redemptive work. The word *seven* or *seventh* is used 583 times in Scripture and is always linked to the things of God, the kingdom of God, or the prophetic future as it relates to God.

One other number commonly found in the Bible is the number forty. This number has represented a period of testing. It is alluded to in the story of Noah's flood, where the rain fell for forty days and nights. After the rain concluded, Noah experienced a second period of testing as he waited in the ark an additional forty days before the dove returned with an olive branch. Later we read where Goliath taunted the Hebrew army for forty days before being slain by David. Christ was tempted of the devil for forty days in the desolate Judean wilderness! Clearly, the number forty is a number of testing and chastisement; Israel wandered through the wilderness for forty years—one year for every day that they doubted God!

THE MEANINGS OF COLORS

The law of first mention is also found in the presentation of colors, metals, and fabrics found in the Scriptures. When Moses was building the tabernacle in the wilderness, God instructed him to use purple, blue, red, and white dyed fabrics. Without entering into a detailed study of the fabrics of the tabernacle, blue is heavenly, purple is royalty, red is redemption, and white is righteousness. A scarlet (purple) robe was placed on Christ at His trial while the soldiers mocked Him as the king (Matt. 27:27–29). A red cord was hung in the window of the harlot Rahab's apartment, marking her house for redemption and protection from destruction (Josh. 2:17–18). In heaven, the saints will wear white robes, which represent the "righteousness of the saints."

When it comes to metals, three are mentioned frequently in the Scriptures: gold, silver, and brass. Gold is the most precious, representing deity. Gold never tarnishes, never needs cleaning, is eternal (never aging), and just as God is sinless, never needs to repent of any sin. Silver is a precious metal that represents redemption. Under the old covenant, a silver shekel was collected from all men over twenty years of age, called the *shekel of redemption*. The entire collection was placed in the temple treasury and was used for repairs of the tabernacle and, later, the temple in Jerusalem. When Jews celebrate the yearly Passover, four silver cups are used for the fruit of the vine, each cup representing an aspect of the redemption from Egypt.

BIBLICAL SYMBOLISM

Some of the most common forms of symbolism found in Scripture are animals that are used to identify nations or individuals. You may wonder why Scripture uses the animal kingdom as symbolism so frequently. I believe the simple answer is that God used what the people of ancient history were most familiar with. The same could be said of Christ's outdoor teaching ministry. When Christ spoke of a man sowing seed in a field, the wheat and tares, and the thorns, His Galilean audience was completely familiar with the objects He used in His famous illustrated messages.

The biblical symbolism of objects and animals is similar to the symbolism of numbers, metals, and colors in that the first mention of the object or thing usually sets the pattern for the cryptic, mystical, or symbolical understanding of that particular object or thing.

The first created creature that became prominent in the Bible was the serpent, which was "more cunning than any beast of the field which the LORD God had made" (Gen. 3:1). Notice that the Bible does not use a term like "reptile" or "slithering thing" but places the serpent with the "beast of the field." Today when we think of a beast in a field, we picture a large ox, a bull, a cow, or other large animal that roams in the field. However, the serpent was more than a skinny snake. He was subtle or crafty and was also able to communicate in some manner with Adam and Eve. Because a serpent initiated the first deception, the fallen angel, Lucifer, called the devil and Satan, became a picture of a deceiving serpent. In fact, he is called a serpent in Revelation 20:2.

One of the most commonly mentioned animals in Scripture is the lamb. The word *lamb* or verses using the word *lamb* first appear in Genesis 22, where Abraham predicted that God would "provide for Himself the lamb" (Gen. 22:8). However, the main story of a lamb that connects this precious creature with Christ is the Passover narrative recorded in Exodus 12. A perfect pet lamb was chosen from the flock. Its blood was sprinkled on the left, right, and top post of the outer door of each Hebrew home, forming an invisible hedge that restrained the destroying angel from taking the firstborn Hebrew.

The entire lamb was then roasted, and all parts were eaten by the family prior to departing from bondage to their homeland. This was not just an exodus but also a redemption from bondage and slavery. It was a preview of coming events—when Christ would appear as the "Lamb of God" taking away the sins of the world (John 1:29). In the Book of Revelation, the word *lamb* is used twenty-seven times, and in all instances but one (Rev. 13:11), the lamb is Christ.

The Bible uses other symbolism that is often found in a spiritual dream. In the Bible we read of wheat and tares. The wheat alludes to the good seed that produces children of the kingdom, and the tares are the bad seed that produces the children of the devil (Matt. 13).

There are certain animals that I call the "odd flock." They are the sheep, goat, and pig—each representing a different type of believer. The sheep always refers to believers or individuals who faithfully follow the shepherd. Sheep are never spoken of in a negative manner in the New Testament and are to be protected, loved, and cared for by their spiritual shepherd. On the opposite end are the goats. Goats are actually a part of the flocks in the Middle East, but they are separated from the sheep, as they can become difficult to get along with at times. A goat can allude to someone in the flock who has a negative attitude or refuses to obey the instructions of a shepherd. As a youth, I knew members in churches where my father was the shepherd who were definitely *goats*. They were always causing some type of difficulty through their stubborn and stiff-necked attitude. The other creature is the pig. In Judaism, a pig is considered a very unclean animal, and religious Jews will not eat any form of pork. In 2 Peter 2:20–22, a pig is a metaphor used to describe a backslider, or someone who returns to their old filthy ways.

Most believers know that the Holy Spirit is symbolized as a dove, and for good reason, when we compare a natural dove to the characteristics of the Holy Spirit.

One form of dove is pure white in color, which represents the purity of the Holy Spirit. A dove is an affectionate bird that expresses its emotions through cooing. It is also a gentle creature, a perfect imagery of the gentleness and affection of the Holy Spirit. When a dove is attacked, it does not retaliate but simply cries in distress. Believers who are filled with the Holy Spirit are instructed never to retaliate against our enemies. The Holy Spirit makes intercession for us in prayer with "groanings" (Rom. 8:26).

The great Christian minister Vance Havner once pointed out that a dove has nine main feathers on each wing and five main feathers on its tail. It is noted in Scripture that there are nine gifts of the Holy Spirit (1 Cor. 12:7–10) and nine fruit of the Spirit listed in Galatians 5:22–23. The tail feathers are similar to the rudder of a plane and assist in guiding the dove in flight. The five feathers would well be a picture of the fivefold ministry of apostle, prophet, pastor, teacher, and evangelist—the fivefold ministry provided to the body of Christ (Eph. 4:11–12). The dove is also unique from other birds because instead of its wings pointing toward its tail, they actually point toward the head. The Holy Spirit does not speak of Himself but points believers to Christ.

In the parables, the field where the harvest grain is maturing is symbolic of the world itself. Water is symbolic of the Holy Spirit when He is manifesting within the life of a believer, as indicated when Christ compared the infilling of the Spirit to someone with living water flowing from their innermost being (John 7:38).

When a believer experiences a spiritual dream with the meaning veiled with symbolism, the meaning of the dream can be understood by using the Scriptures to interpret the symbolism. On occasions I have heard sincere individuals attempting to bring understanding to a dream that was actually nothing more than a strange dream. There was no order, no instruction, and no biblical symbolism. It reminds me of the woman in my father's church who said to him, "Pastor, I had a strange dream. I saw the congregation here at the church, and instead of having normal heads, they all had large, round cabbages sitting between their shoulders." With concern on her face, she inquired, "What do you think this means?"

Dad paused and in a serious tone replied, "Sister, I believe you had too much pizza before you went to bed."

I recall a self-acclaimed dream interpreter interpreting the dreams that people phoned in. From a purely biblical standpoint, most of the dreams made no sense. Yet the person in charge made every dream a spiritual revelation and had the most elaborate system for interpretation that I had heard. However, the colors he used were totally opposite of the biblical patterns, and at that point I realized he was stretching the meanings in order to provide some form of comment for each caller.

In a spiritual dream that is meant as a warning, it is common to see serpents, wolves, tares, dark clouds, hurricanes, fish, churches, and other symbols that are used in the Bible.

THE EFFECTS OF A SPIRITUAL DREAM

When the king of Babylon arose from his dream of the metallic image, we read:

> Now in the second year of Nebuchadnezzar's reign, Nebuchadnezzar had dreams; and his spirit was so troubled that his sleep left him.
> —Daniel 2:1

During my many years of ministry, one common factor in any warning or instructional dream from the Lord was the fact that after waking up, I could not go back to sleep. The dream continually remained with me for days, weeks, and months. A warning dream remains in your mind and spirit. At times there were parts of the dream that I could not remember, but I always recalled the major details of the dream or vision. I have learned by experience that the average nightly dream will occur and often be forgotten after awaking or before the day concludes. For example, last night I dreamed, but at this moment I cannot recall any details, in part or in whole, of the dream. However, a dream from God will remain in your mind or spirit for long periods of time.

WRITING DOWN WHAT YOU SEE

King Nebuchadnezzar's prophetic dream of the metallic image was so dramatic, yet when he awoke, he could not recall what he had dreamed. When Daniel began his explanation, the king remembered all of the details and exalted Daniel in the kingdom (Dan. 2). I have discovered by experience that the moment you awake from a dream, and you believe it may have a spiritual connotation, it is important to write it down on paper. For many years I have kept either a notebook or paper and a good pen on the nightstand beside our bed near the lamp. At numerous times I would awaken after dreaming or actually hearing a word or phrase spoken in my ear, and I would turn on the lamp, grab the pen, and begin to write down the word or the events seen in the dream.

On the other hand there were a few occasions that I would awaken and think, "I will remember that in the morning," as I was too exhausted to get up and make the effort to record the dream. Sadly, there were times when I awoke and could not recall the details that may have been a significant part of the meaning of the dream. Occasionally that day I would be traveling and would see or hear something that would trigger my memory, like a small light from a flashlight suddenly appearing in a dark room. The small *memory jolt*, however, was not enough to bring any substantial light to reflect on the dream.

If you are spiritually sensitive, you should keep a notebook and pen close to you at all times, even when traveling. You may be in the presence of someone who will speak a word during a spiritual or biblical conversation that will be exactly what you need to hear. The best avenue of recall is to write the insight on paper or in a journal. I have three offices, two in ministry facilities and one at home. In each location are numerous file cabinets with drawers stacked full with notebooks and notes from thirty-four years of ministry. To this day I will occasionally pull a stack of white or yellow notepads and muse over the handwritten nuggets on the paper. At countless times I have gleaned a phrase, a title, or a series of outlines from notes that were written years earlier.

I have more than sixteen Bibles that I have used over the years when preaching in revivals and conferences. In each Bible the inside and backside pages are filled with small handwritten notes and nuggets, some of which were deep words I heard in my spirit in prayer. In 1979 I was a teenager traveling in Virginia and ministering in revivals. While I was in Richmond preaching, a youth group gathered around me and began praying for my protection and for a major spiritual breakthrough. Suddenly I grabbed a pen and wrote in the back of my Bible, "The Lord says that you will see the great breakthrough in three weeks!" The next meeting was in Pulaski, Virginia, and the revival continued for three weeks. At the conclusion it was said to be one of the greatest revivals in the church's history, and it was also the revival that opened the door of opportunity for me to minister in other states. To this day I see the small inscription in the back of my old Bible, and I can recall all of the details of that moment and weeks following—all as a result of writing it down!

At times you will personally receive a special word from the Lord, and at other times someone you have confidence in will receive a warning or an instruction for you. If you are a husband, that person is often the one person closest to you—your wife.

TELLING OTHERS YOUR DREAMS

In the event of a spiritual warning or a dream with spiritual symbolism, a person must exercise wisdom and discretion when sharing any dream with a second or third party. When Joseph related his double dream to his father, Jacob, his dad successfully interpreted the meaning, since Jacob himself had experienced spiritual dreams (Gen. 37:10). However, when the lad told his brothers, he was ridiculed and mocked, and they envied him, eventually selling him as a slave, all because of his dreams (Gen. 37:8, 11, 26–28).

Believers are at different levels of spiritual understanding and maturity, just as children are at various levels. There are some children who reach age twelve and are as mature mentally and emotionally as if they were eighteen. Others reach eighteen and are as mature as a twelve-year-old! This was true in biblical times, as we see when Christ was twelve years of age and confounded the doctors of the law at the temple (Luke 2:42–47). Believers are either *milk drinkers* or *meat eaters*. The milk drinkers are the babes in Christ who are unskilled in the Word of God and must hear the simple and basic teachings from Scripture (Heb. 5:13). The meat eaters are those who understand the deeper knowledge of the Scripture, such as the major biblical doctrines, the Hebraic roots of the faith, the prophetic teachings, and other subjects that require deep and detailed study and biblical research, which produces spiritual growth.

I suggest the one thing that a new convert or *babe in Christ* should not immediately do is begin his or her study of Scripture in the books of Daniel or Revelation! However, anyone who has been raised under strong *meat* teaching should have at least a basic understanding of the symbolism found in these apocalyptic books. New believers need to understand their relationship with God and how to pray, worship, and walk by faith before engaging in the in-depth study of things to come.

I recall years ago sharing a major spiritual dream with my son, who I thought would be interested in hearing the unusual warning I felt the Lord had given me. He became quite despondent and discouraged after I shared this warning with him. Later I realized that this type of dream was not intended to share with a young man who was attending high school and had limited understanding or, for that matter, little interest in some strange warning given to his father. As my son, he interpreted the dream as just more *negative stuff* that Dad was seeing. This was an important lesson for me. He needed to be encouraged and built up as a young person. On the other hand, I sat down with my father and shared the same word, and he interpreted the meaning and began to pray about the information the Holy Spirit had revealed through the dream. The difference between these two reactions is the spiritual and emotional maturity level of the person.

You may have a dream that something bad is going to happen to someone. The last thing to do is to worry the person by screaming over a phone demanding he heed the warning before it is too late. The first thing to do is what Daniel did when he received a troubling vision or dream: he set his heart for prayer and understanding. (See Daniel 9.) Pray first before sharing this type of dream. Now, if a person comes to you with his or her dream and asks for a possible meaning, then you have more freedom and permission to search for the understanding. When I was eighteen, I was earnestly seeking God during a fast, and the Holy Spirit revealed to me many forms of ministry I would use to reach entire nations. All of the words

He gave me then have since come to pass after thirty-four years of ministry. I was so excited, and I recall that at ages eighteen and nineteen I sat with other groups of ministers and told them what I saw and felt that the Lord would accomplish through my efforts. Some read this *revelation* as some form of pride or arrogance, which was not in my heart. Their response and actual rejection of the information could have discouraged me. Wisdom later taught me that it is not wise to publicly tell all the *secret things* God reveals to you. When the angel told Mary she was pregnant, she went to the one person who would understand her strange circumstances, her cousin Elizabeth (Luke 1). After all, can you imagine Mary, an unmarried virgin, running through a Jewish community yelling, "I'm pregnant! I saw a vision of an angel, and I'm pregnant, and the Lord did it—*the Lord did it*"? First, who would believe it was the *Lord alone* who helped her conceive? Second, imagine how Joseph would have been persecuted and Mary forever rejected if the community thought she was pregnant out of wedlock! There are times to make information known and times to hide and ponder things in your heart (Luke 2:19).

If you have a believing spouse, it is always good and in order not to hide *personal secrets* from one another, but to have such a trusting relationship that you can share with each other your personal feelings, desires, dreams, and visions—both visions and dreams of your plans and destiny, and visions or dreams that are messages from heaven.

thirteen

FOUR TYPES OF SPIRITUAL VISIONS

Then the LORD *answered me and said:*

"Write the vision
And make it plain on tablets,
That he may run who reads it.
For the vision is yet for an appointed time;
But at the end it will speak, and it will not lie.
Though it tarries, wait for it;
Because it will surely come,
It will not tarry."

« Habakkuk 2:2–3 »

When I say the word *vision,* what comes to your mind? There are several ways in which this word is used in the English language. The common meaning is a person's eyesight, or their ability to see. The second most common usage deals with an individual or a church's plans for the future, as in: "We have a vision for the future; we are going to build a new facility." This meaning of *vision* alludes to the ability to imagine, or create a plan or idea for the future, and to make it occur. However, the spiritual meaning of the word *vision* from the prophetic and biblical stories is far deeper than the two meanings above.

There are three Old Testament prophets who mention the word *vision* more frequently than other prophetic books. They are Isaiah, Ezekiel, and Daniel. In Isaiah, the word *vision* is mentioned in seven verses. In Ezekiel, it is referred to thirteen times, and in Daniel, the word is mentioned twenty-two times—more than by any other prophet. Among the prophets, a vision was a divinely inspired visual scene that a prophet saw either during prayer, during sleep, or at times when they were wide-awake. The wide-awake vision is perhaps the most rare and unusual. We read that the prophet Balaam saw "the vision of the Almighty, falling into a trance, but having his eyes open" (Num. 24:16, KJV).

Many of these visions were so remarkable that they are difficult for the average human mind to comprehend. When King Uzziah died, Isaiah saw into the heavenly throne room where the seraphim were flying above God's throne, each with six wings: two were covering their eyes, two were covering their feet, and two they were using to fly (Isa. 6:2). On the other hand, Ezekiel saw a whirlwind coming from the north, with the appearance of a fire descending. Within it the prophet saw the throne of God being carried on the shoulders of four cherubim. On several occasions Daniel saw Gabriel and numerous other strange symbolism as he witnessed beasts rising up, representing empires.

There are four different types of words found in Daniel to describe the different methods by which a vision can be received.

1. The word chazown

This word refers to a *mental sight, dream, revelation, or oracle.* It is found in Daniel 1:17, where it states that Daniel had "understanding in all visions and dreams." It can also be found in Daniel 8:1–2, 13, 15, 26, and in other references.

2. The word chezev

This Aramaic word simply means *sight or vision.* This word is used in Daniel 2:19, when Daniel received a secret from the Lord in a night vision and was later brought before the king and interpreted the famous dream of the metallic image. This form of a vision occurs while a person is asleep.

3. The word mar'ah

This word, found in Daniel 10:7–8, is also translated as "vision," and is used to describe *seeing a reflection in a mirror.* Daniel was near the river Hiddekel in Babylon when he was suddenly overtaken with a shaking that brought him to his face. He then saw what is considered in theology as a *theophany,* the appearance of Christ in the Old Testament. The man Daniel saw in the vision was clothed in linen held by a golden belt. His eyes were like lightning, his arms and his feet like brass, and his voice like the sound of many waters. Parts of this description are parallel to John's vision of Christ in Revelation chapter 1!

4. The word mar'eh

The fourth word means *sight or appearance* and is used in Daniel 10:1 where Daniel had received a vision but did not have the understanding. He privately fasted for three complete weeks and broke through the spiritual opposition that existed in the atmosphere where a demonic prince of Persia was restraining the revelation from reaching him. (See Daniel 10:1–12.)

The various words indicate that visions occur in different ways. In the Scriptures, the prophets would be in exile near a river when suddenly the inspiration of the Spirit would overcome them, and they would be "caught up" in spiritual ecstasy. John was on the isle of Patmos surrounded by the Aegean Sea when he was "in the Spirit" on the Lord's day (Rev. 1:10). To be "in the Spirit" indicated to suddenly be into the very mind of thinking of God Himself!

Ezekiel was a political prisoner in Babylon near the river Chebar when suddenly the heavens opened, and he saw the visions of God. The prophet describes the occasion as "the hand of the LORD was upon him there" (Ezek. 1:3). The seer then describes in detail the appearance of cherubs carrying the throne of God and how they traveled, moving like a "wheel within a wheel" (vv. 1–28). These are called "open visions," since they occur when the visionary is fully alert, awake, and aware of his physical surroundings. Most scholars would agree that this is the highest form of ecstatic revelation. The prophets were living on a higher dimension of holiness and sanctity, which enabled them to move from speaking to their fellow men to immediately being carried away in the Spirit into the mystical realm of the cosmic heavens and the throne of God.

The next dimension of visions is when the prophets were asleep, and they received an open vision in the night:

> In the first year of Belshazzar king of Babylon, Daniel had a dream and visions of his head while on his bed. Then he wrote down the dream, telling the main facts. Daniel spoke, saying, "I saw in my vision by night, and behold, the four winds of heaven were stirring up the Great Sea.

And four great beasts came up from the sea, each different from the other."
—DANIEL 7:1–3

At times it may be difficult to distinguish between a dream and a vision. These revelations of the four beast empires occurred while the prophet was asleep, in a dream stage, and yet is seen in his vision. He is asleep and yet seems awake at the same time. These dreams/visions occur when a person is sleeping.

The fourth type of vision is the unfolding of spiritual insight that emerges within the mind while a person is completely awake. This is more common, and often a person may not recognize when it occurs. Every person, especially when young, spends time daydreaming. This can cause disruptive behavior during school hours, as the child is present in body but absent in mind. Children may be sitting behind a desk, and at the same time, mentally they are back home in the yard, perhaps splashing in their plastic swimming pool. This is not a vision but simply the imagination at work. The human mind has the ability to create images (the root word for imagination) and can, with a simple change in the brain, take you to any place in the world where you can shop at the finest boutique, dine in world-class restaurants, and rest under silk sheets—all without paying a dime!

At the same time, a Spirit-filled believer can begin to meditate upon the Lord and pray while sitting at a desk, walking down a sidewalk, or lying in a bed. Suddenly the believer may sense a strong feeling that something is wrong. The weight of the thought presses into his or her spirit and creates a burden. As the person begins to pray, he visualizes a situation about which he knows nothing. As he further enters into deeper intercession, the believer realizes he is praying for a particular family member or a negative situation. Later, the situation he visualized is proven true. This is a form of a spiritual vision.

This occurred many years ago when I was visiting in Oregon at a state park with an extinct volcano that was in the middle of a large lake. That afternoon I did a foolish thing, and instead of following the established walking trail to the boat dock, I went in the opposite direction and ended up on the back side of this extinct island volcano. I came to an opening where volcanic lava once flowed into the lake. It was as slick as glass, and I began falling. Lying on my stomach, I was holding on with the fingers of my hand clawing into the hard surface. I knew I could face death and began praying.

The following week I learned that on the same day, at the same time I was in danger, my father and mother were driving through Knoxville, Tennessee. Suddenly Dad saw a sudden mental vision of me in danger, and he shouted to Mom, "We need to pray. Perry's life is in danger." Dad interceded for one hour, often crying and pleading with the Almighty that wherever I was, I would be safe. It took me one hour to get across the slick side of the island, and I knew it was prayer that sustained me.

When my wife and I were searching for property to construct a new ministry center, she and I were at our desks—I was studying, and she was engaged in bookkeeping. Without any warning I sensed that I should get out of the building and drive our van to the opposite end of town. I saw a piece of property in my spirit that I had never seen before. After convincing her that I had a word of knowledge from the Lord, we drove to a part of town we never knew existed. There we found the house we lived in for five years and the property on which we have built two major ministry centers!

THE DIFFERENCE BETWEEN DREAMS AND VISIONS

All men, women, and children are tripartite beings, consisting of a body, soul, and spirit. Dreams seem to emerge or develop more in the realm of the soul, whereas visions are deeper manifestations, which are conceived within the spirit of the person.

Whenever there is a strong outpouring of the Holy Spirit, there will always be an increase of spiritual revelation. In the last days, the Lord will pour out His Spirit upon "all flesh; your sons and your daughters..." (Joel 2:28; Acts 2:17). It is difficult to determine the actual age of a "son or daughter" from the actual Hebrew or Greek words. In most instances, a son and daughter is one who is not married and still under the influence of the parent. My son and daughter can be married and still remain my son and daughter; however, the children they have become my "children's children" or my children's "seed." Today, children who have become young adults are marrying much later than they did in my day or even my father's day.

Why would *young* men see visions and *old* men dream dreams? Why is it not reversed to read, "Young men shall dream dreams and old men shall see visions"? Does it really matter? I believe it is because the Spirit will be poured out on the youth, and this intensive movement of the Spirit always increases the intensity and the sensitivity of the human spirit to the things of God. I believe the second reason has to do with the level of spiritual maturity. Because of years of personal experiences with the Lord, the old men have their senses trained to correctly discern the spiritual from carnal, whereas a youth may not have the maturity to correctly discern or understand the deeper truth.

Young men need a vision—one so dramatic and clear that it becomes impossible for a young man to doubt it was from the Lord. An older, more experienced believer has a fine-tuned spirit and can quickly determine if the dream was from the Lord or not, and should know the symbolism in the Bible to determine the meaning of any spiritual dream.

THE IMPORTANCE OF *VISION*

In our lives a *vision* is required to bring about all possibilities and desires in our heart. To build anything, including a home, an office, a business, or a marriage, demands that the participants have some form of vision. The largest things built on Earth began with a mental image in someone's mind. The plan is transferred from the image of the mind to a blueprint on paper, followed by a team of individuals prepared to take the written design and create a visible, three-dimensional object.

> ► A visionary has the ability to see something finished before it ever begins.

> ► A visionary has the strength to call those things that are not as though they already were.

> ► A visionary continues to believe in the vision despite all opposition and hindrances.

> ► A visionary never lives in the past, but from past mistakes learns to never repeat them in the future.

There is a powerful scripture in Proverbs 29:18 that says, "Where there is no vision, the people perish" (KJV). Another translation reads, "Where there is no revelation, the people cast off restraint" (NIV). A revelation can involve insight concerning your future or your destiny as designed by God. If a doctor tells a patient that he or she has only two months to live, that patient will either resign himself or herself to face death, or the person will fight the disease to live longer. When a person feels he has nothing to live for, then a spirit of hopelessness will often grip him. Proverbs 13:12 says, "Hope deferred maketh the heart sick: but when the desire cometh, it is a tree of life" (KJV). For example, cancer patients have been known at times to extend their lives for many years beyond expectation because of *desire*—a desire to remain longer with their companions, a desire to see their grandchildren grow up, and a desire to continue to enjoy life. Lack of hope can kill, but desire can become a tree of life.

A *vision* always concerns the future and seldom, if ever, the past, as God's kingdom and human life always move forward and never look backward. We cannot undo the past, but we can pursue the future. You may spend your entire spiritual walk and never experience a literal night vision while in deep sleep. However, you must continually live with dreams and visions and desires to be blessed, to be a blessing to others, and to fulfill all that the Lord puts in your heart.

When Moses died, Joshua his servant filled his shoes. The Lord promised Joshua, "As I was with Moses, so I will be with you" (Josh. 1:5). About thirty years later we read these wonderful words concerning Joshua: "He left nothing undone of all that the LORD had commanded…" (Josh. 11:15). The purpose of a *practical* vision is to cause you to pursue your future. A spiritual vision often announces a warning to prepare you for what is coming. Always remember, a warning is never to scare you but to prepare you.

fourteen

DREAMS—AMAZING PURPOSE FOR THESE REVELATIONS

And it shall come to pass in the last days, says God, that I will pour out of My Spirit on all flesh . . . your young men shall see visions, your old men shall dream dreams.

« Acts 2:17 »

If you were to interview the average church attendee in North America and ask, "How does God speak to His people today?" a vast majority would reply that He no longer speaks to us except through Scripture. Of course, God's ultimate and complete revelation is revealed to mankind through the sixty-six books of the Bible. The Holy Scripture *is* God's final instruction for mankind and a revelation of His redemptive covenant through Christ. However, the reason so many Christians believe God no longer speaks to His people is because they perceive the word *speak* as being "audible words" coming from out of the atmosphere instead of God speaking to us through our own inner spirit. Since most believers have never heard an audible, deep, booming voice piercing the atmosphere, they assume God is silent—except through His written Word! Unfortunately, many Christians deny the possibility of God speaking to a person because they are continually bombarded *from the pulpit* with statements like: "God does not speak today." "God spoke only to the original apostles." Or, "We do not need God to speak since we have His Word."

A minister who denied that God speaks to anyone today was asked, "If God does not speak today, then how can any sinner be saved, since they must be convicted of their sin by the Holy Spirit?" Conviction is more than mentally agreeing with a sermon from a pulpit. It is a deep feeling of remorse that leads to repentance. Who brought that feeling? What was that still, small voice that said, "This message is for you. Believe this Word"? That was the voice of the Holy Spirit! No man can come to the Father unless he or she is drawn to Him by Christ through the Holy Spirit (John 6:65; 15:26–27).

FIVE WAYS GOD STILL
SPEAKS TO HIS PEOPLE

There are five methods God uses to communicate personally to a person, if that person has the spiritual ears to hear His voice.

1. He speaks to the conscience of a person.

We are warned that in the last days there will be a release of "seducing spirits" in the earth (1 Tim. 4:1, KJV). These spirits are activated to remove men and women from the truth. As men and women are deceived and reject the truth, Paul wrote that these individuals would have their "conscience seared with a hot iron" (v. 2). This statement alludes to the effects of a hot iron upon the skin, which would cause the skin to be become rigid and hard, and the nerves damaged and dead to sensibility. The conscience is part of the human soul and reacts to a person's moral or ethical actions by judging them to be either right or wrong. A moral conscience should exist in all Christians. It also exists in many morally upright non-Christians.

Through the Holy Spirit, God often penetrates the awareness of the conscience of men and women, both converted and unconverted, and directs them in the right direction related to moral and judicial decisions. For example, when a jury of twelve sits in a box in a court-room, listening to the testimony of a man who raped a child, even an unbeliever knows by his conscience that such an act is immoral and wrong. Something *inside him or her* tells that unbeliever that the criminal deserves a guilty decision and a penalty. Each time a sinner is converted, the Holy Spirit has pierced the mental and spiri-tual *veils* and spoken directly to the conscience of that individual, leading the person to Christ.

2. He speaks to the inner spirit of a person.

The Bible says, "For as many as are led by the Spirit of God, these are sons of God" (Rom. 8:14). Paul wrote about the "inward man" (Rom. 7:22; 2 Cor. 4:16), and Peter mentions the "hidden person of the heart" (1 Pet. 3:4), which alludes to the conscience and soul of each human. The human spirit is the seat of spiritual influence in the same manner that the physical heart is the center of the human body. This inward part is often identified with the phrase "the heart." This brings confusion, for the physical heart pumps blood throughout the body; thus, how can the heart discern or have thoughts?

The Hebrew Scriptures use three Hebrew words to describe the activity of the heart. The Hebrew word *chedher* is translated "reins" and refers to the deepest seat of the breast, bowels, or the deepest seat of emotions. The King James Bible uses the word *reins* (Prov. 23:16). The Hebrew words *tuchoth* and *qereba* mean the middle or the midst of the heart.[1] The ancient cultures saw the *heart* as the center of all emotions and thought. In realty, the human spirit is the seat of all emotions and a filter for all thoughts. When the Holy Spirit begins to speak to a believer within the spirit, the believer will experience strong feelings, which some call *intuition*, that bring a sense of warning, danger, or excitement concerning an individual or a situation. These feelings in the spirit can become strong burdens, which are internal weights or pressures that a person feels around the heart. A burden is often interpreted as a feeling of anxiety or stress, as it can be felt within the body.

I have learned by experience that the only way to determine if the burden or weight is a spiritual matter is by spending time in prayer and intercession. Spiritual weights can only be lifted by the hand of the Lord. After intense prayer I often sense the burden being lifted, and this becomes a signal that the Holy Spirit is moving on behalf of those things I am unaware of.

3. He speaks by using others' wise counsel.

The Bible says, "Where there is no counsel, the people fall; but in the multitude of counselors there is safety" (Prov. 11:14). A counselor is an advisor who gives advice to resolve conflicts, to instruct in business, or to warn about and weigh possible dangers. Solomon, king over Israel, understood that: "For by wise counsel you will wage your own war, and in a multitude of counselors there is safety" (Prov. 24:6). In the Old Testament, kings like King Ahab surrounded himself with *yes-men* and false prophets who were hired for pay and enjoyed dinner at the king's table. It was difficult for such men to warn the king or rebuke him when he was wrong, as negative words were not accepted and often led to a long month in chains in a dungeon under the palace. (See 2 Chronicles 18.)

Often a person on the outside of a situation can see more clearly than those within the organization or situation, because their vision is not blurred by numerous opinions. Many years ago I was engaged to be married to a talented, young woman whom I had dated steadily for about two years. For some reason, everyone who personally met her did not feel that she was the *right one* for me. If only two or three people had indicated this, I would not have thought too much about it. However, this became consistent for months. We both agreed to break off the engagement, and I later married a wonderful young woman named Pamela and have been in love for more than thirty years!

The individuals *counseling* me were on the *outside looking in*, but it did not mean they were not properly discerning my situation. When we become emotionally linked to a person or situation, our focus becomes narrowed, and we are unable to view the broader field of play. At times the Holy Spirit can and will bring a person to speak into our situation, one who is speaking not only the will of God but also giving us possible warnings to avoid a pitfall or a trap that could be set by someone close to us. If you are preparing to become engaged, I suggest some godly wisdom before making a life-changing decision! If you are beginning a business, don't jump just because it looks good. Weigh the positives and negatives, and remember that the Holy Spirit can direct someone to you with a word in season. Isaiah wrote:

> The Lord GOD has given Me
> The tongue of the learned,
> That I should know how to speak
> A word in season to him who is weary.
> He awakens Me morning by morning,
> He awakens My ear
> To hear as the learned.
>
> —ISAIAH 50:4

4. God speaks today using the vocal gifts of the Spirit.

I realize that there will be some reading this section who will disagree with my comments, based upon your church tradition, denominational persuasion, and personal experiences. However, when the Holy Spirit was given as a gift to the body of Christ (Acts 2:38–39), He brought with Him nine fruit of the Spirit (Gal. 5:22–23) and nine gifts of the Spirit (1 Cor. 12:7–10). I find it interesting that ministers believe in the Holy Spirit as a person but teach that the miraculous gifts listed in 1 Corinthians 12 have somehow ceased in our time. Yet they still believe and teach that all nine fruit of the Spirit are for our time!

Paul wrote that the "gifts and the calling of God are irrevocable" (Rom. 11:29). Once God has issued a gift for the body of Christ, He will not withdraw that gift. We are also informed that we should "come short in no gift, eagerly waiting for the revelation of our Lord Jesus Christ" (1 Cor. 1:7). These verses indicate that the gifts (Greek, *charisma/charismata*) are given and will continue until the return of Christ—despite what is being taught in some circles of unbelief.

The three main vocal gifts mentioned in 1 Corinthians 12 are *different kinds of tongues, interpretation of tongues,* and *prophecy.* I have personally witnessed my precious father, Fred Stone, on numerous occasions as he began praying the prayer language of the Spirit and was understood by a person from another nation who spoke the same tongue my father was praying in! In the early 1970s, Dad pastored in Arlington, Virginia. One particular Sunday, a medical doctor, Dr. Spence, and his wife, Mary Ann, were visiting our little church on Fillmore Avenue. That morning Mary Ann came forward for prayer for a special need. As Dad prayed for her, he began praying in the prayer language of the Holy Spirit. After prayer, Mrs. Spence looked at him and asked, "Where did you learn to speak such fluent German?" Dad replied that he had never studied German, but this was the prayer language from the Holy Spirit. She and her husband were amazed. Dad had spoken in perfect German, praying for her and even giving details about her family that only she knew! This incident so impressed this couple that they began attending Dad's church and became wonderful members!

I cannot recall the number of occasions when an operation of one of the vocal gifts—either through a direct word to a foreigner (1 Cor. 12:10), an interpretation of a tongue (1 Cor. 14:1–5), or a prophetic word of encouragement and edification (v. 3)—were manifested in the church and brought spiritual warning, insight, and comfort to the church, as well as a "sign...to unbelievers" (v. 22). Because these gifts operate through human vessels, the words given must be judged by others in the church who have experience and wisdom in spiritual matters and are grounded in the Word of God (v. 29). No word that is truly from the Holy Spirit will ever contradict the sound teaching from the Bible! However, God can and will use humble and godly vessels through which to let His gifts flow.

5. God speaks through dreams and visions.

I was amused recently when a near relative was witnessing to another individual about the deeper things of the Holy Spirit. My relative was informing this particular *spiritual unbeliever* of how the Lord had warned me on several occasions about events that would come to pass in the nation, including my 9/11 vision of the twin towers and the dream-vision of the oil crisis in the Gulf of Mexico off the coast of Louisiana. This skeptic said he did not believe that God spoke to anyone in our day in any fashion except through the Bible. The relative then asked, "How do you explain Perry's receiving these warnings, which were so direct and clear that it could not be denied that they were 100 percent accurate?"

The answer was, "He has some type of psychic powers!" I was amazed that according to this man, a person could have some type of counterfeit power, but God was helpless to use His own power to reveal the future!

These same accusations were thrown at Christ when He performed miracles. The religious Pharisees accused Him of being possessed with a demon and of performing His miracles by the power of Beelzebub (Matt. 12:24). This lie was intended to frighten the multitudes from following Christ, as no one wants to be associated with anyone operating through a demonic influence.

The Bible teaches that in the last days God will pour out His Spirit upon all flesh, and this deluge of God's presence will be accompanied by "your young men shall see visions, your old men shall dream dreams" (Acts 2:17). Today's prophetic ministers continually remind people that we are in the *last days*, pointing out numerous prophecies related to the "last days" to undergird their statement. However, these same men cannot avoid this *Acts 2* promise from the Lord. To indicate that a particular verse is a "last days prophecy prediction for our time" and then turn around and say, "But this verse in Acts is not for today," is not only spiritually dishonest, but it also hinders people from believing God will reveal warnings and personal instructions in visions and dreams!

GOD COMMUNICATES WITH US
THROUGH DREAMS AND VISIONS

For four thousand years of biblical history, from Adam to the Christ, God revealed insights and revelations to holy men through visions, dreams, and mental inspiration. The agent of these revelations was the Holy Spirit. That same Spirit is covering the earth today as nations of hungry individuals study the Word of God and see events that will come to pass through the means of visions and dreams. God still speaks today!

The Book of Job introduces Job as the "greatest of all the people of the East" (Job 1:3). His wealth portfolio included houses, land, seven thousand sheep, three thousand camels, five hundred female donkeys, and five hundred yoke of oxen. He was blessed with ten children and servants (Job 1–2). Satan planned a strategy against Job with the intention of destroying his integrity and causing him to profane and curse God (Job 1:10–11). During the attack Job lost all his children, their homes, and all of his material wealth. In a second wave of assault from the adversary, Job was stricken with boils and endured severe physical trauma (Job 2:7).

From the moment of his attack, Job sought for answers to the enigma of why the righteous suffer. Three friends visited Job during his loss and engaged in a long discussion about life, faith, and suffering. It is evident that Job was seeking God for a divine revelation to his dilemma. As we read the narrative, there are some eye-opening passages that reveal how God speaks to men.

Now a word was secretly brought to me,
And my ear received a whisper of it.
In disquieting thoughts from the visions of the night,
When deep sleep falls on men,
Fear came upon me, and trembling,
Which made all my bones shake.
Then a spirit passed before my face;
The hair on my body stood up.
It stood still,
But I could not discern its appearance.
A form was before my eyes;
There was silence.

—Job 4:12–16

The first point is the use of the phrase "deep sleep." There are many passages in Scripture about a prophet who was being given a divine revelation from a visit of the Lord that indicate the prophet entered a "deep sleep." In Genesis 15:12, a deep sleep came over Abraham as the sun was going down, and the Lord spoke to him. In Daniel 8:18, Daniel remarks that he was in a "deep sleep with my face to the ground" when the angel of God touched him. He repeats the same concept about deep sleep in Daniel 10:9. After he entered this deep sleep stage, he heard the words of a messenger of the Lord.

Just what is a "deep sleep"? The Hebrew phrase can allude to being "sluggish" or entering some form of a "spiritual trance." In my own life, there have been several times when I experienced a true spiritual vision. Usually I was extremely exhausted when this occurred. I believe that this tiredness sometimes causes the fleshly or carnal man—who is always busy and going nonstop—to be more suppressed, thereby enabling the inner spirit of a person to become more alert or aware.

NOW I LAY ME DOWN TO SLEEP

Sleep is a very important part of living a long life. When a person is under stress or mental anguish, it is difficult to rest. A continual lack of sleep is called *insomnia*. A person who sleeps but continually tosses and has difficulty breathing may have *sleep apnea*. Excessive sleep, to the point that a person wants to sleep and not get up, can be symptomatic of *narcolepsy*. All three of these forms of sleep disorders are very unhealthy and should be treated. These disorders not only interrupt normal sleep patterns but can also cause irregular and bizarre dreaming patterns to occur.

During normal sleep, there are five stages of sleep that a person will enter. The first is the drowsy stage, which, with most people, will last a period of about ten minutes. This is followed by a second stage of light sleep, where the heart rate decreases along with a decrease in the body temperature. This state is followed by the third and fourth stages, called "deep sleep," in which the body enters a deep sleeping state and the brain waves begin to slow down. The fifth stage is called *REM* (rapid eye movement) sleep, characterized by eye movement, increased respiration rate, and increased brain activity.[2] This last stage is considered the dream level, when most people dream.

I have discovered that visions can occur at any given time, but dreams usually occur during the time of deep sleep, usually between two to five in the morning. Dreams always transpire when sleeping, whereas a vision can occur with a person's eyes opened. (For more information on visions, see chapter 13.)

THE EAR IS OPENED

The inspired writer of Job speaks of the "ear" being opened to receive a secret word in Job 4. If a person has normal hearing, he will receive all information through the avenue of hearing. We all have physical ears; however, there are also *spiritual ears*. Your physical man has the capability to hear and dissect information, but we must have a spiritual *inner ear* to correctly hear the revelation of the Word of God and the voice of the Holy Spirit! This fact is clear when reading about the seven churches in Revelation. Repeatedly the writer says, "He who has an ear, let him hear what the Spirit says to the churches" (Rev. 2–3). The fact that Christ had to repeatedly instruct His own followers (church members) to pay attention and hear indicates that there can be hearing problems that arise with your spiritual ear—or spiritual discernment. Our natural ears are always *turned on*, but our spiritual ears also need to be continually open.

When we are physically asleep, an amazing thing occurs. The human ear is able to close out any small noises and allow the mind to enter into rest. Of course, any sudden or loud noises can immediately shock a person out of a deep sleep! I have been with a group of people driving in a vehicle when one of the passengers fell asleep. Others would carry on the conversation, but the sleeping passenger heard nothing that was said. This idea of hearing and dreaming is unique, especially as it relates to someone with a physical disability.

WHAT ABOUT A COMA VICTIM?

For many years the medical community has been curious as to the neurological activity occurring in a person who is comatose, or in a coma. A coma is usually caused by a traumatic head injury, often through a fall or an accident. The person appears to be inactive, like they are sleeping. It is noted that at times a comatose individual will have a muscle reaction, such as twitching or squeezing a person's hand. Doctors often inform hopeful family members that this is simply a muscle reaction and not an indicator of the person's response.

One of the interesting aspects of a person in a coma is that if the auditory nerve that runs from the brain to the ear is still intact, it is quite possible for the injured person to actually hear the conversations that are occurring around them. In 1998, my beloved grandfather John Bava was taken to surgery in Elkins, West Virginia. He experienced three strokes, which affected his brain, and he was never able to move, open his eyes, or communicate again. However, his doctor told us to speak directly in his ear, because hearing was the last thing to go when a person was dying! The family placed a cassette player near his bed and began playing his favorite gospel songs. The heart monitor showed his heart beat going from a low 60 beats a minute to as high as 120 beats a minute when the music was playing. When the room was quiet, the heart rate slowed dramatically. When he heard our voice, our singing, or the music, his heart rate immediately increased. I knew he was unable to move, but I also knew he could hear us speaking. His brain may have been impacted by three strokes, but his inner spirit was alive, and he heard—not just with his natural ears but also with his spiritual ears!

I found it interesting that when a person is about to depart this life, under normal circumstances their hearing is the last physical responder to cease. This is important information for any family member standing near the deathbed of a dying loved one. If that individual never made a public profession of faith, then the believer should speak into his or her ear and instruct the dying loved one to pray a prayer in his or her mind. As long as the spirit has not departed from the physical shell (see 1 Corinthians 5:3; 2 Corinthians 5:6), God knows the "thoughts and intents of the heart" (Heb. 4:12) and can hear a prayer of repentance prayed from a person's mind. In the Bible we read where it says, "Jesus, knowing their thoughts…" (Matt. 9:4).

Richard Madison, a minister friend of mine, was in a terrible head-on collision on April 13, 1986. He was rushed to the hospital and was pronounced brain dead upon arrival. Due to numerous serious injuries and broken bones, he remained in a brain-dead coma for twenty-seven days. His Christian mother would come into his room every four hours and anoint him, believing God to raise him up—which God did! Richard describes how on one occasion his soul came out of his body and walked down the hall of the hospital, going to the hospital chapel where his mother and others were praying. He could hear his mother praying, and he actually stood beside her, watching her pray as she asked the Lord to "save Richard and bring him out of the coma." It was at that moment—while he was out of his body—that Richard prayed and asked Christ for help! On another occasion he actually heard a nurse use profanity and rebuke him for being in the coma. She was upset because it was New Year's Eve, and she had to work that night and was going to miss a party! Imagine her shock when Richard woke up out of the coma and walked out of his wheelchair ten weeks later. When he recovered, he told the nurse her entire conversation in his room that New Year's Eve! Despite the coma, Richard's soul and spirit could still hear the words and voices in the room from time to time.

The writer in Job said that when a person went into deep sleep, his "ear received a whisper of it" (Job 4:12). Even in sleep there is an *inner ear* linked with the spirit of an individual, which continues to hear. This is the *ear* that the Lord uses to give His instructions. This is the reason Christ addressed the seven churches in Revelation by saying: "He who has an ear, let him hear what the Spirit says to the churches" (Rev. 2:7).

A second passage in Job reveals several unique reasons, seldom discussed, why God gives His followers a dream:

> For God may speak in one way, or in another,
> Yet man does not perceive it.
> In a dream, in a vision of the night,

> When deep sleep falls upon men,
> While slumbering on their beds,
> Then He opens the ears of men,
> And seals their instruction.
> In order to turn man from his deed,
> And conceal pride from man,
> He keeps back his soul from the Pit,
> And his life from perishing by the sword.
>
> —JOB 33:14–18

The first reason given is that God "seals their [man's] instructions." The Hebrew word here for *instructions* means an *admonition* or some form of *direction*. This passage was written about the time of Moses, before the entire Bible was ever compiled and the written Word of God placed in the hands of common men. Some ministers who refuse to believe that God can still speak today to and though His people would suggest that God no longer uses visions and dreams, since we have the Bible and these visionary methods were ancient, *pre–New Testament methods*. These ministers should consider the following:

▶ Does the Bible specifically tell you the woman that you should marry—other than a believer?

▶ Does the Bible reveal which life occupation you should pursue—other than to be a witness to others?

▶ Does the Bible reveal the place you should live—other than living by faith?

▶ Does the Bible reveal where you should serve Him— other than to always be a giver to the kingdom?

▶ Does the Bible tell you if you should drive, fly, or avoid that trip you are planning?

The Bible is God's inspired Word, and it gives us promises, prophecies, and practical teaching for living on Earth while walking with God. However, there are many practical aspects in life that must be discovered through prayer and intercession or through a word of wisdom or knowledge (1 Cor. 12:7–10), including a word of instruction given in a dream or vision. It was a dream that opened the door for Joseph to initiate a plan of provision in the time of famine!

The second purpose of a dream or vision is to turn us from our own direction ["deed"] to the direction of God. A dream or vision can reveal God's will or plan for your life. When the wise men came to Jerusalem, inquiring of Herod as to where the Hebrew prophets said the Messiah would be born, Herod consulted the religious Pharisees, who in turn reported back that Bethlehem was the anticipated town. Herod instructed these Persian Magi to return to him once they knew of the whereabouts of the infant child (Matt. 2:8).

After a visitation with the holy family, the wise men were returning to Jerusalem when an angel of the Lord warned them in a dream not to return but to depart another way (v. 12). In this instance the Lord was interrupting their prearranged plans and providing protection for them through an alternative route. The same angel would later warn Joseph to get out town with the infant Christ and His mother, because Herod was sending soldiers to slay all children under two years of age (v. 13).

Another reason for visions and dreams is to keep our soul from the "Pit" and the "sword." The pit can be the literal pit of an eternal hell, but it could also allude to a snare that is set by the enemy. The sword is a metaphor for war, fighting, and violent destruction. In Ecclesiastes 7:17 we are asked, "Why should you die before your time?" I believe it is possible to depart this life prematurely. It can occur through illegal drug addiction, alcoholism, gang-related violence, and accidents. It is possible to be at the *right place at the right time* and *the wrong place at the wrong time*. When my father was traveling to Ohio to visit his parents late at night, he stopped at a rest stop. There was one van in the parking area with tinted windows. As Dad stepped out of his car, he had a sudden flash (mental vision) that informed him that four long-haired men were watching him from the van, and if he entered the men's room, he would be robbed and wounded. Dad immediately snapped his fingers as if he forgot something, unlocked and opened his car door, cranked up the engine, and pulled out. As he did, the van door swung open, and four long-haired men jumped out and attempted to catch up with his car but failed! Obedience to the sudden mental vision saved his life. Paul said, "I was not disobedient to the heavenly vision" (Acts 26:19). Obedience brings a positive outcome in all instances. The writer of Job taught that visions and dreams are heavenly visitations to give instructions, warnings, and directions.

Conclusion

DREAMS AND VISIONS—
GOD'S VOICE OF INTIMACY

In summing up the reasons for dreams and visions, I believe that understanding the true purpose of God in revealing the future and giving instruction in dreams and visions involves four aspects of our walk with God. These four aspects are found in Genesis 22, where Abraham offered Isaac to God on Mount Moriah.

1. There is the plan of God.

2. There is the place of God.

3. There is the provision of God.

4. There is the purpose of God.

THE PLAN OF GOD

The Bible says, "For I know the thoughts that I think toward you, says the LORD, thoughts of peace and not of evil, to give you a future and a hope" (Jer. 29:11). We are also told that our thoughts are not God's thoughts and our ways are not His ways (Isa. 55:8). God desires to make His thoughts toward you known, and He does this primarily through His Word (v. 11). However, there are practical plans for us that must be known to us.

In Genesis 22:1 the Lord initiated a plan that would test Abraham's faith and obedience. God instructed, "Take now your son, your only son Isaac, whom you love…and offer him there as a burnt offering" (v. 2). This was the plan—to offer Isaac. When the Lord brings a spiritual revelation to you, it is for the purpose of a plan. He may not always give you the reason why He is asking you to attend a certain church, take a missions trip, work with children, give a special offering, and so forth, but obedience always involves His plan.

When Abraham led Isaac three days away from home to the land of Moriah (v. 4), notice who was missing from the story—Sarah was not present. The reason is obvious. Isaac was actually in his thirties at the time and was so attached to his mother that he had not met his future wife or gone on his first date! If Abraham would have informed Sarah, saying, "The Lord spoke to me to take Isaac and offer him up as a sacrifice," a war would have broken out, and Sarah, no doubt, would have prevented Abraham from following through with the act. This is why you don't always tell everyone your vision until the right time. God's plan always comes in vision form, whether it is a literal vision, a mental vision, or a dream vision that you see in your spirit.

THE PLACE OF GOD

God had a plan, but He also had the place. Abraham was to go to the land of Moriah and offer Isaac on one of the mountains that the Lord would show him (Gen. 22:2). The land of central Israel in and around Jerusalem is surrounded by mountains—but God chose a specific mountain! Years before Isaac's birth Abraham had offered tithe to the first king and priest of the Most High in Jerusalem—Melchizedek (Gen. 14:20; Heb. 7:9). Thus, the areas of Moriah and Jerusalem were set apart as holy to the Lord and to Abraham. It was a special place, a place marked by God. The phrase "the place" is found in Genesis 22:3–4, and 9.

As a believer, you can be at the right place at the right time, the right place at the wrong time, and the wrong place all of the time, unless you know God's will for your life! When Moses was discouraged with Israel's sins in the wilderness, he desired to see the glory of the Lord, and the Lord said, "Here is a place by Me" (Exod. 33:21). Moses entered a cleft of the rock and experienced the glory of the Lord when he entered the "place" God had marked (vv. 22–23). Hundreds of years later, a depressed prophet, Elijah, ran to the same mountain (Mount Horeb) and entered a cave, where he experienced the still, small voice of the Lord instructing him (1 Kings 19:8–12). I personally believe that Elijah found the same cave—that "place"—where Moses had met with God hundreds of years before.

God's blessing for you will be discovered when you find your *place* in His purpose. God spoke in dreams and visions to the early patriarchs, directing them from one place to a different place. As they sought out that special place, they found themselves in the center of the will of God.

GOD HAS THE PROVISION

Our generation is very *provision* oriented. Often believers will accept any type of promise or blessing, try any type of prosperity package, and seek out someone who has an alleged anointing to pray finances into their lives. A need being met is for the present, but the meaning of provision is to provide, prepare, or supply something for future needs. Men and women express their concerns about having the proper provisions for the future.

When God tested Abraham on Mount Moriah, the loving father carried the knife for the sacrifice and the fire for the altar, and Isaac carried the wood to the top of the mountain (Gen. 22:5–6). Once they reached the top of the mountain, Abraham built the altar. Just before Abraham pierced his son with a dagger, the angel of the Lord stopped the process and pointed to a ram that was caught in a thicket by its horns (vv. 9–13). This ram would become the provision for Abraham and would become a picture of the future sacrifice of a lamb that would one day become the final offering for all mankind upon that same mountain (vv. 7–8).

Notice in the narrative that this ram was caught in a thicket by the horns. This is interesting, as at this time Abraham was more than 135 years of age, based upon the age of Sarah at her death in Genesis 23:1–2. It would be difficult for such an old man to wrestle with a ram if that ram was free and not caught in the thicket. In fact, any ram could have outrun Abraham, had he attempted to chase it down. By catching this large animal in the thicket, God took the *fight* out of the blessing!

When you have discovered the plan and found the place, there will always be provision at that place, and God will take the battle out of the blessing. The provision is at the place, and the place where you should be is revealed from the Scriptures and through the inward leading of the Holy Spirit and at times through visions and dreams.

GOD HAS A PURPOSE

This is the divine order: the plan, the place, the provision, and the purpose. Abraham was unaware of the ultimate purpose of this test at the time. However, because God's covenant man, Abraham, was willing to give up his only son to God on the altar (Gen. 22:12), God

Himself would one day give up His Son as a sacrifice on the cross for man's redemption (John 3:16). In this narrative Abraham somehow received either a vision of God's plan and purpose, or it was revealed to him as the Bible records: "And Abraham called the name of the place, The-LORD-Will-Provide; as it is said to this day, 'In the Mount of The LORD it shall be provided'" (Gen. 22:14). I am uncertain what Abraham saw or experienced that day. However, he did predict that "God will provide for Himself the lamb" (v. 8).

In the New Testament, Christ was referring to this incident when He said, "Your father Abraham rejoiced to see My day, and he saw it and was glad" (John 8:56). The purpose of this test concerned the future. The entire scene on Mount Moriah in Genesis 22 is a picture of what was to come with the crucifixion of Jesus Christ!

We all have a tendency to want to know the purpose or the reason *first*. We ask: "Why must I do this, Lord?" "Why are You leading me to this, Lord?" "Why help this person?" On and on the questions of *why* continue. We are motivated to obey if we know the purpose. However, if we knew why, we would not be walking by faith—we would be walking by sight (2 Cor. 5:7). If the Holy Spirit revealed the details of what was coming to you, both the good and the bad, you would try to speed up the good and would intervene to prevent the bad. When God brought Israel out of Egypt, He never told them about the walled cities, the giants in the land, and the seven Canaanite tribes they would need to conquer until they went in to spy out the land. God knew that if the people were aware of the coming battles, they would resign themselves to remain in Egypt and destroy the destiny of the children and their nation! Thus God only reveals the future in bits and pieces, or, as Paul said, "We see in a mirror, dimly" (1 Cor. 13:12). The purpose can only be revealed after we have followed the process!

Our personal lives must be rooted and grounded in the Word of

God. Dreams or visions or even prophetic words and spiritual gifts are not intended to replace the inspired Word of God. They serve as complements to the teaching and preaching of the Scriptures and act as tools for the Holy Spirit to assist in directing us during special seasons of our lives. However, a person should never despise these spiritual visitations and must learn to properly discern them. I hope this book has helped you in this matter. God bless you.

Appendix

DETAILED BIBLICAL SYMBOLISM IN DREAMS

T his section will present numerous objects and symbols found in the Scriptures that are also part of a spiritual dream. I will give the first place in Scripture where the word is found and give a generally possible meaning of each word. Please understand that the general *meaning* may not be the only meaning but is the most common possible meaning.

OBJECT: **ARROWS**

First Reference: Numbers 24:8—Moses wrote that God defeated His enemies by using arrows.

Possible Meaning: We no longer use a bow and arrows, but arrows were used in battle to defeat the enemy.

Just as a sword can represent the Word, the individual arrows being shot can be a cryptic reference to individual scriptures that are quoted and *shot* toward the enemy. They become the *arrows of*

God in the hands of a mighty man. If someone is shooting an arrow at you to harm you, it may be destructive words that are being said (Ps. 64:3–4; Jer. 9:8). If the arrow pierces your body, especially in your heart, it can represent words that are spoken to bring pain to your heart and spirit.

OBJECT: **BIRD(S)**

First Reference: Genesis 15:10—Abraham sacrifices birds without dividing them on the altar.

Possible Meanings: In the Bible, birds are not always viewed positively. When the birds ate the food from the basket on the head of the baker, Joseph said the head of the man would be removed by Pharaoh and the birds would eat his flesh (Gen. 40:17–22). In the New Testament parable of the sower and the seed, the birds come to eat the seed as soon as it is planted in the heart of a person. Christ said these "fowls" (birds) were evil spirits (Mark 4:1–20). Birds eating seed can represent something that is attempting to steal the Word from your heart. Birds are also used as a metaphor for evil spirits (Rev. 18:2).

In a dream, if a bird is picking at your flesh, it can mean that you will encounter difficulty with your flesh, either through temptation or through a physical ailment. If the bird is pecking your home, it can refer to something or someone working their way into your home that will become a problem for you later.

OBJECT: **BOATS/SHIPS**

First Reference: Genesis 49:13—Jacob predicted Zebulun would be a haven for ships.

Possible Meaning: We think of traveling when we think of a ship or a boat. In the New Testament, many of the disciples were fishermen who owned their own boats (Matt. 4:21–22; Luke 5:3–7). Because fish were caught in nets and boats transported the catch, boats can allude to the ministry vessel used to bring in the souls. The boat is the vehicle used to minister.

OBJECT: **BREAD**

First Reference: Genesis 3:19—God said man would eat his bread by the sweat of his face.

Possible Meaning: Bread is a basic staple that sustains life, especially among empires of antiquity. In the New Testament, Christ taught that we should pray for our "daily bread" (Matt. 6:11). Bread can allude to the Word of God (Matt. 4:4). Christ is called the "bread of life" (John 6:35). While bread can be literal food or refer to the food supply, in a spiritual dream, bread is the gospel that feeds the multitudes and satisfies the soul of a person.

OBJECT: **BULL**

First Reference: Genesis 32:15—Jacob's list of animals consisted of ten bulls.

Possible Meanings: A bull can be an aggressive beast. In Psalm 22:12, the writer said the "strong bulls of Bashan have encircled me." A bull can be a type of an aggressive spirit or a situation that will cause you agitation. I once dreamed of many bulls running during a crisis, and it alluded to the stock market whose emblem outside of Wall Street is a brass bull.

OBJECT: **CATTLE**

First Reference: Genesis 1:24—Cattle are listed by name on the fifth day of Creation.

Possible Meanings: In the Bible, cattle were significant with personal prosperity, as they were the chief desired beast of the field. They are mentioned 151 times in the King James Version of the Old Testament. They were used for milk and meat. Joseph saw seven strong, then seven weak cattle, indicating a coming famine. Cattle can allude to your personal or business prosperity.

OBJECT: CHAINS

First Reference: Genesis 41:42—Pharaoh put a gold chain around Joseph's neck.

Possible Meanings: In the Old Testament, a chain has two meanings: the first is where a gold chain is placed around the neck of a leader (Dan. 5:7); the second is where chains are placed upon someone to bind him (Lam. 3:7; Ezek. 16:11). The man of Gadara was bound with chains (Mark 5:3). Peter was bound in prison in chains (Acts 12:6–7), and fallen angels are bound in chains (2 Pet. 2:4).

In a dream, someone in chains can refer to a bondage of some sort that is binding the individual. If you are in chains, it can illustrate an attempt of the adversary or individuals to place you in some type of spiritual bondage, captivating or binding you. If the chains are on your feet, they mean a hindrance in carrying the gospel. On your hands, they are stopping the work you are doing. If they are over your mouth, they are attempting to silence you.

OBJECT: CORN

First Reference: Genesis 27:28 (KJV)—Isaac blesses Jacob, telling him he will have plenty of corn and wine.

Possible Meanings: The King James translation of the Bible (1611) uses the word "corn," and in the West we think of tall stalks of corn in a cornfield. The Hebrew word is *dagan*, and refers to grain. In the West, however, corn is a main grain that is grown nationally for food, fuel, and other purposes.

In the 9/11 vision in 1996, the five grayish tornadoes took out five rows of corn. In this instance, it was a prediction that the economy would be impacted by these storms, as corn being grown, sold, and eaten is a part of our national and global economy. Thus, a field of corn is still a harvest, but it can allude to the economic impact of a certain event upon the area seen in the dream or vision.

OBJECT: **DESERT**

First Reference: Exodus 3:1 (KJV)—Moses is on "the backside of the desert" watching sheep.

Possible Meaning: Israel wandered through the wilderness/desert for forty years because of unbelief (Deut. 2:7), and Christ was tempted of the devil in the wilderness for forty days (Matt. 4:1–2). Evil spirits are said to walk "through dry places" (Luke 11:24). A dry desert can refer to a time of trial or temptation that will be encountered. It can also mean isolation and a period of loneliness and standing alone in your faith.

OBJECT: **DOG**

First Reference: Exodus 11:7—God said not even a dog would move against the children of Israel.

Possible Meanings: In America, dogs are pets. David rebuked Goliath for considering David a "dog" (1 Sam. 17:43). Among Jews in Christ's day, Gentiles were considered "dogs" (Matt. 15:26). Paul wrote, "Beware of dogs" (Phil. 3:2), which were evil-minded people. In ancient times, dogs were mostly without masters, wandered around, and were considered unclean. In a dream, a filthy dog is an unclean person, and a vicious dog is a violent person.

OBJECT: **DOOR**

First Reference: Genesis 4:7—God told Cain that "sin lies at the door."

Possible Meanings: If the door is locked, it indicates a closed opportunity or a hindrance to your progress. An opened door is an open opportunity or the opening you should travel (Rev. 3:8; 4:1). In my dreams of churches, sometimes there are no doors but only openings like a doorway. This indicates that Christ Himself is the door to the church (John 10:9).

OBJECT: **EARTHQUAKE**

First Reference: 1 Kings 19:11—Elijah experienced an earthquake that shook the mountain.

Possible Meaning: A dream of an earthquake can be very literal, as the first simple interpretation. An earthquake is a shaking that causes disruption and damage, depending upon the magnitude of the quake. In a spiritual dream, an earthquake can refer to a sudden and unexpected shaking that will occur. If you are in a church, it may not be the physical building but the body of believers who will experience a shaking. Earthquakes divide land, and a severe spiritual quake could mean a division of some sort is in the future.

OBJECT: **A FIELD**

First Reference: Genesis 2:5—God speaks of the herbs and plants in the field.

Possible Meanings: Ancient Israel was built upon agriculture and planting cycles. The fields were used for barley and wheat (Deut 8:7–10). In the New Testament parables, the field is the world and the harvest is the souls of men who are represented by the wheat and the tares (Matt. 13:38). In several dreams and visions in the past, I have seen large fields, some with grain and some without. In these cases, it represented the entire United States as a whole. In one instance there were piles of grain stacked in the field with a Bible on top. However, grain was still standing in the corners. This, of course, was the gleaning of the fields, which occurs at the very end of the harvest cycle (Lev. 23:22).

OBJECT: **FIRE**

First Reference: Genesis 19:24—God rained down fire on Sodom and Gomorrah.

Possible Meaning: Fire is referred to 549 times in the KJV translation of the Bible. In many instances it is used to describe a judgment (Gen. 19:24), fire for a sacrifice (Gen. 22:6), or refers to God as when He manifested in the form of fire (Exod. 13:21–22). Isaiah's lips were cleaned by coals of fire from the altar (Isa. 6:5–7). Uncontrolled conversation (the tongue) is compared to a fire (James 3:5–6). Certain types of trials and temptations are called "fiery trials" (1 Pet. 4:12).

A fire can refer to a trial, negative words being spoken, a purging of someone, or some situation that is going to occur.

OBJECT: **FISHING**

First Reference: John 21:3—The disciples were fishing after the resurrection of Jesus.

Possible Meanings: Fish are mentioned in both Testaments. Ezekiel speaks of spreading nets to catch many fish (Ezek. 47:10). Several of Christ's disciples were fishermen and lived in fishing communities (Luke 5:1–7). Christ said He would make them "fishers of men" (Mark 1:17). In a dream, fishing is usually an indication of ministry and reaching souls. If the lake is small, it is a smaller ministry; if large, a large church or ministry is indicated. A fishing pole symbolizes a local church ministry, but a net indicates a global impact.

OBJECT: **FLOWERS**

First Reference: Exodus 25:31—Flowers are mentioned when describing the gold menorah and the beaten gold flower design on top.

Possible Meanings: Flowers appear once the winter is past and the spring arrives (Song of Sol. 2:11–12). Flowers indicate a fresh beginning, a passing of the old, and initiation of the new with a season of refreshing and rest. Flowers that have not bloomed indicate the early or infant stages of the new beginning.

OBJECT: **FOXES**

First References: Judges 15:4—Samson caught three hundred foxes, using them to set the Philistines' fields on fire.

Possible Meaning: Foxes are small animals known to be crafty and subtle. They sneak in, do their damage, and then get out before being detected. Song of Solomon speaks of the "little foxes that spoil the vines" (Song of Sol. 2:15). A fox can represent a person who is working behind your back, unnoticed by you, but slowly hindering what you are doing by what they are doing. By "spoiling the vines," the spiritual growth or flow of the Holy Spirit is being disrupted and the fruit that should come forth will not manifest.

OBJECT: **GOAT**

First Reference: Genesis 15:9—God required Abraham to offer a she goat as an offering.

Possible Meanings: Goats were used twice to deceive. First, when Jacob placed goat's hair on his arms, posing as Esau to deceive his father (Gen. 27:16), and second, when Joseph's coat was dipped in goat's blood and presented as a sign that he was slain by an animal (Gen. 37:31). A goat is a negative image in the New Testament and can represent someone who is in the flock of sheep but is not real and can be deceptive by nature. The sheep and goats will be separated at the judgment (Matt. 25:33).

OBJECT: **JEWELRY OR GEMSTONES**

First Reference: Genesis 24:53—Rebekah was given jewelry of silver and gold from Abraham's servant.

Possible Meanings: Jewelry or gemstones were handed over from the Egyptians to the departing Hebrews, who used the gold, silver, and jewelry for the building of the tabernacle in the wilderness (Exod. 11:2; 12:35; 35:22).

At the believer's judgment, good works will be rewarded with "gold, silver, and precious stones" (1 Cor. 3:12).

To dream or see precious stones or precious metals is a good sign that there is coming a great blessing in some form, including but not limited to financial blessing or rewards for your faithfulness. This is what most believe will be a part of the reward.

OBJECT: **LAMB**

First Reference: Genesis 22:7–8—Abraham predicted God would provide a lamb for the offering.

Possible Meanings: Throughout the Bible, a lamb symbolizes the ultimate sacrifice, Jesus Christ (John 1:29). Jesus, the Great Shepherd, told Peter to "feed My lambs" (John 21:15). Thus, lambs in a spiritual dream indicate a flock of believers or the church.

OBJECT: **LAMP**

First Reference: Genesis 15:17—God passed between Abraham's sacrifice with a burning lamp.

Possible Meaning: A lamp provides light in darkness. The commandments and the Word of God are compared to a lamp (Ps. 119:105; Prov. 6:23). In the parable of the ten virgins, all had lamps, but five virgins lacked the additional oil and had no light when the call came (Matt. 25:1–8).

A lamp burning is a sign that the light of the Word is present. A lamp gone out can allude to the light or truth not being presented or received.

OBJECT: **LEFT HAND**

First Reference: Genesis 13:9—Abraham tells Lot to chose between the left and right side of the land before them.

Possible Meaning: In Job 23:9, Job recalls God's blessing and his present trials and implies that although he cannot see God, when he is on God's left, God is at work with His left hand. Some rabbis teach that God created light with His left hand and darkness with His right. The left hand refers to a time of trial or seasons where it may appear that God is not working for us.

OBJECT: **LIGHTNING**

First Reference: 2 Samuel 22:15—Speaks of God's power, which includes sending lightning to discomfort His enemies.

Possible Meaning: The meaning of lightning depends on the setting and circumstances in a dream. When lightning strikes in the natural, it can cause fires and destruction, can shut down power, and so forth. In a spiritual dream, if lightning is striking on a clear day, it can indicate a coming storm that you do not see at the time. If striking during a storm, it indicates the violent or very troubling events that will unfold during the time of the spiritual storm.

OBJECT: **LIMPING/INJURY**

First Reference: Genesis 32:25—The angel touched Jacob and his hip socket was out of joint permanently.

Possible Meaning: In his earlier days, Jacob was on the run, but with a limp he was slowed down, and it caused him to depend more upon God than upon himself. When experiencing a limp, it means something that will affect your spiritual walk.

The people of Israel were warned that if they followed the Canaanite idols, these false gods would become "scourges on your sides and thorns in your eyes" (Josh. 23:13). If a person has a moral failure, that person receives a form of a limp.

OBJECT: **LOCUSTS**

First Reference: Exodus 10:14—God sent a plague of locusts to the Egyptians.

Possible Meanings: Locusts devour anything that is green and growing. A swarm can wipe out plants and the leaves of trees (Exod. 10). A locust is an insect that if not destroyed can slowly destroy entire crops (Joel 1:4). Locusts are small, but when joined as a swarm, they are a great agitation.

In a spiritual dream, a locust is a small creature and can be the imagery of small things combining together to agitate and create many hindrances that you need to battle. You need to protect the spiritual growth in your life and guard against letting little things agitate and become big destroyers.

OBJECT: MEAT

First Reference: Genesis 27:4—Isaac asked Esau to prepare his favorite "meat" (KJV).

Possible Meanings: In the KJV, meat is first used in Genesis 1:29: "Every tree…shall be for meat." This word in Hebrew is *oklah* and means food. The word *meat* in Genesis 27:4 refers to actual animal meat, which is the main meaning throughout much of the Bible. In the New Testament, the two levels of understanding and receiving the Word of God are "milk and meat" (Heb. 5:12–13, KJV). Milk is the simplicity of the Word received by immature or young believers, whereas meat is the stronger doctrine of the Scriptures.

Dreaming of meat in a spiritual dream can allude to the deeper teaching or instruction from the Word of God or to more mature believers.

OBJECT: MOUNTAIN(S)

First Reference: Genesis 7:20—The flood waters prevailed above the mountains during Noah's flood.

Possible Meanings: Mountains have numerous applications. Sitting or living on a mountain can allude to a great victory or accomplishment, as the ark "rested" on the mountains of Ararat (Gen. 8:4). Being at the bottom of a mountain and attempting to climb can allude to a situation that will take time and effort to deal with. Mountains can be difficulties that need to be removed by faith (Matt. 17:20). The seven mountains in prophecy are seven major kingdoms of prophecy (Rev. 17).

OBJECT: **OIL**

First Reference: Genesis 28:18—Jacob poured oil on top of a rock to mark the spot of visitation by the angel of the Lord.

Possible Meanings: Throughout the Bible, oil became the substance used to mark a sacred spot or to anoint sacred objects, including kings, prophets, and priests (Exod. 28:41; 1 Sam. 16:12; Zech. 4:14). James instructed the elders to pray over the sick, "anointing him with oil in the name of the Lord" for their healing (James 5:14). Oil is a very positive symbol in a spiritual dream and is linked to ministry, the anointing of the Spirit, or the calling of God for His work and service.

OBJECT: **PROSTITUTE**

First Reference: Genesis 34:31—Simeon and Levi are angry that their sister was treated like a harlot.

Possible Meaning: In the Old Testament, a harlot is a symbol of religious unfaithfulness and spiritual adultery. In Revelation 17, a harlot is riding on the beast representing the final kingdom. To dream of a harlot indicates seduction from the truth or turning from righteousness. The seduction can come through a person or through a spirit that will rise and work against your mind and your beliefs.

OBJECT: **RAIN**

First Reference: Genesis 2:5—In the Garden of Eden, the Lord had not yet caused it to rain on the earth.

Possible Meaning: With the exception of the flood of Noah (Gen. 7–8), rain by itself (without flooding or lightning) is a good indication of the blessing of the Lord in your life, ministry, or church. The terms "early and latter rain" refer to the outpouring of the Holy Spirit (Joel 2:23; James 5:7). A businessman once dreamed of supporting our ministry and of gold raindrops falling upon him. As he did begin to support our ministry, his business began to flourish and prosper. Rain also brings growth and fruit to plants and trees.

OBJECT: **RIGHT HAND**

First Reference: Genesis 13:9—Abraham told Lot to choose the land between the right and left hand.

Possible Meaning: The Genesis 13 reference deals with deciding between two choices. Later in the ancient culture, the right hand represented authority or power. The mother of James and John wanted Christ to seat her sons on His right hand (Matt. 20:21). Christ is in heaven seated at the "right hand of God" (Acts 7:55–56). Christ has seven stars in his right hand (Rev. 1:20), and the seven-sealed book is in the right hand of God (Rev. 5:1, 7).

The name *Benjamin* means "son of my right hand," as the right hand is symbolic of having favor, receiving authority, and position.

OBJECT: **RIVER**

First Reference: Genesis 2:10—In the Garden of Eden, four rivers flowed from one source to water the garden.

Possible Meanings: One of the famous biblical rivers is the Jordan in Israel, mentioned 182 times in the Old Testament in the King James Version. It serves as a border between two nations: Israel on the west and Jordan on the east. When the Jordan was crossed, it represented a new beginning, as Joshua crossed with Israel (Josh. 3–5). Elijah crossed the Jordan and was translated (2 Kings 2:6–13), and Christ was baptized in the Jordan (Matt. 3:13). Crossing the Jordan also alluded to a picture of death and resurrection.

If a river is flooding in a destructive manner, it can indicate a literal flood or a flood of difficulties. If it is dark water, it is a trial, but clear flowing water in a river can indicate a coming transition that will be smooth.

OBJECT: **ROCK(S)**

First Reference: Exodus 17:6—Moses stood upon the rock in Horeb to bring forth water from the rock.

Possible Meanings: Scripture teaches that God is our rock (Deut. 32:4) and that the rock that brought forth water in the wilderness was Christ (1 Cor. 10:4). Stumbling on a large rock can represent a spiritual offense either in the Word or an offense caused by believing in Christ (1 Pet. 2:8). A rock foundation means a strong spiritual foundation in the Word of God.

OBJECT: **SAND**

First Reference: Genesis 22:17—God promised Abraham that his seed would be as the sand upon the seashore.

Possible Meaning: The stars are heavenly, but sand is earthly. The "spiritual seed" of Abraham is the church, whose promises are heavenly. The earthly seed are the natural Hebrew people, as their promises from God are earthly (the land of Israel, Jerusalem, and so forth). Stars can *fall from heaven* (which is what occurred with Lucifer, Isaiah 14:12–15). Sand can also be shaken by wind and moved by water. Christ taught that any foundation built upon the sand will eventually collapse (Matt. 7:26–27).

To dream of sand presents several possible meanings. Walking in sand is to walk into, or through, a possible unstable situation. To be buried in sand is earthly, indicating carnal surroundings that are attempting to choke you spiritually. To build on sand indicates one who "hears these sayings of Mine [Jesus], and does not do them" (Matt. 7:26).

OBJECT: THE SEA

First Reference: Genesis 1:26—Man was given dominion over the fish of the sea.

Possible Meanings: In prophetic application, the sea can allude to nations of the earth (Isa. 17:12). The beast of Revelation 13:1 rises up from the sea, or from the nations around the Mediterranean, called the Great Sea in Daniel (Dan. 7:1–4). When Daniel saw the winds "stirring up the Great Sea," it was indicating conflict among the nations (v. 2).

OBJECT: SERPENT

First Reference: Genesis 3:1—The serpent in the garden tempts Eve to eat from the forbidden fruit.

Possible Meanings: Satan used the serpent in the garden, and thus throughout the Scripture a serpent is the imagery of Satan or the powers of darkness. In Revelation, Satan is called "that serpent of old, called the Devil" (Rev. 12:9; 20:2). A spiritual dream involving serpents is never a good omen and alludes to an attack or a very difficult time. If the serpent bites you, it means the problem will have an effect upon you emotionally, physically, or spiritually.

OBJECT: SMOKE

First Reference: Genesis 19:28—Smoke "like the smoke of a furnace" want up when the cities of Sodom and Gomorrah were burning.

Possible Meanings: Smoke is the result of a fire. Smoke is never a positive imagery because it represents the remains of something that has burned. David spoke of being "like a wineskin in smoke" (Ps. 119:83), referring to a wineskin hanging in a tent near a fire that the smoke dries out.

Smoke can create discomfort and block what you are attempting to see. Where there is *smoke there is a fire,* and this can refer to a situation that creates stress and confusion.

OBJECT: STARS

First Reference: Genesis 1:16—God made the lesser light such as the moon and stars.

Possible Meanings: Stars are imagery of lights that shine in darkness. They also symbolize eternal promises such as when God said that Abraham's seed would be as the stars of heaven (which cannot be numbered, Gen. 15:5). Seeing stars often represents the promises of God, especially provision during dark or difficult times.

OBJECT: STORMS

First Reference: Job 21:18—The writer of Job speaks of how a storm carries away the chaff with the wind.

Possible Meaning: Scripture speaks of escaping the storm (Ps. 55:8), of God being a covering, or shelter, in the storm (Isa. 4:6), and of God performing His will through a storm (Nahum 1:3). In the Gospels, storms would arise on Galilee; one nearly capsized the boat of the disciples (Mark 4:37; Luke 8:23).

A spiritual storm that God allows can help a person search his or her life and remove the excessive chaff from the life of a believer. A storm created by your circumstances will cause you to search your life to determine your spiritual level of faith. A storm created by demonic powers is intended to capsize your faith, as when Satan desired to sift Peter as wheat to destroy his faith (Luke 22:31–32). A storm in a dream indicates conflict, a time of difficulty, or a challenge that is come into your life, family, or church. If it damages trees, it can allude to individuals getting hurt because of the situation.

OBJECT: **SWINE**

First Reference: Leviticus 11:7—God classifies the swine as an unclean animal.

Possible Meaning: In the New Testament, the evil spirits in the man of Gadara went into the swine (Matt. 8:32). Christ instructed His followers not to "cast your pearls before swine" (Matt. 7:6). In 2 Peter 2:22, a backslider is like a dog returning to its vomit and a swine that is washed returning to the mud. In a dream, a swine is a very unclean person or situation and can allude to a backslider who once knew Christ but has returned to his or her life of sin.

OBJECT: **SWORD**

First Reference: Genesis 3:24—The cherubim with flaming swords were guarding the tree of life in Eden.

Possible Meaning: This flaming sword was a picture of the future power of the Word of God. Ephesians 6:17 teaches that the "sword of the Spirit" is the Word of God. Hebrews 4:12 says the: "word of God is quick, and powerful, and sharper than any twoedged sword" (KJV).

I've had numerous dreams of using a double-edged sword, and in every instance I was using it to fight a spiritual adversary—meaning I would defeat the adversity by reading, quoting, and believing the Word of God.

OBJECT: **TORNADOES**

First Reference: 2 Kings 2:1—Called a "whirlwind" in the Bible, tornadoes are mentioned twenty-seven times in the Old Testament.

Possible Meanings: A whirlwind is very sudden and very destructive, and it always represents either a literal storm of sudden disaster that is coming or a spiritual storm. Each time I have dreamed of a tornado it was a sudden disaster, often on a national level. I saw the five tornadoes in the 9/11 vision in 1996 and the oil tornado in the Gulf of Mexico in July of 2007.

Jeremiah 23:1–20 mentions the destruction caused by whirlwinds, which would also cause many deaths. Jeremiah was possibly alluding to the swiftness of the Babylonians who entered Israel and wreaked havoc on the temple and the city of Jerusalem. I once saw a leader over the U.S. State Department who was being followed by three huge tornadoes; I knew it represented three major nations or national problems she would deal with in her administrative position.

OBJECT: **TREE(S)**

First Reference: Genesis 3:2—Eve spoke to the serpent concerning the trees in the garden.

Possible Meanings: Trees actually have several meanings. Literal fruit-bearing trees can allude to success (if they have fruit, Ps. 1:3) or to economic and business difficulties (if they are withered, Joel 1:12). An individual tree could also allude to a person, as when King Nebuchadnezzar saw a large fruit tree cut down to the ground and Daniel interpreted the dream to mean that the tree was the king, and he would be cut down for seven years (Dan. 4).

The type of tree is significant also. A palm tree represents the righteous (Ps. 92:12), and a cedar can allude to the righteous in ministry, as cedars were used in the temple (2 Chron. 1–6). A weeping willow can represent a time of sorrow (Ps. 137:1–4). A mustard tree can allude to faith (Luke 17:6), and a fig tree has prophetically alluded to Israel as a nation (Hosea 9:10). A barren, dead tree can allude to total death in the home, job, a person, or a situation.

OBJECT: **VALLEY(S)**

First Reference: Genesis 14:17–18—Abraham met the king-priest Melchizedek in the Valley of Shaveh.

Possible Meaning: Most Old Testament battles were fought in the valleys, including the battle of the five kings (Gen. 14:1–3), Joshua's fight in the Valley of Aijalon (Josh. 10:12), and David slaying Goliath in the Valley of Elah (1 Sam. 17:2). Thus, valleys can indicate a time of conflict, struggle, and some form of clash. In Psalm 84:6 we read of godly men who "as they pass through the Valley of Baca, they make it a spring." A valley is something to pass through in order to get to the next destination.

OBJECT: **VESSELS**

First Reference: Genesis 43:11—Jacob told his sons to take fruit, spices, and nuts to Egypt in vessels.

Possible Meaning: There are numerous references to vessels throughout the Bible. In the New Testament, Paul wrote that the spiritual character of individuals is compared to vessels of gold, silver, wood, and earth (2 Tim. 2:20). There are "vessels of mercy" (Rom. 9:23) and even vessels of wrath (v. 22). Humans are compared to vessels, as we are containers that can hold righteousness, peace, joy, and the presence of God within our spirits (Rom. 14:17). When a person dreams of a shattered vessel, it can indicate a trial that will cause great brokenness. Picking up pieces can indicate you will assist in helping heal a bad situation. A full vessel can be a full blessing. The metal gold is associated with the priesthood or ministry (Ezra 1:1–11).

OBJECT: **WALKING BAREFOOT**

First Reference: 2 Samuel 15:30—David left Jerusalem barefooted, running from a conspiracy to overthrow him.

Possible Meaning: Dreaming of being barefooted can represent not being prepared for a situation. David had to leave the city quickly to prevent a possible assassination (vv. 30–32). I have dreamed of being barefooted, and in each case something happened very swiftly and unexpectedly. When you wear your "gospel shoes," your feet are "shod with the preparation of the gospel" (Eph. 6:15).

OBJECT: **WATER**

First Reference: Genesis 2:10—Four rivers went out to water the Garden of Eden.

Possible Meanings: Throughout Scripture, water was needed for survival among the ancient tribal families. A lack of water created famines. Water usually alludes to the Holy Spirit, as when Jesus spoke of the Holy Spirit, He said, "He that believeth on me...out of his belly shall flow rivers of living water" (John 7:38–39, KJV). Water purifies, quenches thirst, and causes life to flourish—all three examples of the work of the Holy Spirit. A well of water is your inward source of blessing from the Spirit. A full well is fullness of the Spirit, and a dry well is a dry, empty spirit.

OBJECT: WEIGHT SCALES

First Reference: Job 31:6—Job spoke of being evenly weighed in God's balance.

Possible Meaning: The Old Testament uses the word "balance" when referring to scales. The Scriptures speak of a false balance (Prov. 11:1, KJV) and a just weight (Prov. 16:11, KJV). Daniel interpreted the handwriting on the wall, which said, "You have been weighed in the balances, and found wanting" (Dan. 5:27).

A dream or vision of a balance identifies God's plan to weigh something or someone to see if it is just or unjust and if the blessing or disfavor of God will rest upon it.

OBJECT: WHEAT

First Reference: Genesis 30:14—Reuben brought mandrakes from the field during the wheat harvest.

Possible Meanings: Many of the local wars that Israel fought with the Philistines and other tribes occurred at harvest time. The enemies desired the grain that had been collected. This is why Boaz was sleeping at his grain pile to prevent thieves from stealing the work of an entire month (Ruth 3:7). The wheat was very precious and valuable and sustained life for the people throughout the long winters.

In the New Testament, the wheat represents the children of God in the kingdom (Matt. 13:38). Wheat also represents the local, national, and worldwide harvest of souls who need to be reached with the gospel. In nearly every example, a full wheat field is a full harvest, a dead wheat field is an area that has been spiritually destroyed by events that have hindered the effectiveness of the gospel, and a diseased wheat field can mean that the message preached in an area has been corrupted or perverted. Gathering in grain indicates you will have an ingathering of souls. Losing grain indicates people will depart from you, your church, or ministry.

OBJECT: **WIND**

First Reference: Genesis 8:1—When the wind sent from God blew over the earth, it dried up the floodwaters in Noah's day.

Possible Meanings: There are two types of wind: wind that comes from heaven as a manifestation of the Holy Spirit, such as the "mighty rushing wind" on the Day of Pentecost (Acts 2:1–4), and wind that brings destruction and death, as when Satan produced the wind storms that destroyed the house of Job's family, bringing death to ten children (Job 1). In a dream, if a wind is tearing up the surrounding area, it indicates a time of severe trouble is coming. If the wind is gentle and brings a positive feeling, it can allude to a move of the Holy Spirit upon a situation.

Journaling Section

Use these pages to record what you are learning about how to interpret your dreams and visions.

Notes

CHAPTER 1
THE LAST DAYS—TIME TO PIERCE THE VEIL

1. Elizabeth Dias, "In the Crystal Ball: More Regulation for Psychics," September 2, 2010, TIME.com, http://www.time.com/time/nation/article/0,8599,2015676,00.html (accessed September 14, 2010).

CHAPTER 2
THE DREAM FACTOR

1. Flavius Josephus, *Antiquities of the Jews*, book 10, chapter 7, Christian Classics Ethereal Library, http://www.ccel.org/j/josephus/works/ant-10.htm (accessed December 13, 2010).

CHAPTER 3
WHY ARE SOME DREAMS DELAYED IN COMING TO PASS?

1. Jaquetta White, "BP Oil Spill May Cost Louisiana Fishing Industry $172 million," *New Orleans Times-Picayune*, October 15, 2010, http://www.nola.com/business/index.ssf/2010/10/bp_oil_spill_may_cost_louisian.html (accessed October 18, 2010).

2. Stephen C. Fehr, "Gulf States Fear Long-Term Fiscal Effects of Oil Disaster," Stateline.org, June 24, 2010, http://www.stateline.org/live/details/story?contentId=493859 (accessed October 18, 2010).

CHAPTER 4
NIGHTMARES AND DIRTY DREAMING

1. Answers.com, "What Is the Origin of the Word *Nightmare?*" http://wiki.answers.com/Q/What_is_the_origin_of_the_word_nightmare (accessed December 13, 2010).

2. Emil G. Hirsch, "Lilith," JewishEncyclopedia.com, http://www.jewishencyclopedia.com/view.jsp?artid=421&letter=L (accessed September 15, 2010).

3. W. E. Vine, *Vine's Complete Expository Dictionary of Old and New Testament Words* (Nashville, TN: Thomas Nelson, 1984), s.v. "demon, demoniac," 158.

4. Ibid., s.v. "renewed," 960.

5. Perry Stone, *Breaking the Jewish Code* (Lake Mary, FL: Charisma House, 2009), 94–95.

6. *Israel Today* magazine, no. 75, April 2005, 12.

7. *Israel Today* magazine, no. 49, February 2003, 12.

8. Stone, *Breaking the Jewish Code*, 103–104.

CHAPTER 6
THE PSYCHIC VOICES VERSUS THE PROPHETIC VISIONS

1. William Patalon III, "Psychic Friends Network Firm Goes Bankrupt," *The Baltimore Sun*, February 5, 1998, http://articles.baltimoresun.com/1998-02-05/business/1998036093_1_psychic-friends-infomercial-bankruptcy (accessed October 7, 2010).

2. No current source information available.

3. James Henry Breasted, *Development of Religion and Thought in Ancient Egypt* (Philadelphia: University of Pennsylvania Press, 1972), 211. Viewed at www.books.google.com on October 7, 2010.

4. Adam Clarke, *Adam Clarke's Commentary*, electronic database (n.p.: Biblesoft, 1996), s.v. "Exodus 1:16."

5. Josephus, *Antiquities of the Jews*, book 2, chapter 9, http://www.ccel.org/ccel/josephus/works/files/ant-2.htm (accessed December 14, 2010).

6. Ibid.

7. Gaius Suetonius Tranquillis, *The Lives of the Twelve Caesars*, trans. by Alexander Thomson, rev. and corrected by T. Forester (n.p.: BiblioBazaar, 2008), 57.

8. Plutarch, *Plutarch's Lives of the Noble Grecians and Romans*, vol. 2, trans. by John Dryden (New York: Random House, 1992), 240.

CHAPTER 8
LEARNING TO LISTEN TO YOUR WIFE'S WARNING DREAMS

1. *TIME*, "Worship: Gospel According to Claudia," April 12, 1963, http://www.time.com/time/magazine/article/0,9171,828101,00.html (accessed December 14, 2010).

2. Henry Forman, *The Story of Prophecy* (New York: Tudor Publishing Co., 1940), 97–98, referenced in Perry Stone, *Unusual Prophecies Being Fulfilled*, no. 7 (Cleveland, TN: Voice of Evangelism, n.d.).

CHAPTER 9
WHAT IT MEANS WHEN DREAMING OF A DEPARTED LOVED ONE

1. Ward Hill Lamon, *Recollections of Abraham Lincoln, 1847–1865* (Chicago: A. C. McClurg and Company, 1895), 113–114. Viewed at www.books.google.com on December 15, 2010.

2. Ibid., 117–118.

3. Jill Stefko, "Abraham Lincoln and the Paranormal," April 19, 2007, Suite101.com, http://www.suite101.com/content/abraham-lincoln-and-the-paranormal-a19245 (accessed October 8, 2010).

4. Perry Stone, *Angels on Assignment* (Lake Mary, FL: Charisma House, 2009), 61–62.

CHAPTER 14
DREAMS—AMAZING PURPOSE
FOR THESE REVELATIONS

1. Dwight Mallory Pratt, *International Standard Bible Encyclopedia*, electronic database (n.p.: Biblesoft, 1996), s.v. "inward part."

2. Kendra Cherry, "Stages of Sleep," About.com.Psychology, http://psychology.about.com/od/statesofconsciousness/a/SleepStages.htm (accessed October 12, 2010).

BOOK II

OPENING THE GATES OF HEAVEN

PERRY STONE

CHARISMA
HOUSE

DEDICATION

I consider myself highly blessed to have been led by the Holy Spirit into full-time ministry, having witnessed three other generations of ministers before me. I am also highly honored to be the son of Fred Stone, the son of a West Virginia coal miner, converted to Christ in the 1949 Coal-field Revival—a little-known revival that lasted for forty-two months, birthed in McDowell County, West Virginia, near the time of the outbreak of the Korean War (1950–1953).

I carry my dad's name, Perry Fred Stone. However, with two people who had the same name in the house, to prevent confusion Dad was always identified by his middle name, Fred, in our home. His closest West Virginia friends and family affectionately called him, "Brother Freddie." Dad was the greatest example of demonstrating the power of prayer, the joy of worship, and the blessing of giving that I have ever known. He prayed prayers that were answered! I often said, "It seemed he walked under an open spiritual window and could access the throne at any moment and see results almost instantly." During his lifetime, when I encountered any type of difficulty, he was the first person I would call, as I always felt he had some type of a *hot line* that connected directly to God.

He taught me how to pray by example and not just by quoting a scripture. In this book, among many important keys, I will also share twelve things my father taught me about prayer, which I believe will inspire you and assist you in your prayer life. I will also dig deep into the concept of financial blessing through obedience and prayer and the subject of God's favor—what favor is and how it works. It is my goal to teach you about opening the gate of heaven, but not just opening the gate, but walking under an open window. Dad is in heaven now, but his example will be taught to hundreds of thousands of future intercessors and prayer warriors!

A PROUD SON OF FRED STONE,
PERRY STONE JR.

CONTENTS

INTRODUCTION

IT MAY COME as a spiritual surprise to some that after more than thirty-five years of full-time ministry, including meeting and preaching to hundreds of thousands of believers, I have discovered that it is actually possible to pray prayers that, although heard by people sitting in the same pew, are *not heard in heaven*! It is also possible to offer God words of praise and even financial offerings that are accepted by earthly ministers but are not recognized in the heavenly temple, the dwelling place of the Almighty (Rev. 4). In some cases, the prayers, praise, and financial gifts become *a systematic routine-based ritual* that may make the participant feel better about himself or herself, but eventually it gives birth to frustration. Weeks or months may pass while the participant's life remains void of answered prayer with no demonstration of any major financial, spiritual, or personal breakthrough. The outward worshiper may appear healthy, but a growing, gnawing void exists inwardly. For some, the heavens—where all spiritual blessings originate—are figuratively *covered in brass*, preventing any heavenly blessing from being released to the earth zone.

Throughout the inspired Word of God the Almighty occasionally sent rebukes and correction to the spiritual lives of His covenant people, Israel, including the priests ministering daily at Solomon's temple. By the time of the prophet Malachi, the daily rituals and sacrificial offerings had become mere routine, and there was a boredom and weariness overshadowing the minds of the priests (Mal. 1:12–13). At that time, what men were offering God was not being received by God (Mal. 2:13). The religious routines seemed outwardly right but were inwardly wrong, because all prayer, worship, and giving must come from a righteous heart and pure motive.

1

Too many believers are stuck in a weekly routine where you enter the church smiling as you grip the greeter's hand, but privately you know you will endure ninety minutes of inner boredom in a performance that many call a *worship service*. Others, when inviting friends to attend church, brag on the *new facility* or talk about the *good music* or *inspirational speaker* instead of telling their friends that the service will change their lives as they experience a *God encounter* and enter the very presence of the Lord. It is quite possible to promise *living water* to thirsty souls only to discover the river has gone dry in the Sunday morning service. In many places, the former days of vibrant spiritual fire have cooled to mere embers of *holy smoke*!

The lack of breakthrough occurs not just in the realm of meeting spiritual, emotional, and physical needs, but it can also be seen in the area of tithes and offerings. Today there is more preaching from pulpits and during a combined twenty-four hours of Christian television programming on the subject of money—sowing offerings and giving tithes—than at any time in the previous six thousand or so years of mankind's existence! Thousands of sincere believers have consistently and in faith *planted their best seed offering* in hopes of receiving the promised "hundredfold...sixty...and thirty" return (Matt. 13:23), only to find that three years later they are still receiving the same amount in their weekly paychecks.

One older believer told me that he gave almost eight thousand dollars over a period of two years in hopes of getting a major financial breakthrough that had been promised on a telecast. He came to a crisis point where he could not pay for his wife's needed medication. When he contacted two ministries, asking in honest sincerity why he had not received the predicted blessing that had been announced by the minister, one responded in a letter by saying, "You do not have enough faith." The second letter said, "There must be some sin in your life!" This older gentleman and his wife had served God for many decades, and his moral and spiritual life was an example of purity to others. He wept and fell into self-appointed condemnation, not from the Lord, but from the piercing words of the two ministers who wrote to him.

The lack of answered prayer, the shortage of needed financial break-throughs, and the seemingly brass heavens seem to indicate that those "windows of heaven" prophesied in Malachi to open over us and "pour out…blessing" (Mal. 3:10) are now closed, and the gate of heaven's blessings has been slammed shut.

I believe it is the will of God that when we pray, we eventually should receive an answer or at least an *inner assurance* from the heavenly Father. (See John 16:23–26.) Based upon Scripture, we can know that it is the will of the Almighty that when we freely give tithes and offerings through the leading of the Holy Spirit, our needs will be met and a measure of blessing will flow to us, not only for personal provision but also to bring additional increase to be a blessing to others (Gen. 12:2).

Although a *closed heaven* is a reality for many, God promises that He will "open for you the windows of heaven and pour out for you such blessing that there will not be room enough to receive it" (Mal. 3:10). You do not have to be bound by the frustration of empty prayers, a cold heart, and miracle-less living. You can experience His tangible presence in your life during your times of worship. Daily needs are a reality, but God's ability to meet your needs—and to pour out an overflow of blessing—is a part of His covenant with you.

I want to take you on a journey to discover not only how to open the windows of heaven but also how to walk in and under the favor of God. We will explore the significance of the gate of heaven and then proceed to journey on a road that leads to the fullness of God's blessing. In the first chapter we will see that reaching up in prayer is similar to climbing a ladder—a picture seen in the life of Jacob.

CHAPTER 1

The Man Who Saw the Gate of Heaven

*And Jacob called the name of the place
where God spoke with him, Bethel.*

—GENESIS 35:15

JACOB, THE GRANDSON of Abraham, was in serious trouble. He had deceived his brother, Esau, and his father, and he had taken the blessing intended for the firstborn son from Esau (Gen. 27:41). Fearing physical reprisal, Jacob went into exile, traveling far from home, and eventually arrived at a location near a place called Luz (Gen. 28:19). One evening as the sun was setting, Jacob stopped for the night and, using stones as a pillow, lay down to sleep. Late that night as he drifted off to sleep, he experienced a mysterious and wonderful dream.

In his dream Jacob saw a ladder whose base was setting on the earth, but the top of the ladder reached into heaven. When we think of a ladder, we picture a stepladder with steps that one climbs to reach the roof of his house. The Hebrew word *ladder* is *sullam* and is actually a *staircase*. This is evident, as Jacob saw angels going up and coming down the ladder. This supernatural ladder may have been in the form of a spiral, a common heavenly design. Through the Hubble Space Telescope, scientists have observed that in the galaxy in which we live, and in other galaxy forms, a "majestic disk of stars and dust lanes" can be seen in the form of spirals.[1]

When Solomon constructed his temple in Jerusalem, there was a winding (spiral) staircase that wound from the ground floor to the second tier chamber, and a second winding staircase led from the middle to the third story of the sacred building (1 Kings 6:8, KJV).

One of my ministry partners, when hearing me speak about this ladder, made an interesting observation. She noted that the double-strand molecules of nucleic acids such as DNA were in the form of what is called a *double helix*. The double helix appears as a twisted ladder that is held together by base pairs that are like steps from the top to the bottom of the helix.[2] While the DNA *ladder* is found in the blood molecules of all humans linked to life itself, Jacob's ladder was a ladder of *life*, linking and connecting the heavenly to the earthly, or the world of men with the world of angels and the supernatural. Since the galaxies of the universe are spiral, perhaps this heavenly staircase was in the form of a spiral, linking to the DNA spiral of life that God implanted in the first Adam at the beginning of Creation!

The dream of this ladder stunned Jacob. We read his reaction after he awoke:

> And he was afraid and said, "How awesome is this place! This is none other than the house of God, and this is the gate of heaven!"
>
> —GENESIS 28:17

Two important points are noted in his statement. The term "this place" identified the land on which Jacob had slept that night. For years I pondered on the exact location of the *place* Jacob was speaking of where the dream occurred. The Bible says he called the name of the place *Bethel*, which in Hebrew means "house of God" (Gen. 28:19). He identified the land where he laid his head as the "gate of heaven." At the time of the dream, no physical "house of God" had been set aside for the Hebrews (Jewish people) in the land, as the Hebrew family only consisted of Isaac, Rebekah, Esau, and Jacob. It would be centuries later, after Israel expanded to six hundred thousand men (Exod. 12:37), that Moses constructed the traveling wilderness tent called the tabernacle (Exod. 25:9). Generations later David's chosen son, Solomon, built the sacred temple in Jerusalem (2 Chron. 3). However, centuries earlier than the building of either the tabernacle or the temple, Jacob had identified the site where he had the dream—*this place*—as the "gate of heaven."

THE HOLY MOUNTAIN OF THE GATE OF HEAVEN

There was only one location on earth set apart from ages past where God placed His name (Deut. 12:5, 11, 21). That place was Jerusalem (Salem), which was also the place where Melchizedek, the first king and priest of righteousness, lived (Gen. 14:18–24). In Jacob's time there was no holy temple set aside for worshiping God that we know of, just altars that were built by Abraham from natural stones, where special sacrifices were offered (Gen. 8:20; 12:7; 13:18; 22:9).

The man Melchizedek was personally known to Abraham. According to Jewish tradition recorded in a religious Jewish writing called the Book of Jasher (mentioned in Joshua 10:13 and 2 Samuel 1:18), Melchizedek was still alive in the time of Isaac and during the early years of Jacob's life (Jasher 26:5, 10; 28:18).[3] In the city of Jerusalem (called "Salem" in Genesis 14:18 and Psalm 76:2), there was a sacred mountain called *Mount Moriah*. It was this mountain to which God Himself led Abraham to test him by commanding him to offer his covenant son, Isaac, on an altar (Gen. 22:2). It was upon this same mountain, Mount Moriah, that Solomon constructed the elaborate and expensive temple, one of the most expensive buildings in world history (2 Chron. 3:1).

For many years I believed that Jacob was at or near Mount Moriah when he experienced his dream, for he called the place the "gate of heaven." From Jacob's family history, he understood that Moriah was the place where his grandfather Abraham had paid tithes to Melchizedek (Gen. 14:20; Heb. 7:9). He was also aware that his own father, Isaac, had been placed upon a stone altar by Abraham and that a ram had taken his place (Gen. 22:13). Thus the land of Moriah (Jerusalem) was not a strange or new territory for Jacob. It had been designated as the location for the future house of God—the temple, where future offerings, sacrifices, and holy incense would be offered and the holy smoke would ascend toward the gate of heaven for generations!

In the early 1990s I was in Jerusalem in an office near the famed Western Wall discussing the vision of Jacob's ladder with Yehuda Getz, the head rabbi. He was asked by a young minister, Scott Thomas, where Jacob had the vision of the ladder reaching from heaven to earth recorded in Genesis 28. The rabbi replied, "Jacob was sleeping somewhere on the Mount of Olives, and the ladder was sitting on the Temple Mount, on Mount Moriah." Personally I had always believed this, but I knew that in the biblical narrative there were no specifics as to the name of the place, other than it was called *Luz* (Gen. 28:19). The word *Luz* refers to some type of a nut tree—perhaps an almond tree. In Moses's day, the almond was considered as a holy fruit. The rod of Aaron was made from the branch of an almond tree (Num. 17:8).

Rabbi Getz referred to the religious and sacred history found in the Book of Jasher:

> And Jacob went forth continuing his road to Haran, and he came as far as mount Moriah, and he tarried there all night near the city of Luz; and the Lord appeared there unto Jacob on that night, and he said unto him, I am the Lord God of Abraham and the God of Isaac thy father.
>
> —Jasher 30:1

The fact that Luz is linked to Jerusalem can be discovered by carefully reading Genesis 35:6:

> So Jacob came to Luz (that is, Bethel), which is in the land of Canaan, he and all the people who were with him.

The name *Luz* was identified with *Bethel,* a Hebrew word meaning "house of God." This story reveals that while at Luz, Rebekah's nurse died and was buried under an oak tree (v. 8). God later revealed Himself again to Jacob, and Jacob built a pillar and called the place Bethel (the house of God). The following verse reveals a clue:

> Then they journeyed from Bethel. And when there was but a
> little distance to go to Ephrath, Rachel labored in childbirth,
> and she had hard labor.
>
> —GENESIS 35:16

The area of Ephrath is today Bethlehem. In fact, Bethlehem is called Bethlehem Ephrath (Ephrathah) (Mic. 5:2). Today near the entrance to modern Bethlehem is the traditional grave of Rachel, who died while giving birth to Benjamin (Gen. 35:19). Genesis 35:16 says "there was but a little distance" from Bethel to Ephrath. If the Bethel in Jacob's dream was Jerusalem, and Bethel was a "little distance" to Ephrath, which is Bethlehem, then the distance of about eight miles between Jerusalem and Bethlehem would be considered a "little distance."

The rabbinical traditions and the textual evidence indicates that Luz was an early city near Mount Moriah, later called the "house of God" by Jacob. It is interesting that after Jacob saw the angels, knowing he was headed into Syria for an unspecified time, he vowed to God that if He would bring him back safely to the land of his fathers, he would offer God the tenth (Gen. 28:22). This word *tenth* in Hebrew is the word *'asar*, which is a word linked to the tithe (*ma'aser*) and refers to the *tenth* offered to God (Lev. 27:30, 32).

Twenty years passed, and the angel appeared to Jacob instructing him to return home to Canaan (Gen 31:13, 18). Notice the words of the angel:

> Then the Angel of God spoke to me in a dream, saying, "Jacob."
> And I said, "Here I am." And He said…"I am the God of Bethel,
> where you anointed the pillar and where you made a vow to Me.
> Now arise, get out of this land, and return to the land of your
> family."
>
> —GENESIS 31:11–13

God recalled the angelic visitation twenty years prior, reminding Jacob of Bethel and of his vow when he anointed the stone pillar. In the Old Covenant, when altars were built and anointed, the spot became sacred and was marked by God Himself. By reminding Jacob of his vow and the anointing of the pillar, He was recalling Jacob's prayers, promises, and covenants made at these altars.

When Jacob returned from Syria twenty years later, there still was not a physical house of God in Jerusalem or anywhere else in Canaan. However, generations later it would be one of Jacob's sons, Levi, who was selected to lead the holy priesthood, and the children of Jacob (called the children of Israel) would present tithes and offerings in the same area when Melchizedek ministered and where Abraham offered Isaac and Jacob saw the ladder. This location was a gate, *a portal into the spirit world,* and an opening in the atmosphere enabling angels to ascend and descend to carry the tithe and offerings before God and to release the blessing back to earth.

In reality, this gate of heaven was positioned over the Temple Mount itself. The base of the stairway sat on the solid rock of the Temple Mount platform, and when ascending upward, it led to the entrance of the temple of God in heaven. Thus the city of Jerusalem became known as the "city of God" (Ps. 46:4) and the city of the "great King" (Ps. 48:2). The mountain where the temple was constructed is called the "holy mountain" in sixteen Old Testament passages, including Isaiah 11:9; 56:7; and 57:13. The blessings released to the high priest, Levites, and Israelites on the mountain and at the temple were the result of an open heaven, a spiritual ladder reaching from the holy of holies to the throne room of the Almighty in the third heaven (2 Cor. 12:2; Rev. 4:1–2). This stairway to heaven enabled God's chosen people to have access to reach up to God, and in return, God had access to reach down to man.

THE OTHER SIDE OF THE LADDER

Jacob revealed that the house of God was the gate of heaven, meaning there was a portal or spiritual opening above the sacred mountain. When the apostle John was on the island of Patmos, he heard a voice saying, "Come up here," and he saw "a door standing open in heaven" (Rev. 4:1). The Greek word for "door" is the same word for "door" used throughout the New Testament—*thura,* meaning a portal or an opening. John actually saw the other side of the "ladder," or the "gate" side (entrance) of God's heavenly temple. When he entered through the door, he was "in the Spirit," meaning caught up in the ecstasy or visionary gift of spiritual vision through the influence of the Holy Spirit (v. 2).

John then described "the other side of the ladder" as he entered the open portal door and was standing upon a massive floor of crystal, called a "sea of glass" (v. 6). When light strikes a cut diamond, there are sharp colors of blue, green, orange, and red that actually flash from the sparkling cut stone. A crystal prism catches light and produces the same colors of a rainbow. The floor of the heavenly temple radiates the light of the Eternal One, sitting upon the throne in the center of the heavenly temple. The Almighty dwells in a glorious light that no man can approach (1 Tim. 6:16). As the light radiates throughout the temple, the reflection on the crystal floor flashes beautiful colors.

In Revelation 6 John can actually see under the clear floor and observe the souls of martyred saints under the golden altar, clothed in white robes (Rev. 6:9). Later, in Revelation 15:2, the glass floor has the appearance of being mingled with fire, which has a reddish and orange glow when burning.

John also saw a throne and described the one sitting on the throne to be like a *jasper* and a *sardius* stone in appearance. The throne was and is the central feature in the heavenly temple. John said:

> And He who sat there was like a jasper and a sardius stone in appearance; and there was a rainbow around the throne, in appearance like an emerald.
>
> —REVELATION 4:3

On the breastplate of the high priest of the earthly tabernacle there were twelve individual precious gemstones—three stones positioned in four rows in a golden breastplate (Exod. 28:15–21). The first stone was a sardius (v. 17), the stone representing Jacob's first son, Reuben. The jasper was the last stone on the breastplate (v. 20) and was the stone for Jacob's last son, Benjamin. The fact that these two stones are the first and last stones on the breastplate of the high priest reveal that the

Almighty is the first and the last. It is written, "I am the Alpha and the Omega, the Beginning and the End" (Rev. 1:8).

These two stones also hold a clue concerning Christ Himself. The Hebrew name *Reuben* means, "Behold a son," and the name *Benjamin* means, "Son of the right hand." Christ was introduced at His baptism as God's Son (Matt. 3:17). After His resurrection He ascended to heaven and is now seated at the right hand of God (Acts 2:33). Thus, the first and last sons of Jacob represent Christ's earthly ministry and His heavenly ministry.

John described a rainbow that was like an emerald (Rev. 4:3). The emerald is sea green and, according to some, was the stone used to identify the tribe of Judah in ancient Israel.[4] The emerald was also considered a wedding stone. The rainbow is mentioned as a covenant sign given after the flood of Noah, indicating that God would never again destroy the earth by water. On earth when we see a rainbow, we only witness half of the bow—as the other half remains in the heavens, around about the throne.

THE SAPPHIRE STONE

When Ezekiel saw the throne of God, he wrote:

> And above the firmament over their heads was the likeness of a throne, in appearance like a sapphire stone; on the likeness of the throne was a likeness with the appearance of a man high above it.
> —EZEKIEL 1:26

The appearance of a sapphire is interesting, as this beautiful royal blue stone is referred to in several places where God revealed Himself to Moses and the elders. In Exodus 24:10, when Moses and the elders saw the Lord, the pavement under His feet was paved with sapphire. The same occurred in Ezekiel's vision above, where he describes the firmament above the heads of the cherubim as the appearance of a sapphire. There is a Jewish tradition that when God wrote the original commandments with the fiery finger of His hands, they were inscribed on stone tablets of sapphire.[5]

This may seem more of a tradition. However, I have a man on my ministry board of directors who is a specialist in laser research and development. Years ago he shared with me how it would be theoretically possible for the original stones of the Ten Commandments to actually be sapphire. He explained how a percentage of the earth's crust contains aluminum oxide, and sapphires can form in rocks poor in silica and rich in aluminum. When aluminum oxide is heated to a high temperature, it forms sapphire crystals. Thus, when God wrote with the fiery finger of His hand (Exod. 31:18; Deut. 33:2), the fire from God's finger could have caused the stone tablets to form some type of sapphire crystals.[6]

In Ezekiel's vision, the prophet continued describing the interior of God's throne as the color of amber, with fire moving inside the throne (Ezek. 1:27). Later Ezekiel described the one on the throne with the appearance of fire from the waist up and fire from the waist downward (Ezek. 8:2). This may have been what the writer to the Hebrews alluded to when he wrote, "Our God is a consuming fire" (Heb. 12:29). The Hebrew word for "amber" is *chashmal*, and it probably means, "a *bronze*-type color." This is likely, since in John's vision the feet of Christ appeared as brass that had been polished through a fire (Rev. 1:15).

THE LIGHTNING, THUNDER, AND VOICES

As John's eyes continued to view the magnificent heavenly scene, he observed three phenomena occurring in connection with the throne of God.

> And from the throne proceeded lightnings, thunderings, and voices. Seven lamps of fire were burning before the throne, which are the seven Spirits of God.
> —REVELATION 4:5

Thunder, lightning, and rainbows are associated on earth with storms and rain. In John's vision, the thunder and lightning indicated the coming upheavals and judgment to be initiated on earth shortly. The voice of God, however, was also identified with a sound like thunder when it was heard upon the earth (John 12:28–30). Lightning is one of nature's most powerful and, at times, dangerous forces. In Psalm 144:5–6, lightning demonstrates this great power of God as it is released through a manifestation.

The rainbow is the symbol of God's covenant to man (Gen. 9:13). The voices heard coming out of the throne may be the voices of *praise and worship* that ascend up the ladder, arriving at the throne of God. We read that God inhabits the praises of Israel (Ps. 22:3), giving us a picture of God as He sits enthroned on the praises of His people. Isaiah saw the Lord "high and lifted up" and described the seraphim crying, "Holy, holy, holy is the LORD" (Isa. 6:1–3). We could say that God is sitting upon His throne and riding upon our praises!

THE TEMPLE—CENTER OF THE UNIVERSE

John was the last of the biblical prophets to see a vision of the temple of God in heaven, recorded in the Book of Revelation. This is the same temple where Ezekiel revealed that the anointed cherub, Satan, once worshiped on the holy mountain and walked up and down in the midst of the stones of fire (Ezek. 28:14). This is the same temple where Moses stood on Mount Sinai, piercing the veil and catching a glimpse of the sacred furniture, which he then constructed for the tabernacle, using the pattern of the furniture he saw (Exod. 34:2). It was the same heavenly temple that David tapped into when he drew the building plans for the temple Solomon would build, including the ark of the covenant, called the pattern of the chariot of the cherubim (1 Chron. 28:18). In the year that King Uzziah died, Isaiah looked upward and saw the seraphim with six wings, flying through the heavenly halls of the temple of God in heaven, crying "Holy, holy, holy is the LORD" (Isa. 6:1–3). From this same holy mountain, Ezekiel viewed four "living creatures" carrying the throne of God from the northern part of the universe upon their shoulders, moving it like a chariot (Ezek. 1). While in Babylonian captivity, the prophet Daniel tapped into the realm of the spirit and witnessed the Ancient of Days sitting upon His throne surrounded by thrones (Dan. 7:9–10). It would be the apostle John, six hundred or more years later, who would describe those sitting upon the thrones as twenty-four in number and identifying them as elders (Rev. 4:4).

One day, at the great gathering together and the resurrection of the dead in Christ, a multitude that no man can number will be thrust instantly through this supernal portal, entering the temple of God, standing on the crystal sea, and viewing the other side of the ladder (1 Thess. 4:16–17; Rev. 5:11). However, we need not wait to have access to the literal presence of God! By understanding the process of opening the heavenly gate, we can access the divine counsel and presence of the Creator through our prayer life. This process is accomplished through the ability of the Holy Spirit.

CHAPTER 2

The Five Gates of the Holy Spirit

Lift up your heads, O you gates!
Lift up, you everlasting doors!
And the King of glory shall come in.
Who is this King of glory?
The Lord of hosts,
He is the King of glory. Selah.

—Psalm 24:9–10

THE MOST IMPORTANT parts of the temple compound in Jerusalem were the many gates leading in and out of the temple facility. The main outer walls of the city of Jerusalem were built upon layer after layer of large ashlars, cut stones taken from a quarry. The Jerusalem from the time of Christ had large limestone ashlars, some weighing four hundred tons.[1] The gates were openings in the walls where large, thick wooden doors were hung. The sacred side of the temple was the east side, and the double wooden doors leading to the holy place were layered in Corinthian bronze. When the sun arose from the east over the peak of the Mount of Olives and struck the gates on the east, the gates glowed with a brilliance that reflected like gold.

The gates at the temple were opened in the morning and closed in the evenings. The closing of the gates at night prevented stray and unclean animals from entering the compound, but it also kept out possible thieves, robbers, and spies who would be scoping out the temple late at night. The chambers on the side stored wood for the altar, grains, oil, and the monetary offerings of the people. Certain priests, called *watchmen,* were assigned the duty of carefully guarding the walls and the gates; this was especially important during the night watches (after the sun set and until the sun arose). If any priest was caught sleeping, he could be stripped of his clothes and expelled from the priesthood. This is what Christ meant when He told the seven churches in Revelation 16:15, "Behold, I am coming as a thief. Blessed is he who watches, and keeps his garments, lest he walk naked and they see his shame."

In the time of Christ there were numerous gates that were positioned on the outer walls of the city of Jerusalem. Inside the inner walls of the temple compound, there were designed entrances that led a person to the top of the sacred platform. From the east entrance, the main entrance facing the holy place, there were three gates—the main eastern gate on the outer wall, the gate leading into the brass altar, and the doors of the temple itself.

The Jewish *Mishnah* describes five gates that one could use to enter the Temple Mount:

> There were five gates to the Temple Mount: the two Huldah Gates on the south, that served for coming in and for going out; the Kiponus Gate on the west, that served for coming in and for going out; the Tadi Gate on the north which was not used at all; the Eastern Gate on which was portrayed the Palace of Shushan.[2]

The Book of Ezekiel describes a future temple to be constructed during the millennial reign of the Messiah. The prophets saw five gates on the walls leading into the temple platform, two to the south and one on each of the other three sides.[3] There is a spiritual significance to the number five linked with these five gates.

THE FIVE GATES OF THE HOLY SPIRIT

Biblical numbers all hold a meaning that is maintained throughout the Scriptures. The number five is considered to allude to *grace* and *redemption.*[4] God's grace and redemptive knowledge is taught through a fivefold ministry team, mentioned in Ephesians 4:11–12. We read:

> And He Himself gave some to be apostles, some prophets, some evangelists, and some pastors and teachers, for the equipping of the saints for the work of ministry, for the edifying of the body of Christ.

This list identifies five specific ministry gifts for the church: apostles, prophets, evangelists, pastors, and teachers. Each ministry gift opens a different gate to spiritual understanding and blessing.

- An *apostle* is a "sent one" whose voice impacts entire nations and ethnic groups. The apostolic door also links other ministries together.

- An *evangelist* leads souls through the gate of salvation with his message of redemption.

- The *prophet* opens the gate to the manifestations and operation of the vocal gifts of the Holy Spirit (1 Cor. 12:7–10).

- The *pastor* leads the sheep through the gate of feeding and caring for the flock, protecting them from danger.

- The *teacher* opens the gate of spiritual understanding through the gate of biblical knowledge.

Now consider the important routines required at the temple to maintain the flow and operation of the ministry. These included cleaning the ashes from off the brass altar each morning from the previous burnt offerings, inspecting the wood that would be used on the brass altar for burning the sacrifices, keeping the three fires stirred on the altar, and inspecting the sheep for sacrifice, along with creating the ingredients for the holy incense.[5]

It is the job of the fivefold ministry to maintain the divine order of the house of God. The *apostle* clears the ashes off the altar by plowing into new areas and ministering in burnt-over fields, thereby reestablishing the message of the kingdom of God. The *prophet* is an inspector of the wood as he examines the spiritual condition of those in the church and in the ministry, exhorting and rebuking when needed. The *pastor* deals with the flock, the sheep, and leads them into the temple area, preparing them for ministry, including dealing with the need to offer themselves as a "living sacrifice" upon the brass altar of sacrifice. The *evangelist* is a bringer of good tidings, and evangelists are known for stirring up or relighting the fires that have gone out. Someone in the ministry must guard and maintain the fire on the altar, and anointed evangelists are capable of doing this. The *teacher* instructs the sheep how to approach God through prayer and worship, which is identified through the symbolism of the golden altar where incense that has been compounded at the apothecary is mixed with the coals of fire from the brass altar. The teacher knows how to build layer upon layer of biblical truth and present teaching in a clear fashion.

The Five Senses and the Five Pieces of Furniture

In my earlier ministry I heard extended teaching on faith that emphasized the importance of operating by *faith* and not by *sight* (2 Cor. 5:7). At that time there was a strong emphasis that believers should never lean at all upon any of their five senses, as faith was the opposite of *sense knowledge* and hindered *spiritual knowledge*. I was once told, "Don't pay any attention to your five senses." I later realized that without my God-given five senses, I would be considered physically dead! I do realize that we must set a guard on what we see and hear. There are spiritual *eyes* that must be opened to understand spiritual truths (Eph. 1:18) and spiritual *ears* that must be opened to hear what the Spirit is saying. When addressing the seven churches in Revelation, seven times Christ said, "He who has an ear, let him hear what the Spirit says to the churches" (Rev. 2:7, 11, 17, 29; 3:6, 13, 22).

Notice the words Paul wrote about the *senses* in Hebrews 5:14:

> But solid food belongs to those who are of full age, that is, those who by reason of use have their senses exercised to discern both good and evil.

The Amplified Bible explains the verse in this manner:

> But solid food is for full-grown men, for those whose senses and mental faculties are trained by practice to discriminate and distinguish between what is morally good and noble and what is evil and contrary either to divine or human law.

The fact is that all information and knowledge must first come though the five main senses of seeing, hearing, smelling, tasting, and touching before we can learn anything. We learn the danger of a hot stove through the sense of touching. We understand foods we like and dislike through the sense of taste. We select colognes, perfumes, and body lotions by the sense of smell. Through the sense of touch we are stimulated and experience feelings of affection and love. The light of the entire body is the eye (Matt. 6:22), and what we *see* impacts us mentally, emotionally, spiritually, and, for a man, even physically.

These five senses are actually gates where outside information enters and is passed to the mind and eventually into the human spirit. It is amazing to see how each human sense has a relation to the five different pieces of sacred furniture used in the daily ritual at the temple.

- The brass altar was the first piece of sacred furniture upon which three fires continually burned. It was a place where the sense of *smell* would have been impacted. The burning flesh of the sacrifice and the smoke from the altar would have filled the air the moment the worshiper came near the altar.

- The sense of *touch* would be the chief sense at the second piece of furniture, the brass laver, where the water was used for washing the feet and hands of the priest performing the ministry at the temple.

- When the priest entered the holy place, the menorah would be lit, providing light in this inner chamber, requiring perfect vision using the sense of *sight* to see the illumination from the seven-branched candlestick.

- The next furniture in line is the table of showbread, where twelve flesh loaves were baked each week and laid in rows on the golden table. The priests were permitted once a week to eat the bread, which was replenished every seventh day. A priest would require a sense of *taste* to experience the taste of the bread.

- And finally, the golden altar was the site of the offering in incense, where *hearing* was required to offer the verbal prayers up to God—the golden altar is the place of intercession and prayer.

The five senses were used each day when ministering at the temple and performing the daily rituals. The five senses can be used for either carnal or spiritual purposes. The word *carnal* is used in the New Testament English translation eleven times and refers to the flesh nature or literally the old Adamic nature that at times acts in an unregenerate manner. Both the carnal and spiritual man receive information from the five senses; thus they were given by the Lord to each human being for the purpose of learning.

We discover life as we grow by using our senses. The Bible teaches us to train our five physical senses to discern good and bad, right and wrong, and truth and lies, thereby training them to follow spiritual laws and truth. When your ears hear profanity, how do you react? If your eyes see pornography, how does your spirit react? If you are using your taste to experience illegal drugs and alcohol, how does your spirit react? If you are carnal, you will enjoy the small *flesh sins* that tickle your flesh nature. If you are spiritual, your senses will come into agreement with your spirit and will cut off the things feeding off your flesh.

In the Scriptures we read how the five senses should be used as gates through which the Holy Spirit can flow. When it comes to the ears and hearing, we read: "He who has an ear, let him hear what the Spirit says..." (Rev. 2:7). David mentioned the sense of taste when he wrote: "Taste and see that the LORD is good" (Ps. 34:8). Our spiritual eyes can be opened, and we can experience "eyes of your understanding" (Eph. 1:18). Even the sense of touch is significant, as the woman with the issue of blood said, "If only I may touch His garment, I shall be made well" (Matt. 9:21). Afterward she "felt in her body that she was healed" (Mark 5:29). Even Christ is "touched with the feeling of our infirmities" (Heb. 4:15, KJV). Paul wrote of the sense of smell in Philippians 4:18, speaking of an offering as "sweet-smelling." Thus our financial giving is viewed as a "sacrifice" in the New Testament. Just as the burning offering on the altar at the temple gave a sweet fragrance to the worshipers, our giving is a sweet fragrance to the Lord Himself. The human sense of smell can actually save your life. If you smell a gas leak in your house, you know there is danger. The sense of smell can figuratively be the spiritual ability of discerning danger or spiritual truths.

These five senses are often called "gates" to the soul and spirit. The senses must be exercised or trained in the fields of spiritual discernment and spiritual application. For example, tasting is connected to the tongue. The human tongue is divided into sections, with one section more sensitive to something sweet and another part sensitive to something sour. Even hot sauces are more intense on certain areas of the tongue. The tongue is also called "an unruly evil" (James 3:8) because it has caused strife, contentions, wars, and divisions when individuals speak hateful or negative words. The Holy Spirit, however, enters the human spirit and endues us with power from on high (Luke 24:49). Upon His entrance, the Holy Spirit imparts a special prayer language through which He takes rule over the unruly tongue, providing a new effective way to worship and pray "in the Spirit" (1 Cor. 14:2).

It is the Holy Spirit who also impacts the human eye gate by the method of spiritual illumination. The Greek word for "illumination" is the word *photizo*; it means, "to shed or give light, brighten up and to enlighten." The older method of taking pictures required a camera to have light-sensitive film. Once the shutter opened, the image was sealed on the film through the amount of light coming through the shutter. Too much light could cause overexposure, and too little light could cause underexposure. In either case, an otherwise good picture would be ruined. Overexposure to illumination can cause some people to become puffed up with pride (1 Cor. 8:1), while underexposure can cause a person to remain "in the dark" spiritually.

There are three important words related to how we receive the Scriptures: *inspiration, revelation,* and *illumination.* Inspiration is how God gave the Word to man: "All Scripture is given by inspiration of God, and is profitable..." (2 Tim. 3:16). The word *inspiration* in Greek is *theopneustos,* from *theos,* meaning, "God," and *pneo,* meaning, "to breathe." Thus, God breathed upon the prophets to write the Scriptures. *Revelation* is a word meaning, "to unveil something that is hid." The operation of spiritual revelation occurred when the prophets penned onto parchment the exact words God spoke, and it became the written Word of God. Finally, there is *illumination* by which we receive the light or the insight in our spirit of what has been written.[6] It takes illumination to form understanding.

All men have physical eyes, but the "eyes of understanding" are the ability to properly understand spiritual and biblical information that others miss or may not comprehend. In Christ's day, people continually misunderstood His messages and teachings. He once said, "Unless you eat the flesh of the Son of Man and drink His blood...," and the entire synagogue filled with people became offended, with many eventually ceasing from following Him except His original twelve disciples (John 6:53–69). He was speaking of communing with Him in the form of the Lord's Supper, the bread and the fruit of the vine, but the masses took His message wrong. On another occasion Christ said, "Destroy this temple, and in three days I will raise it up" (John 2:19). Christ's enemies used these words to accuse Christ of threatening to destroy the temple in Jerusalem, when He was actually speaking about His own body being the temple of the Lord and of His resurrection from the dead (vv. 19–22). Christ taught that these people were "blind leaders of the blind" (Matt. 15:14), and their eyes (spiritual perception) were closed (Matt. 13:15). Through the light-giving illumination of the Holy Spirit, your spiritual eye gate can be opened to receive impartation from the light giver.

The ear gate is how all information we hear is received and processed. Hearing is an odd thing: four different individuals can hear the same message preached by the same minister on the same night, and all four will hear a different emphasis or receive the same message four different ways. This is because some have true hearing ears, and others have natural ears that are spiritually closed. I have had conversations with a group of people in one room, and after I left the room, several in the meeting would discuss the conversation. I would hear things repeated that had been filtered through the perception of the hearer and not actually said by the speaker. This is why it is important to have not only *clean* ears but also *spiritual* ears that are in tune with God's truth.

Humans filter information through the filters of our upbringing and traditions. This is how we select the type of preaching, worship, and even the style of music we hear. Often we filter out what we should be hearing and hear what we should be filtering. The Pharisees were notorious for being the kings of the ear filter. They only heard what agreed with their doctrines and traditions, and they rejected anything that was in conflict with their upbringing. Jesus spoke in parables that at times were difficult to interpret. However, Christ gave the reason by saying, "Therefore I speak to them in parables, because seeing they do not see, and hearing they do not hear, nor do they understand" (Matt. 13:13). Truth can never change your spirit if your ears have shut the door.

The area of touch involves feeling. I grew up in a full-gospel denomination where there was great freedom in the Spirit and worship was encouraged and practiced. As time progressed, we were continually reminded that we are not to *live by feelings* but *by faith*. Good advice and very true. However, among some denominations, spiritual leaders refuse to allow, or they place certain restrictions upon, any form of emotional expression during a church service. Some believers are reminded from the pulpit, "God is not deaf and doesn't require hearing your noise." I once reminded a minister that neither is God nervous, and holy noise has never frightened Him!

The Holy Spirit is not just an invisible force of supernatural energy, a cloud, a fire, or a fog (Exod. 13:22). He is a person, identified with the personal pronoun He (John 16:13), and His presence can be felt when He comes near. The sense of touch is significant for several reasons. If certain flesh sins were not *fun* or exciting, they would never attract sinners like a magnet to metal. Men and women become addicted to illegal drugs because of the feeling (the high) they get from some counterfeit chemical. Drunks can act like fools one night, and then the next morning not remember how dumb they were acting the night before. They act that way because they thrive on feelings. Actually, they are fooled by a feeling. They remind me of Isaac, whose eyes were dim and he "believed" his hands feeling the hairy arms of Jacob, thinking he was Esau. He was *fooled by a feeling*. (See Genesis 27:1–29.) The adversary is the master of deception; he is capable of using your feelings to get you high and then dropping you low!

The Holy Spirit uses the five gates of the human temple, or five senses, to help us discern good from evil and to experience the presence of the Lord in our lives. All spiritual blessings originate and are activated within the eternal spirit of a man. However, the Lord uses the natural to reflect the spiritual. The results of experiencing His visitation impacts your mind and spirit, bringing "righteousness and peace and joy..." (Rom. 14:17). The five human senses are five gates leading into the innermost part of your spiritual man, the holy of holies of your physical temple (1 Cor. 3:16). Just as temple priests were watchmen for the gates of the temple, the Holy Spirit is the watchman for every gate and entrance through your physical senses.

Because the mind tends to operate more from the carnal and fleshly senses, allowing fear, unbelief, doubt, and skepticism toward spiritual things to build a mental wall between your prayer and your faith, it is important for a believer to learn to cast down any mental picture (imaginations) that would exalt itself against the spiritual knowledge gained through the inspiration and illumination of the Holy Spirit (2 Cor. 10:5). In Paul's words, we must, "Cast down imaginations" (KJV). The phrase "casting down" means, "to violently lower something to the point of demolishing it." It is an aggressive word that indicates a person is taking charge of his or her thought life and seizing any invading opponent that would disrupt the righteousness, peace, or joy he or she is enjoying! By stopping the thoughts from gaining a foothold, a person is *shutting the door* on the negative forces that often enter the gates of the five senses, creating spiritual hindrances. Thus, *YOU* become the watchman over your own temple.

Understanding how the Holy Spirit uses the five senses is the first step. Understanding the types of prayers you and the Holy Spirit can pray is the next step as we climb the ladder to the gate of heaven.

CHAPTER 3

Prayer Types and Secrets

*Therefore I say to you, whatever things
you ask when you pray, believe that you
receive them, and you will have them.*

—MARK 11:24

T HE SECRET TO answered prayer is a great mystery. After family members pray intently for someone who is sick to be healed, and that person passes away, believing family members often ask why. "Why didn't God answer our prayers?" "What did we do wrong?" "Is there something in my life that prevented it from coming to pass?" "Is there some hidden sin, and is God angry with me?" In this chapter I am going to attempt to tackle the greatest enigma that most Christians experiences at some point in their lives—the matter of unanswered prayer.

PRAYER FROM THE HEBRAIC PERSPECTIVE

In the Old Testament, the word *pray* is found in the English translation 245 times. The word *prayer* is identified in 83 references, and the past tense form, *prayed*, is found 31 Times. The word *praying* is used 6 times. Twice the word *prayers* is used. Thus the main words of *pray*, *prayer*, *prayers*, *prayed*, and *praying* are alluded to in 365 references. How unique, that there are 365 days in a solar year, and there are 365 times when the main forms of the word *pray* are alluded to! To me this indicates the importance that prayer should be a daily activity, and not just once a week on the Sabbath day.

The common Hebrew word translated in the English Bible for *prayer* is *tefilah*, which comes from the verb *pallel*, "to judge." When using the reflexive verb *lehitpallel* ("to pray"), it means, "to judge oneself." Thus, times of prayer are times of self-judgment and self-evaluation, as we cannot have confidence in our own prayers if we have condemnation in our own hearts (1 John 3:20–22). The idea of prayer involves "to beg, to beseech and to implore" the Almighty. Prayers are often centered around our needs, but prayer is a commandment from the Lord. The Jewish sage Maimonides taught that the reason for prayer was to "...establish firmly the true principle that G-d takes notice of our ways, that He can make them successful if we serve Him, or disastrous if we disobey Him; that the success and failure are not of chance or accident."[1] If we never prayed, how would we know it was God that sent us the blessing?

Some Jewish sages identified Jacob's ladder with angels going up and coming down with prayers. "G-d showed Jacob that prayer is like a ladder which connects the earth with the heaven, man with G-d. The meaningful words of prayer, the good resolutions which prayer brings forth, are transformed into angels which go up to G-d, and G-d sends down angels with blessings in return."[2] The imagery of the ladder is important, because the first step begins at the base, or the bottom of the ladder, and each step of intercession then ascends upward toward God.

If the ladder is a picture of our prayer life, then we must begin with the basics of understanding prayer as a communication between man and God. If you were raised in a Christian family, your parents taught you the basics of prayer at an early age. You prayed over meals, "God bless this food..." You were instructed how to pray before you went to bed, "Now I lay me down to sleep..." However, as you grew physically, you also grew spiritually, and spiritual maturity moved you up the ladder as you discovered the various types of prayers and how to speak to God using your words. As your knowledge became mixed with your spiritual experience, you should have eventually moved from a self-taught ritual to a self-motivated routine of worshiping and praying. Each type of prayer is a rung on the ladder, moving us upward.

THE TYPES OF PRAYER

Many believers say that all prayer is the same. This is like saying all miracles are the same. They are not. There are healing miracles, creative miracles (turning water to wine, for example; John 2:3–9), miracles dealing with nature (calming storms on Galilee; Mark 4:37–41), and miracles that defy nature (the sun standing still; Josh. 10:13). There is the example of Christ walking on the water in Matthew 14:25–26. The resurrection of Lazarus was a miracle defeating death, a *rung* at a much higher level on the ladder of miracles (John 11).

Prayer involves words, but not all prayers are the same. Our example is taken from the golden altar, which was positioned before the veil in the tabernacle and the temple (Exod. 40:26–27). One of the rituals of the priest was to enter into the holy place and mingle two fistfuls of holy incense with the coals from the brass altar, burning the incense in a golden bowl that fit in the golden altar situated before the veil. This daily ritual represented the prayers of the high priest, the Levites (priests), and the Israelites going up from the holy place to the heavenly temple (Ps. 141:2).

I am friends with several rabbis at the Temple Institute in Jerusalem, a Jewish organization researching the history of the Jewish temples, and have visited there. The institute used Jewish artisans to re-create the sacred vessels from the past for possible use in the third temple. On display at the institute are the different spices that were used in the compound mixture for the priest to burn on the golden altar.

Incense in the temple was made from eleven different ingredients, four of which are mentioned in the Bible (Exod. 30:34). The first is *stacte,* a fragrant sap gum from a tree on Mount Gilead. Some suggest this may have been myrrh. Next is *onycha,* which may have been some form of shellfish taken from the depths of the Red Sea. It was rare and costly. The third was *galbanum* and was derived from a sap or gum that came from a broken shrub in the highlands of Syria. It had a disagreeable odor and was used to drive away insects and reptiles.

Fourth was *frankincense*, which was a sap that flowed from a particular tree pierced at night.[3] The Institute says that salt was added to preserve the quality of the spices. The other seven ingredients have been passed down by oral tradition in the Talmud and the Siddur. The eleven spices used are shown in the table below:

The English Word	The Hebrew Word
Balsam	*Ha'tzri*
Onycha	*Ha'tziporen*
Galbanum	*Ha'chelbenah*
Frankincense	*Ha'levonah*
Myrrh	*Mor*
Cassia	*Ketziyah*
Spikenard	*Shibolet nerd*
Saffron	*Kharkom*
Costus	*Ha'kosht*
Aromatic bark	*K'lufah*
Cinnamon	*Kinnamon*

As Psalm 141:2 teaches, our prayers come up before God as incense. These eleven different ingredients are all distinct and separate, yet they merge into one substance called incense. Just as there are eleven different individual types of spices and ingredients in the temple incense, the New Testament identifies at least eleven different types of prayers.

Type of Prayer	Reference
Prayer of confession of sin	1 John 1:9
Prayer of confessing our faults	James 5:16
Prayer of agreement	Matthew 18:19
Prayer of faith for the sick	James 5:15
Prayer of binding	Matthew 16:19
Prayer of loosing	Matthew 16:19
Praying in the Spirit	Ephesians 6:18
Praying in the Spirit with understanding	1 Corinthians 14:15
Prayer of thanksgiving	Philippians 4:6
Prayer of intercession	1 Timothy 2:1
Prayer for general supplication	Philippians 4:6

THE SILVER CHALICE FOR THE INCENSE

In Revelation 5:8, the prayers of the saints are stored in golden vials or bowls. This imagery was understood by the Jewish reader, who knew of the procedure used by the priest when burning incense on the golden altar at the temple. We read:

> He whose lot it was to burn incense took a vessel containing the quantity of three caps, in the midst of which there was a censer full and heaped up with incense; over which there was a cover.[4]

At the Temple Institute in Jerusalem there is a beautiful silver chalice that was re-created from the Jewish traditions handed down for generations. The chalice has a circular base and at the top has a lid that opens and closes. When touring the institute, I observed a small silver ring connected to the top that is used to open and close the cover. The student demonstrating the use of the chalice made two significant points. First, when the selected priest was preparing to enter the holy place, he placed two fistfuls of incense into the chalice. He then took his *pinky finger* and began striking the silver ring against the top cap, making the sound of a dull bell. He then showed our group a silver tray in which the chalice was set to prevent any of the incense from falling on the floor.

When I questioned him as to why the *noise* was made, he replied, "You never enter a person's house without knocking on the door or ringing the doorbell. Likewise the priest could not enter God's house without making a holy noise, letting the Lord know he was coming into His presence." This was significant when considering that prayers and worship are both *words*, and your words are the *holy noise* that tells the Lord you are entering His presence.[5]

The second comment concerns the silver tray. Silver is identified as the metal representing redemption (Num. 3:47–49). The incense is holy and must be handled in a proper manner. For example, at the time of the Passover, the blood of the lamb was *not* placed on the floor of the house but on the top post and two side posts of the doorway. This was to prevent the Hebrews from trampling the redemption blood under their feet. In Hebrews, the backslider is pictured as one who tramples the Son of God underfoot (Heb. 10:29–30). According to the Temple Institute, it was important that the incense not fall to the ground and be trampled under the foot. The tray served to catch any small pieces, ensuring that all eleven spices burned on the golden altar. The significance is that God does not allow one word that you speak to fall to the ground. The words of holy men and women, who handle the Word of God and pray, always go up and never down.

One good example is Samuel, who heard the Lord speak to him as just a child, telling him about the wicked house of Eli and his vile sons, who served as priests. God was going to destroy Eli and his entire house. Eli requested that Samuel give him the Word of the Lord:

> And he said, "What is the word that the LORD spoke to you? Please do not hide it from me. God do so to you, and more also, if you hide anything from me of all the things that He said to you." Then Samuel told him everything, and hid nothing from him. And he said, "It is the LORD. Let Him do what seems good to Him." So Samuel grew, and the LORD was with him and let none of his words fall to the ground.
>
> —1 SAMUEL 3:17–19

In a short time Eli's two sons, Hophni and Phineas, were slain in a battle, and the ark of the covenant was seized by the Philistines (1 Sam. 4:10–11). Eli heard of his sons' deaths, and he fell backward off a wall and broke his neck (v. 18). Thus Samuel's words never "fell to the ground." What he spoke came to pass. All of Israel knew that Samuel was a prophet and that the Lord was with him. They knew that when he spoke, the Lord fulfilled it. The mark of true saints and people of the Most High God is that when we pray, God answers our prayers. This is how others who are outside of the faith know that our God is with us—when we seek God He is found, when we knock on the door He opens, and when we ask He gives us our petitions (Matt. 7:7).

THE AVTINAS AND THE SMOKE

According to Jewish writings, the method of preparing the incense was a secret guarded by a family called the Avtinas. This family, selected by the Sanhedrin, knew the exact measurements and mixture, and they also knew a family secret concerning a special herb used in the mixture called *ma'aleh ashan,* meaning, "that which causes smoke to rise." This mysterious herb is said to have caused the smoke of the incense to rise in a straight pillar or column off the golden altar. The family was given a chamber on the south side of the temple over the water gate, called the Chamber of the Avtinas.

The family was criticized for not sharing their secrets with others in the temple. When asked why, they responded, "Our fathers passed on a tradition to us, that one day the Holy Temple will be destroyed. We did not want to teach our secret, so that it does not fall into the wrong hands...then be used for idolatry."[6]

I have seen several artists' renditions of how the priest would stand over the golden altar once the incense was burning. He held his hands over the smoke in the form of the Hebrew letter *shin,* which is the twenty-first letter of the Hebrew alphabet; it was also the letter representing the name of God and the letter placed on every Jewish mezuzah, the object on the right side of the doorposts of a Jewish home and business. The priest's hands were formed similar to the letter *W* in the English language. The initial smoke of the incense would travel upward through his hands and into the atmosphere. The belief was that all of the prayers from God's covenant people went to the temple over the golden altar, and once the incense was burned and formed the smoke, the words went up into the heavenly realm toward the temple in heaven.

In what is classified as *extra-biblical literature,* the gate of heaven is mentioned as being linked with prayer. In 1 Enoch 9:10, prayers go to the gate of heaven. In 3 Baruch 11:1–9, it is written that the gates of heaven are opened to receive prayer, an idea also confirmed in Testament of Adam 1:10.[7]

In Revelation 5:8 (KJV), the golden vials have prayers of the saints described as "full of odours." The word *odours* means, "the fragrance burned by incense." In most churches, we no longer use incense when offering prayers, but in the sight of God the words of our prayers become the individual spices and herbs that form a sweet-smelling fragrance before God's throne. In the Old Testament we read where the sacrifices were a "sweet aroma" ("sweet savour," KJV) before the Lord (Exod. 29:18, 25). The incense is also called "sweet incense" (Exod. 25:6; 30:7; 31:11). "Sweet savour" (KJV) is found forty-two times in the Old Testament and usually refers to the smell of the smoke from the sacrifice or the incense once it is burned on the altars.

In Revelation 8 an angel is standing at the golden altar in heaven:

> Then another angel, having a golden censer, came and stood at the altar. And he was given much incense, that he should offer it with the prayers of all the saints upon the golden altar which was before the throne. And the smoke of the incense, with the prayers of the saints, ascended before God from the angel's hand.
>
> —Revelation 8:3–4

This angel has incense in a golden chalice—similar to the same imagery found with the priest at the earthly temple. The angel offers the incense with "the prayers of all the saints" upon the golden altar. If the twenty-four elders have golden vials full of odors, "which are the prayers of the saints" (Rev. 5:8), then this passage in Revelation 8 implies that the angel has opened the vials and is now offering all prayers at one time on the heavenly golden altar. Even the imagery found in the heavenly temple reflects the manner of how the words of our prayers ascend from where we are and make their way into the golden vials of the heavenly temple.

Amazing Prayer Stories

Many years ago, when I was preaching in Mentor, Ohio, a pastor who had gone on a forty-day fast, Pastor Hess, related this story to me. At the end of his fast, he was lying on the floor in his church when suddenly he felt the presence of God overcome him. When he opened his eyes, the Holy Spirit had taken him "in the Spirit" into the heavenly temple, where he was looking face down from heaven to the earth.

(See Revelation 1:10; 4:2; 17:3; 21:10.) He saw what appeared to be large arrows, like missiles, shooting off the earth toward the throne room of heaven. When he asked, "What are these?," he heard the Lord say, "These are the prayers and praises of My people." He began to see that there were some arrows that were very thin and short, and some that were large and very tall. He saw some go into the atmosphere and disintegrate, while the larger ones came through the crystal floor past his head and entered into the heavenly temple realms.

He told me that he just knew that the largest arrows were coming from the many Christians in the United States! However, when he saw the outline of the continents, he saw that the arrows falling back toward earth and not making it through the floor of heaven were coming from America. He saw that the greatest missiles were coming from the Soviet Union and areas where there was great persecution of saints on earth (this was before the fall of Communism). He said, "Lord, this is impossible, because these people are atheists and are not Christians."

He heard these words, "You don't know how many true believers are in those nations!" When he inquired why so much praise from America never made it to heaven, he heard the Lord say, "It is because in America too many worship Me with their lips, but their hearts are far from Me!" At that moment he turned over and saw a light of God's glory and observed the large arrows of praise entering the light and being received by the Lord Himself!

Another time when I was preaching in Nairobi, Kenya, at the Lighthouse Church, I listened as one of the ministers on staff shared an amazing event. He was taken to the hospital at the point of death. He was lying on a medical bed and being worked on by doctors and nurses. Suddenly he could hear the voices of his mother, his pastor, and others praying for him—and they were not in the room! He could hear them crying out for God to heal him and raise him up. He said it was the oddest thing, because he heard them praying all at once but could also hear them praying individually. He also saw an angel of the Lord at the foot of his bed. He was sharing this story after he was completely healed and had returned to the church to testify.[8]

My first impression was that if he could hear many, many voices of family and friends, praying all at once, and yet hear each voice and what each was saying, then the spirit world has the ability to see many things at once and hear many things all at once. Other people have testified to departing from their bodies and actually seeing the words of their families' prayers in the heavens and of hearing their voices as they prayed for them.

There are times when we pray simple prayers, and there are other occasions when we must intercede for an extended period in a deeper form of prayer or travail. As we learn how to communicate with God and gain personal experience through our prayer lives, we progress upward on that spiritual ladder, from prayers in the house of God to answers at the gate of heaven.

PRAYER IS WORDS
AND NOT JUST THOUGHTS

In the biblical narratives of both testaments, prayers consisted of words and not just thoughts. I say this because there are many people who speak of *silent prayers* in order to be politically correct and not offend someone of another faith. So they say, "Let us bow our heads for a moment of silence," or "Let us pray a silent prayer." In reality, we can bow our heads and meditate about someone or something, as the word *meditate* in Scripture means, "to muse, ponder or to think in deep thought about something or someone." (See Psalm 119:15.) Through God's Word we know that God knows "the thoughts and intents of the heart" (Heb. 4:12) and can read our thoughts, knowing what we have need of before we even ask (Matt. 6:8). This is important to understand if we are praying for a loved one who is in the hospital and cannot communicate with his or her mouth or speak with audible words.

When my grandfather John Bava was in his final hours at a hospital in Elkins, West Virginia, he was unable to physically move, open his eyes, or speak to us because he had experienced three strokes in his brain. However, based upon the heart monitor, his heart would beat faster every time we spoke or sang. Thus we believed he could still hear us. The doctor came into the room and said to us, "The very last sense that goes prior to death is the hearing. Get up close to his ear and speak into his ear, because he can still hear what you are saying." We placed a CD player with his favorite Gospel music beside his bed, where he could hear.

Allowing the sense of hearing to remain until the moment of death is a demonstration of God's mercy for the dying. Believers are able to speak to the person and invite that person to pray in the mind and repent of sins. Certainly God knows the thoughts and intents and will hear these thoughts just as He hears a person who is physically able to speak. This is clear when Jesus looked at the Pharisees; we read, "Jesus, knowing their thoughts..." (Matt. 9:4).

When my father, Fred Stone, was in his final days of life, he was in a special care facility. He had not eaten in two weeks and had not drunk anything in seven days, as he was unable to take in any liquids. However, his mind was still clear, and he could nod and open his eyes slightly. On one occasion we placed Dad's hands on my head and the head of youth pastor Mark Casto to release a blessing. I said, "Dad, you cannot speak but you can think, and I want you to ask God to bring an anointing on me and Mark, as he is leading the youth ministry of OCI" (Omega Center International). We knelt down, and both Mark and I could feel a strong anointing and even felt Dad's hands become quickened by the Spirit of the Lord. We believed this was a transfer just as in 2 Kings 2. Someone said, "A man in his condition cannot release any form of the anointing." I reminded that person that Elisha had such a level of the Spirit that after he died, they threw a dead man into the tomb on his bones, and the soldier was raised from the dead (2 Kings 13:21). There are times when those unable to speak can still pray in their minds, and God knows their thoughts.

We must understand that prayer is not silent for those who are *able to speak*. Meditating on the Lord and His Word can be done silently, but saying a silent prayer is like saying there is *silent worship*. Worship is an attitude of the heart, yet out of the "abundance of the heart the mouth speaks" (Matt. 12:34). If praise for God is in your heart, then the praise will manifest with words from out of your mouth. Praise always consists of *words that are spoken* and not just *thoughts that go unsaid.* Prayer consists of words from the heart that are spoken with the mouth. When a person is converted to Christ, or "born again" (John 3:3), the first process is to believe on the Lord Jesus Christ, which is followed by confession with the mouth (words):

> That if you confess with your mouth the Lord Jesus and believe in your heart that God has raised Him from the dead, you will be saved. For with the heart one believes unto righteousness, and with the mouth confession is made unto salvation.
>
> —Romans 10:9–10

We humans only see what occurs during the *act* of prayer on earth and not the *arrival* of the prayer in heaven or the *action* of the Lord upon hearing the sinner's petition. Yet, the moment a sinner confesses Christ and believes he or she is made clean and righteous through Christ's atoning work, the prayer is instantly received, immediately processed in the heavenly temple, and the *action* is twofold: the sinner is released from the guilt and condemnation of their sins (Rom. 8:1), and the record books in heaven are cleared of any wrong committed by the seeker while, at the same time, the repentant person's name is penned into the heavenly book called the Book of Life (Phil. 4:3; Rev. 3:5).

The prayer of repentance of sins is the first and most important prayer a person will ever pray. The act of forgiveness is immediate, as indicated with the thief on the cross who asked Christ, "Remember me when You come into your kingdom," and Christ replied, "Today you will be with Me in Paradise" (Luke 23:42–43). The swiftness of God's forgiveness is a witness of His mercy. Those in the throes of death, with only seconds to live, can receive a sudden and quiet acquittal of their lives of iniquity by a simple prayer and confession to God.

Once you have received Christ, it is important to understand the various types of prayers mentioned in this chapter and to target your request in the direction of your need by being specific. Prayers are often viewed as words that are simply spoken from the mouth and shot into the atmosphere like bullets from a gun. However, as the next chapter reveals, there are important spiritual laws linked to prayer that are established in the Scriptures.

Seven Spiritual Laws
for Answered Prayer

*There is therefore now no condemnation to those
who are in Christ Jesus, who do not walk according
to the flesh, but according to the Spirit. For
the law of the Spirit of life in Christ Jesus has
made me free from the law of sin and death.*

—ROMANS 8:1–2

BELIEVING IS THE first step, and confession seals the believing. Believing and confessing are spiritual laws that create a supernatural result for the believer and the confessor. Just as there are natural laws of gravity, aerodynamics, and life and death, there are also laws of the Spirit (Rom. 8:2), including spiritual guidelines for prayer.

1. You must ask.

Christ taught that you must ask: "Ask, and it will be given to you" (Luke 11:9). We use the word *ask* every day; for example: "May I *ask* you a question?" "Did you *ask* for directions?" "May I *ask* you a favor?" Asking involves saying something; you cannot ask with your mouth closed. While there are different forms of prayer, all prayer involves asking or petitioning God.

Asking comes in several forms. At times a person will pray a simple prayer, similar to a normal conversation between two people sitting across a table from each other. Asking in prayer can move to a level similar to when a person desperately cries out for help. Many of the people healed in Christ's ministry became so desperate for Christ's healing touch that they literally cried out with loud voices to gain His attention (Matt. 20:30; Mark 1:23; 9:24).

There is a spiritual principle throughout the Bible that God does nothing to meet a need for a believer on the earth until He is first asked. God spared Lot because Abraham petitioned God on Lot's behalf (Gen. 18). God spared Israel from complete destruction because Moses interceded (Exod. 32). King Hezekiah was given a death sentence. However, when he asked for God to extend his days, the Almighty added fifteen more years to his life (Isa. 38:5). When Peter was in prison with plans for his execution to take place following the Passover, the church did not cease from praying, and God released an angel of the Lord to free Peter (Acts 12). The first law of prayer is this: *praying means to ask*, or to form words from your heart and speak them as a petition and request before God.

2. You must ask in faith.

There are different levels of faith. There is the simple measure of faith. We read, "God has dealt to each one a measure of faith" (Rom. 12:3). The word *measure* is the Greek word *metron* and is a term used for measuring. In this case it refers to a *set measure* of faith.[1] One of the nine fruit of the Spirit is the fruit of faith (Gal. 5:22, KJV). Fruit will automatically grow on a healthy tree. The fruit of the Spirit, all nine, should grow and develop in the life of every believer as he or she matures in his or her walk with Christ. This type of faith should mature with a person's spiritual growth. There is also a *gift* of faith, listed as one of the nine gifts of the Holy Spirit (1 Cor. 12:7–10). This gift is a supernatural impartation of faith that is often combined with the gifts of healing and the working of miracles.

As a teenage evangelist, I recall spending days fasting and hours daily in prayer, beseeching for God to touch the people attending a revival in Alabama. It was a Saturday night, and I had preached a faith-building message on Christ's healing power. Suddenly I sensed a surge of faith that was so strong that at that moment I felt no unbelief or doubt anywhere in the sanctuary! I immediately began forming a prayer line to minister to the people's needs. In that one service, practically everyone was either healed or received a visible touch of the Holy Spirit. This is an example of the gift of faith in action.

When we pray, we must exercise the *measure of faith* we have been given. To seek the face of God through prayer does not require the "gift of faith," but simple childlike faith. Christ said that if we have faith "as a mustard seed," we can ask for a mountain to be moved, and it will be not only removed but also cast into the sea (Matt. 17:20; Mark 11:23). In the natural, it is impossible to remove a mountain from its foundation unless you have massive earth-moving equipment, dynamite, and a crew working continually. However, the *mountain* figuratively alludes to the difficulty or problem that has become a mountain in your life. Each person has a "measure." This is evident when preaching overseas in foreign nations where people have never heard the gospel. A simple message from the Bible will stir up the measure of faith that God has imparted like a small seed in every living person.

When you pray, you must ask, but you must ask *in faith*. When exercising faith, you maintain a sense of expectation. After praying, your faith begins to tell you God has heard your prayers, and He is working on your situation. Expectation helps maintain confidence in God's willingness and ability to move on your behalf.

3. You must ask in faith, nothing wavering.

The New Testament writer James spoke of asking God for wisdom:

> But let him ask in faith, with no doubting, for he who doubts is like a wave of the sea driven and tossed by the wind. For let not that man suppose that he will receive anything from the Lord; he is a double-minded man, unstable in all his ways.
>
> —JAMES 1:6–8

The King James Version of verse 6 reads, "...Let him ask in faith, nothing wavering." There are two different Greek words translated as "wavering." One is found in Hebrews 10:23, where we are told to "hold fast the profession of our faith without wavering" (KJV), which means "without blending or mixing." The word in James means ask in faith and *do not withdraw* from your belief and do not *stagger* or doubt.[2]

Wavering would be if you said in the morning, "I believe God will do it," and before the sun was setting, you are saying, "It just looks like nothing is going to happen!" For example, a father brought his epileptic son to Christ's disciples, requesting them to expel the spirit from the lad. The disciples prayed, and nothing happened. Later Christ showed up, prayed, and the child was delivered. Christ told the dad that if he believed, all things were possible. The father replied, "I believe; help my unbelief" (Mark 9:17–24). This statement sounds like a contradiction: "I believe; help my unbelief." A fountain cannot produce both bitter and sweet water, and a tree cannot grow both sweet and bitter fruit (James 3:11–12).

The father had faith when he brought his sick child to the disciples for deliverance. When their prayers failed, the father was discouraged. This is why he said, "Help my unbelief." The father did not turn around and take the little fellow home in discouragement. He may have wavered because of the failure of the disciples to bring deliverance, but he continued to believe in the power of Christ and did see his son set free. If you believe today, then believe tomorrow, and continue to believe in the days ahead. This is "holding fast your confession." In fact, the word *believe* does not indicate just a one-time moment of faith. Believing is a continual act, not a one-time event!

4. You must be in full agreement with another.

> Again I say to you that if two of you agree on earth concerning anything that they ask, it will be done for them by My Father in heaven. For where two or three are gathered together in My name, I am there in the midst of them.
>
> —Matthew 18:19–20

I love the word *agree*. In Greek it is the word *sumphoneo*, which is derived from two words: *sun*, meaning together, and *phone*, a sound. Together they mean, "to sound together or say the same thing or be in one accord." From this word we derive the English word *symphony*, such as a symphony orchestra. In an orchestra, it is important for the instruments to be in tune and for the musicians to have the correct music set before them. One player out of tune or playing the wrong notes will disrupt the unity of the others.

I have heard ministers receive prayer requests and then instruct their congregations to "agree in prayer" hundreds of times. People often pray for everything and everyone except the names that were given in the prayer requests moments earlier. That does not demonstrate a true prayer of agreement. If I were to say, "Let's pray to be able to buy this land for our new church," then everyone must be specific about what to pray for. Are we to ask the Lord to give us the land, or should we just ask for God's will to be done, or perhaps ask the Lord to block the deal? If three groups are praying three different ways, then they are not in agreement. Thus if the property sells to the church, a third of the group will say their prayer was answered. If the purchase is blocked, then another one-third of the people will thank God for hearing them. The other group will believe God's will was done no matter how it turns out!

At times when I ask a group of individuals to come into agreement, I will ask the people to not say anything, but to agree in their inner spirits with the words I am speaking to God. Or I will have them listen and say, "Amen," or "So be it," or "Let it be," so as to not speak varied words in all different directions. A prayer of agreement only requires two people. In the Torah, God required two or three witnesses to establish a crime (Deut. 17:6). By the agreement of two or three witnesses, every word is established, or settled (Deut. 19:15).

Prayer agreement must be more than agreeing with the mind or with words; it must be an agreement deep within your spirit—an assurance and unity that cannot be broken by outward circumstances that may appear to be working contrary to your prayers.

5. You must ask the Father in Jesus's name.

Under the first covenant, Hebrew men approached God in prayer by addressing Him as the "God of Abraham, Isaac, and Jacob" (Exod. 3:16; 6:3; 32:13; 33:1; 1 Chron. 29:18; 2 Chron. 30:6). These three names are the three patriarchs of the faith with whom God confirmed and reconfirmed His covenant. When praying in the name of these three men, it reminded God of His everlasting promise toward the seed of Abraham. When God prepared to destroy Israel in the wilderness and raise up a new nation through Moses, the prophet Moses reminded God of Abraham, Isaac, and Jacob and of His covenant—and God immediately relented (changed His mind) and spared Israel (Exod. 32:13–14).

Under the new covenant, we approach God through the name of Jesus Christ, because Christ initiated a new covenant through His death and resurrection:

> Whatever you ask in My name, that I will do, that the Father may be glorified in the Son. If you ask anything in My name, I will do it.
>
> —JOHN 14:13–14

> You did not choose Me, but I chose you and appointed you that you should go and bear fruit, and that your fruit should remain, that whatever you ask the Father in My name He may give you.
>
> —JOHN 15:16

> And in that day you will ask Me nothing. Most assuredly, I say to you, whatever you ask the Father in My name He will give you. Until now you have asked nothing in My name. Ask, and you will receive, that your joy may be full.
>
> —JOHN 16:23–24

Christ is the heavenly High Priest, ever living to make intercession for us (Heb. 7:22–25). He is today at the right hand of God. Normally, when the high priest presided over the ceremony on the Day of Atonement, after he completed his assigned duties he was seated. Christ is "seated" at God's right hand, indicating He completed the redemptive covenant (Heb. 1:3). However, when making atonement for Israel, the high priest must stand up to intercede and perform the Day of Atonement rituals. When Stephen looked up into heaven, he said, "I see the heavens opened, and the Son of man standing on the right hand of God" (Acts 7:56, KJV). When Stephen was being stoned, he asked God not to lay the sin of the men who were stoning him on them. Christ as the High Priest stood in the heavenly temple to make intercession as Stephen was requesting forgiveness for his murderers.

As we ascend the ladder of prayer, through our words we petition the Father in the name of Jesus and thereby gain legal authority to approach the gate of heaven where the throne of God sits. This is the same throne Daniel saw when he described God as the Ancient of Days, sitting on a fiery throne with burning wheels. The Almighty appeared in white garments with hair white like snow, and in this setting the "judgment was set" (Dan. 7:9–10, KJV). God's throne is more than a large holy chair. It is a seat of judgment where decisions are made, blessings released, and judgments applied.

When we use the name of Jesus in prayer, we give Christ the authority to present our petition at God's throne of decision. In return, the Father releases answers back to earth through angelic messengers, the movement and inspiration of the Holy Spirit, and by speaking through individuals who are willing to hearken to God's voice and assist you in areas of your life. The heavenly throne room is similar to an earthly court. God is the judge (Ps. 50:6). Jesus is the advocate or lawyer (1 John 2:1). There are twenty-four elders who serve as the jury (Rev. 4:4). Satan appears in the heavenly court as the "accuser of the brethren," or a prosecutor (Rev. 12:10). The primary purpose of the heavenly temple is to deal with the issue of the forgiveness of sins for those who believe upon the Lord. The same temple, however, is a throne of judgment in which life and death decisions are made for humanity.

In John 16:24, Christ gives the ultimate reason for the Father in heaven to hear and answer your petition: "that your joy may be full." Just as there are different levels of faith, there are also different levels of joy. There is the simple *joy of the Lord*, which every believer should experience (Neh. 8:10). This joy is a continual peace in knowing you will spend eternity with Christ. Then there is *great joy*. We read where a revival broke out in Samaria, bringing the entire city to Christ and causing great joy. Luke reported, "There was great joy in that city" (Acts 8:8). When the wise men saw the star in the east, indicating the child King's birth, they "rejoiced with *exceedingly great joy*" (Matt. 2:10, emphasis added). Finally, there is a level of joy when there is an overflow of God's presence called "*joy unspeakable* and full of glory" (1 Pet. 1:8, KJV, emphasis added). The Amplified says: "with inexpressive and glorious (triumphant, heavenly) joy." The greatest level of joy, however, is when you pray and see your prayers answered, especially when a loved one is converted to Christ! This is the "fullness of joy," as there is no greater joy than the salvation of a lost soul. Even the angels in heaven will rejoice with joy over one sinner who repents (Luke 15:10).

6. You must hold fast your confession.

> Let us hold fast the confession of our hope without wavering, for He who promised is faithful.
> —HEBREWS 10:23

The Greek word for the phrase "hold fast" is *katecho*, which is a compound of the two words *kata* and *echo*. The first word, *kata*, implies, "something that comes down hard, heavy and overpowering," indicating that the force comes in with an overwhelming influence to subdue and conquer. The second word, *echo*, means, "I have," and denotes possession. The word paints the imagery of a person searching a long time for something or someone, then when suddenly finding it, they seize hold of it without letting go. The Greek word means, "to hold on to something tightly."[3]

The King James Bible uses the word *profession*, and other translations use the word *confession*. The Greek word here is *homologia*, from two words: *homou*, meaning, "the same kind," and *logos*, the Greek word for "words." It means to speak and say the same words. In this case, it would mean to speak and confess the Word of God, and by speaking it, you are coming into agreement with God.

As a teenage minister, I recall a strong teaching that emerged in the late 1970s and early 1980s explaining the importance of *confession*. After hearing many messages on the subject and watching people at times confessing some of the most unusual and selfish things, I realized some were turning a spiritual principle into a religious ritual.

An individual can speak and confess all he wishes until he loses his voice, but if faith and agreement are not in his heart, and the promise has no biblical basis, the sounds emitting from his voice are simply flat words without power.

There is a deeper reason why a person must "hold fast the confession …without wavering." It has to do with time—light travel. Understand that distance does not matter in prayer. If God lives two blocks down the road or lives, as He does, billions of light-years from you, it does not matter—distance has no meaning in the realm of spirits. One reason is because spirit beings operate in a different realm than human beings. They not only travel at the speed of light (Ezek. 1:13–14), which is more than 186,000 miles per second, but spirits also can transport themselves at the speed of thought, which enables them to move from the top of heaven's ladder to earth and back to the gate of heaven within seconds of time.

I once heard an explanation of why *distance* has no bearing on prayer. The speaker explained, "Picture a long hollow tube stretching from your home to the center of the throne room in heaven, filled with marbles. There is a second tube twelve inches long that is also filled with marbles. If one person stood at the bottom of each tube, each person holding a marble in his hands, and on the count of three, each person pushed their single marble into their tube, what would happen at the top?"

I answered, "A marble would be pushed out at the top."

The man noted, "And both marbles would come out of the top *at the same time!*" I knew his point. Distance did not matter, because God can hear the moment we open our mouth from anywhere on the planet—at the same moment and time.

There is also an interesting concept based upon the theory of how fast light travels through the universe. Light travels through the vacuum of space at 186,282 miles per second. At this speed, light can travel at approximately 700 million miles per hour. At this speed it would take 100,000 years to travel across the Milky Way. Let me explain these distances using a single sheet of paper. The thickness of one piece of paper represents the distance from the earth to the sun, which is approximately 93 million miles. From the earth to the nearest star, the stack of paper would be 71 feet high. To cover the diameter of the Milky Way, the stack would be 310 miles high. To reach the edge of the known universe, the stack would increase to 1 million miles high.[4]

We know that the dwelling place of God—the gate of heaven, the entrance of the heavenly temple—is far beyond the visible edge of our galaxy. The distance is so far that the region is identified by Paul as the "third heaven" (2 Cor. 12:1–4). When we compare the distance from earth to heaven and the words of our prayers, it almost seems ludicrous to the natural mind that one person can open his or her mouth and pray on earth, and at the same time the words can be heard in a far-flung galaxy called heaven. What an amazing enigma that God, who is billions of light-years away, can hear the slightest cry of one of His earthly children!

One of the explanations of how God can hear your words in an instant may be explained with what is known as "time-light mysteries," or, as some call it, "Time Dilation Theories." The theory suggests that if an object were to travel through space while gradually increasing its speed to the speed of light, then time would slow down as the speed increased. The illustration used is that of a man in a spacecraft who set out to travel into the deepest part of the universe, traveling at the speed of light. To reach his first destination, Alpha Centauri, the closest star from earth, it would take three years and six months going from earth to the star. However on earth, ten years would have passed. If the spacecraft moved from earth to the center of the Milky Way, then the journey would take twenty-one years; however, on earth fifty thousand years would have transpired! If the same man traveling at the speed of light traveled to the Andromeda Galaxy (earth's nearest galaxy), the trip would take twenty-eight years on the spacecraft, but more than two million years will have passed on earth.[5]

It has also been speculated that if a thirty-year-old man could remove himself to a planet thirty light-years away and then point a telescope back to earth, he could see himself being born.[6]

I use this illustration to demonstrate the distances from earth to the far-flung galaxy when traveling from earth at the speed of light. However, this theory also brings up an interesting possibility as it relates to the importance of your verbal confession after you have prayed. Consider this: Angels have access to heaven and earth and can travel these astronomical distances faster than the speed of light. What could be faster than the speed of light? Answer: the speed of thought. This would indicate that angelic beings are able to think of the geographical regions they desire to travel to, and as quickly as they think of the region, they are transported from one location to another. This is the only *logical* explanation of spirit travel, as angels can be in heaven one moment and then manifest on earth within a moment's time.

Prayer consists of words, but the words are also a dynamic spiritual force. Jesus said, "The words that I speak to you are spirit, and they are life" (John 6:63). How can words be "spirit"? A spirit being is invisible to the natural eye, and words can be heard but are not seen (invisible) to the natural eye. A spirit can travel at the speed of thought, and your words travel from earth to heaven at the speed of thought. A spirit can be felt when its presence is near you, and your words have the power to create a negative or positive presence. Just as angelic spirits travel from the bottom of the ladder to the top of the ladder from earth to heaven, as quickly as thoughts, your words actually travel with such speed and distances.

Maintaining your confession

Picture yourself on earth praying a prayer of faith to receive a needed answer from the Lord. You have petitioned the Father in heaven, and you are thanking Him for hearing your prayer. For the next several weeks you begin to speak faith words indicating your expectation of a possible, sudden visitation from God bringing a much-needed answer to prayer. However, the weeks turn to months, and the months turn into a year.

After a year passes by, your faith begins wavering, and your confession changes. You begin to say, "God is not hearing me. I am weary of waiting and tired of believing...I am going to give up..."

In your earthly time dimension, twelve months have passed. But how has God perceived this twelve months that has passed? Scripture indicates that one day with the Lord is as a thousand years, and a thousand years is as one day (Ps. 90:4; 2 Pet. 3:8). One thousand *solar years* consist of about 365,250 days. Those days translated to hours is 8,766,000 hours. That's a lot of time. Yet to God, this time can be equal to one day in the eternal dimension. Theoretically, if you pray a strong prayer of faith and believe for an answer consistently, but experience no answer, you must continue to hold on to your confession, nothing wavering (Heb. 10:23). If in twelve months you change your confession to one of unbelief, in the eternal realm it is possible that the Lord heard your prayer and then heard your words of unbelief within the same time! He heard, "Thank You for answering"..."I don't know what You are doing"..."Are You doing anything about what I am praying?" The unbelief of your words will always cancel out the answer and blessing to your intercessions. Because God exists in the past, present, and future, time for God does not have the significance that it does for us in the earth realm. We must be consistent in believing and be steadfast in our verbal agreement with what we have prayed.

7. You must agree in line with the will of God.

There are three types of *wills* on the earth. There is the *will of God*, the *will of Satan*, and the *will of man*. The will of God is revealed in the Word of God. The ultimate will of God is that none perish but that all come to God through repentance (2 Pet. 3:9). The will of Satan is "to steal, and to kill, and to destroy" (John 10:10) and to prevent a person from turning to God though repentance. The will of man includes the mental and spiritual ability to choose between eternal life and eternal punishment, to follow or reject the truth, and to choose between good and evil. God never forces His will upon an individual, but He provides each person the option of accepting Him by submitting his or her will to God by believing, or rejecting Him by choosing to not believe.

> He who believes in the Son has everlasting life; and he who
> does not believe the Son shall not see life, but the wrath of God
> abides on him.
>
> —JOHN 3:36

Satan does not play by the same rules and will use temptation, trials, and other circumstances as mental and spiritual pressures build to cause a person to make wrong choices.

It is important to understand that when the human will shifts, so does the spirit world. Once a sinner chooses to repent, the adversary is rendered powerless to prevent the transformation (Rom. 8:35–39). The power of the will was present when Christ was in Gethsemane prior to His physical scourging and crucifixion. He prayed to the Father that if it was possible, to let the cup (of suffering) pass from Him. Then Christ said, "Nevertheless not My will, but Yours, be done" (Luke 22:42). Because He submitted to the will of the Father, Satan was rendered powerless in His life, as we read in John 14:30: "The prince of this world is coming. He has no hold on me, but the world must learn...that I do exactly what my Father has commanded me" (NIV). Once Christ submitted His will to the Father's purposes, the sins of mankind were placed upon Him (2 Cor. 5:21), and He entered a time of agony where His sweat became great drops of blood (Luke 22:44). The spirit world shifted, and according to Paul, God spared Christ from death in the garden. Hebrews 5:7–8 describes how this agony almost led to Christ's death:

> Who, in the days of His flesh, when He had offered up prayers
> and supplications, with vehement cries and tears to Him who
> was able to save Him from death, and was heard because of His
> godly fear, though He was a Son, yet He learned obedience by
> the things which He suffered.

It was the will of God for Christ to receive a physical scourging in order to initiate the provision of physical healing through Christ's atonement (Isa. 53:5; 1 Pet. 2:24). The will of God was manifested at Christ's crucifixion for the redemption of mankind (John 3:16). God has provided a promise of sanctification in His written will, the Word

(1 Thess. 4:3), and included in His will is that you prosper (3 John 2). God sent another Comforter for you, the Holy Spirit—a promise for you, your children, and all who are afar off (Acts 2:39). The greatest promise in His will is the promise of eternal life for all who will receive Christ (John 10:28).

Our prayers must be in agreement with the will of the Heavenly Father:

> Now this is the confidence that we have in Him, that if we ask anything according to His will, He hears us. And if we know that He hears us, whatever we ask, we know that we have the petitions that we have asked of Him.
>
> —1 JOHN 5:14–15

When we begin understanding these basic laws of the Spirit concerning prayer, we can all pray with more faith, confidence, and expectation. The power of expectation cannot be underestimated. Often we minimize our expectations as we fear disappointments—"What if it doesn't happen the way I have prayed?" However, throughout the four Gospels those who received miracles were those filled with expectation when Jesus was passing by. In Nazareth, His hometown, the people's expectations were low, because He grew up there. Thus Christ could do no "mighty works" because of their unbelief (Matt. 13:58).

Christ taught:

> Therefore I say to you, whatever things you ask when you pray, believe that you receive them, and you will have them.
>
> —MARK 11:24

We must believe we have received when we are praying. There must be a feeling of expectancy. In 1981 I preached a five-week revival in Pulaski, Virginia. One afternoon, two hours before service, I was praying in the sanctuary and saw a woman sitting near the front on the left side. I approached her and noticed her hair was shaved and one of her eyelids was closed. She had a scar on the side of her head—the same side as her closed eyelid. I learned that her name was Mrs. Thacker and that she had undergone surgery for a brain tumor in Roanoke, Virginia. The doctor used a laser to remove the tumor and in the process had severed her optic nerve; thus she was blind in her right eye. She said, "I need God to heal me, and I'm here to receive a healing from Him."

Immediately I felt faith strike my spirit. I told her to sit on the second row in front of the pulpit. She did, and that night I preached a faith message. During the altar service, she came to the platform assisted by two godly women from the church, Bea Ogle and Birdie Viars. I remember placing both of my thumbs over both her eyes and praying. I could sense high expectations coming from her. After prayer she said, "I feel something odd moving in my eye where the nerve was severed. It feels like small insects moving in the eyeball!" I knew something was occurring. I asked the two women to help her walk the aisle of the church and begin praising God for her healing. Within about thirty minutes, as I was on the platform, I felt a set of hands grab me around the chest. It stunned me for a moment, and I turned to see Mrs. Thacker lifting her *bad* eyelid with her thumb and saying, "I can see outlines of things...I can see...some color..." Then she yelled, "Oh, my, I can see you!" Not only was she healed, but she remained healed until her death. Her son, Jackie Thacker, is a minister, and he always comments on how that moment changed his mother's life!

I remember the expectation I felt that something good was going to happen that night. I recall her excitement and her anticipation to receive prayer.

My father came out of the great revivals in the 1940s, which had a healing emphasis. One of the often overlooked keys to the revival was the spirit of expectation that built in the hearts of the people. They believed that if they could get to the big tent and be prayed for, the Lord would touch them. This is the same expectation the woman with the issue of blood had, who said to herself, "If only I may touch His [Christ's] garment, I shall be made well" (Matt. 9:21).

The spiritual principles and laws of prayer listed above are keys to receiving answers to prayer. However, if you pray without the anticipation that the answer is coming, you may lose the joy of expectation, which is the breeding ground for the answer you are waiting for!

These spiritual laws and principles of prayer are not complicated; they are simple enough for a child to understand. There has never been any question concerning answered prayer, but there is an enigma concerning why at times when believers pray it seems the heavens are closed. Sometimes no answer manifests for weeks, months, or years. This mystery must be discussed and understood.

CHAPTER 5

Who Closed the Heavens
Over My Head?

*And thy heaven that is over thy head shall be
brass, and the earth that is under thee shall be
iron. The Lord shall make the rain of thy land
powder and dust: from heaven shall it come
down upon thee, until thou be destroyed.*

—DEUTERONOMY 28:23–24, KJV

GOD'S BLESSINGS FLOW from heaven to earth like rain falling
from the clouds. When the children of Israel walked in obedience, they received "rain in due season" (Lev. 26:4, KJV).
If their actions were contrary to God's commandments and statutes,
the Almighty would cause the heaven over their heads to "be brass,"
a term indicating not one drop of water would fall from the sky. This
punishment of dry heavens transpired in the days of Ahab, because
the wicked king and his wife worshiped Baal and began slaying the
true prophets (1 Kings 17:1). God closed the heavens over Israel, and
a forty-two-month drought struck the nation (2 Kings 18; Luke 4:25).
For many years old-time ministers used the phrase "The heavens have
turned to brass" figuratively when saying that the heavens seemed
closed to the blessings of God. Many believers think this could not
occur; however, there are types of actions that can hinder our prayers

from being received and being answered. Thus, the gate at the top of the ladder can be opened or closed.

In the parable of the ten virgins, all ten were asleep (Matt. 25:5) when the call of the bridegroom's arrival was heard. Five had additional oil and five did not (vv. 3–4). The five wise virgins with oil trimmed their lamps and were able to travel at midnight to the wedding supper. The five foolish had to go buy oil, which is odd in the parable, as no shop or store would be open at midnight. The only place to buy oil would be from neighbors sleeping at that time who would need to be awakened by the five foolish virgins. When the five foolish virgins finally arrived at the wedding, the "door was shut" (v. 10).

God controls the doors—the *door* of heaven (Rev. 4:1), the opening and closing of the *windows* of heaven (Mal. 3:10), and the *gate* of heaven (Gen. 28:17), as well as the access of angels going up and down the ladder (v. 12). This is evident when Christ addressed the faithful church at Philadelphia in Revelation 3:8:

> I know your works. See, I have set before you an open door, and no one can shut it; for you have a little strength, have kept My word, and have not denied My name.

The faithfulness of this church to maintain its spiritual strength, keep the Word of God, and confess the name of Christ inspired Christ to open a door of opportunity and blessing for the believers. Notice that what God opens, no man can shut. However, the opposite is also true: what God closes, no man can open. At times Christ is on the outside of our lives or situations trying to get inside to commune with us, but we have closed Him out. He told the lukewarm church at Laodicea: "Behold, I stand at the door and knock. If anyone hears My voice and opens the door, I will come in to him and dine with him, and he with Me" (Rev. 3:20). This is the door of our heart, which must be entered through the gates of our spiritual senses, using open spiritual ears and open spiritual eyes to hear the knock and answer the call.

To open or close any door requires a key. The key can lock and unlock the door, inviting someone in or keeping someone out. The Lord said He opened a door that none could close and informed the church He had the "key of the house of David." This expression in Isaiah 22:22 is a reference to the Messiah: "The key of the house of David I will lay on his shoulder; so he shall open, and no one shall shut; and he shall shut, and no one shall open." This alludes to the spiritual authority that has been given to Christ. All authority is given to Him, both in heaven and in earth (Matt. 28:18).

The expression "God opening doors" has been understood for generations and is often repeated when something good happens for us. We will comment to other believers: "God opened the door for this new job." "God opened the door for me to take a new church." "God has opened a new opportunity for me to walk through." "God opened the door for me to witness to this person." When we pray, we should ask the Lord for "open doors," as these doors will lead us into the deeper measure of God's will for us.

When it appears a door is closed, after we have prayed for an opening, the tendency is to question God as to why our prayer was not answered. You may say, "I prayed to get that job, and someone else did instead. God did not answer my prayer!" Or you say, "I prayed to be able to do thus and so, and God didn't answer." He *did* answer, but not in the manner you expected. He answered by shutting the door! This may seem like a strong statement considering that you may have believed that door could possibly have been a great blessing to you by increasing your income, getting you a larger house, or even bringing you temporary joy. However, you must believe that:

> The steps of a good man are ordered by the LORD,
> And He delights in his way.
> Though he fall, he shall not be utterly cast down;
> For the LORD upholds him with His hand.
>
> —PSALM 37:23–24

The Hebrew word for "ordered" is *kuwn*; it means, "to erect something and make it stand up." The word implies that you are being *set up* with every step you take. This setup is, of course, contingent upon you seeking the will of God and praying, "Your will be done on earth as it is in heaven" (Matt. 6:10).

For example, one person once said he had the opportunity to move to another state and double his income. The positive result would be more money for him and his family. The negative result would be that they would have to leave the church their children loved and leave their best friends. After prayer, they rejected the move. They later learned that the job, which would have taken them out of state, would have eventually shut down, meaning they would have lost everything had they moved. Remember: what looks good is not always God's will.

Years ago a mother wrote me about praying that her son would be accepted to a certain university. It was family pride that drove the desire for him to attend that school. He was rejected, and she became angry at God, reminding Him that she had paid tithes and gone to church, and still He had let her down.

I wrote her and said, "So God doesn't know what He's doing? What if the woman your son is to marry was not at *your* chosen school but at the one he is now going to? Is it not possible that the Lord may desire him to go to the other school in order to be in *HIS* will and not yours?" We must learn to trust God in prayer and to understand that just because it appears the heavens are brass and we are not getting what we *want* it is by no means a signal of defeat.

WHEN GOD SAYS NO!

There are two primary examples in the Scriptures of men who prayed specific prayers and the Lord replied that He was not going to do what they were asking. The first example was Moses, whose sister, Miriam, had mocked the wife Moses had married, and a critical spirit had overcome her. The Lord knew that verbal criticism was like leaven in bread, and it would spread. Moses was God's anointed prophet, and to speak against this humble servant was to speak against God. The Lord struck Miriam with leprosy. Moses cried out to the Lord, "Please heal her, O God" (Num. 12:13). Remember, this is the man who could raise his rod and open the Red Sea, speak and God would send plagues, and a man God knew face-to-face (Exod. 33:11). Yet when he cried out for a healing, God said no! God required Miriam to spend seven days shut outside the camp by herself (Num. 12:15).

The second case is recorded in 2 Samuel 12. David committed adultery, and Bathsheba, the wife of Uriah, became pregnant. David attempted to cover up the sin and eventually sent Uriah into battle to be killed in order to marry his wife. As the birth drew near, the Lord sent Nathan the prophet to expose David and to inform him the child would die. After the birth, the infant became sick, and David spent seven days in fasting and prayer, interceding for God's mercy to heal his little son. The heavens became *brass*, and the child died. The Lord allowed this as an act of judgment on David for killing an innocent man and taking his wife. Nathan the prophet also had informed David that although he would not die because of the sin, but because he had caused people to blaspheme God's name, the sword of the Lord would never depart from his house (v. 10). David lost four sons because of this word of judgment.

In the first case, the Lord said no to Moses for several reasons, but the primary one, I believe, was to teach Miriam how to control her tongue and not speak evil against God's prophet. In David's case, the child was already under a death sentence before it was born, and thus the death was the fulfillment of God's chastisement to David (2 Sam. 12:14). Notice that Moses did not blame God or become angry, and after the death of David's son, the king arose from the dust, washed himself, worshiped God, and ate a meal (v. 20). David said he could not bring the infant back from the dead, but one day he would go to where the infant was—speaking of paradise, the home of the righteous departed souls (v. 23; 2 Cor. 12:1–4).

Notice, however, the outcome of each situation. Moses was told that God would not heal Miriam; however, she was healed seven days later after setting outside the camp and, no doubt, learning the importance of guarding her words (Num. 12:15). David could not raise his departed son from the grave, but God in His mercy gave David and Bathsheba another son named Solomon, meaning, "beloved of God," and this son became the king of Israel after David's death (2 Sam. 12:24; 1 Kings 1:43).

God said no, but He still worked His plan. There will be times when we pray and it will seem that God is not moving in the direction we are asking. This is often because God works in three dimensions and we humans work in one. Our earthly realm operates only in the now. We cannot undo the past, we cannot see or predict events for the future, but we can only live for the moment. We may plan for the future, but often what we plan is not where things end up. Every day I plan for 15 percent of my day to be taken up with the unexpected events. The future is uncertain in the sense we can plan, we can prepare, but we can't go out into the future, alter it, and return to the now with the assurance of knowing exactly what will occur. However, God has been in ages *past*, lives in the *now*, and knows the *future*. Let me say again, the Lord knows the future—all of it. This is how He calls things that do not exist as though they did (Rom. 4:17). Christ was called the "Lamb slain from the foundation of the world" (Rev. 13:8). This expression means He was ordained from the beginning to become the final offering for mankind (Heb. 10:10). God planned the crucifixion and resurrection of Christ when He formed the world!

A "No" Is Just for "Now"

There are also times when God's no may not be a permanent no but means, "No, just for now." King David desired to build a house of God (temple) and amassed the spoils of war (gold and silver), actually preparing plans to construct a massive temple. Nathan the prophet came to David and told him to do all that was in his heart, for the Lord was with him—a word indicating to move forward with the building project (2 Sam. 7:3). Later that same night the Lord informed Nathan that David would *not* be the man to build God's house, but God would permit a son after David to fulfill the plan (vv. 4–29). This prediction came to pass with Solomon (2 Chron. 3).

David had previously pitched a tent on Mount Zion and hosted nonstop worship, even moving the ark of the covenant to Jerusalem (2 Sam. 6:12). This tent was called by scholars the *tabernacle of David* and was a continual place of singing and worship. The Book of Psalms is a songbook of words that were originally sung and not just read from a scroll. They were written under divine inspiration while priests and singers ministered at David's tabernacle in Jerusalem.

(See 1 Chronicles 15 and 16.) With a place like that and with such a desire to please and worship God, why would the Lord not permit David to build a permanent temple on the Temple Mount? In reality, David was already worshiping God in a tent on or near the holy mountain, so why the restriction from the temple?

The answer was that David was a man of war and a man of blood. His hands were filled with blood from being a warrior and a fighter. His worst moment was when he set up Uriah, the husband of Bathsheba, to be killed. Uriah was one of David's faithful mighty men and was loyal to the king. David shed the innocent blood of his faithful soldier and thus forfeited the right of being the builder of the temple (1 Chron. 28:3). However, the *NO of David* became the *YES of Solomon*, David's son. The name *Solomon* in Hebrew is *Shelomoh* and comes from the root word *shalom*, meaning "peace." Solomon was not a man of war but a king of peace, and his administration initiated peace in Israel for the first time in many generations. The Law of Moses taught that no iron tool should be used when building a stone altar (Deut. 27:5). Solomon followed this principle when precutting the stones at a rock quarry and bringing them to Jerusalem, so that no hammer, ax, or iron tool was heard (1 Kings 6:7). The metal of iron figuratively speaks of war and fighting, and the new temple was to be a house of peace and blessing. What David could not do, his son was enabled to do.

The point is that God prevented David from doing what he wished in his heart to do—build God a house. However, the dream of David was passed on to his son, and David's dream was eventually fulfilled.

Moses was unable to enter the Promised Land for his one act of disobedience of striking the rock twice when the Almighty instructed him to simply "speak to the rock" (Num. 20:8–11). The rock is a type of Christ, the true Rock (1 Cor. 10:4). The first striking of the rock, early in the Exodus, is a picture of Him who was stricken for us (Exod. 17:5–6; see also Isa. 53:4). But this second event was meant to be a symbol of the victory of the Resurrection. In his anger, by striking the rock instead of speaking to it, Moses was saying that Christ's sacrifice had not been enough; something more was needed. Moses exalted himself and Aaron in the eyes of the congregation by implying he and Aaron ("Must we…," Num. 20:10) were the ones providing the water instead of God. Spiritual unbelief had impacted all of Israel, as the entire generation who departed from Egypt died in the wilderness—except two men, Joshua and Caleb (Num. 14). Joshua was Moses's minister, and he received the impartation and blessing of replacing Moses at his death and leading Israel into the Promised Land (Josh. 1:1–7). The *NO* of Moses became the *YES* of Joshua!

The prayers you are praying that are based upon your dreams and visions of the future may be only partially fulfilled in your lifetime, but they may be fulfilled through your children and their children's children! My grandfather John Bava was called the "Coal Miner Preacher," working in the West Virginia mines and also preaching, singing, and using the radio to reach entire towns in northern West Virginia. At one time he held the copyrights on more than one thousand songs that he had written, and he printed a magazine called *Musical Echoes*. My dad was a musician, singer, and preacher and was very gifted in understanding the operation of spiritual gifts.

Our ministry, the Voice of Evangelism, has two large facilities and a seventy-eight-acre piece of land with plans for constructing the Omega Center International, a youth church and a major Christian youth camp facility. Years ago Dad came by the office to see all the Lord had done through His blessing upon the ministry. Dad said, "Son, I would have loved to have accomplished this in my ministry, but I did not have the faith to believe for finances and the strength to do what you have done." Here was a man who had prayed a prayer of faith and had seen sixteen people healed of cancer in the last fifteen years of his ministry, yet he had difficulty believing for finances on a large scale! I have not stepped out into any ministry project until I have heard from the Holy Spirit, but I have also never been concerned about finances. I believe that if God plans it, then He pays for it! That's just my personal faith level.

There will be times when your answer to prayer will be linked to the proper *timing* of the event or situation. Thus your answer can be delayed but not necessarily denied. At age seventy-five Abraham received the promise of God for a son. Ten years later Sarah was still barren and Abraham was still fatherless (Gen. 16:3). Finally, at age ninety-nine, the Lord appeared to Abraham and reconfirmed a son through Sarah, nearly twenty-four years after the initial promise. I always questioned the reason for such a long delay. Then I read:

> Now Abraham and Sarah were old, well advanced in age; and Sarah had passed the age of childbearing.
> —Genesis 18:11

Literally, Sarah had gone through menopause and was past the age of having a child. This was the purpose for a twenty-five-year wait for Isaac to be born. (Abraham was one hundred, Gen. 21:5.) God desired for the circumstances to be completely impossible for the couple to have a son. That way both Abraham and Sarah—and all who would hear—would know that the child was a gift and promise from God. The Almighty delayed the timing so that He alone would be glorified. The name *Isaac* means "laughter," as Sarah laughed when God told her she would bear a son in her old age (Gen. 18:13–15). In Hebrew, his name is *Yitzach*; a person cannot say *Yitzach* without opening their mouth and saying a phrase that sounds like you are laughing. *Yitz-ahh-ch*! Delayed answers are not denials—they are simply pauses in the action.

There are reasons God puts you on hold. In 1988 I was in Zephyrhills, Florida, preaching for Pastor Tom Jammes. One night Tom and I went to the church at 11:00 p.m. to have an all-night prayer meeting. We were burdened for the body of Christ, as breaking news had announced the moral fall of a world-renowned minister. As I was in a spirit of prayer at 3:00 a.m., I heard an inner voice say, "Manna-fest." Then these words followed, "This is the title of your television program."

At the time I did not have a studio or studio lights; I had no cameras and tripods, no taping or duplication equipment. In fact, I had no interest in a television program and had not been a guest on any programs up until that time, so I could not comprehend the words I heard. The next morning I told my wife about the name *Manna-fest* and the word I received. We said nothing to no one but did as Mary did when she heard Jesus at age twelve talk about doing His father's business; she "kept all these things in her heart" (Luke 2:51).

Although I knew the Lord had spoken to me, I did not go out and begin purchasing equipment and running up a bill for television airtime. The future was hidden in my heart but was not yet activated in my spirit. The delay of twelve years from the time the word of the Lord came in Zephyrhills until the first telecast of *Manna-fest* in the year 2000 was preparation time for me. During this time my office manager, Charlie Ellis, taught himself how to tape programs, edit them, and produce a completed program. We also met a wonderful woman, Dorothy Spalding, and her husband, Russell, who were experienced in designing and building television sets, and they constructed our first television set in a small studio. In those early days we taped prophetic videos that were offered on Christian stations for numerous years. Over time this provided income to purchase our own television equipment. The entire process took twelve years.

We initiated the *Manna-fest* program with a Hebraic/prophetic format, including programs taped on location in Israel. It was during one of those times that I remembered a statement I had made in the early 1990s. Since age eighteen I have published a newsletter called *The Voice of Evangelism*. It began as a simple four-page leaflet and has turned into a twenty-eight-page, full-color, bimonthly publication. In each early issue I spent time researching a prophetic update, detailing events according to Bible prophecy. After years of this process, I once told my wife, "Why am I wasting time doing this? Only a few people are reading what I am spending hours studying."

She replied, "Maybe the Lord is going to use what you are learning down the road at some point." Twelve years later when I saw the format that the Lord laid out for us for the weekly telecast, I knew He had directed my footsteps.

God's no is not always a no; it can be a delay, such as with Moses and Miriam and David and his son. The second point is that God's no to you may be a yes to someone in your bloodline.

THE UNEXPLAINABLE "NO"

The third point is that some noes are simply unexplainable. One of the unexplainable events in life is the death of a child or a loved one. When a child or loved one passes unexpectedly through an accident or a terminal illness, sincere believers attempting to comfort the mourner will often make statements such as: "God took them because He needed another angel." "God needs more workers to prepare for the marriage supper." "God took them to spare them from all the trouble on earth." These strange comments, meant to comfort at that moment, can actually agitate the mourner as he or she often smiles in response and walks away.

I know of minister friends who prayed for their children's protection, asking God to build a hedge around them (Job 1:10) and not allow premature death to take them out before their appointed time. They claimed the *protective* scriptures for a long life and yet received a dreaded phone call that changed their world in a split second—as the voice on the other line released the news that the child had been killed in an accident.

It is appointed unto men once to die.

Here is fact number one: it is appointed unto men once to die (Heb. 9:27). This is a spiritual law that cannot be broken. Only two men have escaped death, Enoch (Gen. 5:24) and Elijah (2 Kings 2), and they will experience death at the hand of the future Antichrist when they return as the two witnesses to Jerusalem (Rev. 11:7). There are also those who will be "caught up" at the time of the gathering together (1 Thess. 4:17); a group of living saints will be changed from mortal to immortal (1 Cor. 15:52–54), escaping the normal form of death. However, sooner or later all men will pass away, so it's not a matter of *if* but *when*. Some will pass later in life and some sooner.

We live in a violent world.

Fact number two is this: we live in a violent world that is still under the curse. Because of human criminal elements, good people often become the victims of violent crimes. Because the earth is presently under the curse (Gen. 3:17–19), hurricanes, tornadoes, floods, and disasters can strike good people. Christians can lose their homes and possessions, just as Noah did during the Flood and Lot did when Sodom was destroyed (Gen. 6; 19), and even, at times, their lives. Jesus taught: "He…sends rain on the just and on the unjust" (Matt. 5:45). Trouble comes to both the righteous and the unrighteous.

We can override warnings.

Fact number three is: in some tragedies, it may have been possible the person(s) ignored warnings from people and/or from the Holy Spirit. The Holy Spirit will show you things to come (John 16:13). This can mean warnings through a vision, a dream, a close friend, visible circumstances, and inner signals that come call *premonitions*. If the Lord shows you impending danger and you act in a way that voids that warning by walking toward the danger or ignoring the warning, I call it *running red lights*! A red light means *stop*. It does not mean slow down; neither is it a yellow light but a red light. People try to beat the signal all the time, running red lights and crashing their vehicles. In such cases you can't blame the red light for changing at the wrong time; you must blame the person for ignoring the signal.

God is sovereign.

Fact number four: God is sovereign, meaning He is the highest, royal reigning chief, and there is none above Him. He is also the Creator, and we are the creation. The Almighty holds the power of life and death and can control or unleash natural forces by His spoken Word. I have observed that among Christians, there is a concept that if we follow God, only good will follow us!

The theory of "it's always good" goes something like this. If you are strong, you will always win every battle. If you are fast, you will always come in first in the race. If you are smart enough, you have guaranteed success in business, and if you are wise, you will always escape trouble. If you live righteous, you will never be attacked by Satan. (But don't tell old Job that; see Job 1 and 2.) If you have faith, you will always be healed. And if you attend church, you must be a Christian!

Wrong ideas produce wrong thinking. Opposite groups of people will say: If you *are* sick, you don't have enough faith for your healing. If you are having financial struggles, it is because you are not sowing enough seed (money). If there is a shortage of answers to prayer, then you must be praying wrong. Any trouble with rebellious children must be because you are not disciplining them correctly. The personal trouble in your life is allegedly a result of some door you opened to the adversary.

If you have fallen into a trap, *it's your own fault,* nobody else's! These incorrect *super spiritual* commentaries on the explanation for your trouble remind me of Job when he lost his health, wealth, and family (Job 1; 2). Three friends came to reveal the reasons for Job's numerous disasters, explaining that the door of trouble was opened because he had sinned, because of pride, and because God wanted to bring him down a notch and teach him a lesson. All three opinions of these friends were wrong according to God Himself (Job 42:8).

One of the best scriptures explains all of these negative things that happen to good people. It was written by Solomon in Ecclesiastes 9:11–12:

> I returned and saw under the sun that—
> The race is not to the swift,
> Nor the battle to the strong,
> Nor bread to the wise,
> Nor riches to men of understanding,
> Nor favor to men of skill;
> But time and chance happen to them all.
> For man also does not know his time:
> Like fish taken in a cruel net,
> Like birds caught in a snare,
> So the sons of men are snared in an evil time,
> When it falls suddenly upon them.

Time and chance happen to all men. The word *chance* here is not *luck,* but it is the Hebrew word *pega'* and means, "impact, or something that has an impact." Life-changing events that impact us for good or bad happen to us all. Jesus said it well when He said that God "sends rain on the just and on the unjust" (Matt. 5:45).

We are bombarded with positive opinions as to how good things should be and given weird explanations of what went wrong when the outcome crushed our expectations. The fact is, there will be times when there is an unexplainable *no!* On numerous occasions I have observed that when a very godly and pure-hearted believer is stricken with cancer or some disease, and other believers stand in the gap through intercession, calling on God on that person's behalf, still the individual passes away. Basic explanations may be given, such as, "It was just his or her time to go." But we must always believe that God is sovereign. There are things we may never know this side of heaven. God may have been protecting that person from future crisis and sorrow.

Living for and Dying With Integrity

Many years ago a noted television minister fell into a sin that was publicized to the world, devastating the body of Christ and shocking sinners. The fallout was so intense that thousands quit attending churches and many disappointed people said they would never watch another television minister again. I commented to my wife, "Would it have been better for the Lord to take this person on before this terrible sin developed in his life?" The event made me think of King Hezekiah, who was told he was going to die and then prayed for a life extension. God added fifteen more years to his life (Isa. 38:5). After he was healed, Hezekiah invited several Babylonian *ambassadors* to see all of the wealth in his house and the temple. He revealed *God's secrets* to the enemy. Afterward Isaiah the prophet rebuked the king and informed him that in the future the Babylonians would invade and destroy Jerusalem, taking Hezekiah's future seed (descendants) captive and seizing the golden treasures and sacred vessels of God's house. (See 2 Kings 20.)

I have pondered over the fact that if Hezekiah had died with the sickness, then the Babylonians would not have visited him, and the gold of the temple would have remained hidden from public eyes. Eventually, destruction would have come, but would it have been delayed? Was the extension of his life a negative result for Israel, opening the door to the Babylonians? It is a theological debate.

I knew one minister who always said that he would prefer the Lord to take him on early rather than let him live and bring a reproach to the name of the Lord by sinning in his latter years. When he died, the assumption was, "God must have seen something coming that was bad and spared him from the trouble." This is possible. However, I would prefer to live long and believe that God can *keep* and *preserve* me, for Jude wrote:

> Now to Him who is able to keep you from stumbling,
> And to present you faultless
> Before the presence of His glory with exceeding joy.
>
> —JUDE 24

At times there will be no visible reason why events play out as they do. It has been suggested that since God knows the future, He can allow some to arrive in heaven at an earlier age to prevent them from experiencing future trouble that could cost them their eternal destiny.

I recall when a noted television minister lost his daughter and son-in-law in a plane crash, leaving three children behind. This was an international minister who was the president of a leading university. He was known for seeing answered prayer, and prior to the crash he had taught the body of Christ about forming a prayer hedge around their families. I still have many of this minister's older magazines, and in the issue prior to the departing of his daughter, he wrote a powerful article articulating the spiritual principles of the prayers of protection. Then, subsequently, he lost his own daughter and son-in-law.

Love and prayers began pouring in to his ministry, along with the critics' questions. Some wrote that the minister's preaching did not work since his daughter was taken in this accident. This would be like saying that Jesus had no power over death because He could raise Lazarus but died Himself! The minister and his wife went on their weekly television program to share their grief with the world. He told that when he began to ask the Lord why this happened, the Holy Spirit responded and revealed to him that there were things that happen in this life that a person will never know the answers for until they arrive in heaven. That settled the issue for him and his wife. He would not ask why again, knowing that once he began asking why, one question would lead to another, and the questions might never end.[1]

The point is that we will all eventually pass away, and when the moment of our appointment comes, we will go on to our final eternal destination despite the amount of prayer being offered on our behalf. We are told in Scripture, "The days of our lives are seventy years; and if by reason of strength they are eighty years, yet their boast is only labor and sorrow; for it is soon cut off, and we fly away" (Ps. 90:10). There is no limitation set on an exact number of years we can live. We should, however, strive to live a good life with integrity and to pass with a good name.

This point was made clear to me with the passing of my father. Before going to heaven, he told me, "Son, I regret that I don't really have anything materially to leave you children."

I responded, "Dad, you are leaving all four of your children something more valuable than silver or gold; you are leaving us a good name!" You see, my dad was known to all as one of the greatest men of prayer and integrity many people had ever known. Thousands of e-mails and individual messages came to us, and those who knew him spoke of his godly life, his integrity, and his humility. During the funeral I was suddenly struck with a burden in my heart I had never experienced before: I carry his name. His name was Perry Fred Stone, and he was senior and I am Perry Fred Stone Jr. I realized that I must guard my name the same as he guarded his.

While you do not know the future, you must trust God through the good and the bad. Always remember, there are noes you may never understand. However, you can still go to heaven with a no for an answer, but you cannot go to heaven with sin in your life (Ezek. 18:4, 20).

Praying Through the Battle of the Firstborn

Then the Lord spoke to Moses, saying, "Consecrate to Me all the firstborn, whatever opens the womb among the children of Israel, both of man and beast; it is Mine."

—EXODUS 13:1–2

FROM THE VERY outset of human time, there has been an unexplainable battle over the firstborn. Part of this conflict stems from the special genealogical *birthright* and spiritual *blessing* that marked the firstborn from the moment of their births. For some reason, the adversary has a great hatred toward the firstborn and often sets a target upon them from the moment of birth—especially firstborn sons.

THE LAW OF THE FIRST

On the *first day* of Creation God separated the light from the darkness (Gen. 1:4–5). The "law of the first" is a law of "separation." The firstborn of the animals were to be separated from the flock and set aside for God (Exod. 13:2). The firstfruits of the harvest were marked in the fields and on the trees and were cut from their stems, vines, and trees to be presented to the Lord as a firstfruits offering (Deut. 26:2). God went so far as to say, "Consecrate to Me all the firstborn, whatever opens the womb among the children of Israel, both of man and beast; it is Mine" (Exod. 13:2).

It appears that God's original plan was that every firstborn male child born into twelve Hebrew tribes would be called into the priesthood. God said to Israel:

> Now therefore, if you will indeed obey My voice and keep My covenant, then you shall be a special treasure to Me above all people; for all the earth is Mine. And you shall be to Me a kingdom of priests and a holy nation.
> —EXODUS 19:5–6

When Israel sinned with the golden calf, Moses asked who was on the Lord's side, and the Levites assembled around him. Moses instructed these men to slay the idolaters, which they did (Exod. 32:26–28). Instead of choosing *all of the* firstborn sons to form a kingdom of priests, the tribe of Levi—the tribe of Moses and Aaron—was chosen. The Levites were given charge of the ark of the covenant and the tabernacle (Deut. 10:8–9). The sons of Levi were not given a land grant in Israel, because they were to live and minister at the tabernacle and, later, in the temple of Solomon. Prior to the high priest's passing, his oldest son would receive the garments of his father, the anointing oil was poured upon his head, and any secret that the high priest knew was passed from the mouth of the father to the son (Num. 20). Without a son, the high priest could not have passed on his priestly ministry!

THE BLESSING AND THE BIRTHRIGHT

The firstborn was granted two unique honors: the birthright and the blessing. The Jewish sage Rashi commented that when Esau gave up his birthright, he was forfeiting the right of his future firstborn to become the priesthood through his lineage, as it would be the firstborn in the future to carry the responsibility of the priesthood.[1] The birthright was a heritage grant from the father to his firstborn son and imparted to the firstborn son a double portion of the estate blessing, including the houses, lands, trees, and animals on the father's estate. When Esau returned from the field, he was hungry, and he asked his brother, Jacob, to fix some soup of lentils (Gen. 25:30). Esau was covered with red hair, and in Hebrew the text reads he wanted the "red stuff," speaking of the soup he desired to eat. The word *Edom* means red, and Esau eventually lived in Edom and became the father of the Edomites (Gen. 32:3; 36:1).

The "blessing" was to be imparted near the moment of death. When Jacob was dying, he called his sons together and gave each one a strong message in the form of a prophetic blessing. (See Genesis 49.) The same occurred with Moses prior to his death near Mount Nebo. He spoke a major prophetic blessing to the individual tribes of Israel. (See Deuteronomy 33.) In Genesis 27:1, Isaac's eyes were dim, and he assumed he was dying (v. 4), so he asked for a final meal of his favorite meat stew. Esau, Isaac's oldest son, went hunting and, after returning home, discovered his brother, Jacob, had posed as him, tricking his father, Isaac, into giving Jacob Esau's blessing (Gen. 27). When reading the "blessings" of Genesis 49 and Deuteronomy 33, the significance of the blessing becomes clear when observing that Jacob, Moses, and Isaac spoke not just a blessing such as, "May the Lord bless you all," but within the words of their blessings are prophetic statements that reveal the future of the individual or the tribe. Thus, the blessing of the father was more than just a *prayer*; it was also a *prophecy*.

The most important person in the ancient patriarchal family was the firstborn son. He was marked as holy and set apart with the favor of the father, the family, and the additional spiritual blessing. This blessing also carried a heavy responsibility, as all blessings do. The firstborn was responsible to be the leader over the other children and to set the example to them. He was also to become the spiritual leader and provider in the event of the father's death. Only if the firstborn son were to dishonor the family did he lose the birthright and blessing. This occurred with Jacob's oldest son, Reuben. This firstborn committed fornication with his father's concubine, and in the final message given to his sons, Jacob told Reuben he was unstable as water:

Reuben, you are my firstborn,
My might and the beginning of my strength,
The excellency of dignity and the excellency of power.
Unstable as water, you shall not excel,

Because you went up to your father's bed;
Then you defiled it—
He went up to my couch.

—Genesis 49:3–4

Thus, in this case, the firstborn son of Jacob, Reuben, was not honored by a special blessing because he had dishonored his father.

Satan Hates the Sons

There are two major examples of global leaders coming after the Hebrew sons. The first was Pharaoh in Egypt, who made a decree concerning all of the newborn sons born to the Hebrew women (Exod. 1:22). One reason for Pharaoh's *legalized abortion* may have been a dream of Pharaoh that revealed Egypt was soon to be brought down.

In a dream:

> Pharaoh slept, and saw in his sleep a balance, and behold the whole land of Egypt stood in one scale, and a lamb in the other; and the scale in which the lamb was outweighed that in which was the land of Egypt. Immediately he sent and called all the chief magicians, and told them his dream. And Janes and Jimbres (see 2 Tim 3:8), who were chief of the magicians, opened their mouths and said to Pharaoh, "A child is shortly to be born in the congregation of the Israelites whose hand shall destroy the whole land of Egypt." Therefore Pharaoh spake to the midwives...[2]

Here is what is written by Josephus:

> One of those sacred scribes [said to be Jannes or Jambres in the Targum of Jonathan], who are very sagacious in foretelling future events truly, told the king, that about this time there would be a child born to the Israelites, who, if he were reared, would bring the Egyptian dominion low, and would raise the Israelites; that he would excel all men in virtue, and obtain a glory that would be remembered though the ages. Which thing was so feared by the king, that, according to this man's opinion, he commanded that they should cast every male child, which was born to the Israelites, into the river, and destroy it...that if any parents should disobey him, and venture to save their male children alive, they and their families should be destroyed.[3]

Pharaoh was afraid that a future Hebrew son would eventually bring down the kingdom of Egypt. The same was true with Herod, who set out to kill all infants under two years of age in and around Bethlehem. Herod was an egotistical narcissist who was threatened by any individual who could take his position of authority. He murdered his wife and two of his sons.[4] When he was informed that an infant king was born in Bethlehem, he eventually marshaled Roman soldiers to initiate a house-to-house search in and around Bethlehem and slay all infants under two years of age (Matt. 2:16). This Herod built a fortified palace atop a small mountain near Bethlehem for his personal tomb. This palace, called *Herodium*, which still exists today, was first positively identified in 1838 by Edward Robinson, who compared his observations with those of first-century Jewish-Roman historian Flavius Josephus. The palace fortress once reached close to 199 feet high and was surrounded by double concentric walls accented by four cardinal point towers.[5] While Herod's egotistical desire for power and recognition appears to be the reason for the slaying of infants, Herod no doubt felt threatened by a possible future king of the Jews!

Why does the adversary despise the sons? While there is no direct scripture to explain this hatred, there are observations that can be made. First, a son can carry on the family name, but a daughter will give up her name for her husband's name. In the Old Testament, if a man passed away without children, his brother was to marry the widow to raise up children and carry on the departed brother's name (Deut. 25:5–6). The sons were important in the aspect of procreation. God's promises for the Hebrew nation were given to the "seed of Abraham." The term *seed* is used in certain verses in reference to the unborn children who are promised to a man. This term *seed* is used for the fruit of a tree (Gen. 1:12), a natural seed that is planted in the ground (v. 11), and the seed that is in the loins of a man giving him the ability to create another living being (Gen. 13:16, KJV). It is the man who carries the seed of promise that enables the woman to become impregnated with child.

A third clue is given in Hebrews, when God speaks of the priestly ministry of the sons of Levi, the Levites (Heb. 7:5). The writer speaks of Abraham paying tithes (the tenth) to the first king and priest of Jerusalem, Melchizedek (Gen. 14). We read a powerful revelation concerning this event:

> Here mortal men receive tithes, but there he receives them, of whom it is witnessed that he lives. Even Levi, who receives tithes, paid tithes through Abraham, so to speak, for he was still in the loins of his father when Melchizedek met him.
>
> —Hebrews 7:8–10

Consider this: the tenth was presented to Melchizedek on behalf of Levi; however, Levi was to be born two generations later! First came Isaac, then Jacob, then Levi, one of Jacob's twelve sons (Gen. 29:34). The tithe act of Abraham was actually impacting Abraham's future seed, who would be assigned as ministers of the tabernacle and the Jewish temple. The spiritual principle is that the words, deeds, and actions stemming from obedience, and even disobedience, a man commits can impact future generations even when those generations are still in the loins of the father in the form of the male seed. One of the biblical warnings stated that the sins of the fathers were transferred to the third and fourth generations (Exod. 20:5; 34:7). The spiritual leadership of a family lies with the responsibility of the father, grandfathers, and the elders to teach their sons the commandments and instructions of the Word.

Without the male seed there would be no procreation. In today's culture there is almost an obsession with the same-sex lifestyle. When men are in physical sexual relationships with men—which is strictly forbidden in Scripture (Lev. 20:13; Rom. 1)—it is impossible for two men to produce another human. As the sinful culture expands its immoral influence, more and more young men are encouraged to move toward these forbidden relationships. The more radical elements in this lifestyle would love to see every man reject the traditional and biblical man-woman, husband-wife relationship, choosing instead another man. If the entire population suddenly rejected the husband and wife relationship for a man with man relationship, in a century all human life would cease. Men with men cannot produce natural offspring!

Sons become husbands and eventually fathers, and those fathers create families. This was the divine plan of God from the beginning. God desired to be a Father and to have sons who could bring forth families (Eph. 3:15). The heavenly Father gave His only Son, Christ, and those who believe in Him become the adopted sons of God (John 3:16; 1 John 3:2). Before the creation of Adam, who was called the "son of God" (Luke 3:38), angels were given the title of "sons of God" (Job 1:6; 38:7). This would mean that at the beginning of Creation, Satan, the angel called the "anointed cherub" (Ezek. 28:14), held a position of a "son" in the relationship with the other angelic messengers. Since his fall from heaven, the adversary lost his position of authority and is no longer an angelic son to the heavenly Father. This exile from the heavenly temple and abandonment from God could, and I believe did, certainly create a violent animosity toward mankind—especially the *sons*!

THE STRUGGLE WITH THE MINISTER'S SEED

It should come as no surprise that some of the adversary's chief targets are the children of anyone who is in ministry, especially the sons of ministers. I believe one reason is the spiritual principle God established among the Levites, that the blessing and office of ministry were handed down to the next generations of sons—from fathers to sons. There is a definite threat to the kingdom of darkness from children raised under the influence of godly and anointed biblical instruction, especially when they lived in the home of the minister. If a minister's children—male and female—obey the spiritual instruction, then the minister has successfully duplicated himself to carry on his ministry following his death. His words and influence will continue expanding to future generations. The only way for the enemy to prevent this transfer is by either disrupting the destiny of a child through sin and disobedience or by setting up circumstances that lead to a premature death through accident.

I have personally known of at least eight great men of God (some are internationally known) whose firstborn sons passed away through different circumstances (between the ages of sixteen to thirty-five). Some of the children would have been future heirs to the ministry of their fathers, just as an Old Testament high priest passed his priesthood to his son. While the circumstances of their deaths differ in each instance, the departure of the possible heir of the *ministry mantle* caused great sorrow, anguish, and many questions. In most cases, the child had great knowledge of God and was taken to heaven, which is the ultimate comfort for any parent.

There is no doubt that the children of ministers seem to struggle and are targeted at a different level than the others. All individuals have a certain realm of influence as believers. However, a minister reaches larger numbers of souls, which becomes a threat to the kingdom of darkness.

THE PRAYER FOR THE FIRSTBORN

The death angel in Egypt was assigned to slay the firstborn sons. God provided supernatural protection for the Hebrew nation by commanding them to apply the blood of a slain lamb on the left, right, and top posts of the outer door of each Hebrew house. The power of Israel's obedience and the blood from the lamb restrained the angel of death (called "the destroyer" in Exodus 12:23) from crossing the threshold into the Hebrew home. Thus the firstborn sons were preserved as they remained in the house, while the Egyptians lost all of the firstborn sons the same night (v. 29).

How could the blood of thousands of lambs provide a supernatural hedge against death itself? The answer is that this narrative was a *type and shadow* (Heb. 8:5) of the redemptive covenant provided by Christ on the cross. When by faith and confession we receive the finished, redemptive work of Christ through His blood, we have redemption and the forgiveness of sins (Eph. 1:7), we are justified (Rom. 5:9), we have peace (Col. 1:20), and we have boldness to enter the heavenly holy place (Heb. 10:19)!

There is a wonderful and marvelous mystery concerning the process of how Christ's shed blood can be applied and actually cleanse, forgive, and bring salvation to a sinner. When we ask for forgiveness, we do not see literal blood flowing out of heaven. However, there is a revealing scripture in Hebrew 9:23–26:

> Therefore it was necessary that the copies of the things in the heavens should be purified with these, but the heavenly things themselves with better sacrifices than these. For Christ has not entered the holy places made with hands, which are copies of the true, but into heaven itself, now to appear in the presence of God for us; not that He should offer Himself often, as the high priest enters the Most Holy Place every year with blood of another—He then would have had to suffer often since the foundation of the world; but now, once at the end of the ages, He has appeared to put away sin by the sacrifice of Himself.

The "things in heaven" refer to the original sacred furniture in the heavenly temple, such as the seven-branched candlestick (Rev. 1:20), a golden altar (Rev. 8:3–4), and the ark of the covenant (Rev. 11:19). This temple is the original temple of God that preexisted prior to Adam's creation. In this temple the sons of God (angels) rejoiced and sang during the creation of the heavens and the earth (Job 38:4–7). Satan was among them, perhaps even directing the worship on the holy mountain (Ezek. 28:14). When Satan made his attempt to direct a rebellion in heaven against God, it occurred in the presence of the throne room in the sacred holy mountain (vv. 14–15). Thus, sin originated with Satan, and the sacred vessels in the heavenly temple needed to be purified with the blood of Christ.

> But Christ came as High Priest of the good things to come, with the greater and more perfect tabernacle not made with hands, that is, not of this creation. Not with the blood of goats and calves, but with His own blood He entered the Most Holy Place once for all, having obtained eternal redemption.
> —Hebrews 9:11–12

This heavenly purification occurred between the moment that Mary saw Christ early resurrection morning (John 20:1) and when the disciples saw Christ later that same day (v. 19). This is why Christ told Mary not to touch Him, that He was ascending to the Father (v. 17). Just as the high priest sprinkled the sacrificial blood of chosen animals on the sacred furniture on the Day of Atonement, Christ made ascension to the temple in heaven and sanctified the holy furniture by His own blood! This process, mentioned in Hebrews, was the event that opened up heaven to mankind, giving us direct access to God!

Under the first covenant, the mediator (the go-between) who stood between man and God was the high priest. Today, our High Priest is Christ alone, the mediator of the better covenant established on better promises (Heb. 8:6). When a sinner calls out to God for forgiveness of sin and uses the name of Christ, he or she immediately gains access through the "forgiveness gate" where the heavenly priest uses *His own blood* to remove the stains of sin and erase the sinner's guilt. Because Christ is seated at the right hand of God, He can actually view the holy furniture and the bloodstained mercy seat of the ark of the covenant.

When we confess Christ's blood, we are not speaking vain and empty words from a spiritual imagination, but we are speaking a powerful statement that activates heaven itself on our behalf. In prayer, we must continually pray for our families and our children. Because the firstborn son would receive a double portion of the estate, we must *double up our prayers* for the firstborn sons and all firstborn children. Often siblings will carefully watch and mimic the ways of the older ones in the family. If the adversary can chain a bondage around the firstborn, then the younger siblings see the captivity and may be drawn into a similar prison.

The battle for the firstborn will never end—at least in this life. However, the weapons to defeat the adversary are at our disposal.

BREAKING THE SATANIC HEDGE

If you have two children, one may be compliant and the other defiant. One may be easy to discipline, and the other may challenge your authority. Often in a large family, one child will struggle more with addictions, rebellion, and personal sins than the others. Why is it difficult to penetrate their intellect to understand the truth? What is the unseen hindrance that prevents them from reaching out for help?

Sometime back while meditating on this question, I saw in my spirit how the adversary attempts to build a *hedge* around your unsaved children (or child), almost like an invisible cage, to prevent you from reaching them and to prevent them from getting out of their bondage. I compare this type of hedge to the hedge surrounding Job. The man Job was the greatest man in the East (Job 1:1–3), with massive wealth including land, animals, houses, and ten children. When Satan attempted to attack Job, he was *unable to penetrate the hedge* that surrounded Job and his possessions on every side (v. 10). Only when the hedge was removed was Satan permitted to steal and destroy, beginning with the animals, then the children, and eventually Job's health (Job chapters 1–2). In Job's case, the words of Solomon rang true: "He who digs a pit will fall into it, and whoever breaks through a wall will be bitten by a serpent" (Eccles. 10:8). I personally believe the hedge was an encampment of angels, for angels are assigned to encircle those who fear the Lord (Ps. 34:7). This angelic force would have prevented any form of destruction or danger from entering Job's property lines.

I believe that the adversary uses circumstances and especially wrong influences to create mental barriers and unhealthy soul ties, which often prevent a sinner from coming to Christ. Negative and sin-encouraging individuals are like the armor bearer of Goliath. This Philistine giant already had the advantage of being nearly twice the size of the average Jew and was armed with huge weapons of destruction. Yet there was a shield bearer who went before him. Any assailant would need to pass the armor bearer to get to the giant (1 Sam. 17:7). To prevent a parent from reaching his or her child, there are demonic armor bearers, so to speak, that are placing walls between the deliverer and the one bound.

CALLING ON ANGELIC MESSENGERS

The kingdom of Satan consists of principalities, powers, rulers of the darkness of this world, and wicked spirits in heavenly places (Eph. 6:12). As parents, we are used to distractions, bad attitudes, and times of rebellion from a child. These are dealt with through discipline. But when a child is under a satanic bondage, it takes more than *discipline*—it takes *deliverance.* When we are battling a stronger spirit, it may require a higher intervention from an angel of the Lord to break through the barrier. When Daniel was praying for twenty-one days, the answer was hindered until Michael the archangel broke through the barrier in the heavens and released the angel of the Lord (perhaps Gabriel) to bring the revelation (Dan. 10). It required supernatural assistance to bring the breakthrough. God has numerous angels capable of bringing supernatural assistance to us if we will ask when we pray.

One Scripture passage that has inspired me to ask the Lord for the assistance of angelic messengers is Hebrews 1:13–14:

> But to which of the angels has He ever said: "Sit at My right hand, till I make Your enemies Your footstool"? Are they not all ministering spirits sent forth to minister for those who will inherit salvation?

I examined this passage and various translations only to discover a great illumination. God has countless ministering spirits to minister for those who will (in the future) inherit salvation. In Acts 10, an angel came to the Roman centurion Cornelius and later appeared to Simon Peter in Joppa, linking the two men together—one Jew and one Gentile—and the rest is history! Cornelius was the first Gentile to be grafted into the new covenant, and the angel of the Lord set up the entire meeting. Angels can lead a person in the right direction and connect your unsaved child with the right person, or even prevent your child from meeting someone who would be detrimental to your child's future.

Angels are released through prayer. When Peter was arrested and Herod planned to behead the apostle after Passover, the church prayed nonstop. An angel of the Lord went into the inner prison, removed the chains, opened the gates, and sent Peter on his way to the prayer meeting where they were praying for his release (Acts 12:5–12). When Peter knocked on the door, the prayer warriors did not believe it was Peter.

> But they said to her, "You are beside yourself!" Yet she kept insisting that it was so. So they said, "It is his angel." Now Peter

continued knocking; and when they opened the door and saw
him, they were astonished.

—ACTS 12:15–16

When they said it was "his angel," this indicated they believed
Peter had a personal angel that went with him. We would call them
guardian angels today. If you are a believer and are attempting to raise
your household in the faith, then I believe there is an angel of the Lord
that is assigned to your family. Years ago my father saw in a vision his
brother Morgan being killed in a car accident in West Virginia. After
prayer for more than an hour, the Holy Spirit told Dad that he was
praying for Him to protect a person who had willfully turned from the
truth and was no longer walking in the covenant. As Dad continued
praying, he recalled a vision of an angel he had seen many years earlier while pastoring in Northern Virginia. The Lord impressed Dad to
ask *his* angel—the one assigned to him—to go to West Virginia and
protect Morgan from death. Dad prayed a mighty prayer with a strong
unction. Later that day Dad discovered that Morgan came close to
being hit by a coal truck and killed. The event brought Morgan back
into a relationship with the Lord. Dad had been praying for Morgan's
salvation for forty years!

When we are in a battle for our firstborn, or a battle for any child or
grandchild, we must continually ask the Lord for supernatural protection from angels to prevent a premature death. One young man came
to me and said, "I should have died several times, but I know it was
the prayers of my parents that have kept me alive."

HEDGING THEM IN

If Satan attempts to use wicked people, sin, or addictions to form a
hedge to prevent you from reaching your children, you should also
pray for a hedge around them that makes it uncomfortable to go out
and be disobedient to the truth of God's Word. I saw this example in
the Old Testament story of Hosea and Gomer. The prophet Hosea was
instructed to marry a woman who was a prostitute. Gomer, Hosea's
wife, would have children through him, yet she would go out and

sin against her husband by committing adultery. She was a picture of Israel's unfaithfulness to God. In Hosea 2:6 we read:

> Therefore, behold, I will hedge up your way with thorns, and wall her in, so that she cannot find her paths.

The imagery here is what a Middle Eastern shepherd does each night when gathering sheep into a cave for the night. The good shepherd will often place large thorn bushes at the entrance of the cave to prevent a curious sheep from straying from the flock and heading into the dangerous darkness where a bear or lion could be lurking. There is no comfort when brushing up against a thorn bush, and a stubborn sheep will only become frustrated, but in the process it will be protected from danger.

In Gomer's case, the Lord was going to make it difficult for her to leave her husband and enjoy sinning. Eventually, just as in the story of the prodigal son, she would realize how good she had it with Hosea and become weary of her lifestyle and turn to God.

There have been several times when I would, or would suggest that others, pray two prayers. The first is to commission angels to go forth and begin to penetrate the hedge of the adversary and break into the mind and heart of the sinner to where the light of the gospel and the rays of God's love can be shed abroad in that person's spirit. The second prayer is for God to form a spiritual thorn hedge around the person so he or she becomes uncomfortable with sin and addiction and surrenders to the Holy Spirit, who is able to deliver that person from bondage.

PLEADING THE BLOOD

When a sinner is repenting and turning to God, he may say a prayer asking the Lord to "cleanse me by the blood of Christ" or "wash me in the blood of Jesus" (Rev. 1:5). During the prayer, there is no visible sign of blood dripping from the heavenly temple and covering the new believer. However, the words and faith create a new person as God recalls the sacrifice of His Son on the cross.

Years ago it was common for older saints, when praying for a person struck by illness or under a sudden attack, to "plead the blood" over the situation. Their influence for their aggressive petition came from the verse: "They overcame him [Satan] by the blood of the Lamb and by the word of their testimony…" (Rev. 12:11).

In order to be saved or born again, we read, "With the heart one believes unto righteousness, and with the mouth confession is made unto salvation" (Rom. 10:10).

Under the old covenant, the priest offered a lamb in the morning and a lamb in the evening. The imagery is that with the blood of a lamb, the Israelites would begin their day, and with the blood of a lamb the people would conclude their day (Num. 28:4). In the time of the Exodus, the blood of the chosen lamb on the outward doorpost of the house prevented the destroying angel from taking the life of the firstborn (Exod. 12). Today, we do not offer animals for sacrifices because Christ is the final and complete offering for mankind. However, the blood of Christ has been given all power over all of the power of the adversary, and the blood is applied by prayer and confession.

I often pray that through the power of the blood of Christ my wife and children will be protected, our home will be preserved from danger, and we will have traveling mercy. I pray this because there are spiritual forces from the kingdom of darkness at work, making strategies and plans of which we are unaware, which can only be defeated through the authority of the name of Christ and the power of His blood.

The battle for the firstborn and for all of our future children and grandchildren will continue until the time of the end. However, through prayer, confession, the ministry of angels, and the power of the blood of Christ, we have weapons to defend our children and defeat our adversary! The believers' array of weapons is designed to make the impossible *possible*!

CHAPTER 7

Miracle Prayers—Making the Impossible Possible

So Jesus said to them, "Because of your unbelief;
for assuredly, I say to you, if you have faith as
a mustard seed, you will say to this mountain,
'Move from here to there,' and it will move;
and nothing will be impossible for you."

—Matthew 17:20

I F YOU ARE one of those individuals who accept the theological theory that the only prayers God answers are prayers for salvation and that He no longer heals the sick or performs miracles through prayer and faith, I suggest you simply skip over this chapter, as staunch unbelief is seldom changed. However, if you have been taught that miracles have ceased but deep within your spirit you know God has never changed and you want the knowledge of praying for impossible situations, then this section will be of benefit to you.

If you were raised in a Christian environment that doctrinally taught the ceasing of miracles after the Canon of Scripture was completed, then anyone's claim today that God healed them or preformed a miracle after prayer may seem delusional, deceived, or just *lucky* to you. If you were like me—raised in the home of a faith-filled, anointed man of God who prayed and saw the Lord heal and deliver many—then belief in the supernatural power of God is as normal as breathing air.

DOUBT PEDDLERS AND JOY KILLERS

If you needed your car repaired, you would not visit a local surgeon in the hospital and say, "Can you X-ray my engine and see what the problem is?" If, on the other hand, your arteries are clogged and you need bypass surgery, you would never go to a carpenter in a subdivision and say, "Hey, brother...you got a saw that can cut through my chest and a few small wires to clean this plaque out of my heart?" The same is true with spiritual matters. If you desire a possible healing or need a special miracle, you should refrain from reading the words of a theological doubt peddler whose writings are filling you with more questions than you can answer and more unbelief than your spirit can contain.

I have questioned how two ministers can read the same Bible, including the same passages and verses, and yet end up with totally opposite views. Part of this problem is that we all read the Bible with our own denominational filters. All evangelical denominations basically hold to the same major doctrines of the New Testament, including: Christ's virgin birth (Matt. 1:23), that Christ was the Son of God (Luke 1:35), the Crucifixion and the Resurrection (Mark 15:15; 16:6), the initial coming of the Holy Spirit (Acts 2:1–4), the believers' judgment (Rev. 11:18), the return of Christ (Rev. 19), and the new heavens and new earth (2 Pet. 3:13; Rev. 21). These are basic doctrines upon which evangelicals can agree.

The greatest difference from some mainline churches and certain full gospel groups stems from the opposing opinions concerning whether God performs the supernatural today, or if the supernatural was simply to assist the first-century church. The doctrine of miracles ceasing is called *cessationism*, meaning "coming to an end." There are two common teachings from the schools of the cessationists. One group believes that the supernatural gifts of the Spirit (1 Cor. 12:7–10) and the miraculous ceased after the death of the apostle John, somewhere around A.D. 96. They hold that only the apostles were given the ability to perform signs and wonders; thus, when John, the last of the original twelve apostles, passed, the miracles passed with him. The second group traces the time of cessation to when the biblical canon (books) were compiled in the fourth century. They suggest that when the Scriptures were completed in book form, there was no further need for healings, spiritual gifts, or the miraculous. The full gospel school teaches that there is no such thing as a day of or season of miracles, only a God who never changes and who still answers prayers and performs His mighty works. The ability for full gospel people to believe in the miraculous, I believe, is linked to their prayer life.

If you were raised in a *classical full gospel church*, which would include any of the eight major Pentecostal denominations that were birthed from 1886 to 1932, then you remember that older *saints* were the *prayer warriors* in the church. As a child, when my dad pastored in Big Stone Gap, Virginia, it was common for the women and the men to have separate prayer rooms, and these very godly believers would often pray for one hour or more before services. After exiting the room to the small main sanctuary, the glory, presence, and peace of the Lord would come over the congregation. You felt the tangible presence of God. I remember that one of the effects of the divine presence was such JOY among the believers. Deep intercessory prayer always builds your confidence in God's ability.

THE SPIRIT OF A DOCTRINE

The question "Does God still perform miracles through prayer?" is still being asked today. One man said, "I don't believe God does miracles today."

I replied, "Then you are not really saved, because the act of salvation is in itself a miracle!"

My dear friend Pastor Paul Zink teaches that when a person judges doctrine, he or she must also judge the *spirit of the doctrine*. When the ten spies came back from spying out the Promised Land, two of the original twelve, Joshua and Caleb, expressed faith and not unbelief—for they had "a different spirit" (Num. 14:24). In Christ's day, the Samaritans despised the Jews and the Jews despised the Samaritans. On one occasion Christ was going to pass though the city, and the people did not want him there. James and John requested Christ to "command fire to come down from heaven and consume" the

Samaritans (Luke 9:54). Jesus rebuked these two "sons of thunder" and said, "You do not know what manner of spirit you are of" (v. 55). Their motive was wrong, and their request was refused.

Scholars note that the Old Testament law had what was termed the *letter of the law* and the *spirit of the law.*

> Who also made us sufficient as ministers of the new covenant, not of the letter but of the Spirit; for the letter kills, but the Spirit gives life.
>
> —2 CORINTHIANS 3:6

In Christ's time, the Pharisees were followers of the *letter of the law.* These religious men actually made serving God a burden, and when Christ taught contrary to their man-made opinions and traditions, they publicly announced that He was not from God and His miracles were performed through the power of an evil spirit (Matt. 9:33–34). Christ was healing on the Sabbath and telling people to take up their beds and carry them back home (Matt. 12:1–12; Mark 2:2–12). The Pharisees knew the Law taught, "Remember the Sabbath day, to keep it holy" (Exod. 20:8), and that you shall "do no work on it [the Sabbath day]" (Jer. 17:24). The Pharisees were so strict on the *letter* of the law that they accused Jesus of breaking the Sabbath by curing the sick and asking a healed man to roll up his cot and go home. They missed the *spirit* of the law, which was simply that the Sabbath was made for resting (Exod. 23:11–12). Jesus was delivering people from sin, sickness, and bondage and giving them physical, emotional, and spiritual rest for their bodies and souls by healing them! But the Pharisees were so caught up in the letter of law and tradition they refused to recognize the Messiah in their midst! Their eyes were veiled with traditional filters (Mark 7:9–13).

When ministers begin to teach that God no longer performs miracles and heals, anyone who understands the *nature* and *character* of a loving and caring God must examine the spirit of that doctrine. The "no miracles today" theory does not encourage you to seek God for help, nor does it produce faith in your spirit, and it certainly does not create any hope! You just accept what comes and put up with what is happening. Christ answers prayers that our "joy may be full" (John 16:24). Christ's desire is that His disciples have "My joy fulfilled in themselves" (John 17:13). When healing occurred in the New Testament, there was "great joy in that city" (Acts 8:8). When the Holy Spirit came, the disciples were "filled with joy and with the Holy Spirit" (Acts 13:52). Paul wrote that the kingdom of God is not meat and drink but "righteousness and peace and joy in the Holy Spirit" (Rom. 14:17).

If all we have are religious forms, rituals, and routines, then we have a form of godliness and deny the power; Paul said we must turn away from such a religion that denies the power of God (2 Tim. 3:5). Compare the congregations of those who accept the anointing and the power and those who teach against it. Which group appears to have more peace, joy and enjoyment in their fellowship? One encourages you to believe for the impossible, and the other teaches you to accept the impossible! One group teaches with God nothing is impossible, while some in the other group imply that with God nothing is possible to change the impossible! The spirit of the "no miracles and healing today" teaching, proclaiming the miraculous gifts and manifestations of God have ceased, is contrary to the *spirit of the entire Bible*. Both Old and New Testaments reveal God as a Savior, healer, and deliverer! Why would God reveal His power for four thousand years and then retire His manifestations after the death of John, the last apostle? Look at the Greek word for "save." When I say, "I am saved," you simply think, "He is saying he is forgiven of sins and has eternal life." Did you know the Greek word *save* is *sodzo*, and it has a much broader meaning than just forgiven of sins?

According to notes in *Vine's Expository Dictionary of New Testament Greek Words*, "to save" is a verb, and the noun *soteria* is translated as *salvation*. The meanings are: "of material and temporal deliverance from danger and suffering (Matt. 8:25; Mark 13:20; Luke 23:35); the spiritual and eternal salvation granted immediately by God to those who believe on the Lord Jesus Christ (Acts 2:47; 16:31)." The word is used in a broad sense of being made whole, being saved from danger, and being delivered.[1]

Greek scholar Rick Renner commented on the Greek word *sodzo* by saying it means, "'to be saved or delivered. It suggests something that is delivered, rescued, revived, salvaged, and protected and is now safe and secure.' One expositor suggests that the word *sodzo* could actually depict a person who was on a verge of death but then was revived and resuscitated because new life was breathed into him."[2] The ultimate and most important act of being saved is to be rescued from sin and given eternal life. However, it would be a disservice to the Lord to limit His power and teach that He is unable to save, heal, deliver, and perform the impossible while you are still living on the earth!

THE IMPOSSIBLE SITUATIONS

In life there are situations that become impossible for man to alter. Some deal with health issues, addictions, or life-and-death struggles. However, what is impossible with man is possible with God, for with "God all things are possible" (Matt. 19:26). It is impossible for an entire nation to cross the Red Sea, but not when Moses raises his rod and commands the sea to open (Exod. 14:16–22). It is impossible to feed six hundred thousand men in a dry desert, but not when God has angel's food called *manna* being baked in heaven and sprinkled on the ground six out of seven days a week for forty years (Exod. 16:35). It is impossible to break a forty-two-month famine in one day, but God reversed the poverty of Samaria using four men with leprosy (2 Kings 7:3–10). Three hundred men cannot take on a foreign army, but Gideon took three hundred and did the impossible (Judg. 7:7). The entire Bible is a book of the impossible made possible.

I have met numerous individuals who have bumped into a solid wall of impossibility and turned their attention to God to find a divine intervention that made the impossible possible. The first thing a person must do is realize that with God nothing is impossible (Luke 1:37). The reason we don't always ask God to perform the impossible is because we are afraid to ask because we fear failure. "What if I pray and it doesn't happen? If it doesn't happen, I may become discouraged and be disappointed in God!" The fact is, when things are at the impossibility level, what harm will it do if you have to ask God and believe Him for a divine reversal?

When the Syrian general Naaman had leprosy, he preconceived in his mind how he would be healed. Elisha would walk outside his house, lay his hand over Naaman's head, and cure him. Instead, when the chariots of this leper and his team arrived at the prophet's house, Elisha stayed in his house and sent his servant to tell him to go "jump in the river!" Actually, he told him to go dip seven times in the Jordan. The pride of this military leader was crushed, and he was about to return to his home. However, when a servant reminded him he was dying anyway, so what would he lose by getting soaking wet in a dirty river, he obeyed Elisha's instruction and was cured (2 Kings 5:5–14). He was dying anyway, so why not make the faith leap into the river! The worst that could happen is he would be a wet leper—but the best that could happen is he would come out a healed man!

RITUALISTIC PRAYERS VS. REAL PRAYERS

Among the more traditional churches and groups, it is common to have a prayer book and to say certain prayers for significant occasions. There is certainly nothing wrong with this, if the prayer is offered from the heart and not just from the paper. After all, the Lord's Prayer is a prayer with a set pattern of words. However, Christ told us not to pray prayers of "vain repetitions."

> And when you pray, do not use vain repetitions as the heathen do. For they think that they will be heard for their many words.
> —MATTHEW 6:7

The Greek word used for "repetitions" is only found here in the New Testament. The word is *battologeo*, which means, "to repeat idly." It may come from an Aramaic phrase meaning, "not mechanically repeating the same phrases over and over again."[3] This reminds me of ministers I have heard on certain radio stations who, when they preach, say the word *amen* after every sentence. "God said, amen…that He would help you…amen…and you need to know…amen…He's alive…amen…and is here now…amen." After a while, the repetition of "amen" becomes an agitation to a listener. We call these *fill-in words*, used when the speaker doesn't know what to say next! The same is true in prayer. Prayer must be from the heart and must be words that have meaning.

The Anointing—the Main Key

In my earlier years, a very seasoned and highly anointed minister, Dr. Ray H. Hughes, preached a message called, "The Anointing Makes the Difference." I was listening to the cassette message when suddenly I felt the hair on my entire body rise up! Some would call this *emotionalism*, but emotionalism cannot destroy a cancer, raise up the infirm, or deliver addicts from lifetime bondages. However, the *anointing* will break the yokes of bondage (Isa. 10:27). The anointing is not a Pentecostal or charismatic thing—it is a gift of God for individual believers upon being baptized in the Holy Spirit. My definition of the anointing is this: the absolute life of God that God enables a person to experience and feel! However, it is much more than that, and the anointing will make a difference in your worship, prayer life, and personal ministry to others. Since childhood, I have observed many altar services and thousands of prayers that were prayed for the needs of men and women. The most effective prayer is prayed with the *anointing* of the Holy Spirit.

The word *anoint* is first mentioned in the English Bible in Exodus 28:41, where Aaron and his sons were anointed with holy oil. The Hebrew word for "anoint" is from the root *mashach*, which means "to rub with oil." Olive oil was the main substance used in the process of anointing a man. The anointing was used as a public mark of separation unto God. Scripture records that Saul, David, and Solomon were anointed with oil as the first three monarch kings prior to the division of the Northern and Southern tribes (1 Sam. 10:1; 16:13; 1 Kings 1:39). The high priest was to be anointed with oil (Lev. 8:12), and the prophets were anointed, although the biblical record indicated the anointing of the prophets and judges was imparted directly by the Holy Spirit Himself (Judg. 3:10; 6:34; 11:29; 14:6).

There are two ways to *preach*, *sing*, and *minister*—with the anointing of the Holy Spirit, and without the anointing of the Holy Spirit. In 1 John 2:20, we read, "But you have an anointing from the Holy One, and you know all things." This Greek word for "anointing" is *chrisma,* meaning "something that is smeared upon." Figuratively it alludes to a special endowment of God's graces and gifting. We derive the English words *charisma* and *charismatic* from the root word *chrisma.* The Greek name for *Christ* is *Christos,* which refers to Jesus being the "anointed one."

In the Old Testament three individuals could be anointed with the holy oil:

1. A king—1 Samuel 15:1; 16:12; 1 Kings 1:34

2. A prophet—Zechariah 4:14

3. A priest—Exodus 28:41; 30:30; Leviticus 16:32

Samuel was commissioned by the Lord to anoint Saul with holy oil (1 Sam. 9:16). Once Saul received the sacred oil, the Holy Spirit's inspiration, like a mantle, was placed on this first king of Israel, and he was given "another heart" (1 Sam. 10:9). In another verse he was "turned into another man" and given the gift of prophecy (v. 6). Saul was not interested in being king, as he was "hidden among the equipment" (v. 22). The anointing of the Spirit will turn a shy person into a bold person and exchange a stony heart for a soft heart.

When Saul failed God, Samuel was sent to the house of Jesse to anoint his youngest son, David. David was already noted as a warrior, having protected his father's sheep by slaying a bear and a lion (1 Sam. 17:34–36). However, when Samuel poured an animal's horn filled with oil over David's head, the Spirit of the Lord immediately came upon him (1 Sam. 16:13). The Holy Spirit gifted David to write hundreds of psalms, many recorded in the Book of Psalms, and anointed him to play the harp with such an unction that evil spirits departed from tormented King Saul (v. 23). David's anointing also made him invincible in battle and gave him the gifting of inquiring of the Lord and receiving divine instruction (1 Sam. 30:8).

The First Time I Felt the Anointing

My earliest memories of the precious anointing, when I actually felt the presence of God, goes back to the state of Virginia, when our denomination hosted an annual "camp meeting" under a large open-air metal tabernacle. I was eleven years of age and recall watching Dr. T. L. Lowery praying for individuals in what we termed a *prayer line*, which was simply a long single line of men and women seeking individual prayer from Dr. Lowery, a highly anointed man of God.

This night a man approached TL, walking with a cane and limping. One of his legs was damaged, and he was in pain. The man of God laid both hands upon the man's head. Suddenly the fellow went backward on his back and then bounced up on both feet like a rubber ball! TL grabbed the cane from his hand and threw it in my direction! The fellow began shaking his injured leg, screaming, "I'm healed! I'm healed!" He began running at full speed across the platform. I never will forget that moment, as that was when I first felt the sacred unction, the anointing of God. I began to shake and felt like crying for joy. I had *bumps* on my arms. I had witnessed a true miracle of instant healing!

One of the most dramatic moments of my life came when I was eighteen years of age, at the same tabernacle in Virginia. It was again camp meeting time, and I was assigned as an altar worker, assisting in praying for seekers who came to the altars for prayer. As I walked in front of the wooden altar benches, for a brief second I saw an actual manifestation of the Spirit in the form of a small spinning cloud (like a miniature tornado) hovering over the right corner of the altar. Without thinking, I ran my right hand through the white spinning mist, and suddenly the hand of the Lord came mightily upon me. I began to pray for everyone around me and was actually so caught up in the Spirit that I did not realize how many people I prayed for. About an hour later, as I looked around, there were men and women lying out under God's Spirit all over the concrete floor, weeping, praying, and receiving a divine impartation.

If a person has never experienced a tangible anointing, the feeling and unction are impossible to explain in human terms. However, as my father always said, "God never wastes His anointing!" At times I believe the full gospel churches have painted the anointing as some mystical feeling or invisible power that causes the receiver to act in odd ways. However, the anointing is not just a feeling, but it also teaches a person "all things" (1 John 2:27). Most early full gospel ministers had little if any formal training, some not even completing high-school-level educations. Yet when they preached, it was evident that the anointing was their teacher, and you would have thought they had attended both college and seminary. They were self-taught men (and women), and they amazed even their critics with their knowledge.

In Acts 10:38 we read, "God anointed Jesus of Nazareth with the Holy Spirit and with power, who went about doing good and healing all who were oppressed by the devil, for God was with Him." Christ was anointed to preach but given power from the Holy Spirit to perform miracles.

THE USE OF HANDKERCHIEFS AND APRONS

Now God worked unusual miracles by the hands of Paul, so that even handkerchiefs or aprons were brought from his body to the sick, and the diseases left them and the evil spirits went out of them.

—ACTS 19:11–12

It is impossible for a minister bodily to be in two places at once. If Christ was ministering in Capernaum, He could not at the same time be in Nazareth. A human is limited to the ability to be in one location at a time. In one biblical narrative, a Roman centurion beseeched Christ to heal his dying servant. When Christ said He would go to the man's house to heal his servant, the military commander told Jesus to simply "speak a word," and his servant would be healed (Matt. 8:8). A centurion commanded one hundred men under his authority, and whenever the centurion spoke, his men followed his orders. This centurion recognized that Christ was a man with authority in His words; thus he knew that if Christ said, "Be healed," the spoken word would travel to the centurion's home and a miracle would occur, just as Psalm 107:20 states: "He [God] sent His word and healed them." Christ could physically lay hands upon people and heal them, but He could also send His word to heal them.

In Acts 19 we see another method established to assist the oppressed and suffering when they were unable to receive personal ministry through the laying on of hands. The method was for Paul to pray over a handkerchief or an apron and then send the anointed cloth to the suffering individual. The "apron" was a narrow linen covering that was worn over part the body, used especially by servants and workmen. The implication seems to be that people were bringing certain clothing from those who were sick or oppressed and asking Paul to pray over the object for the person's deliverance. The word *handkerchief* indicates a cloth for wiping the face (Luke 19:20; Acts 19:12) and is the same Greek word that can be used for a head covering for the dead (John 11:44), translated as *napkin* in the King James Version.[4] It appears from the text that many people were unable to travel to receive personal ministry, but through the *anointed cloths* and Paul's prayers, these individuals were healed, as demons departed and the sick were cured.

How can this type of prayer—praying over a linen cloth—be effective? First, God watches not only our words but also our actions. James wrote: "Faith without works is dead" (James 2:20). The word *works* in Greek is *ergon*, which means "to toil or work" and, by implication, means "to act." We would say, "Faith without corresponding action is dead." When the men carrying a paralyzed man on a cot were prevented by the crowd from entering a house, they went up the side steps and tore the roof off, lowering the man into the center of the room where Christ was ministering. The Bible says that "Jesus saw their faith" and cured the man (Mark 2:2–12). They put action behind their believing! It required faith for a person to present an apron or handkerchief to be prayed over and faith for the person to present the prayer cloth to the suffering individual.

Not only does God watch your actions, but also the anointing is the tangible presence of God and is transferable. When a believer prays for another by laying on of hands, the anointing is transferred to the person receiving prayer if that person has faith to believe. The woman with the issue of blood touched the hem of Christ's garment and was cured. Christ acknowledged that He felt "virtue" come out of Him and enter the woman's body (Mark 5:30, KJV). The word *virtue* is the Greek word *dunamis* and is the same word used in Acts 1:8, when Christ said we would receive "power [*dunamis*] when the Holy Spirit has come upon you [us]." This word is used in the New Testament in references to the miraculous power of God that operates to perform miracles (Mark 6:5; 9:39; Acts 2:22; 8:13). If the *dunamis* (power) of God is released through the prayer of faith and the laying on of hands (James 5:14–15), the same anointing can be transferred to a cloth that is prayed over by faith. When these prayer cloths were taken to the sick and possessed in Paul's day, even the evil spirits departed from the possessed (Acts 19:12).

PRAYING OVER THINGS

There are many people who love Christ, but their particular denomination does not accept the view that miracles can occur today. They would teach that these prayer cloths were "special miracles just for the apostle Paul," and we should not attempt to copy this type of ministry in our contemporary time. However, what do these skeptical individuals do with the following verse?

> Assuredly, I say to you, whatever you bind on earth will be bound in heaven, and whatever you loose on earth will be loosed in heaven. Again I say to you that if two of you agree on earth concerning anything that they ask, it will be done for them by My Father in heaven. For where two or three are gathered together in My name, I am there in the midst of them.
> —MATTHEW 18:18–20

This is a new covenant promise, giving the believer spiritual authority over the powers of the enemy. Christ said if two or three agree as touching "anything that they ask"! Years ago I saw the word "anything" and realized there was no limitation placed upon the "thing" we pray and agree over. "Anything" is a broad word, meaning we can agree in prayer concerning personal needs, other people, our circumstances, the need for healing, financial breakthrough—literally *any need* becomes *anything*!

When I was a teenage evangelist, I read Matthew 18:18–20, noticing that I could agree as "touching anything." Suddenly a supernatural faith was burned into my spirit, and I believed that if we could pray over "things" that belonged to sinners, then the Lord could convict them, bringing them to the revival where I was speaking, where the Word of God and the Holy Spirit would bring them to Christ. At different times there were three churches where extended revivals occurred due to the spiritual results of such prayer: Daisy, Tennessee, went seven and a half weeks; Lafollette, Tennessee, went eleven weeks nightly; and Pulaski, Virginia, continued for almost five consecutive weeks. In each of these great revivals, hundreds came to Christ, and many of the conversions were a result of a believing family member bringing something that belonged to the unsaved loved one, having it prayed over, then taking it back home. Everyone was amazed at how the Lord was performing special miracles of salvation through the same method Paul used centuries ago.

The inspiration to pray over items and return them to the sinner without their knowledge of the prayer came to me after reading the story of Paul and the handkerchiefs and aprons. I was so burdened because people were inviting loved ones to the revival, but they refused to attend. I read the verses in Acts 19:11–12 and thought, "If they won't come to us, then we will take what's happening to them!"

We began by requesting that families place a photograph of unsaved family members in a large box. Each day for hours intercessors would hold up the pictures and "send the word of conviction" to the person whose picture they held, demanding that the adversary's influence be broken over the sinner. Within days these individuals began attending the revival with their loved ones, and many received Christ. In one revival there were more than five hundred unconverted souls who came to Christ. One woman said, "I want to pray over my husband's shoes. I believe that when he wears them, God will begin to convict him of sin!" We prayed that when he wore them, God would watch over the prayer and perform a miracle of salvation; we were "agreeing as touching anything"! In a few days, he attended the revival and received Christ.

I began to comprehend how important this type of special miracle was. I realized that there are many times a person will not attend church or for physical limitations cannot attend and be prayed over or ministered to. Here we were in a live church service, receiving the Word and giving an opportunity for personal ministry, and yet many were unable to be present and desired the same touch of God we were experiencing. This is one of the other reasons for the special prayer cloth ministry.

One young man was struggling with heavy addictions and mental attacks from Satan. His parents were at "wits' end" (Ps. 107:27) and were stuck in a spiritual battle, concerned for their son. The family contacted a major youth group that continually prayed and interceded for the lost. The dad requested that the youths pray over prayer cloths that could be placed in the mattress and in other places in the young man's room. Prayer was offered for hours, and the cloths were sent and scattered in his room without the knowledge of the young man. After years of his parents praying and believing for his salvation, within ten days the young man asked for prayer—and change occurred. He had literally been sleeping on the prayers and faith of a group of young people who believed God for his deliverance!

It is important to understand that this is not some religious form or ritual, as without a pure faith it becomes a mere routine. I am reminded of a group of Jewish men who saw Paul casting out evil spirits and decided to imitate the man of God. They found a deranged man and spoke to the devil in him, saying, "We exorcise you by the Jesus whom Paul preaches" (Acts 19:13). The evil spirit rose up in the man, saying, "Jesus I know, and Paul I know; but who are you?" (v. 15), and tore the clothes off these seven men, who ran streaking out of the house (vv. 16). The seven men were the sons of one of the leading chief priests (v. 14), yet they failed to expel the demon. It is clear that these seven sons of Sceva had religious knowledge but no relationship with Christ!

There is only one type of prayer God will answer when a person is not in any type of relationship with Him, and that is the prayer for forgiveness of sins (Matt. 9:2–7; Luke 7:44–48). It requires faith to believe that God can forgive sins, and when a sinner asks for forgiveness, it initiates a believing process that leads to salvation and justification by faith (Rom. 5:1). Christ always addressed the sin issue first and the healing issue second (Matt. 9:2). When Christ healed one man, He told him to go and "sin no more, lest a worse thing come upon you" (John 5:14). Forgiveness can help bring healing to a person's spirit, emotions, and even to the body (James 5:16).

My father had a great anointing and strong compassion to minister to the sick and anyone who was hurting physically. He loved praying for people, and at times he spent hours in an altar service, staying until the last person was prayed for. One of our relatives had a granddaughter who had an afflicted leg that she painfully dragged around. Dad anointed a prayer cloth and told the grandmother to place the cloth over the leg. The girl was healed! It is so exciting to realize that this method of prayer can be used to reach those who cannot reach us.

I know some will say, "I don't believe in all of that." Well, as the old-timers used to say, "The proof is in the pudding." Those who saw their loved ones saved as a result of their faith and obedience will never be convinced that it doesn't work; they saw the proof with their own eyes that God honors faith and obedience.

GOD USES PEOPLE AND THINGS

Moses was commanded to use his *rod* as a sign of God's power (Exod. 4:17). Moses also built a *brass serpent,* and those bitten by poisonous vipers were cured when they looked upon the brazen serpent on the pole (Num. 21:8–9). Gideon took three hundred *clay pitchers* with *lamps, jars,* and three hundred *trumpets* and defeated the Midianites (Judg. 7:16–22). Samson took the *jawbone* of a dead donkey and slew a thousand Philistines (Judg. 15:15). Shamgar defeated six hundred men with the weapon of an *ox goad* (Judg. 3:31). David's faith tool was his *slingshot,* which he used to deck Goliath (1 Sam. 17:50). King Hezekiah was cured after placing a lump of *figs* on his diseased wound (Isa. 38:21). God gave the king an amazing sign of his healing by allowing the *sundial* to go backward ten degrees (v. 8). On one occasion Christ spat on the ground and put *mud* over the eyes of a blind man, and he was cured (John 9:6–7).

Why was it necessary for there to be a rod, a brass snake, a slingshot, trumpets, a jawbone, an ox goad, figs, and mud used to assist in the miracles of the Bible? Jesus healed other blind men without using mud (Matt. 9:28–29). After Goliath was slain, years later four other giants were slain without anyone using a slingshot (2 Sam. 21:15–22). The brass serpent was preserved in the tabernacle of Moses, and later the temple, for almost nine hundred years and never cured anyone again. It was destroyed by King Hezekiah (2 Kings 18:4).

God has allowed men to use *things* as faith tools to hold in the hand or to display in public view as the object God would use to demonstrate the person's gifting, power, or ability. In some instances the object was a type or symbol of the coming Messiah—such as the rod or the brass serpent (John 3:14). However, the Almighty also ensures that once He used an object for a major miracle, that others following do not take the same object and think they can repeat the exact miracle from generation to generation, as this would lead to idolatry. The brass serpent healed Israel in the wilderness (Num. 21), but it never healed anyone after the major healing crusade in the wilderness. Yet Israel preserved the brass snake, placing it in the temple of Solomon and burning incense to it as a sacred relic (2 Kings 18:4). It is *possible* that at Christ's crucifixion, when the Roman soldiers were gambling for Christ's seamless outer garment, they may have believed it held some supernatural healing power, and perhaps one of them could use it for personal gain (John 19:23–24). However, it was not the garment that cured the woman with the issue of blood (Matt. 9:20–21) but the anointing and virtue dwelling in the Man who wore the garment!

The handkerchief or apron is a very simple and common object that holds little if any monetary value and is actually quite insignificant. This makes the answered prayer all the more interesting, and the fabric on the cloth can never receive credit for the healing. It is very unlikely that someone is going to worship a small piece of fabric that may have a few tears or drops of anointing oil on it. This is how God uses "the weak things of the world to put to shame the things which are mighty"

(1 Cor. 1:27). It is how He demonstrates that "the natural man does not receive the things of the Spirit of God, for they are foolishness to him" (1 Cor. 2:14).

You can always pray prayers in which you speak the Word, and God will "hasten my word to perform it" (Jer. 1:12, KJV). The method of anointing a cloth has a New Testament basis and can be used in faith as it was centuries ago. "According to your faith be it unto you" (Matt. 9:29, KJV).

In the New Testament, the Lord gave us several faith tools, such as the power of agreeing, the anointed prayer cloth, and agreeing as "touching anything," that will enable us to send the Word and speak the Word in the manner that Christ, our example, did when He spoke a healing word to the centurion's servant in spite of the fact that the servant was at home and Christ was perhaps miles away from the house (Matt. 8:5–13). When your faith is stirred, use the various biblical methods to minister to those in need. Some may suggest these methods are foolish—in reality that's the whole idea, for God desires the glory when He intervenes in your situation!

Praying in Whose Name— Jesus or Yeshua?

And in that day you will ask Me nothing. Most assuredly, I say to you, whatever you ask the Father in My name He will give you. Until now you have asked nothing in My name. Ask, and you will receive, that your joy may be full.

—JOHN 16:23–24

OUR MINISTRY IS internationally recognized in two major fields of biblical research: the study of Hebraic roots, and the message of the coming of Christ through the study of biblical prophecy. These two unique subjects are both exciting and, among some, quite controversial. Often certain aspects of these teachings are considered controversial among those who disagree. I have learned that some disagreements are actually based upon misunderstandings, misinterpretations, or, at times, traditional interpretations presented by a denomination to protect their own beliefs more than what the Word itself actually teaches. In other words, it is not usually the plain biblical truth that initiates disagreement but someone's opinion of that truth. This is true especially with the Hebraic root of Christianity.

The study of Hebraic roots is a broad yet specific study revealing to the Gentile Christian community how the foundation of the New Testament is found in the Old Testament through types, shadows, patterns, and symbolism used by Moses and the prophets. It studies the feasts, Sabbath cycles, and the ancient prophecies of the Hebrew prophets. Paul revealed that the Jewish faith is the original olive tree of which the wild olive tree branches of the Gentiles were grafted in (Rom. 11). The Sabbaths, new moons, feasts, and narratives found in the first five books of the Bible (the Torah) are all a picture of Christ, His redemptive work, and future prophetic events.

There are many Gentiles who, instead of simply gleaning the truths from the roots and using it to enhance their understanding of their spiritual heritage, take the teaching and bring other Gentiles into almost a type of spiritual bondage, demanding them to follow the details of every law established by Moses. For example, the original Sabbath (seventh day) was Saturday, and God required Israel to rest and worship Him on the Sabbath. In the Western culture, the seventh day is the last day of the week, or Sunday. Thus most Western Christians worship on Sunday. The Sabbath has nothing to do with a person's salvation, redemption, or entrance into heaven. However, some teach that anyone not worshiping on Saturday will be lost for eternity. I will not take up space to debate either position, other than saying each person must "work out your own salvation with fear and trembling" (Phil. 2:12). As Paul wrote:

> Who are you to judge another's servant? To his own master he stands or falls. Indeed, he will be made to stand, for God is able to make him stand. One person esteems one day above another; another esteems every day alike. Let each be fully convinced in his own mind. He who observes the day, observes it to the Lord; and he who does not observe the day, to the Lord he does not observe it. He who eats, eats to the Lord, for he gives God thanks; and he who does not eat, to the Lord he does not eat, and gives God thanks.
>
> —ROMANS 14:4–6

There is one area, however, of concern. There are some within Christian-Messianic circles who are causing quite a division in the body of Christ by saying that all believers must pray in the Hebrew name of *Jesus*, which is *Yeshua*. The teaching says that if you do not pray in Christ's *original Hebrew name*, not only will God not hear your prayer, but also you are praying in a pagan name! Since we are instructed by Christ to "ask the Father in My name" (John 16:23), then we must understand the name of Christ.

THE AUTHORITY OF THE NAME

Being a student of Hebraic teaching, I am fully aware that the Hebrew name of Jesus is actually the name *Yeshua*. When the angel Gabriel came to Mary at Nazareth and said to her, "You shall call His name Jesus," he actually said His name would be *Yeshua*. Some well-meaning believers argue and debate fellow Christians as to what name they are using in prayer. I have received letters and e-mails from people who teach that the English form of His name, *Jesus*, is a pagan form of the name *Zeus* and should not be used.

In Christ's day there were three languages spoken. The Jews spoke Hebrew, the Romans spoke Latin, and the Greeks spoke Greek. When Christ was crucified, an inscription was placed above His head in each of these three languages:

> Then many of the Jews read this title, for the place where Jesus was crucified was near the city; and it was written in Hebrew, Greek, and Latin.
> —JOHN 19:20

The English name *Jesus* is *Yeshua* in Hebrew and is spelled with the following Hebrew letters: *yod, shin, vav, ayin*. The pronunciation is *Ya-shoo-ah*. This Hebrew name is a form of the English name Joshua, which means, "He will save." Thus even the Old Testament story of Joshua indicated the coming One! *Yeshua* is in the present tense, meaning "God is now saving."

We can take a look at how the name Jesus was transliterated from the original language into the English language. Here is the etymology of the word. Yeshua is a Hebrew name, and the Greek scriptures translate it as Iesous (pronounced *ee-AY-sus*). The English name *Jesus* comes from the Latin transliteration of the name Iesous. The reason the letter *I* is used is that the Greek has no letter *Y*, and the Latin *I* is both an *I* and *J*.

Scholars state that Jesus is a transliteration, or a copy, of the Greek name. It is a derivation of the Hebrew name *Ieshoua*, a common Jewish name in Christ's time. There is also no *J* in the Hebrew alphabet. In the English language God's name is Jehovah and Christ's name is Jesus. In Hebrew the letter *J* is actually *yod*, which is *Y* in the English language. Therefore God's name and Christ's name begin in Hebrew with the letter *Y*.

One of the earliest English Bibles was the Geneva Bible. The 1560 edition did not use the letter *J* but the letter *I* when spelling *Jesus*—*Iesus*. The letter *J* was inserted in the English translation in the eighteenth century. This is how the name was transliterated:

- Hebrew—Yah-shu-a

- Latin—Ie-s-us

- Greek—Ie-s-ous

- English—Je-s-us

By the third century, the names for Jesus and Christ were shortened into monogram form. The name of Jesus was identified with the letters *IHS, which* is said to represent the phrase "Jesus, Savior of Men" in Latin. The second monogram, and believed to be the oldest, is the Chi-Rho, or the labarum. These letters are the Greek letter *chi* (χ) and the letter *rho* (ρ), which are the two letters of Christ's name in Greek. In modern culture among the Catholics, the IHS is seen on the priest's staff.

One of the main challenges comes with the translation of the Bible into other languages other than the original Hebrew and Greek. In the English Bible the Old Testament is translated from Hebrew, with small portions of Daniel and Ezra being written in Aramaic, and the New Testament from the Koine Greek. Every translation must use the letters available in their alphabet to translate the letters from the original manuscripts. This is a challenge for Bible translators, because many of the primate tribal languages consist of grunts, breathing sounds, and even odd noises when communicating among themselves.

There are those who insist that a person never say the English name *Jesus* in prayer or worship. The name of Christ is pronounced differently in different languages because of the transliteration from the alphabets. For example, one of the Hebrew names for God is *EL*. This name is recorded thousands of times in various forms in the Old Testament. The most common name of God in the English Bible is the Hebrew name *Elohim*. There is another name for God, found in the Hebrew Bible when combining the Hebrew letters, *yod, hei, vav, hei*, or YHVH. In English the name is pronounced as *Jehovah*; however, the Jewish rabbis are emphatic that this sacred name for God cannot and should not be pronounced, as the actual pronunciation has been lost in history.

In English, the name *God* can represent any god from any religion. Should Christians quit praying and saying "Praise God" or "Glory to God" because the heathen also say god or use the word *god* to identify their deity? The answer is no, because the true God looks at the *heart* of the individual doing the worshiping and the petitions. Paul once saw a monument dedicated to the "unknown god," and Paul used this ignorance to his advantage when telling the audience in Greece who this unknown god was—the God of Abraham, Isaac, and Jacob (Acts 17:23–24).

When a person argues that we cannot say the English transliteration of the name *Jesus*, then we must ask ourselves the following question: multiple millions of Christians prayed a sinner's prayer asking Jesus into their hearts; are they all lost and deceived because they used the wrong name? When being baptized in water, some say in the name of the Father, the Son, and the Holy Spirit (Matt. 28:19), and others baptize in Jesus's name (Acts 2:38). If the name of Jesus is used in the baptism, then does not using the Hebrew name void the baptism? In evangelistic meetings held overseas, powerful missionaries preach and minister to the sick using the name of Jesus. There have been countless millions of individuals in foreign nations who have received a miraculous healing or assistance after prayer being offered in the name of

Jesus. How is it possible that this name, if it is some form of a pagan idol's name, holds such authority and power when it is spoken?

On a personal note, my father, Fred Stone, was known throughout the body of Christ as an intense prayer warrior, spending hours at a time in prayer prior to ministering in a church or convention. During his sixty-two years of ministry he prayed hundreds of thousands of prayers and saw countless numbers touched and healed through the prayer of faith. In every instance he would pray in the "name of the Lord Jesus Christ" or "in Jesus's mighty name!" The power of the name was demonstrated by the answers to his prayers.

There is ample evidence that God looks at the heart of each seeker. When we say, "in Jesus's name," the heavenly Father recognizes the word coming from the pure heart and knows we are praying in the name of His Son. It is also important to understand that it is always in order if a person chooses to pray in the Hebrew name of Jesus, *Yeshua*.

There are about 1.4 billion professing Christians in the world. As believers in Christ they will pray in the name of Jesus; below is a list of languages and how each spell the name of Jesus (spelled phonetically):[1]

The Language	The Phonetic Spelling
Creole	*Jezu*
Filipino	*Hesus*
Galician	*Xesús*
Irish	*Íosa*
Italian	*Gesù*
Kenyan	*Yesu*
Luganda (Uganda)	*Yezu*
Malaysia	*Yesus*
Mandarin Chinese	*Yeu-su*
Maori	*Hehu*
Polish	*Jezus*
Romanian	*Isus*
Russian	*Iesus*
Swahili	*Yesu*

The Language	The Phonetic Spelling
Turkish	*İsa*
Vietnamese	*Giêsu*
Zulu	*Ujesu*

The blood of Jesus Christ deals with *sin*. But the name of Jesus deals with *sickness* and *spiritual attacks* of the enemy.

HEALING COMES THROUGH HIS NAME

The first healing in the New Testament after the initial outpouring of the Holy Spirit on Pentecost was the miracle of the lame man at the Eastern Gate. Born lame from his mother's womb, he was a thirty-eight-year-old beggar who survived by the occasional coins he collected from compassionate people entering the temple in Jerusalem.

When Peter and John saw him, Peter said:

> Silver and gold I do not have, but what I do have I give you: In the name of Jesus Christ of Nazareth, rise up and walk.
>
> —ACTS 3:6

The fact that this man was instantly healed demonstrated that Jesus was alive! A *dead Jesus* would not have the power to answer a prayer that was prayed in His name! We are told the key to this miracle was faith in the name of Jesus:

> And His name, through faith in His name, has made this man strong, whom you see and know. Yes, the faith which comes through Him has given him this perfect soundness in the presence of you all.
>
> —ACTS 3:16

Notice that faith in the name brought the miracle. The Hebrew name of Jesus, *Yeshua*, is actually a form of the name of Joshua (*Yehoshua*), the same name as the servant of Moses who brought Israel into the Promised Land. This name means, "Jehovah saved." The point is that whether we say *Yeshua* or *Jesus*, it still takes faith in His name to see a miracle occur.

HIS NAME IN FOREIGN NATIONS

Perhaps the most interesting and profound proof of the authority in the name of Jesus can be observed when a person ministers overseas. Missionaries report that in every nation of the world—including nations in Asia, Europe, and the Middle East, as well as the nations where the major religion is Hinduism, Buddhism, or Islam—the evil spirits that possess and control men and women *all* recognize the name of Jesus! When missionaries pray over the individual possessed by a demon, it is common for the evil spirit to say, "Do not say that name," or to begin to curse the name of Jesus. Moments later, however, the power of that name is manifested as the person is delivered from satanic oppression and demonic possession.

God knows whose name we are praying in when we say the name of Jesus. The Most High Father is looking down upon us to see our faith in His Word and our faith in the name of Jesus. It is: "God also bearing witness both with signs and wonders, with various miracles…" (Heb. 2:4).

SO WHICH NAME DO WE USE?

There are more than one billion Christians on the earth, scattered across every continent and nation on the planet. The teaching of Hebraic roots—including the insight into the Hebrew name of Jesus—is known among many in North America and parts of Western Europe, Australia, and in Israel among the messianic groups. However, there are multiple hundreds of millions of believers in places such as Africa, China, South America, and other lands that simply have a Bible and say the name Jesus in their particular tongue. It is evident from the tangible presence of the Lord in their services that the Holy Spirit is moving in their hearts, and many are being converted to Christ and baptized in the Holy Spirit.

I have messianic friends who only pray using the Hebrew name *Yeshua*. I know of many colleges whose students and teachers pray in the name of Jesus. The fact is, heaven is very familiar with all of the world's languages, as it was God who distributed the languages at the tower of Babel (Gen. 11). The Almighty is very familiar with various translations and transliterations of the Bible and the name of Christ. I suggest that a person must follow his or her individual conscience concerning this issue. It is obvious that the biblical Sabbath is Saturday; however, the seventh day in our culture has become Sunday. Thus if a person feels he must worship on Saturday, there is no biblical restraint in doing so. However, Paul was meeting and receiving offerings on the "first day of the week," which was Sunday (Acts 20:7, 18; 1 Cor. 16:2). In the Book of Acts, the Gentile believers were being persecuted in the synagogues and expelled from sites because of their faith in Christ. It became difficult for the Gentiles to worship with the Jews because of arguments and persecution, thus Sunday became the traditional Christian day of worship.

Never place more confidence on a day or a feast than in the blood of Christ. It is Christ's redemptive work that is the primary message to preach and proclaim—not arguing about which day is the right day. God knows His Son, knows your heart, knows your level of understanding, and, whether we use the English name or the Hebrew name, the fact is that His name is worshiped in both languages—anywhere in the world.

What to Do When You Don't Know How to Pray

Likewise the Spirit also helps in our weaknesses. For we do not know what we should pray for as we ought, but the Spirit Himself makes intercession for us with groanings which cannot be uttered. Now He who searches the hearts knows what the mind of the Spirit is, because He makes intercession for the saints according to the will of God.

—ROMANS 8:26–27

IN JOURNALISM AND writing there are five words used as an outline when answering questions in a major article or a documentary. They are *who, what, when, where,* and *how.* In Romans 8, Paul did not say, "We do not know *who* to pray for," because when praying for an individual we normally know that person's name. Neither does he say, "We don't know *when* to pray," for the Bible says to "pray without ceasing" (1 Thess. 5:17) and to be "ready in season and out of season" (2 Tim. 4:2). The *when* is never the issue, as we can pray at any place and at any time. We can also pray anywhere; therefore the verse does not read, "We know not *where* we should pray." The *where* is insignificant.

With some individuals there are questions on *how* to pray. Even Christ's disciples said, "Lord, teach us [*how*] to pray" (Luke 11:1). This is somewhat of an odd question coming from men with Jewish backgrounds, who would have been familiar with synagogues and would have sat in a Jewish synagogue often. Both the synagogue and the temple were places of prayer. However, in both sites the prayers were often more of a routine or ritual, repeating the same words and phrases daily, weekly, or during a feast. No doubt the followers of Christ observed that His prayers were actually answered and were not some rustic formula handed down for generations. They wanted to know how to pray, and Christ gave them a pattern (Luke 11:1–4).

In Romans 8 Paul said we do not know *what* to pray for as we should. In the context of the chapter, Paul is speaking of creation and expresses that all of creation is travailing and groaning for the day of deliverance (vv. 21–22). In verse 23 he states that even believers, who have the firstfruits of the Spirit, also travail, waiting for the redemption of the body—the day when we receive a resurrected body and are delivered from this body of death. He reveals that "we do not know what we should pray for as we ought," revealing that it is the Spirit who "makes intercession for us with groanings" (v. 26).

This can be witnessed in the lives of mature believers as they reach their later years. Some have great health and live ten to twenty years longer than others. Others may experience a serious illness that begins to affect their bodies. When this occurs, what should we pray for? Should we pray for healing, for additional years to be added, for physical strength? Or should we just say, "Whatever You wish, Lord"? Because we don't know what to pray for, we may be tempted to refrain from praying at all.

Paul gives a solution to this challenge by telling us that the Spirit, "helps in our weaknesses" (v. 26). This indicates not only spiritual weaknesses but also weakness in every area of our lives, including physical infirmities and even moral struggles. The word *helpeth* (KJV) is from a Greek word meaning, "to take hold of together." It can be used for someone who assists in carrying a burden.

The will of a man is known to the mind of a man. The will of God is revealed by the mind of the Holy Spirit. The Holy Spirit makes intercession for us. When a person intercedes for another, it is a legal implication of someone standing in court defending a person. The Holy Spirit intercedes for us.

THREE TYPES OF PRAYER LANGUAGE

By Scripture and experience I have learned there are three types of prayer language given to those who have received the Spirit.

1. Praying with your understanding

To pray with your understanding, you must pray in your natural, native language. There are individuals trained in speaking numerous languages. One man I know in the Middle East can speak four major languages. He can actually move from English, to Hebrew, to Aramaic, and to Greek without hardly pausing to think. I have wondered what language he hears in his mind when he is tempted by the enemy or when the adversary throws a thought into his mind. The answer is the original, initial language that he learned as a child. To pray with your understanding would be to pray in the words of your primary language. In my case, it would be the English language.

The weakness of praying in the English language is encountered when your mind begins to doubt the words you are saying. We know that we must pray believing, and pray in faith, nothing wavering (James 1:6). Thus, when we are uncertain how to pray, we are provided a second method of intercession, praying "in the Spirit."

2. Praying in the Spirit

Praying in the Spirit, or "praying in the Holy Ghost," is a phrase used in Jude 20: "But you, beloved, building yourselves up on your most holy faith, praying in the Holy Spirit." The Holy Spirit has a prayer language of His own, which He imparts to believers who are baptized in the Holy Spirit (Acts 2:1–4; Acts 10:45–46; Acts 19:1–7). The Bible teaches that man consists of a body, a soul, and spirit (1 Thess. 5:23). When a believer prays "in the Spirit," he or she is praying in the language the Lord has imparted to the individual's inner spirit. In 1 Corinthians 14:14, we read: "For if I pray in a [*unknown*] tongue, my spirit prays, but my understanding is unfruitful" (emphasis added).

Just as the human body has a voice box with vocal cords, the human spirit has an inner voice of its own. The human body communicates in learned languages, but the human spirit can communicate in unlearned languages that are imparted by the Holy Spirit Himself. This form of communication involves your spirit speaking directly to God (1 Cor. 14:2).

3. Praying with groanings

Paul taught that we make intercession with groanings that cannot be uttered. The Amplified says: "…the Spirit Himself goes to meet our supplication and pleads in our behalf with unspeakable yearnings and groanings too deep for utterance" (Rom. 8:26). I understand the meaning of the prayer language called *praying in the Spirit* or speaking with tongues, but what does the word *groaning* mean? The word means, "to sigh or to cry out." During times of great grief, it is common for a living loved one of the departed to cry out in an agonizing moment of grief or sorrow. At times there are no specific words said, as the sounds are not articulated words but painful groans, signaling loss, from deep within the soul. This is an example of "groanings which cannot be uttered."

The majority of our prayers are prayed with our understanding and in our native language. At times a Spirit-filled believer will begin to pray in the prayer language of the Spirit, often during worship (1 Cor. 14:15) or in times of deep intercession (Rom. 8:34). There will, however, be occasions when great heaviness or grief strikes the soul like an iron hammer hitting an anvil. Sudden and unexpected events overwhelm us and cause a weakness to the point of not knowing how to pray. In these seasons, often a sigh or a groaning from the soul is the only way a person can communicate to the heavenly Father.

All three of these methods can be operative today, as the Holy Spirit is still on earth working through the body of Christ and enduing individual believers with power from on high.

WHAT TO DO WHEN IT SEEMS YOU
ARE WAITING TOO LONG

It only takes a brief second for you to initiate a prayer, and it only takes a moment for God to hear you. However, it may take an extended time for God to answer your prayer. This is especially true when your answer is connected with someone else—that person may not be serving Christ or presently be in God's will. It may require time for God to set up the circumstances and to alter on earth what He has decreed in heaven before you will be able to experience the answer.

When Job lost his ten children, their home, all of his livestock, and his health, three of his friends arrived to share in his grief. After seven days, all three began a series of discourses to give their personal explanations as to why God had sent such devastation to Job. God knew that Job had integrity (Job 2:3). However, the friends felt they needed to defend God's integrity and gave a series of *spiritual* reasons for the disasters. Like many others, they believed there must be a reason why bad things happen to good people.

THREE WAITING ZONES

After many years of ministry, I have discovered that you may need to travel through three *spiritual zones* prior to your prayer being completely answered. Let's look at these *waiting zones.*

The wilderness zone

The father of John the Baptist, Zacharias, was given a detailed prophecy concerning the birth of his son, including his name before he was ever conceived (Luke 1:13). Scripture indicates that after John's birth, he grew strong and was "in the deserts till the time of his manifestation to Israel" (v. 80). When time came for John to minister, the people came to him in the desert instead of him going into the synagogues. The most important item in the deserts of Israel is water, and the Jordan River was the sanctuary of John!

Your wilderness zone is the place God hides you from public view while you prepare for His purposes; it's the place where you write your words in private, practice singing in front of a mirror, or preach to the animals in the house. Does this sound odd? When I was eighteen years old, I found a beautiful mountain behind a church campground in Roanoke, Virginia. I recall laying twelve stones in the form of an altar and painting the names of God on the surface. It became my private prayer mountain, and only three people knew it was there. I would pray, preach, and imagine the trees were people. No one was watching except the Lord and perhaps a few angels that were smiling at the zeal of this young boy! You may feel you are being hidden for a season, but then the time comes the Lord will bring you out of the hiding place to the place He desires for you

The warfare zone

The warfare zone will be experienced by every believer. At times the war is a battle over doing the will of God. Many times we become frustrated because we cannot fulfill our own expectations, which are often expectations we place upon ourselves that God is not requiring. Thus a mental battle ensues, and we place self-pressure, creating our own battle. Other conflicts are caused by our struggle against demonic agents that may be assigned as hindering spirits, similar to Paul's "thorn in the flesh," the messenger of Satan that buffeted him (2 Cor. 12:7). The mental or spiritual battles will always be a part of our life experiences. However, just as Daniel held firm for three weeks, later discovering the heavens were raging with a cosmic conflict that was eventually broken by the intervention of the archangel Michael (Dan. 10), we must hold fast our confession until we experience a complete breakthrough.

The waiting zone

The third zone is the waiting zone. This can be the most difficult as we are a generation of instant messaging: e-mails, texting, and Twitter. In seconds we can communicate with anyone around the world. We have come to expect instant answers to questions and comments. When we pray, there will be an earthy time element from the moment the Father hears until the moment we see the manifestation. The waiting zone is where we will either hold on or give up. The ability to wait requires patience, the ability to remain in faith over an extended period of time when you see no results from your believing.

TRUSTING THAT GOD KNOWS BEST

There will be many times in your life when you will question why God would allow certain things to happen, especially bad things happening to good people. This is where trusting God is important. Lazarus was a close friend of Christ. We read: "He whom thou lovest is sick" (John 11:3, KJV). Christ's love was emphasized when we read He loved Martha, her sister, and Lazarus (v. 5). Yet Christ didn't show up to prevent the death, nor did He send an anointed cloth or "speak the word" as He did with the centurion's servant. He remained where He was.

Jesus didn't show up when they requested or anticipated His arrival. Yet He loved Lazarus. When you don't see Christ moving in your direction, it does not mean He doesn't love you.

PRAYING AND INTERPRETING THE PRAYER LANGUAGE OF THE SPIRIT

Prior to the translating and printing of the Holy Bible, common men and women were in darkness concerning the great doctrines of the Bible. With the Protestant Reformation and the translation of the 1611 English Bible, the distribution of the Word of God and the voices of reformers began to restore great doctrines from the Scripture. This restoration of truth was progressive, as each successive generation began to see truth that the previous generation may have missed.

Each denomination has a central doctrinal emphasis that marks that organization. Among the Lutherans, it was Martin Luther's emphasis that the "just shall live by faith," or justification by faith and not by works. The Baptists became noted for their emphasis on water baptism upon conversion and confession of your faith. The early Methodists were recognized as the "Holiness people," and their early leaders taught a sanctified and holy life after conversion. During the late 1800s and early 1900s, the Pentecostal movement emerged and became noted for its belief in the restoration of spiritual gifts (1 Cor. 12:7–10) and the baptism of the Holy Spirit with the first (initial) evidence of speaking with other tongues. Finally, in 1967, the Charismatic Renewal was birthed and was spread by numerous men and women from more traditional mainline churches that had embraced the operation of spiritual gifts. Charismatics also emphasized the importance of worship and the importance of individual and collective praise and worship in their congregations.

THE CONTROVERSY OF
SPEAKING WITH TONGUES

All of the above movements basically believe the same fundamental doctrines of Scripture. The most significant disagreement has been the belief concerning the operation of spiritual gifts, particularly the manifestation of speaking with other tongues. When I was growing up in the 1960s, the Pentecostals were considered a lower class of Christians, often on the lower economic ladder, and were considered an uneducated bunch whose spiritual *superstitions* led them to believe in miracles and God's supernatural power. As the years have passed, many in Pentecostal/full gospel congregations have received college and university educations and are in positions in the community, the state, and federal government. They have been economically blessed—and the movement includes countless millionaires who worship in their congregations. The majority of people who are charismatics were raised in the church, and they still believe in the gifts and in speaking with other tongues.

Today, there are hundreds of millions of believers around the world who believe in the baptism of the Holy Spirit and speaking with tongues. In the Book of Acts there are three direct and two implied references to individuals and groups of people being filled with the Spirit and speaking with tongues:

- Acts 2:1–4: About one hundred twenty believers,
  including the apostles (Acts 1:15) were initially filled
  with the Holy Spirit on the Day of Pentecost, and they
  all spoke with tongues.

- Acts 10:34–46: Cornelius, an Italian centurion, and his
  entire household were filled with the Holy Spirit and
  spoke with tongues.

- Acts 19:1–6: In Ephesus Paul laid his hands upon twelve disciples of John the Baptist, and they were all filled with the Spirit, spoke with tongues, and prophesied.

The other two references in Acts are Acts 8, where Peter and John laid their hands upon the believers in Samaria to receive the Holy Spirit, and Acts 9, where after Paul's conversion Ananias laid his hands upon him to receive his sight and be filled with the Holy Spirit (Acts 9:17). Later we read where Paul acknowledged that he spoke with tongues (1 Cor. 14:18).

The Greek word for "tongues" in the Acts passages is *glossa* and refers to a language spoken that was received by the infilling of the Holy Spirit. On the Day of Pentecost, the Galilean disciples spoke in actual languages understood by the Jews out of every nation (Acts 2:6). Others began to speak a supernatural language unknown to the person speaking, which was actually a prayer language from the Holy Spirit for that person to speak to himself or herself and to God (1 Cor. 14:2). Paul implied that it was possible for a tongues speaker to speak in the languages of "men and of angels" (1 Cor. 13:1).

There is a common belief among some that the operation of speaking with tongues was only for the first-century church, and then it ceased. This is contrary to Scripture, which clearly states that the gifts and calling of God are irrevocable (Rom. 11:29). We are to "come short in no gift, eagerly waiting for the revelation of Lord Jesus Christ" (1 Cor. 1:7).

Many of our early church fathers spoke about the gifts of the Spirit. Read these examples from their writings:

> For the prophetical gifts remain with us, even to this present time....Now, it is possible to see amongst us women and men who possess gifts of the Spirit of God.[1]
> —Justin Martyr (a.d. 160)

> In like manner we do also hear many brethren in the Church, who possess prophetic gifts, and who through the Spirit speak all

kinds of languages, and bring to light for the general benefit the hidden things of men, and declare the mysteries of God.[2]

—Irenaeus (a.d. 180)

This is He who places prophets in the Church, instructs teachers, directs tongues, gives powers and healings, does wonderful works, often discrimination of spirits, affords powers of government, suggests counsels, and orders and arranges whatever other gifts there are of *charismata*; and thus make the Lord's Church everywhere, and in all, perfected and completed.[3]

—Novatian (a.d. 200–258)

Let Marcion then exhibit, as gifts of his god, some prophets, such as have not spoken by human sense, but with the Spirit of God, such as have both predicted things to come, and have made manifest (1) the secrets of the heart; (2) let him produce a psalm, a vision, a prayer (3)—only let it be by the Spirit, (4) in an ecstasy, that is, in a rapture, (5) whenever an interpretation of tongues has occurred to him; let him show to me also, that any woman of boastful tongue (6) in his community has ever prophesied from amongst those specially holy sisters of his. Now all these signs (of spiritual gifts) are forthcoming from my side without any difficulty, and they agree, too, with the rules, and the dispensations, and the instructions of the Creator; therefore without doubt the Christ, and the Spirit, and the apostle, belong severally (7) to my God. Here, then, is my frank avowal for any one who cares to require it.[4]

—Tertullian (a.d. 207)

Some theologians suggest that the spiritual manifestations, including tongues, ceased when the New Testament was compiled. However, throughout history this manifestation has occurred and continued to reoccur during great spiritual awakenings and religious revivals, as revealed by these historical examples during the past one thousand years.

In the twelfth century, Hildegard of Bingen (a.d. 1098–1179) sang in other tongues, and the manifestation was called the *concerts of the Spirit*.[5] During the fourteenth century, the Moravians spoke in tongues, and the activity was called the "evacuations of the Spirit."[6] In the seventeenth century there were French prophets who spoke in tongues and the interpretation was given by the same person.[7] It is reported that in the seventeenth century the early Quakers spoke as the Spirit gave utterance.[8] Later, in the 1800s the Catholic Apostolic Church under the leadership of Edward Irving began experiencing manifestations of tongue speaking and prophetic utterances.[9] The manifestation occurred in Murphy, North Carolina, in 1886[10] and was also manifest throughout the famous Azusa Street revival in Los Angeles at the turn of the twentieth century. For anyone to suggest that tongue speaking ceased by the fifth century has not studied the subject in detail and certainly has not examined the spiritual renewals and awakenings occurring throughout history.

THE REASON FOR TONGUES SPEAKING

I will not spend page after page attempting to convince a skeptic that the gift of the Holy Spirit accompanied by the prayer language of the Spirit is available today. Instead I will give you the biblical reason for this gift.

After the outpouring of the Spirit on Pentecost, Peter called the manifestation the "gift of the Holy Spirit" (Acts 2:38). The Greek word for "gift" is the word *dorea*, and means a free gift, alluding to a spiritual or supernatural gift. Later, in 1 Corinthians 12:1–7, Paul mentions the *gifts* of the Spirit, using the Greek word *charisma*, a word commonly used for God's special endowment of power and operation of the Spirit upon believers (1 Cor. 1:7; 12:4, 9, 28).

It was Christ who promised that another Comforter would be sent to assist believers (John 14:16; 16:7). This Comforter is the Holy Spirit and was sent on the Day of Pentecost (Acts 2:1–4). Christ predicted that believers would speak with "new tongues" (Mark 16:17), and this manifestation occurred throughout the New Testament when believers were filled with the Spirit (Acts 2:1–4; Acts 10:46; Acts 19:6).

When a person speaks with other tongues, he or she is speaking in utterances from the Holy Spirit, as He speaks forth out of the human spirit directly to God (1 Cor. 14:2). There are numerous reasons given in the New Testament for praying in the prayer language of the Spirit.

Through the Holy Spirit we speak mysteries that the Lord wishes to make known for us (1 Cor. 14:2), as the Spirit can show us things to come (John 16:13). Paul wrote that, "He who speaks in a tongue edifies himself" (1 Cor. 14:4). The Greek word for "edifieth" (KJV) is *oikodomeo* and is the root of the word *edifice*. The word alludes to building a house. Since our body is the temple of the Holy Spirit (1 Cor. 3:16), the edifice that is being built up is the inner spirit of the person that dwells within them.

One of my personal favorites is the twentieth verse in Jude, which reads: "But you, beloved, building yourselves up on your most holy faith, praying in the Holy Spirit." The phrase "building up" means to build upon something that already has a foundation. Believers already have a foundation of faith through their redemptive covenant (Rom. 12:3). However, Scripture indicates there are various levels of faith that move up the spiritual ladder. When a storm was endangering their ship, the disciples had only "little faith" (Matt. 8:26). When people came to be healed by Christ, He often commented that their faith had made them whole (Mark 5:34). The Roman centurion told Jesus, "Only speak a word, and my servant will be healed." Jesus said this soldier had "such great faith" (Matt. 8:8, 10). Praying in the Holy Spirit supernaturally increases your faith and can actually assist in crushing the thoughts of unbelief that can enter the mind like a fiery dart from the adversary (Eph. 6:16).

Occasionally a sincere person will ask me why he should practice praying in tongues when he can pray in the English language, and God can hear that prayer the same as a prayer in some unknown tongue. He may point out that when we pray in the Spirit, our "understanding is unfruitful," or our understanding cannot comprehend what we are saying (1 Cor. 14:14). I can answer this from Scripture and by experience. Paul wrote that there would be times we would experience "infirmities" (the Greek word implies weaknesses of the mind, body, or spirit), and at those times we wouldn't know what to pray for as we should (Rom. 8:26, KJV). Paul then said, "…but the Spirit Himself makes intercession for us." There will be times when you feel mentally weak, emotionally drained, or under a physical attack, and you just don't feel like praying. The Holy Spirit will help your weakness by praying through you in the language of the Holy Spirit.

Some criticize the verse that "our understanding is unfruitful." But consider how many times your understanding actually interferes with your faith. Your understanding wants to walk by sight, but your spirit wants to walk by faith (2 Cor. 5:7). Your understanding doubts the supernatural as possible, but your faith can believe in the impossible. Man's understanding attempts to reason away miracles and words of Christ. This was evident as a pattern, as we can see by the Pharisees continually criticizing the miracles of Christ (Mark 11:31–33). We can pray and believe for simple things and believe the Lord will perform the work, such as: "Lord, bless this day," "Go with my children," "Give me strength," "Bring me peace," and so forth. However, when a major accident has occurred, or a sudden disease strikes, or a disaster hits a family, it is as a believer begins to pray for a supernatural intervention that the negative circumstances appear greater than the words they are praying. At that point praying in the Spirit allows the words to come straight out of your spirit and go directly to the Lord. Your mind does not know what is being spoken, and thus the Lord is able to block your mental reasoning from interfering with your prayer. This is usually the method the Lord uses when a person is in deep intercession concerning a tragedy or is interceding to prevent a person from dying before his or her time.

Praying Excessively in the Spirit

Year ago a terrible national disaster occurred in America. My father was greatly burdened and was praying much in the language of the Holy Spirit. He said, "Son, the Bible predicts that there will be dangerous times at the time of the end [2 Tim. 3:1], and believers must begin to pray excessively in the Spirit." This type of praying in the Spirit is usually practiced when a person is alone with God or in a group prayer meeting setting. Paul indicated that in a local congregational setting, the speaker should speak in the native language of the congregation, and speaking in tongues should be limited to a person speaking to himself or herself or to God, or, if a message in tongues is given in a public service for the edification of the congregation, it must be interpreted (1 Cor. 14). Paul said, "I speak with tongues more than you all," but in the congregation he spoke with understanding in order to teach the people the Word (vv. 18–19). Paul apparently spent much time praying in the Holy Spirit when he was not in a church setting or when he was in a meeting with intercessors.

Thus far during my ministry, I have personally seen more than five hundred thousand souls won to Christ and more than sixty thousand souls baptized in the Holy Spirit. I strongly believe that this spiritual fruit from the ministry has been a result of the thousands of hours spent by myself and other ministry partners praying in the prayer language of the Spirit. During this type of prayer, powerful messages are birthed, and the gifts of the Holy Spirit are activated to operate to meet the needs of the people.

I recall preaching an eight-week revival in Daisy, Tennessee, in 1982. I had spent much of the day in prayer for the service that night. I was at the pastor's house looking out a window and watching people arrive early, parking their cars in the church parking lot. A vehicle pulled in, but no one exited the car. Suddenly I had an open vision, and I saw something by revelation of the Holy Spirit. I immediately called over to the church and asked two young ministers to get over to the house. They literally *ran* up the hill and came inside.

I said, "The Holy Spirit is giving me a warning. In that car is a young woman who will attempt to distract the service tonight. Go to the front of the church and watch who gets out of the car, and keep your eyes on them. Be prepared!" The building was packed, and the service proceeded as normal. Midway in the service someone came to the platform and spoke to the pastor, and he exited the building, reentering from the front. He came up to me and said, "There is a woman in the parking lot who is threatening to harm herself." I looked up, and two men were literally carrying a young girl down the aisle. She was kicking and even cursing. They brought her to the front, and I asked the church to pray. I attempted to minister to her and began rebuking the spirit attacking her. This went on for some time.

Suddenly the Holy Spirit reminded me of the warning prior to service. I looked at the girl and said, "Do you want help?"

She said, "No, I don't."

I replied, "I'm wasting my time and yours."

When I stood up, one of the young men said, "That is the girl who stepped out of the car you told us to watch!"

This is one of many examples of the importance of knowing the mind of God on a daily basis and being prepared in advance through praying in the Holy Spirit.

Interpreting
the Prayer Language

One of the strengths of full gospel churches is their emphasis on the baptism of the Holy Spirit and the need to pray in the Holy Spirit. One of their greatest weaknesses, in my opinion, is the lack of teaching on the importance of interpreting the prayer language.

Based on 1 Corinthians 12:7–10, two of the nine spiritual gifts are different kinds of tongues and the interpretation of tongues. When I was growing up, it was common in a worship setting to hear someone give what was called a message in tongues and for someone to interpret it to the congregation, which is exactly what Paul taught should occur in a worship service (1 Cor. 14). However, a believer can interpret his own prayer language when he is alone in prayer in the same manner the gift operates in a public setting.

At age eighteen I traveled to War, West Virginia, to ask my dad's uncle, Rufus Dunford, to lay his hands upon me and pray for me to be blessed in my ministry. Rufus was healed of a brain tumor in the 1930s and received the gift of the Holy Spirit at the same time. He only had a third-grade education, but he could speak in divers tongues through the Spirit—in at least nine languages fluently. People from the coal fields knew he could go up to foreigners working in the mines and actually witness to them in their own language—and he had never studied any foreign language.

I spent more than two hours with him three months before his death and asked him to pray for me. I bent over his bed, and he laid hands on me and began to pray in the Spirit. He stopped and said, "Son, what is the Holy Spirit saying?" I replied that I didn't know. He rebuked me and said, "The Spirit is praying in Latin, and you need to know the language and how to interpret it!" This was the man my father ministered with in the early 1950s, and he also taught Dad to pray for the interpretation.

I cannot count the times my father would pray in a prayer language and then interpret by the Holy Spirit to me and others in the prayer meeting exactly what the Spirit was revealing. Many times it was a warning of something that was coming in the future for the family, the church, the nation, and, at times, for a foreign nation. My father saw the assassination of Yitzak Rabin by a fellow Jew three months prior to the actual assassination; he even shared the warning with Jewish believers from Israel. After praying in the Spirit, he predicted "great darkness coming from Lebanon," at a time when Lebanon had been stable and in a peaceful state for several years. Weeks later a democratic leader was killed, and the country when into chaos. I recall Dad praying in a home and saying that the Holy Spirit was revealing a clash between the two leading Palestinian groups in Israel. Weeks later the unexpected clashes began.

Praying in the Spirit also opened his mind and spirit to the world of visions and dreams.[11] The gift of interpreting tongues is imparted by the Holy Spirit. However, I believe that when Dad ministered with Rufus, it was this powerful minister who taught Dad the importance of praying for the interpretation.

If you pray in a prayer language, then you may be interpreting what the Spirit is praying without actually realizing it. For example, I always begin my prayers with worship to the Lord and by magnifying His name. Worship then flows into a time of boasting upon the goodness of God and telling Him of my love and appreciation for His blessings. This is always prayed in English, the only language I speak. Eventually, I will begin to focus on a certain aspect of the ministry (perhaps a coming conference or the need for a message to preach), and the language will move from English to a particular prayer language.

As I enter into a deeper level of prayer, my mind will begin to shift from my present focus to perhaps a burden I have for my children or a need a friend has that concerns me. As I pray in the Spirit, I begin to sense the prayer burden shift from my main focus to another situation. This occurred for years before I realized that it was not my mind being distracted, but the Holy Spirit was inspiring my thoughts toward the same direction as the Holy Spirit. When we think of interpreting something, we think of speaking out loud by saying, "Thus says the Lord...," and this is the correct pattern for interpreting tongues in a worship service. However, in private prayer, the mind of the Spirit can be revealed to the mind of the one praying, if the one praying will ask the Lord for the meaning of the words.

WHEN AN INTERPRETATION IS NOT NEEDED

There is one occasion when an interpretation is not needed, and that is when the Spirit is praying in a language known to the hearer. On the Day of Pentecost, those in the upper room were "all filled with the Holy Spirit and began to speak with other tongues, as the Spirit gave them utterance" (Acts 2:4). In the city of Jerusalem at that time, there were Jews representing at least fifteen different nations and regions, and each one heard the disciples speak in his or her own language (v. 6). There was no interpretation necessary, as each hearer was familiar with the language being spoken.

Speaking in tongues is called a sign "to unbelievers" (1 Cor. 14:22). During the outpouring on Pentecost in Acts 2, the Jews in Jerusalem had mixed reactions. Some were "confused," while others were "amazed and marveled." Others were "amazed and perplexed," or even "mocking," and said, "They are full of new wine" (Acts 2:5–13). The fact that uneducated Galileans were speaking in so many different languages was an amazing "sign" to the Jews. These Spirit-filled believers did not know the languages in which they were speaking, but those familiar with each language understood the message. Therefore there was no need for an interpretation, because each *hearer* recognized the language.

The manifestations of "different kinds of tongues" (1 Cor. 12:10) indicate different types of prayer languages—many are human languages that are unlearned by the speaker but inspired by the Holy Spirit. There are numerous faith-building stories where a believer prayed for a person from another nation and spoke in the language of the foreign person. To the Spirit-baptized believer, the language is an "unknown tongue," but the person hearing the speaker understands the language and can translate word for word what was being said.

One of the most dramatic personal illustrations of this occurred in Israel. I was studying the prophetic implications of Islam in the last days and asked my Arab friend Esam to find a knowledgeable Muslim I cold interview concerning Islamic predictions for the last days. He found a man who asked me to meet him at an Arab hotel on the Mount of Olives. After arriving, three Arab men were in a small lobby, and Esam served as my interpreter. After an hour, the call for prayer from the mosque was heard coming from the Temple Mount in Jerusalem. My interpreter said, "They said they must go pray."

I replied, "I am going to pray too."

He said, "You can't go with them because you are not a Muslim."

I shot back, "I am going to pray NOW!"

We stood up, and when I opened my mouth, I was not praying in English but in some form of Middle Eastern dialect. I heard the Muslim man say something to my interpreter, but I continued to pray. The prayer in the "unknown language" (unknown to me) was actually known to the Muslim. After I concluded, my interpreter said, "The man told me he thought you could not speak any language and wondered why you were speaking Farsi, which is the same language spoken among the Persians [in Iran]." He continued, "I told him it was the Holy Ghost and the Spirit of God in you!" I found out that the Holy Spirit revealed to this man that he had a bad heart and needed to be healed. The Lord told him that if he would believe on Christ, he would be cured! According to Esam, the Lord did touch this man.

This is an example of the listener receiving the interpretation in a language he understood, even though I did not know the language in which I was praying.

If a person lacks wisdom and asks God for wisdom, without wavering, the Lord will liberally impart wisdom to any who desire the blessing (James 1:5). Likewise, if a believer who speaks in tongues through the prayer language of the Spirit asks God for the interpretation, the Lord will grant understanding.

Never underestimate the significance of allowing the Holy Spirit to direct your prayer. It begins in the mind, then moves into your spirit. At times the language of your mind (in my case it's English) will shift to the language of the spirit (the prayer language). When this occurs, the Holy Spirit is directing your words and your life into the plan and purposes of God. The Holy Spirit can bring needed insight, encouragement, direction, and warnings. I realize there are some who would reject the very idea of praying in the prayer language. However, heed the instructions of Paul when he said, "Do not forbid to speak with tongues" (1 Cor. 14:39).

Twelve Significant and Effective Insights My Dad Taught Me About Prayer

After this manner therefore pray ye...
—MATTHEW 6:9, KJV

RED STONE WAS the greatest male prayer warrior and intercessor I have ever known. Dad was converted in 1949 in a southern West Virginia *coal field revival* that continued nightly for forty-two consecutive months. My father had only a tenth-grade education, never attended Bible school, but amassed thousands of books, read continually, and was gifted with wisdom that often amazed the highest among the academic elite he encountered. From the time of a teenager until his retirement due to physical disabilities, Dad was noted throughout America as a man who could *get hold of God* and a man to whom God revealed secrets.

In his early ministry he was blessed with several older mentors, but his chief teacher of spiritual gifts and their operation was his uncle, Rufus Dunford. Uncle *Rufe,* as he was called, was miraculously healed of a brain tumor in the early 1930s and accepted a call into the ministry at the moment he was healed. God imparted a unique spiritual gift to Rufus, as this humble man with a third-grade education could witness to foreigners working in the coal mines through the gift of divers kinds of tongues, which enabled him to speak fluently in the language of the other person although he had never formally or privately studied that language. Dad was with Rufus in Norton, Virginia, when he was *impressed of the Holy Spirit* to enter a shoe repair store and speak to a German man working in the store. Rufus had never been in the store, yet he knew *by the Holy Spirit* that a German man worked there. In a brief span of time Dad saw Rufus carrying on a conversation in fluent German, witnessing to the man about the virgin birth, the death, and resurrection of Christ and then inviting him to repent and receive Christ. The man refused, and Rufus instructed Dad that both of them were to leave the store as the man was about to become violent.

It was through observing the old-time preachers pray and the powerful intercessory prayers of Rufus that Dad learned and developed a daily life of prayer, learning the principles for approaching the gate of heaven and receiving answers from the heavenly temple! Just as men and women of God served as his example to pattern, I was honored to live with this great man and observe his actions and methods of prayer, and I have patterned much of my own prayer routines after him. In this section I wish to share the twelve most significant aspects, patterns, and methods of prayer that I learned from my father.

1. Bow Your Knees in Prayer

My dad believed you should bow your knees in prayer. I am a *walker* when I pray. I find it difficult to remain in one spot or location, and thus in a sanctuary, my private office, or basement of my home I often walk when I pray. If I am not walking, I will at times sit in a chair and pray, especially if the prayer is more of speaking to God as a son to his Father. When I am about to engage in an extended period of intercession, I have lain on my face or placed a Bible under my head as I lay on my back with my face toward heaven. However, when Dad prayed, he would always pray in one position: on his knees. If he were in a hotel room, he would kneel by a bed. In an office, he would kneel at a chair, and in the sanctuary, he would bow his knees at the front pew.

After seeing Dad pray in this position for years, I once asked him why he always prayed on his knees. He immediately quoted this verse:

"For this reason I bow my knees to the Father of our Lord Jesus Christ" (Eph. 3:14). He said, "We should pray bowing before the Lord as a sign of humility and honor toward Him." Throughout the Scriptures, when a person in covenant with God was in prayer or was encountering the presence of the Lord in some form, they "bowed their heads" (Exod. 12:27), they would "kneel before the LORD" (Ps. 95:6), or they would prostrate themselves on the ground, especially in the presence of an angel of the Lord (Num. 22:31; Rev. 1:17).

When we bow our knees, not only do we acknowledge the humbling of our spirit and the submission of our will, but we also physically demonstrate to God that we are honoring the verse teaching that "every knee should bow...every tongue should confess that Jesus Christ is Lord" (Phil. 2:10–11) and are submitting to His authority and Lordship. There is no set physical position required when praying, but bowing on your knees is most definitely biblical and honorable.

2. INCLUDE THE LORD'S PRAYER

At some point near the beginning of his prayer, my dad would pray the Lord's Prayer. The disciples of Christ observed that when Christ prayed prayers, they were answered. These were not like the numerous formal prayers offered in the synagogues, but they were prayers from His heart. The disciples approached Christ and requested, "Lord, teach us to pray" (Luke 11:1). Christ gave His followers a pattern to pray:

> After this manner therefore pray ye: Our Father which art in heaven, Hallowed be thy name. Thy kingdom come. Thy will be done in earth, as it is in heaven. Give us this day our daily bread. And forgive us our debts, as we forgive our debtors. And lead us not into temptation, but deliver us from evil: For thine is the kingdom, and the power, and the glory, for ever. Amen.
>
> —MATTHEW 6:9–13, KJV

This prayer begins by honoring God's name and predicting the coming kingdom. It asks for God's will to be released on earth. There is a request for provision, forgiveness, and freedom from the evil one. It concludes by honoring the kingdom of God and recognizing God's power and glory in the kingdom. From a practical perspective, there are four main parts of this prayer that are important on a daily basis:

1. Praying for and doing the will of God on earth

2. Praying for God to provide daily needs in our lives

3. Praying for forgiveness and forgiving others

4. Praying to be free from temptation and evil influences

The prayer recorded in Matthew 6:9–13 is called the *Lord's Prayer* as it was introduced by the Christ Himself. Within moments after Dad bowed on his knees to pray, often the first words out of his mouth were the Lord's Prayer. Since Christ Himself said "After this manner therefore pray..." (v. 9, KJV), Dad felt he should follow the same pattern. He did not consider this some routine, but when he prayed, he literally took his time, slowly speaking each phrase and sentence clearly and boldly. He believed this prayer was almost the introduction to his own prayer and intercession that followed. If he did not begin with the Lord's Prayer, at some point during his prayer he would repeat this biblical prayer, and it never became old to him!

3. PRAYER REQUIRES QUALITY TIME

Dad seldom prayed under one hour when he was in intense intercession. I cannot count the times when I was sitting at my desk with two laptops, a pile of notebooks, and a Bible; digging into the depths of biblical nuggets to compile a special article, message, or a book; and flowing in inspiration for writing, and Dad would enter my large office, lift his left hand, point his finger upward, and say, "Brother [he always called me *brother* even though I was his son], do you want to have a word of prayer?" The first words out of his mouth were not "How are you today?" or "What are you working on?" or "How's everything going?" They were his offer to pray for me! Prayer was literally the main thing on his mind every time he came into my office. Because I am an extremely focused person when studying a subject, his question often interrupted my intended flow. However, I could seldom make any valid excuse to not stop my busy activity and pray.

I knew that once he bowed his knees, it would not be a little prayer meeting—a sort of *meet and greet* with God. He slowly approached the Lord, almost like a dignified diplomat addressing a king. He considered approaching the Almighty the same honor as being invited to approach a royal throne to petition an earthly king. But Dad also understood the difference between praying a general prayer and in-depth intercession. Dad's general prayer consisted of phases of worship, thanksgiving, and general petitions, lasting for fifteen to thirty minutes. His deeper intercession, however, lasted up to one hour or more. Dad always respected my time of study, but when the spirit of prayer came upon him, it was not uncommon to stand up after praying and realize that we had prayed for nearly one hour.

When Christ was entering a season of "agony" in the Garden of Gethsemane (Luke 22:44), He requested for His three chief disciples—Peter, James, and John—to "watch" with Him (Matt. 26:38). The first phase of Christ's prayer lasted an hour, and His disciples were found sleeping. He asked them, "Could you not watch with Me one hour?" (v. 40). Three different times that same night Christ asked His inner-circle disciples to watch with Him, but all three times they fell asleep (vv. 42, 44–45).

There is something to be said about praying for one hour. I will always cherish those times of prayer with my dad, as this taught me that there is nothing quite like spending time in the presence of the Lord. During a church altar call, people often pray for only a few short minutes, perhaps only ten to fifteen minutes, and then the prayer breaks up and they return to their seats. This may be because our minds are geared to television programming, which is interrupted about every thirteen to fourteen minutes for a commercial. You must pray beyond the *commercial breaks* to effectively intercede.

4. Pray as Long as the Burden Stays

Dad never quit praying as long as he felt a *prayer burden*. This is one aspect of prayer that too many Christians ignore. No one enjoys carrying a burden. For some, the burden is a heaviness concerning how they will provide for their families. For others, it is a burden they must live with such as when caring for a family member in ill health. A prayer burden is not a mental pressure, like a depression or a feeling of oppression; it is a spiritual pressure, almost a discomfort in the heart of your spirit or innermost being. You feel a churning within your *belly*. A burden may also be a signal of a change or possible difficulty that is coming.

Dad taught me that one of the ways God informs a person on earth of some form of danger, trouble, or satanic attack is by placing a pressure in a person's spirit that is not some normal type of feeling. The *weight* can become so heavy that a person cannot think or work clearly. It may begin to manifest as restlessness and uneasiness that cannot be explained by any circumstances occurring for that individual at that moment. In fact, the strangest part of the burden is that when you do a *spiritual autopsy* to determine the reason for the feeling, you often see or hear nothing to indicate what the burden is about.

This is the purpose of entering into a season of prayer. Dad taught me that during this season of a prayer burden, a person must remove all forms of distractions and pray unhindered for an extended period of time. Often when engaging in deep intercession, the Holy Spirit will begin to place in your spirit certain leadings or directions toward another person or situation, thereby revealing to you who and what you have been burdened for. Never quit praying as long as your spirit remains restless. Only when the burden lifts should you arise from your prayer position.

5. Pray Without Ceasing

Dad showed me how it is possible to pray without ceasing. When Paul wrote 1 Thessalonians, he gave the church seven things that would assist them in their daily spiritual walk. He told them to:

- Rejoice evermore
- Pray without ceasing
- Give thanks in everything

- Quench not the Spirit

- Despise not prophesyings

- Prove all things

- Hold to the good and abstain from the appearance of evil (1 Thess. 5:16–22, KJV).

Each of these admonitions is self-explanatory except for one. How can a person pray without ceasing? The Amplified Bible says to "be unceasing in prayer." The NIV says, "Pray continually." The instruction is simple: always pray. The Greek word for "without ceasing" can mean, "without interruption, or pray not just occasionally but constantly reoccurring."[1]

When I was a teenage minister, I wondered how a person could "pray without ceasing" when he or she must drive a car to work and concentrate on the road, work a job for eight hours (often with unsaved people), drive home, and eat dinner with the family, along with other daily responsibilities. When we think of prayer, we imagine a person speaking words out of his or her mouth in rapid-fire order. After all, we must say something for it to be *prayer.* Thus, I can't be *praying* and talking to a fellow worker about work at the same time, or be talking on the phone and to God at the same time.

Dad felt that to pray without ceasing, a person could keep his or her mind on the Lord at all times. For example, when driving to work, sing a praise song to the Lord or worship Him with simple words of "Praise the Lord" and "I love You, Lord." To Dad, praying without ceasing meant maintaining a *spiritual mind* and *holding fast* to good thoughts, biblical promises, and words from the Lord.

To pray without ceasing can also have a double meaning—it can indicate praying without interruption. In other words, when you pray, don't pray for ten minutes, get up for a cup of coffee, then go back for ten more minutes, get up to watch the news, and then return for ten more minutes, then get a sandwich from the fridge. Don't interrupt your prayer time with distractions. Really pray without ceasing!

6. Don't Be Influenced by Surroundings

Dad taught me that surroundings don't influence your prayer. This was something I had to learn early in my ministry. At age eighteen I began traveling full-time in three states: Virginia, West Virginia, and Maryland. I ministered in small rural congregations with an average of forty to eighty attendees—mostly present on Sunday mornings. My accommodations were often a small upstairs bedroom or, at times, a cold and moldy basement in the church. At one church I spent the entire week in the attic of an old house, barely able to walk, continually bumping my head against the low beams. The precious people provided what they could, and as a single minister *on fire* for the Lord, I did as Paul and "learned to be content whatever the circumstances" (Phil. 4:11).

I remembered how Daniel prayed in a smelly lions' den (Dan. 6). I recalled Old Testament prophets who received numerous visions while they were in captivity in foreign nations. Daniel was in Babylon (Dan. 1). Ezekiel saw the visions of God while an exile in Babylon (Ezek. 1; 10). Even John, the author of the Book of Revelation, was banished to the desolate island of Patmos (Rev. 1:9), where he saw the apocalyptic vision while in the Spirit on the Lord's day (v. 10). Obviously the circumstances surrounding a prophet praying in a den of hungry lions were far more difficult than enduring a cold and moldy church basement!

I have prayed with Dad in churches, homes, and small hotel rooms, and I have discovered that your surroundings have no dominion for hindering you from visiting the realm of heaven or for heaven visiting you. In Paul's day, the Roman prison was the least desirable place to be. Stone jails were cold in the winter, smelly, and rodent infested. Prisoners were commonly chained to the walls to prevent escape or fighting. Yet it was in this setting that Paul wrote many prison epistles, including a letter to the church at Ephesus, in which he penned the famed armor of God passages in chapter 6. Despite being in jail, Paul never allowed his present circumstances to hinder his intimacy with God. On one occasion he and Silas were beaten and placed in stocks. Both preachers began singing at midnight so loudly that the other prisoners heard them. Suddenly an earthquake struck the prison, setting all of the prisoners free (Acts 16:25–26). When penning the Book of Ephesians, Paul wrote that he was seated with Christ "in the heavenly realms" (Eph. 2:6). Never allow your setting to set the atmosphere of your approach to God.

7. PRAY FOR YOUR
FAMILY'S PROTECTION DAILY

Dad demonstrated the importance of praying for family protection every day. In every prayer that I can remember, toward the conclusion Dad would always pray for the entire family! Daily he called the names of his four children in prayer: Diane, Phillip, Melanie, and Perry. I can still hear him petitioning God by saying, "And, Lord, keep Diane, Perry, Phillip, and Melanie from harm, from danger, and from any disabling accident." This prayer may have come from an experience he had in 1962, when he hit another car from behind while going fifty-five miles an hour. He wrapped the steering wheel around the steering column, and my mother's head broke through the windshield, breaking her jaw. I was thrown against the metal dashboard and ended up on the floor in glass and bent metal. We all survived, but from that moment, Dad always prayed a prayer for protection.

The results of those prayers have been evident throughout our lifetimes, individually and as a family. We have survived several car accidents and have avoided possible life-threatening tragedies because of prayer. As a young teenager, I drove by myself to major cities such as New York to preach in churches. In those days there were only printed maps and pay phones to make calls. There is always a danger in traveling, including unexpected engine problems, flat tires, and accidents. Dad always prayed for angels to protect me as I was traveling. On a few occasions when I had to drive all night long to go from one state to another for a revival, Dad literally stayed up most of the night praying for me. He always said that I was the one who caused his hair to turn from coal black to gray!

8. LEARN TO DISCERN
SPIRITUAL SUDDENLIES

Dad learned how to discern those spiritual nudges and *suddenlies*. A prayer burden will usually come upon a person gradually. It begins as a weight in your spirit, and as the day progresses, the pressure intensifies. There are, however, what I call the *nudges* and the *suddenlies*. These inner urges come very unexpectedly and suddenly. I describe it like being in a room by yourself reading a very important business contract, when suddenly a person you did not see enters the room and screams, "There's a fire!" You nearly jump out of your skin and your heart begins to pound—not just because of the announcement but also because of the unexpected visitor who broke the utter silence of the moment. Dad once said, "Many people have a mouth to speak to God, but not many have the ear to hear from God!"

There were times when Dad and I were driving or flying, or perhaps had just returned home from a morning service and eating lunch. He would be carefree and even laughing. Suddenly he would say, "I need to pray for my brother Morgan…something is wrong!" In my early ministry I would think, "Why can't Dad enjoy his life? It seems he's always sensing things, especially unseen trouble or negative things he was unaware of but could feel in the spirit realm." I was always amazed when, after praying, he later discovered that at the same time he felt the urge to pray, something was occurring that could have been a danger to the person for whom he was praying.

This is why a believer must maintain a spiritual mind at all times. In Ecclesiastes 7:17, we discover that it is possible for a person to die before his or her appointed time. A premature departure can be the result of not caring for your health, being in an accident, or the result of a dangerous addiction. Remember that the adversary comes to "steal and kill and destroy" (John 10:10). A believer can become the target of an evil assignment, either by wicked men or wicked spirits. The sensitivity to the Holy Spirit enables a believer to be able to suddenly change plans or alter circumstances that can save your life or preserve a loved one.

9. Pray in the Spirit

Dad believed strongly in *praying in the Spirit*. "Praying in the Spirit" is a form of prayer that has been experienced by hundreds of millions of believers globally. This act is called the "gift of the Holy Spirit" (Acts 2:38) or being "baptized with the Holy Spirit" (Acts 1:5). Throughout the New Testament, when believers received the baptism or the infilling of the Holy Spirit, a special prayer language was imparted to the person, called, in the King James Version, "speaking with tongues" (Acts 2:4; 10:46; 19:6). The language is called the language of men and of angels (1 Cor. 13:1). The purpose of the prayer language is to enable a person's inner spirit to speak to God (1 Cor. 14:2), to help the believer to build up his faith (Jude 20), and pray the will of God when he is uncertain of what His will is (Rom. 8:26–28).

I will not take the time to defend this teaching, as those who have received need no explanation, and those who have not can find the promise of the Holy Spirit in the New Testament. I will tell you that one of the most important things Dad taught me came from watching his own prayer life as he would change his words from English to praying in the prayer language of the Holy Spirit. If Dad was praying for more than an hour, at least half of his prayer would be in the language that the Holy Spirit had given him. He learned this by sitting under the ministry of Rufus. One of the daughters of Uncle Rufus attends a large Baptist church in Virginia. Years ago she told me that as a child, she would see her father step out of bed and fall to his knees in prayer. As the unction of the Lord came upon him, he would literally bounce on his knees all over the bedroom floor. At times, those downstairs wondered if the ceiling would eventually fall in!

On one occasion Dad was traveling with Rufus during a revival in Beef Hide, Kentucky. There was a young boy who had been born with a birth defect and walked on the ball of his ankle. He could not walk flat-footed and had never run, as it was impossible for him to do so. Rufus prayed for the lad, and nothing happened. He told the church to fast and pray the following day, and he instructed the parents to bring the lad back the next night. The next morning Dad and Rufus went up on a mountain and spent the day fasting and praying. Dad said, "Rufus prayed much of his prayers in the Spirit." The following night the boy sat on the front bench as Rufus began rubbing his ankle and praying for a miracle. Suddenly the bones began *snapping* and the boy's foot went flat! He was so stunned that he began laughing and crying at the same time. He ran around the church and continued to laugh and cry. Dad said the day of fasting and praying in the Spirit had energized the people's faith, and God touched the boy.

I have been with Dad hundreds of times in prayer and have observed a major *atmospheric shift* when he changed from English to the language of the Holy Spirit. At times the hair on my arm would *stand up*, and I would sense a real reverence and holiness of God's presence overshadow the atmosphere. Never underestimate the power of praying the will of God through the prayer language of the Spirit.

10. CONCLUDE WITH PRAISE

Dad always concluded prayers with praising the Lord. Most Christians understand the spiritual principles of approaching the Lord in prayer. Many, however, think very little about how a person should conclude his or her prayer. The simple answer would be, "Say amen." The word *amen* in Hebrew is *'amen*, which means, "truth and faithfulness, or so will it be." The New Testament uses the world *amen* fifty-one times. When spoken, the Greek word for "amen" means, "to put a surety or a firm trust on what has been said." It became a custom to end prayer with *amen*, which indicates agreement, and to set a seal of faith that the words had been heard, they were firm and sure, and they would eventually be answered.[2]

Dad always did more than say "amen" at the conclusion of his prayers. He put the icing on the cake by saying, "Glory to the name of the Lord," "Praise the Lord," and "Hallelujah." This was also the pattern in the prayers of David, as seen in Psalm 106:48: "Blessed be the LORD God of Israel from everlasting to everlasting! And let all the people say, 'Amen.' Praise the LORD." In the Book of Psalms, twelve of the psalms conclude with the words, "Praise the LORD." (See Psalms 104:35; 150:6, for example.) In each instance the word *praise* is the Hebrew word *halal*, which means, "to shine, boast, or celebrate."[3] It is the root for the word *hallelujah*, which means, "Praise the Lord!" It may seem to be repetitious to say "Praise the Lord" or "Hallelujah" over and over. However, consider the living creatures at the four corners of God's throne. They have no rest day or night as they cry out, "Holy, holy, holy, Lord God Almighty" (Rev. 4:8). Certainly the Almighty does not tire or become weary when angels or men give Him continual praise and worship. In fact, when the saints are with God in the New Jerusalem, there will be no more need to pray, because all spiritual and material needs are met, and God and the Lamb dwell with the saints. We will forever worship the King!

11. GOD ANSWERS PRAYERS FOR HIS GLORY

Every time, and I do mean every time, my father concluded his prayer with these words: "For the glory of the Son of God." He emphasized the word *glory*, and his voice always raised slightly, as if to emphasize the word. In earlier years I wondered why he said this phrase each time. Then when I was called to preach and studied the Word, I saw that in the four Gospels, when a person was healed by Christ, we read, "They marveled and glorified God" (Matt. 9:8); "They glorified the God of Israel" (Matt. 15:31); "All were amazed and glorified God" (Mark 2:12). When Christ was asked to come and pray for Lazarus, He told the people, "This sickness is not unto death, but for the glory of God, that the Son of God may be glorified through it" (John 11:4).

Later I consulted with Dad, and he said, "God does not heal and touch someone just because we need a healing or a touch. He does what He does to bring glory to His name and to magnify Himself among the people." Throughout Christ's ministry, after a visible miracle occurred, the multitudes would believe on Him, and many were converted. Before raising Lazarus, we read:

> And Jesus lifted up His eyes and said, "Father, I thank You that You have heard Me. And I know that You always hear Me, but because of the people who are standing by I said this, that they may believe that You sent Me."
>
> —JOHN 11:41–42

Following the resurrection of Lazarus, the Bible says, "Then many of the Jews who had come to Mary, and had seen the things Jesus did, believed in Him" (v. 45). The influence of a miracle performed in the name of Jesus is evident in the large evangelistic meetings on the mission field. Once the people see the visible results that occur through prayer, they turn to Christ, often by the thousands. Paul told the church, "Pray for us, that the word of the Lord may run swiftly and be glorified" (2 Thess. 3:1). The Greek word for "glorified" is the word *doxazo*, which "paints the picture of the triumphant arrival of God's glory, ushering in a new and glorious day in the lives and territories where the Word of the Lord is heard and received."[4]

Always remember this: The purpose of God answering prayer is not just because He is touched by your infirmities and He loves you. He answers for His glory so that you will testify to others and His name will be magnified among the people (Acts 19:17).

12. PRAY IN THE SPIRIT ... WITH THE INTERPRETATION

Dad prayed in the Spirit, and he interpreted his prayer language. This was the real secret of my father's deep spiritual walk with God—he prayed much of his prayer in the prayer language of the Holy Spirit. He would always begin praying in his native English language, calling on the heavenly Father, praying the Lord's Prayer, and entering the gate of heaven into the throne room with worship and words of understanding. At some point deep in prayer, he would begin to pray in the languages imparted to him by the Holy Spirit (Acts 2:4; 10:46; 19:6). It was during this time of "praying in the Spirit" (1 Cor. 14:2) that the Holy Spirit spoke to him and brought him instruction, sometimes for the church, for himself, or for the family. Sometimes the Spirit brought warnings of coming danger or insight into events about to transpire.

He also believed strongly in the gift of interpreting what the Spirit was saying. I will spend an entire chapter explaining the importance and significance of the prayer language of the Spirit and interpreting the words the Spirit is speaking.

THE EXAMPLE FACTOR

There are three general ways of learning: first, being taught by a teacher; second, reading detailed books on a subject; and third, by watching others and following their examples.

We live in a town with a Christian university and a great school of theology. I have many friends who graduated from both. Once they are out of the academic community and rubbing shoulders with hard-hearted sinners, saints in crisis, and disgruntled church members, they often say, "They never prepared me for this in Bible school!" Paul told Timothy, "Let no one despise your youth, but be an example to the believers in word, in conduct, in love, in spirit, in faith, in purity" (1 Tim. 4:12). The word *example* is the Greek word *tupos,* which is an image created by striking a die or a stamp. It is like saying, "Be a *model,* or be the mold that others can pattern after."[5]

Strong models are effective in mentoring students who will act in the same manner as their teacher. When Elijah crossed the Jordan, he rolled up his mantle and struck the water, causing the river to split and form an opening for him and Elisha (2 Kings 2:8). After Elijah's translation into heaven, his student Elisha took the prophet Elijah's mantle and struck the same waters of the Jordan, again causing the waters to open a dry path for Elisha to return to Jericho (v. 14). Paul reminded his spiritual son, Timothy, that he was a by-product of several generations of faith that had been passed on to him: "When I call to remembrance the genuine faith that is in you, which dwelt first in your grandmother Lois and your mother Eunice, and I am persuaded is in you also" (2 Tim. 1:5).

When I was eighteen years of age, Uncle Rufus Dunford laid his hands on me and prayed for me, three months prior to his death, asking the Lord to impart his anointing upon me. After his passing, I began to experience extended revivals, continuing from three to five weeks in length. I could actually detect an increased level of faith when ministering in the altar services. It was my beloved father, however, whose dedicated daily prayer life served as an example for me to follow. Dad was the greatest example of prayer I have ever seen and was the most praying man I have ever known. I hope to follow his pattern.

Please note that these twelve examples are not exclusive for one man. They are twelve patterns that each person reading this book can put into practice. The most important point is to never allow a pattern to become a form that loses its effectiveness because it is coming from a ritual instead of your heart. In all forms of prayer, God desires that your words come from the wellspring of your inner being.

The Power of Meditating Upon the Lord

I remember the days of old;
I meditate on all Your works;
I muse on the work of Your hands.
I spread out my hands to You;
My soul longs for You like a thirsty land.

—PSALM 143:5–6

W E HAVE DEALT extensively with our prayers through the imagery of ascending the ladder from the house of God on earth to the gate of heaven, the entrance to the heavenly temple of the Ancient of Days (Dan. 7:9, 13, 22). The ultimate purpose of prayer is to communicate our praise, feelings, and needs to God and to eventually hear back from Him in the form of answered prayer. In Jacob's dream, angels were going up the ladder and also *descending* the ladder—a picture of God sending answers to our prayers by using His angelic messengers (for example, Dan. 10). In this section I will explain a seldom-taught spiritual concept that will assist you in learning to *hear* from the Lord as He directs instructions and guidance to you after your seasons of prayer or deep intercession. The concept involves *meditating upon the Lord.*

The word *meditate* is first used in the Bible in Genesis 24:63, where Isaac "went out to meditate in the field in the evening." The Book of

Psalms uses the word *meditate* in nine verses (Ps. 1:2; 63:6; 77:12; 119:15, 23, 48, 78, 148; 143:5). In these verses the Hebrew words for "meditate" mean, "to murmur, to ponder, and to study or to muse."[1] People often speak of spending time reflecting upon a person's life or a major personal incident. *To reflect* upon something means to form an image of the object or thing and bring it back into your mind, like looking into a mirror.

There are seven different words used in the Old Testament for the Hebrew word *meditate* and two different words in the Greek New Testament. The most common meaning is: "to ponder and to muse upon something." One of the meanings of mediating on something means "to chew the cud." There are certain animals such as cattle, sheep, and goats that are unable to produce the enzymes required to break down the plant matter they eat. The animal's stomach is made to return a portion of that which was eaten from the stomach back into the mouth to be chewed a second time. The old farmers called this *chewing the cud*. The phrase became an idiom expressing someone who spends time silently meditating or pondering something before making a final decision.

In the Bible God spoke to Joshua and counseled him, "This Book of the Law shall not depart from your mouth, but you shall meditate in it day and night…then you will have good success" (Josh. 1:8). David wrote that the one who meditates day and night in God's Word would be "like a tree planted by the rivers of water, that brings forth its fruit…and whatever he does shall prosper" (Ps. 1:3). In Psalm 63:6 the writer indicates: "I remember You on my bed, I meditate on You in the night watches." It is clear that believers must begin and conclude their day by meditating upon the Lord and His Word.

THE TRUE MEANING
OF MEDITATE

The word *meditate* is a common word used among secular individuals but does not hold the same meaning as the biblical word *meditate*. The secular picture of *meditation* is that of a person sitting on the floor with his or her legs crossed and arms relaxed at the side, eyes closed, and humming a monotone sound. The image is also that of some Asian guru with long hair and a straggly beard, sitting in a room teaching a small group how to relieve stress by blanking out their thoughts or picturing themselves lying on a beach in the Caribbean.

The biblical meaning of meditation is not blanking out your thoughts, breathing deep, and exhaling slowly; the biblical word means to quietly muse, ponder, and reflect upon something you have read in the Scriptures or heard preached, or to simply sit alone or in a group quietly and think about the Lord and His goodness toward you.

THE PURPOSE OF
MEDITATING IS TO HEAR

Meditating on the Word or upon the Lord is for more than resting in His presence. If a person is continually talking or speaking, it is impossible for that person to listen to another person or hear what another is saying. As previously stated, I believe in prayer, including seasons of long prayer and intercessory prayer. However, I am also aware that there are two directions on the ladder—one goes up and the other comes down. My prayers go up, but the answers come down. At times, part of the answer involves acting upon something that the Lord spoke to me in my spirit. This answer comes by being sensitive to the inward leading of the Holy Spirit. There are times we are to be still and know that the Lord is God (Ps. 46:10).

When we allow our minds to cease from mental activities and concentrate entirely upon the written Word of God, then we can glean important nuggets that are dropped into our spirits by the Holy Spirit. Each person should have a special private place, or as Christ said, a prayer "closet" (Matt. 6:6, KJV) in which to meet with the Lord one on one. Through meditating, insight and revelation moves from the mind to the spirit.

TWO POWERFUL EXAMPLES

In November in the late 1970s I was preaching in Danville, Virginia. On this particular afternoon I was praying in the basement of the church. I was lying on my back with a Bible under my head praying very intently. I became very still and quiet. Within seconds I saw a full-color vision of Rev. M. H. Kennedy, who was serving as an administrative bishop for about 450 churches in the state of Alabama. I saw him standing behind his desk in his office in Alabama. I heard him say, "Perry, do not go to the Parkway church…God has another place for you to go to." I was scheduled to preach at a church named Parkway in Alabama in the first of February. The visions faded, and I jumped off the floor in amazement.

That night following the service I called the pastor of the Parkway church and canceled the revival, not knowing where I was to minister. Weeks later I received an unexpected letter from Joe Edwards, the evangelism director for Alabama, inviting me to preach a revival at the Northport Church of God in Northport, Alabama. I placed the Northport church in the empty slot, replacing this church for the Parkway meeting. The Northport revival continued for four weeks, and during this revival I met the young girl who two years later became my wife!

It was in February of 1988, after praying for about four hours, when the Holy Spirit spoke the words *Manna-fest* to my spirit and impressed upon me that this name would be the title of a future television program I would host. When I heard the name, I actually heard the voice of person speaking it, and not just as a thought in my mind. I remember it was about three in the morning, and I was lying across the front pew. I was not asleep and not totally awake. I had been quiet for about twenty minutes after praying for several hours. Without sounding overly sensational, the feeling I had was of being caught somewhere between earthly things and heavenly things, sort of in a spiritual vortex. The phrase came completely by surprise and unexpectedly. However, since 2001 our weekly telecast has carried the name *Manna-fest*.

Both *revelations* occurred at the conclusion of lengthy prayers but also during times when I was quiet and still. Remember, it is impossible to hear from the Lord as long as you are speaking. Your prayers and words are climbing the ladder. However, your answers will be sent from the heavenly temple to you, and it is important to have a spiritually *trained ear* to hear what the Spirit is saying to you.

MEDITATING ON
SOMETHING INSTEAD OF NOTHING

I want to clarify further between the world's method of meditating and the biblical manner of meditating. Both use the same word, *meditate*, but their ideas differ. Secular teachers teach a person how to clear the mind and think on nothing. In the Bible, believers must become quiet or still, but they are to use their knowledge to muse upon or to think about the subject or spiritual matter about which they are concentrating. Joshua and David concentrated upon the Word of God.

Every human from every nation has been given an imagination, which is the ability to picture in your mind things that are not present visibly in front of you. We begin using this as children. Boys use a stick as an imaginary gun and fight invisible wars, concocted only in their own minds. It is the same with a little girl and her dolls; she is the momma taking care of her sick children. When we become teens, the imaginations change to young men who sees themselves riding in the latest sports cars and young girls who see themselves as nurses or teachers even before they attend college. It is true for us as adults also. For example, no church was ever organized before a minister first saw in his spirit the invisible made visible!

Let's compare mental pictures. When I say "God," what do you see? Do you see a bright light, a glowing form on a throne, or an aged figure with a long white beard? I see the images painted by the prophets in Ezekiel 1 and Revelation 4. What is your mental impression when someone says "heaven"? Does your mind carry you into the clouds, into starry outer-space realms, or perhaps to the beautiful images from the Hubble telescope? In my mind I attempt to combine all of the pictures painted by the prophets in both Testaments and lay them upon layers with my finite mind to paint a complete picture of heavenly realities. Believers all see something different when a minister says, "Jesus the Messiah." The minds of some travel back to the city of Bethlehem to a babe in a manger. Others see Mary holding the infant Jesus. Some will visualize the cross or the resurrection. When I see Christ in my mind, I see Him as John did in Revelation 1—wearing a white garment with a golden belt, His eyes like fire, His hair as white as snow, His feet like a polished bronze, and His radiance as bright as the sun (Rev. 1:14–16).

Without a *sanctified imagination*, how could we believe that we receive something when we pray before it actually comes to pass (Mark 11:24)? If I pray for someone in my bloodline to receive Christ, my faith vision must see that person rejoicing in church before they ever pray at an altar. If someone needs a healing, our minds must line up with our spirits as we see health, and not a picture of death and destruction. This is not *mind over matter*, as some suggest, but it is simply meditating upon what you desire to see occur before it occurs. It is impossible to honestly confess with your mouth something that is not in your heart, since out of the abundance of the heart the mouth speaks (Matt. 12:34). The unbelief and mental struggles that chain a person to doubt can be broken when that person begins to muse over and over again upon the promises from God's Word. As you rehearse the passages of Scriptures that are special to you, then the light of revelation will bring rays of illumination to your mind.

MEDITATING IN PLACES OF VISITATIONS

At times when I am meditating upon a message for a major conference and feel *stuck* in one thought zone and unable to break out to receive fresh insight, I will leave the office and walk to the property called the *Omega Ranch* behind our facility. I often end up at the prayer barn, where I sense the peace of the Holy Spirit. This prayer area is where our youth meet each week for intercession, and I consider it a *hot spot* where there is a small *open heaven*. I say this because it is very easy to pray at any time in this area. Instead of reading the Bible, I will simply begin to muse over my thoughts and begin humming a gospel hymn or singing and worshiping God. In a short time I experience a breakthrough and receive the necessary insight to complete the subject I will teach.

You need to discover your *secret place* or *prayer closet* where you can be still and hear from the Lord. Remember that the instruction you receive from the Lord will always agree with the Word of God and never contradict it.

FIND YOUR SECRET PLACE

Your "secret place" is that one special location you select that becomes your consistent meeting place between you and God. At the beginning of Christ's ministry He spent forty days in isolation in the wilderness of Judea praying and resisting the temptations of Satan (Matt. 4:1-2). This "wilderness" consists of brown-reddish rocky and dry mountains several miles from the Jordan River and just behind the city of Jericho. Having visited these very mountains on countless occasions, the silence and solitude are almost like another world compared to the hustle and noise of a town or community.

When Christ was in Galilee, His meeting location with the Father was a mountain where He could be found in times of early morning solitude praying (Matt. 14:23; Mark 6:46). We read in Luke 6:12, "Now it came to pass in those days that He went out to the mountain to pray, and continued all night in prayer to God." It appears that the majority of Christ's prayer time was in the night or the early hours of the morning while the people were sleeping, as during the day multitudes sought Him out seeking healing or blessing.

When Christ was in the city of Jerusalem, He marked a special location for prayer time, the Garden of Gethsemane. This was a garden of olive trees and, during the warm months, flowers located on the edge of the Kidron Valley at the base of the famed Mount of Olives. The disciples, including Judas, knew of this prayer spot: "When Jesus had spoken these words, He went out with His disciples over the Brook Kidron, where there was a garden, which He and His disciples entered. And Judas, who betrayed Him, also knew the place; for Jesus often met there with His disciples" (John 18:1-2). Even in this garden Christ was praying at night when the Roman soldiers arrived to arrest Him

(John 18). Notice that in each region Christ had a specific outdoor location selected for His devotional and prayer time with the Father.

Your personal secret place must be a place that is separate from both the busy traffic path of people and the busyness (cares of life) often accompanied with the daily routine. In Matthew 6:6 (KJV) Christ spoke of a person entering their prayer closet and shutting the door. The word *closet* refers to a chamber in a house or a spot for retirement in a house, such as a bedroom. For example, when I was a teenage evangelist, the churches where I ministered were small rural churches, and I always stayed in the home of the local pastor or a church member. I recall that the bedroom where I slept was also my main "prayer closet," in the sense that I spent the day in study and prayer at a small desk in the room throughout the day. At times I took the verse literally concerning the prayer closet and cleared out a closet to use for prayer time. Many times the church was located next door, and my prayer time was spent walking the aisles of the small church during the day, hours before ministering at night.

It was during these times of prayer that I received the messages I would minister that night in the services. Prayer time would often last one to three hours each day. Each time I sought the Lord in this manner, He honored that time through great results in the altar services the same night. This is because part of the prayer during the day was exercising spiritual authority over the powers of the enemy by rebuking, binding, and commanding the powers of the enemy to loose the people attending the service (Matt. 16:19) and asking the Holy Spirit to convict the sinners. At other times I would meditate upon the Word, and through musing and "chewing" the Scriptures, the Holy Spirit would impart a definite "right now" word for the people. I have not changed this pattern of seeking God to this day.

When you meditate upon the Word, God will speak to you. Your secret place should be the command center for communicating with the Lord and meditating upon His Word. Find your "hot spot" each day and keep it so warm in prayer that each time you walk in the direction of your prayer closet, the angels in heaven are at attention and the Father says, "Get ready—here he comes!"

CHAPTER 12

Releasing the Angel of Blessing

The Angel who has redeemed me from all evil,
Bless the lads;
Let my name be named upon them,
And the name of my fathers Abraham and Isaac;
And let them grow into a
multitude in the midst of the earth.

—Genesis 48:16

J ACOB WAS THE son of Isaac, who was the covenant son of Abraham. In the setting of the above Scripture, Jacob and his sons had journeyed to Egypt during a time of global famine and were fed and preserved by the wisdom of Jacob's son Joseph, the second in command over Egypt (Gen. 41:43–44). Jacob had been unaware that Joseph had fathered two sons, Ephraim and Manasseh, and the old patriarch Jacob, in Genesis 48, was now blessing his two grandsons, adopting them into the Hebrew family.

Jacob requested to God that the same angel who redeemed him from "evil" go with his two grandsons and make them great in the earth (Gen. 48:16). The Hebrew word for "evil" in Genesis 48:16 means, "to be in distress and calamities," referring to the many crises Jacob encountered during his lifetime. Jacob also had a twin brother, Esau, whom he tricked out of a birthright and a blessing (Gen. 27:36). Out of fear of retaliation, Jacob was sent by his mother into exile in Syria for twenty years, where he worked continually and had his wages changed ten times (Gen 31:7, 38). Jacob was blessed with a large family of twelve sons. His daughter, Dinah, was raped (Gen. 34:1–5), and his favorite wife, Rachel, died giving birth to their last son, Benjamin (Gen. 35:16–18). Later Jacob was deceived, thinking his favorite son, Joseph, was devoured by a wild animal (Gen. 37:32–34), and years later he had to survive a severe famine (Gen. 42). Jacob had endured years of distress, living on the run, and had become a gray-haired man full of sorrow, believing he would soon step into the grave filled with all his sorrow (Gen. 44:29–31).

However, Jacob's final years became his best days, spent in Egypt with Joseph, his two grandsons, and his own sons and their children, living in the fertile land of Goshen in Egypt. He was able to watch his sons and their children mature into a large family of seventy souls (Exod. 1:5). Prior to his death, Jacob is calling upon the angel of the Lord that redeemed him from evil to go with his grandchildren.

THE REDEEMING ANGEL

When Abraham was old in years, he sent his servant into Syria to find a bride for his son Isaac. Abraham predicted that God would send His angel before his servant to help find a wife for Isaac. Years later when Jacob was fleeing in fear from his enraged brother, Esau, he encountered a vision of angels going up and down the ladder, as we have mentioned in this book. After twenty years in Syria, the angel visited him and instructed him to return to the Promised Land with his two wives and his children (Gen. 31:11–13). After this angelic message, Jacob prepared a secret escape from Syria. Within seventy-two hours, Laban, his father-in-law, realized he had lost two daughters, huge flocks, and all of his grandchildren, and he pursued Jacob. Laban intended to harm Jacob, but the Lord appeared to Laban warning him not to speak evil or good of Jacob (v. 24). It was this angel that continually redeemed Jacob from evil throughout his lifetime!

Not only did the redeeming angel preserve Jacob from life-threatening incidents, but also this was an angel of blessing. Jacob was exiled from home with basically nothing but the clothes he wore. Over the next twenty years he was blessed with livestock and twelve sons. When he met Esau, he confessed when he met Esau, "I have enough" (Gen. 33:11).

It appears that Jacob's angel may have also been the same angel assigned to Abraham that set up the marriage of Jacob's father, Isaac, with Rebekah. This angel became a personal guardian from God assigned to the family of the patriarchs, as Jacob asked this angel to continue being with his grandchildren. While Scripture does not use the term "guardian angel," we often speak of personal angels assigned to individuals as guardian angels. This personal angel concept is revealed in Acts 12. Peter had been arrested and was under a death threat. The believers gathered in a house to pray for Peter's release. An angel of the Lord entered the prison, released Peter from his chains, and led him out of the iron gate of the city. Peter arrived at the home prayer meeting and knocked on the door asking to be let in. Those *faith-filled prayer warriors* did not believe it was Peter!

> And as Peter knocked at the door of the gate, a girl named Rhoda came to answer. When she recognized Peter's voice, because of her gladness she did not open the gate, but ran in and announced that Peter stood before the gate. But they said to her, "You are beside yourself!" Yet she kept insisting that it was so. So they said, "It is his angel."
>
> —Acts 12:13–15

Those praying told Rhoda it was "Peter's angel." The believers understood the fact that this great apostle had a *personal angel* that was assigned to him. It is rather humorous that the church was praying and believing that God would release Peter, and yet when he was released, they didn't believe it had occurred!

THE ANGEL OF BLESSING

One of the most spiritually transforming moments in Jacob's life was when he wrestled the angel of the Lord until the breaking of the day, in Genesis 32:24–28.

> Then Jacob was left alone; and a Man wrestled with him until the breaking of day. Now when He saw that He did not prevail against him, He touched the socket of his hip; and the socket of

> Jacob's hip was out of joint as He wrestled with him. And He said, "Let Me go, for the day breaks." But he said, "I will not let You go unless You bless me!" So He said to him, "What is your name?" He said, "Jacob." And He said, "Your name shall no longer be called Jacob, but Israel; for you have struggled with God and with men, and have prevailed."

Jacob was returning from twenty years of exile and was preparing to encounter his brother, Esau, for the first time, not knowing the response he would receive. Would Esau plan an assassination against his estranged brother? Would his twin brother set up an ambush to slay Jacob's wives and children? Fear was gripping Jacob. This *patriarch on the run* finally came to the realization he needed a total transformation from being a conniving trickster to a real man of God. When the angel showed up in the form of a man, Jacob began to physically wrestle him. Jacob desired a "blessing."

However, upon hearing Jacob's request, this heavenly messenger did something rather odd. He struck the thigh of Jacob, causing the sinew in his hip to shrink, creating a permanent limp in Jacob's walk. Jacob's *strength* had been his ability to run like a fox from people and from his own troubles. If Jacob had ever planned on running, it would have been the following morning when he met Esau—if Esau was threatening him. Now Jacob would limp to his meeting place and not be able to run and escape. He was now totally dependent upon the Lord. Jacob would find it necessary to trust God alone for his protection and for God to fulfill his future destiny.

The second act of the angel was when he changed the name of Jacob to Israel (v. 28). The name *Israel* has been interpreted to mean, "prevailing with God," or "God preserves." This angel then informed Jacob that he was a "prince with God" as he had prevailed with man and with God (v. 28). His name would no longer be Jacob but Israel! Jacob's sons were known at that time as the sons of Jacob, but after entering Egypt they were named the "children of Israel" (Gen. 45:21; 46:8; 50:25). In that day all names had meanings, and the ancient people were familiar with what the name of the person meant. Many names were linked to the personality of the person. When men began to say *Israel*, they knew it was a name implying prevailing with God and men.

Jacob recognized a third and very important blessing from the angel. Jacob called the place of wrestling *Penial*, meaning, "face of God" (Gen. 32:30). Jacob confessed that he had seen God's face and that God had preserved his life. The fact is that if Jacob's life had been prematurely taken through assassination, either by Laban or Esau, the destiny of the Hebrew nation would have been disrupted and perhaps prevented.

ANGELS OF BLESSING THROUGH OBEDIENCE TO GOD

Your prayers and your financial giving *can* and *will* gain the attention of the Almighty in heaven and the angelic messengers assigned to your situation. The Bible indicates that an Italian centurion named Cornelius "gave alms [financial charity] generously to the people, and prayed to God always" (Acts 10:2). The Almighty sent this precious man an angel linking him up with Simon Peter, who preached in this Gentile Italian's house, introducing his entire family to the redemptive covenant and the gift of the Holy Spirit. (See Acts 10.)

One of the primary methods by which God blesses you is allowing an angel of the Lord to link you up with the right people at the right time. When you give financial offerings, Christ informs us that men will "give into your bosom" (Luke 6:38, KJV). Years ago I invited a gifted young woman to minister in our main yearly conference. She had been singing and ministering often without any remuneration or offerings. That morning a rather wealthy man in the congregation approached her and said he felt impressed of the Lord to pay for her to produce a CD of her singing. God released the blessing as she was in the *right place at the right time.*

Not only is the angel of the Lord moved by your prayers and financial gifts for God's work and assisting the poor, but the angel will also bring a blessing through a *blesser* to you, because you are seeking the kingdom of God first (Matt. 6:33). At times your blessing comes through an individual assigned to your dream or vision. In Christ's ministry, several prominent women whose husbands were wealthy assisted in supporting the traveling ministry of Christ (Luke 8:1–2). Some of these were women who were healed of infirmities through Christ's prayers (Luke 8:1–2). At times your needs may not be financial, but it may be a need for workers and co-laborers to assist you. Paul was blessed to have numerous individuals working alongside of him during his missionary journeys.

The angel of the Lord can also speak words of instruction or warning, if we will *fine-tune* our minds into hearing the little nudges and inspirations that are dropped into our spirit from time to time. Years ago my father, Fred Stone, was traveling late at night through Ohio to visit his parents. He stopped at a rest stop where only one vehicle, a van with tinted windows, was parked. As he was exiting his car, he heard a voice say, "There are four hippies in that van. When you go into the men's room, they will physically rob and harm you!" He immediately stepped back into his car, cranked the engine, shut the door, and locked it with his left elbow. He pulled out, spinning off without delay. As he did, the side door of the van opened, and these rough-looking men stepped out and attempted to stop him from driving away. This voice, who he believed may have been an angel, spared his life.

WHAT RELEASES THE ANGELS?

While growing up and during my earliest years of ministry, I assumed that angelic visitations were totally in the control of the Lord Himself. If God wanted to send an angel, He would simply turn to one in heaven and give His invisible messenger instructions. With that concept, there is nothing we can do to initiate the assistance of angels. The Bible, however, gives a different insight.

When we read the Scriptures, we discover some interesting passages related to this thought. We read, "Bless the LORD, you His angels, who excel in strength, who do His word, heeding the voice of His word" (Ps. 103:20). This "word" can refer here to God instructing the angels, or it can also allude to angels following the Word of God, which we speak from our mouths. The apostle Peter wrote:

> To them it was revealed that, not to themselves, but to us they
> were ministering the things which now have been reported to

you through those who have preached the gospel to you by the Holy Spirit sent from heaven—things which angels desire to look into.

—1 PETER 1:12

The phrase "look into" means, to "lean over or bend as to peer within."[1] Angels are attracted to the preaching of God's Word. To me, the passage has the implication of angels peering into the worship services where the gospel is preached around the world, just waiting for an opportunity to minister. The writer of Hebrews speaks of this ministry when he wrote: "Are they not all ministering spirits sent forth to minister for those who will inherit salvation?" (Heb. 1:14). Angels are assigned to worship Christ (vv. 5–6) and are called "ministers" and "a flame of fire" (v. 7). In Daniel, the angel of the Lord informed the prophet that God had released him to bring a message to Daniel "because of your words [prayers]" (Dan. 10:12).

When you have entered a redemptive covenant with God through Christ, you become a candidate to be assigned angelic assistance. In Scripture, the spoken Word of God and the words you speak in prayer can release the angel of blessing in your life.

We should not seek angels, neither should we be caught up in angel worship, which has occurred from time to time throughout history. Our spiritual, physical, and financial blessings are always released through faith, obedience, and patience. However, just as Abraham, Isaac, and Jacob were given a redeeming angel that ensured their inheritance and blessing, believers today have angels that are on assignment on our behalf, ensuring that God's covenant blessings are released upon His covenant servants.

As a new covenant believer, never be hesitant to exercise your spiritual authority by petitioning God for blessings in your times of prayer. I have met some who suggest that it is wrong to seek God for His blessings; they say that we should just be passive and accept whatever comes our way—good or bad. However, you cannot read the New Testament, especially the promises of Christ, without realizing that it is the will of God for you to be blessed: first spiritually, then emotionally, then physically, and then financially. Angels are a part of the blessing program of God.

> The angel of the LORD encamps all around those who fear Him, and delivers them.
>
> —PSALM 34:7

The Hebrew word for "encamps" is *chanah* and means, "to set an abode or to pitch a tent." The encampment is "round about," which literally means to encircle a person. The man Job "feared God and shunned evil" (Job 1:1) and was provided a hedge of protection, which likely was an encampment of protective angels that prevented the adversary from entering Job's property. Our prayers go up the prayer ladder, and, in return, angels will bring the blessing from the celestial realm to the earthly realm to manifest in various forms on behalf of God's covenant people.

THE MONTH OF ANSWERED PRAYER

In this section I share with you the belief that there are certain seasons of answered prayer. I recall years ago that my dear friend Pastor Bob Rogers from Louisville, Kentucky, shared with me a dream in which it was revealed to him: "August is the month of answered prayer." After Bob shared this spiritual dream in detail, I was very fascinated with the possibility of certain seasons being significant prayer seasons where special blessing could be released. I began to search the Scriptures and Jewish/rabbinical commentaries and history to see if there was some written thought on this concept. I was amazed to learn that there is a unique yearly season recognized by devout Jews, called *Teshuvah*, which often begins in the month of August. The emphasis of this season is repentance, the opening of the gates of heaven, and is the time God makes decisions for His people for the following twelve months.

THE SEASONS OF GOD

It is important to first understand the *seasons of God* and the *Jewish calendar*. Let me establish the fact that God hears and answers prayer every second of every day, every day of the year. However, there appears to be special seasons when major events are assigned to occur. God promised Abraham and Sarah a son during a twenty-four-year period. Sarah was in her late eighties when the Lord said, "But my covenant I will establish with Isaac, whom Sarah shall bear to you at this set time next year" (Gen. 17:21). Notice this was a "set time." We see a similar term used when God was warning of a coming Egyptian plague: "Then the LORD appointed a set time, saying, 'Tomorrow the LORD will do this thing in the land" (Exod. 9:5). When Job was at the peak of his suffering, these words were spoken: "Oh, that You would hide me in the grave, that You would conceal me until Your wrath is past, that You would appoint me a set time, and remember me!" (Job 14:13). A fourth example is when God promised to restore Zion in a future generation. The writer penned: "You will arise and have mercy on Zion; for the time to favor her, yes, the set time, has come" (Ps. 102:13).

These events are "set times." It is a special season when God moves for a specific purpose. In Hebrew, the phrase "set time" is *moed*, which is used of the appointed seasons or feasts of the Lord. In Job 14:13, "set time" is a different Hebrew word, *choq*, which means to make an appointment to bring him out of his captivity—again a specific season or set moment.

God's main seasons and yearly cycles are found in the seven feasts of Israel. In Hebrew these feasts are called *moedim* (plural form), or in English they are called an *appointed season* (*moed* in Hebrew). These seven appointed times occur each year at the same time on the Jewish calendar. The day and the month remain *set* during each year. However, because of the lunar calendar, the months vary as to when the feasts occur. Since the lunar calendar is an average of eleven days shorter than the solar, to keep the spring feast in the spring months, the Jews add an additional month called *Adar II* to the third, sixth, eighth, eleventh, fourteenth, seventeenth, and nineteenth years of the calendar cycle. This ensures that Passover remains in the spring and does not eventually drop back into the winter months. This following chart explains the English and Hebrew names of the feasts, the month they occur, the event they commemorate, and the past or future prophetic fulfillment.

Month	The Event	Prophetic Fulfillment
Passover—*Pesach*		
First month, fourteenth day	Israel out of bondage	Christ's crucifixion
Unleavened Bread—*Hag Ha Matzah*		
First month, fifteen to twenty-first day	No time for leaven	Christ in the tomb
Firstfruits—*Bikurim*		
First Sabbath after Passover	The waving of barley	Christ's resurrection
Pentecost—*Shavout*		
Fifty days after Firstfruits	Receiving the Law	Birth of the church
Trumpets—*Yom Teruah*		
Seventh month, first day	The head of the year	Possibly the Rapture
Atonement—*Yom Kippur*		
Seventh month, tenth day	Atonement for sins	Future Tribulation
Tabernacles—*Sukkot*		
Seventh month, fifteenth day	Wandering for forty years	Christ's millennial reign

Concerning the calendar, Israel's feast cycles are based upon a Jewish lunar calendar and not a solar calendar. The global solar calendar is based upon a year being 365.25 days per year. On a lunar-based calendar, the original calendar believed to have been used prior to the seventh century B.C., there were twelve months of 30 days each month. However, the lunar/solar calendar is based upon 354 days per year. The cycles of the moon play an important part in the Jewish seasons. The Hebrew word for "month" is *chodesh*, and at times it is also translated as *moon* (1 Sam. 20:5, 18, 24). The moon renews itself every 29 to 30 days. It moves from dark to bright in 14 to 15 days, then from bright to waxing dark in 14 to 15 days.

The names of the Jewish months are as follows:

- Nisan (Aviv)
- Iyar
- Sivan
- Tammuz
- Av
- Elul
- Tishri
- Cheshvan
- Kislev
- Tevat
- Shevat
- Adar
- Adar II (every several years)

In the West, we use a standard calendar with 365.25 days per year with a total of twelve months. It can be somewhat confusing, but the Hebrews have both a religious and a civil calendar. It appears that in the beginning of time, the month of *Tishri* was the time of the creation of man and the beginning of the year. However, in the time of the Exodus, which occurred in the spring, the month of *Nisan* became the first month of the year on the *religious* calendar. During this first month, the first feast—Passover—took place on the 14th day of the month and was set at the appointed time each year. This month usually falls in March or April of the solar calendar. It is called *Nisan* in modern Hebrew calendars, but the more appropriate biblical name is *Aviv*. The name *Aviv* means, "springtime," and is associated with the green ears of the barley harvest, revealing that life is coming forth from the dead winter months. God was teaching Israel that He brings life out of death and is the giver of new life and a new beginning.

The Jewish civil calendar starts the year with the Feast of Trumpets, which falls in *Tishri*, the seventh month, on the first day of the month. Among Jews, this day is called *Rosh Hashanah*, also called the *head of the year.*

THE MONTHS OF AV AND ELUL

Prior to the Jewish New Year on the civil calendar, there are two important months for devout Jews—the months of *Av* and *Elul*. Occurring in the mid to latter summer, the month of *Av* precedes *Elul*, which is followed by the month of *Tishri*—the month the Jewish New Year begins. It is during the month of *Elul*, the final month of the Hebrew civil calendar, that a very important season is commemorated by devout Jewish people. In fact, this important spiritually set season is often *linked* with August as being a special month of answered prayer!

WHAT IS TESHUVAH?

There is a season called the *forty days of Teshuvah*. This season is historically connected to Moses and his encounter with God on Mount Sinai. After departing from Egypt and camping in the wilderness, Moses ascended Mount Sinai to receive the commandments from God. In Exodus 34:28, Moses spent forty days on the mountain. After descending into Israel's camp, he saw the children of Israel worshiping the golden calf, and, in anger, Moses broke the commandment stones. Moses then returned to the top of the mountain for a second period of forty days during which he interceded on Israel's behalf to prevent God from destroying the nation. He returned the second time with a second set of commandments written on stone. This second forty days, by tradition, was thought to have begun in the first of *Elul* and concluded forty days later on the Day of Atonement.[2]

The word *Teshuvah* is a word that means to "turn, as to repent and change your direction." In Hebrew the word *turn* is *shuv*, meaning to turn back. The word *shuv* is the root word of the Hebrew word

Teshuvah. The time frame for Teshuvah begins on the first day of the month *Elul* and continues the entire month for thirty days, then for ten more days in the month of *Tishri* prior to the Day of Atonement. Through the entire month of *Elul* the shofar is blown daily to indicate the season of *repentance* has begun. During these thirty days, devout Jews spend time searching their hearts and repenting of any sin or actions that may have affected other people or affected their own spiritual lives. It is also a time to reflect upon your future destiny and to obtain mercy from the Almighty prior to the Day of Atonement, which is set on the tenth day of the seventh month. Thus the forty days begin with the first day of *Elul* and conclude on the Day of Atonement (called *Yom Kippur*).

The thirty-first day of *Teshuvah* falls on the first day of *Tishri*, the seventh month, and the day of the Feast of Trumpets. On this day, one hundred trumpet blasts of the shofar are sounded. Nine days later is the Day of Atonement. The first ten days of *Tishri* are named the "Days of Awe." It is during this season that devout Jews believe God is making not only major decisions concerning Israel's forgiveness or guilt but also important decisions regarding the next twelve months. Tradition indicates that the *gates of heaven are opened* during these ten days.

For clarity, let me sum up these forty days of *Teshuvah*:

- *Elul*—the first day through the thirtieth day are the first thirty days of Teshuvah.

- *Tishri*—the first day is the Feast of Trumpets and also begins the ten "Days of Awe"; the tenth day is the Day of Atonement, the tenth "Day of Awe," and the fortieth day of *Teshuvah*.

The month of *Elul* is considered to be a month of great mercy. As the book *Days of Majesty* points out:

Even though repentance is received at any time, nonetheless from Elul to Yom Kippur, Teshuvah is accepted much more readily. For during these days Hashem (God) pardoned the Jewish people for

173

the *chiet ha'eigel,* the sin of the golden calf. And this period was permanently set aside as Days of Mercy.[3]

—Chayei Adam, Hilchos Rosh HaShannah

It has been taught among devout Jews that the month of *Elul* is a month that overflows with heavenly compassion. This can be seen when examining the Hebrew spelling of the Hebrew month of *Elul:* the Hebrew letters are *aleph, lamed, vav,* and *lamed.* This forms the acrostic, *"Ani LeDodi VeDodi Li,"* which means, "I am my beloved (Hashem) and my beloved is to me (the Jewish people)." It is noted that in Hebrew, the last Hebrew letter of the four words (an *i* in the English translation) is the Hebrew letter *yud,* whose numerical equivalent is the number ten. These four yuds add up to forty, which is also a cryptic reference to the forty days from Elul to Yom Kippur.[4]

On the fortieth and concluding day of *Teshuvah,* climaxing on the Day of Atonement (called *Yom Kippur*), the gates of heaven are then shut (in the spiritual sense that the heavenly decisions for the coming year have been sealed in the heavenly temple). This shutting and sealing is called *neilah,* or "closing the gates." An example of the twelve-month decision period may be alluded to in the story of Nebuchadnezzar, king of Babylon. The proud king was given a warning dream that despite all of his skill as a world leader leading a wealthy empire, in the future he would experience a complete mental breakdown lasting seven years (Dan. 4:10–18). The main verse states:

> This decision is by the decree of the watchers,
> And the sentence by the word of the holy ones,
> In order that the living may know
> That the Most High rules in the kingdom of men,
> Gives it to whomever He will,
> And sets over it the lowest of men.
>
> —Daniel 4:17

This decree to remove the king from his throne was a decision made by the "watchers" and the "holy ones" (Dan. 4:17). The English translation says this was a "decree" by the *watchers.* The Aramaic word for "decree" comes from the root word *gezar,* meaning, "to cut." The imagery is that this decision had been "cut out" and established before the decision actually came to pass. The "holy ones" in Aramaic is *kadishiyn*, meaning, "the set apart ones." It is equivalent to the Hebrew word *kadoshim*, which means, "set apart or holy ones." In the Scripture, the holy ones would refer to the Jewish people who were following God's law and obeying His covenant. Nebuchadnezzar had destroyed Jerusalem, burnt the temple, and seized the golden treasures from God's temple. From this narrative in Daniel 4, it appears that the Jewish saints (holy ones) were making a *demand* (which in Aramaic means a judicial/legal decision or mandate) decreeing that God would judge Nebuchadnezzar for his actions against them, thereby proving to the proud king that God rules over all men. This decree in the form of prayer was heard in heaven, and an angel was assigned to bring the judgment to pass against the king (vv. 31–33).

Months prior to the king's complete mental breakdown, the prophet Daniel interpreted for the king the warning concealed in his dream. However, the judgment did not immediately come to pass. In fact, it was twelve months later that Nebuchadnezzar was walking through his palace boasting of his accomplishments (vv. 29–30) when he was stricken with a rare mental disease that drove him from the palace to live with wild beasts in a field for seven years (vv. 31–33). The significant point is that the prayers were offered and *the decision was sealed in heaven* twelve months before it was issued to be enacted on earth.

This is the same concept to understanding the belief that there is a special appointed season in which the gates of heaven are opened for times of repentance, reflection, and special intercession to God. It helps to explain the belief that major decisions for the coming year will be good and positive for yourself and your family!

JOB'S SEASONS OF REVERSAL

Job experienced a satanic attack in which he lost his wealth, ten children, and his health. (See Job chapters 1 and 2.) After several months of misery he received a word promising a better future and a divine reversal if he would follow certain instructions:

If you return to the Almighty, you will be built up;
You will remove iniquity far from your tents.
Then you will lay your gold in the dust,
And the gold of Ophir among the stones of the brooks.
Yes, the Almighty will be your gold
And your precious silver;
For then you will have your delight in the Almighty,
And lift up your face to God.
You will make your prayer to Him,
He will hear you,
And you will pay your vows.
You will also declare a thing,
And it will be established for you;
So light will shine on your ways.

—JOB 22:23–28

In this passage there are three important elements to bring for a decree to reverse the captivity of Job:

- Return to the Almighty—this is the time of repentance, or turning

- Make your prayers to Him—spend time seeking God in prayer

- Pay your vows—keep your promises (vows) including vows of giving

Now consider the season of *Teshuvah*. Job was to *decree a thing* (v. 28, KJV). The word *decree* or *declare* (NKJV) is *gazar* in the Hebrew, equivalent to *gezerah*, as used in Daniel 4:17 for "decree." The word *thing* comes from the Hebrew word *'omer*, which means, "to speak or to command." In other words, after repenting, you must make a prayer decree concerning your situation and mix your prayers with your financial giving (paying vows). These three things—repentance, prayer and offerings, and making decrees—are all common to the Days of Awe during the season of *Teshuvah*.

HOW DOES THIS APPLY TO US?

Because this concept of a season of repenting and decreeing for answered prayer and blessings is based upon a Jewish concept, many Christians of Gentile backgrounds see no common link or purpose in teaching this concept to Gentile believers. As Gentile believers, however, we must remember that it was God Himself who established the seasons, Sabbaths, new moon cycles, and set the yearly Hebraic calendar. I realize that some will read this chapter and take on the opinion that this is a Jewish concept and has no bearing on New Testament Christians or our prayer lives. However, many patterns in the early church were rooted in the Old Testament.

For example, the Old Testament Scriptures record that men arose early to seek God in prayer. Abraham arose early to seek God (Gen. 19:27), as did Jacob (Gen. 28:18), Moses (Exod. 24:4–7; 34:4–5), Joshua (Josh. 3:1), and Job (Job 1:5). In the New Testament, Christ is found rising a great while before daybreak for prayer, and on one occasion we read where He was awake during the fourth watch, which was between three to six in the morning (Mark 1:35; Matt. 14:25). Thus Christ, founder of the church, set the same pattern as the patriarchs and prophets had done during nearly two thousand years of prayer.

Upon conversion, a Christian is baptized in water in the same manner that John baptized at the Jordan River those who repented in his day (Matt. 3:6). The act of submerging in water was not new in John's day, as every Jewish man entering the temple in Jerusalem was required to briefly disrobe and plunge himself in a *mikvah*, which was a ritual purification bath area cut out of the limestone with stone-carved steps descending into the water. It wasn't called *baptism* but was called *purification*. These two incidents—water baptism and ritual purification—are two separate and distinct acts, but they are similar in their application: submerging under water for spiritual purification or separation.

Many Gentile Christians do not understand the seven feasts, and some are totally unaware that at the return of Christ, those living on the earth during the one-thousand-year reign (Rev. 20:4) will be worshiping on the original Sabbath day, celebrating new moon cycles at the new temple and also participating each year in the Feast of Tabernacles in Jerusalem (Ezek. 46:1; Zech. 14:16–19). The Sabbaths, new moons, and Feast of Tabernacles all originated in the Torah in the time of Moses, yet they continue in the time of the Messiah's rule.

For Gentile believers to ignore or completely reject this season may cause them to miss an important yearly cycle and set time in which they could experience a unique blessing or breakthrough.

I am certainly aware and always teach that God hears and answers prayer continually. Also, a person must not wait until the conclusion of a year or of a one-time season such as the Day of Atonement to repent. Repentance and humility must be expressed the moment a person realizes he or she has transgressed (1 John 2:1). The month of *Elul* usually begins in the month of August and at times may be at the beginning, sometimes in the middle, or toward the end of the month. After Bob Rogers explained how August was the month of answered prayer, and I spent time studying the Jewish feasts and traditions, months later I shared with him how the season of *Teshuvah* begin usually in the month of August, often the month prior to the beginning of the Jewish New Year.

For several years now, I have kept a calendar that informs me when the forty days begin and conclude. During this time I choose to reflect on the past eleven months, to ensure that my heart and spirit are clear toward all men, and that my own heart is in right standing with God. I also make decrees for areas of my life and ministry where I believe God's will is involved for the coming twelve months. In addition, I consider a special offering for the work of the Lord to advance the kingdom of God or a gift for the poor and needy during this season.

Note again, however, that I seek forgiveness, pray continually, and give financially throughout the year. However, although the men of Israel would ascend in Jerusalem to the temple several times a year to present certain offerings for transgressions, for blessings, and to offer specific prayers, during the season of *Teshuvah* they observed special traditions and spiritual patterns. Still today this season is a special time for believers to follow the same pattern.

THE IMPORTANCE OF UNBROKEN PRAYER

Humans have a tendency to pray only when they are in distress, great conflict, or danger. One of the greatest lessons you will learn is to create a set time each day to spend in prayer.

There are traditionally three major prayers recited daily as Jewish prayers: the morning, the evening, and the night prayers. Jewish tradition states that Abraham prayed in the morning, Isaac in the afternoon, and Jacob in the evening. While this is based upon Jewish tradition, Abraham did arise early, as it is written, "Abraham went early in the morning to the place where he had stood before the LORD" (Gen. 19:27). We read also that Isaac "went out to meditate in the field in the evening" (Gen. 24:63). However, Jacob was at times up during the night wrestling with God until the breaking of day (Gen. 32:24).

The three temple prayers were first the *Shacharit*, from the root *shachar*, meaning, "morning light." The second was *Mincha*, named for the flour offering used during the sacrifices at the temple, and the third was *Arvit*, from "nightfall." These three prayers were prayed each day.

When the Jewish temple existed, prayers were offered throughout the day during certain sacrifices. On the Sabbath at the synagogue, numerous formal prayers were offered for fifty-two weeks a year, as the synagogue was a place of study and prayer. When the first Christians had access to the temple in Jerusalem, they continued "daily with one accord in the temple" (Acts 2:46). They were also going from house to house preaching and teaching Jesus (Acts 5:42).

In Acts 3:1 we read, "Now Peter and John went up together to the temple at the hour of prayer, the ninth hour." This "hour of prayer" was a set, appointed time when men would enter the temple for prayer. The ninth hour was about three o'clock in the afternoon. This would have been the afternoon prayer time, as the morning prayers were offered at 9:00 a.m. In Acts 10 we read that Cornelius was a man who gave alms (financial gifts to the poor) and prayed always. About the ninth hour of the day he experienced a unique vision of an angel.

He was living in Caesarea, which is a long distance from Jerusalem. However, the ninth hour of prayer was the same prayer time—three in the afternoon—in Caesarea as in Jerusalem in the Jewish temple. On the following day Peter was on a rooftop praying at the sixth hour, which would have been at twelve noon (Acts 10:9).

In the above events we see two prayer times: the ninth and the sixth hours. While in Babylon, Daniel prayed three times a day—morning, afternoon, and evening, in correlation to the prayers once prayed at the temple in Jerusalem (Dan. 6:10, 13). These times matched the temple prayers, which were offered at the third, sixth, and ninth hours. Please observe that in Acts 10, God released visions to both Peter and Cornelius during the same set time of prayer occurring as in the temple in Jerusalem!

I have traveled to the Middle East more than thirty-four times, primarily to Israel, but also including Egypt and Jordan. I recall the shock I experienced in 1985 when in the early hours of the morning I was awakened by the call to prayer from an Islamic mosque located next to the hotel. In Islamic religious law, it is required for devout Muslims to pray five times a day. During these times Muslims will literally stop whatever they are doing—including carrying on a conversation or doing business—and go into a room and bow down on a prayer rug facing Mecca. In major cities like London, Muslims actually kneel on public sidewalks, blocking anyone from walking by as they bow down in prayer. If a Muslim cannot physically bow or enter the prayer room, mosque, or a selected public place, each has a set of prayer beads called *bismillah* containing ninety-nine beads, which are used to pray the ninety-nine names of God. I have seen Muslim men sitting in chairs moving each bead between their thumb and forefinger. If devout Jews and Muslims pray at set times, and if in the New Testament there were set times, each believer today should have his own set time to spend with God each day!

Several weeks before my father passed away I was in his home, sitting with him next to his easy chair in the living room. He was very, very weak, almost unable to hold up his head. He began to talk about how frustrated he was that he could no longer see to read his Bible, travel to churches, and minister—and most of all, that his strength was gone for spending long times in prayer. He said his body had just worn out. I attempted to comfort him, reminding him that he had been in successful ministry for more than sixty years and had spent literally thousands and thousands of hours in prayer. I simply said, "God understands your situation."

Dad suddenly turned to me, pointed his bony pointer finger on his left hand in the air, and leaned a little forward toward me to say: "Son, there are no reasons for a man not to pray. When you stand before God, He will not accept any excuse for a man not praying every day!" I was put to silence. With that, nothing else need be said.

When the Joseph Ring Is Placed on Your Finger

Then Pharaoh took his signet ring off his hand and put it on Joseph's hand; and he clothed him in garments of fine linen and put a gold chain around his neck.

—Genesis 41:42

WHAT GOES UP will eventually come down. Our words ascend like holy smoke before the throne of the heavenly One, and answers are sent back to the seeker. When God's blessings are released and the windows of heaven are open over you, then God begins to pour out blessings that you will not have the room to contain (Mal. 3:10). These blessings are more than spiritual *bumps* on your arms and feeling good about your relationship with the Father. When God manifests His blessings, it is a visible sign of favor to those observing your life.

We see one of the greatest examples of divine favor in the events in the life of Joseph. There are some important insights concerning God's favor in the story of Joseph's ring.

THE THREE RINGS

There are three main narratives in the Bible where a ring becomes the main feature linking the events of a story. The first was the ring that Pharaoh gave to Joseph:

> Then Pharaoh took his signet ring off his hand and put it on Joseph's hand; and he clothed him in garments of fine linen and put a gold chain around his neck. And he had him ride in the second chariot which he had; and they cried out before him, "Bow the knee!" So he set him over all the land of Egypt.
>
> —GENESIS 41:42–43

The second narrative is when King Ahasuerus, the king of Persia, removed the signet ring from Haman and gave it to Mordecai, the cousin of Queen Esther:

> So the king took off his signet ring, which he had taken from Haman, and gave it to Mordecai; and Esther appointed Mordecai over the house of Haman.
>
> —ESTHER 8:2

The third story is when the prodigal son returned home and the father gave the boy a ring:

> But the father said to his servants, "Bring out the best robe and put it on him, and put a ring on his hand and sandals on his feet. And bring the fatted calf here and kill it, and let us eat and be merry; for this my son was dead and is alive again; he was lost and is found."
>
> —LUKE 15:22–24

All of these stories have one thing in common—a ring was given. Two were presented by the ruler of the nation, Pharaoh and the king of Persia, and the other by a wealthy father to his youngest son.

The word *signet* is from the Latin word *signum*, meaning "sign." The signet dates back to ancient Mesopotamia, the land of Abraham, where special rings were worn by the leaders and men of the house to seal legal documents and letters. The rings were commonly made of brass, but could be made of gold, and in the middle of the metal was an emblem or seal that had either been impressed in the metal or carved and inserted as a precious stone or ivory. For example, wills were rolled and wrapped with leather straps around the parchment and then sealed with the signet ring, which had been dipped in hot wax. Once the signet ring was used, it was illegal for anyone to open that document unless they were the proper authority.[1] The wills of wealthy individuals in Roman times were sealed with seven seals, as was the case with the will of Julius Caesar. In Revelation 5:1–7, a seven-sealed scroll is opened by Christ, who is the only one worthy to loosen the seals and view the contents of the scroll. When a pope dies, his signet ring is destroyed and a new ring is prepared for the new pope, as each pope has his own emblem.

THE TRIALS OF JOSEPH

Joseph was the favorite son of Jacob, the father of Israel (Gen. 37:3). When he was about seventeen years of age, he was stripped of his coat, thrown into a pit, and sold to a traveling band of Ishmaelites. He was eventually sold to a man named Potiphar in Egypt. Despite being rejected and sold as a slave, the Lord was with Joseph, as we read:

> The LORD was with Joseph, and he was a successful man; and he was in the house of his master the Egyptian.
> —GENESIS 39:2

Joseph was a Hebrew servant who had such favor with his master that he was given total control over the entire house when Potiphar was on his business travels. His master began recognizing how his house was blessed because of Joseph! There are probably businessmen right now who are actually blessed, not because of their ability, but because they have righteous men or women working around them who are walking in the favor of God!

Joseph's *fortune* changed when the boss's wife falsely accused him of attempting to force himself upon her. He was placed in the king's prison. Usually, no favor is given to any prisoner; however, look at Joseph:

> But the LORD was with Joseph and showed him mercy, and He gave him favor in the sight of the keeper of the prison.
> —GENESIS 39:21

The hand of the Lord was so firmly upon Joseph that even in prison the Lord extended His mercy to him and gave him special favor in the sight of the head guard! Joseph ended up being in control of the prisoners while he was also a prisoner.

Joseph waited a total of thirteen years for his dreams to come to pass. Eventually he interpreted the dream of Pharaoh and prepared for a famine, and through his obedience, the Hebrew nation was spared.

If you intend to follow Christ and serve Him, I believe it is the will of God that you walk in the favor of the Lord. I call *divine favor* the ability to walk under an open window of heaven. Having a window open and keeping a window open are two different things. Getting a window opened happens because of God's redemptive *grace,* but keeping it open is a result of God's covenant *favor.* It may surprise you to discover the connection between the word *favor* and the word *grace.* In fact, the Hebrew word for "favor" is *chen* and is the same word translated and used for "grace." The New Testament Greek words for "favor" and "grace" are also the same! The word *favor* is the Greek word *charis* (Luke 1:30; 2:52; Acts 2:47; 7:10, 46). The Greek New Testament word for *grace* is also *charis* (Luke 2:40; Acts 4:33; Rom. 1:5) and means, "that which causes delight or favorable regard toward."

While the Greek and Hebrew meanings are the same, there is one major difference between grace and favor in relation to *how it is applied* in certain biblical narratives, and this distinction is important. *Grace is unearned and is a free gift from God,* but *favor may be deserved or gained.* The basic meaning of the grace of God is, "God's free gift of mercy and salvation given to believers." The favor of God is indicated when grace is multiplied or added and called "more grace" (James 4:6), or to be "highly favored" (Luke 1:28).

When God chose Mary to carry the Messiah, the angel told her she was "highly favored." This means she was looked upon with a greater measure of God's favor than other women. While God is "no respecter of persons" (Acts 10:34, KJV), He does choose certain persons over others in the realm of being chosen for an assignment or a special calling. For example, Paul was called a "chosen vessel of Mine to bear My name before Gentiles" (Acts 9:15). Moses was "chosen" to lead the Hebrew nation out of Egypt's bondage, not because he could speak well (Exod. 4:10–15) but because he would have the faith and patience to deal with the millions of people in the wilderness for forty years. God chooses those who will use their gifts, talents, and abilities to advance His purpose.

From a practical perspective, the difference between simple grace and multiplied grace or favor is this: saving and redemptive grace is unearned, and favor can be earned by obedience to God. Both are free gifts of God. One (grace) is the reward for *believing* upon Christ and believing His Word, and favor is a reward for *acting* upon the promises of God. I believed upon Christ; therefore I am saved. As I serve Christ and follow His teachings, I begin walking in the favor of God. His favor is a reward for my actions and obedience.

WHY SOME SEEM MORE "HIGHLY FAVORED"

Gabriel made the announcement to Mary that she would birth the Son of God. Gabriel's introduction to the young virgin was, "Rejoice, highly favored one, the Lord is with you" (Luke 1:28). Why was Mary chosen, as there were thousands of young virgins living in Israel at the time? She fit the right requirements. She and Joseph, her fiancé, were of the lineage and house of David—a requirement for the Messiah (v. 27). Their tribal roots were the tribe of Judah, a second requirement (Gen. 49:10). Their ancestral town was Bethlehem, the location where the prophet Micah predicted the Messiah would be born (Mic. 5:2). At the time, Mary was from Nazareth, a tiny town in Galilee. This fulfilled a fourth prediction, that a light for the Gentiles would come from Galilee (Isa. 9:1–2). The ancient Hebrew prophet also said that this light would come from Naphtali. It is not coincidence that the town of Nazareth is in the tribal region of Naphtali, as Nazareth would be the town where Christ would be raised by Mary and Joseph.

The tribal area also covered the area around the Sea of Galilee, where Christ performed many of His miracles, in Capernaum, Chorazin, and Bethsaida. Mary was at the right place and the right time and had the correct ancestral background to be the mother of Christ!

This question of favor often perplexes ministers. In ministry, some build much larger congregations than others, yet the smaller ministries are just as effective, if not better, pulpit preachers than some with large congregations. I have heard television ministers with large ministries who preach as simply as the average Sunday school teacher, yet they are reaching millions. Some teachers in small town USA have a gift of communication and knowledge, far exceeding television teachers, yet few people are present in the Sunday morning classroom to experience this teacher's ministry.

This is also true in the realm of business. Take three Christian-owned businesses, all involved in the same retail sales and marketing area. One business owner seems to have more business than he or she can handle, while the others are just getting by. Yet the other two are dedicated to Christ and have dedicated the works of their hands over to the Lord.

Is God randomly selecting favorites? I don't believe so. While every Christian has experienced the saving grace of God, not everyone may experience the same level of reward. It is not because God withholds His favor. *It is because we may not be tapping into His favor.* Favor can be obtained from God through acts of kindness and obedience to simple instructions and by following God's will for your life.

Paul was favored of God to be an apostle. He was a highly educated Pharisee who trained under Rabbi Gamaliel. Jewish history reveals that Saul of Tarsus (Paul) was destined to be the next head rabbi of Jerusalem, had he not converted to Christianity. So why did God choose Paul above someone else?

To the Jews, Paul was a Jew, but to the Romans, he was a Roman. This worked well when he was arrested. He would tell the Romans, "Why have you arrested a Roman?" Roman governmental officers would tremble in their shoes; arresting a Roman without just cause could cost the officer his life! When with the Jews, Paul talked about his Jewish upbringing and the Law of Moses. He celebrated the feasts and was knowledgeable concerning Hebrew customs. Paul spoke several languages, was bold, and had great wisdom. God chose a vessel who would best fulfill God's purpose at that time in history.

God often selects people who will use every gift they have for the kingdom of God. In your ministry or business, do you:

1. Dedicate everything you own and have to God?

2. Follow the practical scriptures in Proverbs and the commands of Christ?

3. Discover the will of God in every decision you make?

4. Have the right people working with you who will build up and not tear down?

5. Ask God for His favor on a consistent basis?

THE BENEFITS OF FAVOR

The Scriptures list many examples of favor being poured out on God's children. I have listed a few for you.

Favor can come in strange places.

When the Jewess Naomi returned to Bethlehem after ten years of living in Moab, she was a bitter woman who had lost her husband and two sons and had discovered her husband's property was no longer hers. She had one blessing overshadowing her—her daughter-in-law Ruth. However, Ruth had four things working against her chances for living successfully among the Jews. Ruth was a Moabitess, and there was a curse in the Law of Moses against the Moabites. She was a widow, meaning she had no financial assistance but had to lean on the charity of the community. However, through diligence she gained the attention of Boaz, a single landowner in the city who was the nearest kinsman to Naomi.

When she met Boaz, she saw the man of her dreams. Ruth said to Boaz, "Let me find favor in your sight" (Ruth 2:13). Boaz allowed Ruth to glean in his barley field to help supply her and Naomi's personal needs. After she obtained favor, he gave her "handfuls of purpose" (v. 16, KJV). Afterward, he put six measures of barley in the shawl that she was wearing and "laid it on her" (Ruth 3:15). Finally, she had his attention, and Boaz married her! From their marriage came Obed, the father of Jesse, who was the father of King David (Ruth 4:18–22).

Favor can bring unexpected financial blessing.

The nation of Israel was coming out of bondage and received their back pay from working overtime for the Egyptians! Scripture reveals, "The Lord had given the people favor in the sight of the Egyptians, so that they granted them what they requested. Thus they plundered the Egyptians" (Exod. 12:36).

The Hebrews didn't borrow *a cup of tea*. They took gold, silver, and jewels from the Egyptians. Later, in the wilderness, Moses received an offering for the building of the tabernacle. Much of the gold and precious metals used to build the house of God was given in an offering received by the man of God. The gold of Egyptians became the wealth of the Hebrews and was used in the furniture of the tabernacle! This is a true example of the "wealth of the sinner is stored up for the righteous" (Prov. 13:22).

Two other Old Testament stories demonstrate the unexpected financial blessing that can come with favor. When Jacob was working with Laban in Syria, the financial increase began to pour into Laban's entire household and all his property. Laban admitted that the reason for this blessing was because Jacob, a Hebrew, was working for him. Laban said, "For I have learned by experience that the Lord hath blessed me for thy sake" (Gen. 30:27, KJV). Jacob answered Laban back by saying, "For it was little which thou hadst before I came, and it is now increased unto a multitude; and the Lord hath blessed thee since my coming" (v. 30, KJV).

In the story of Ruth, within twenty-four hours Ruth went from being a single stranger to the most famous woman in the city. Her favor with Boaz brought the blessing of Boaz into her private life.

Favor can stop a national disaster.

When the Jews were in Persia, a wicked man, Haman, set out to destroy the entire nation. Actually, Haman was an "Aggagite," meaning he was descendant of King Agag. This Canaanite king was ruling in the time of Saul and was the king of the Amalekites. Agag was slain by the prophet Samuel. Therefore, Haman was full of revenge and chose to destroy the Jews in Persia as a retaliation against them for the death of his ancestors.

The plot would have succeeded, had not Esther the queen made a decision to appear before the king. This sounds simple. The queen always has access to the king—but not in Persia. The king had condemned his previous wife from his presence, had taken the royal position from her, and was prepared to give her royal position to another because she showed him disrespect, and a law had been passed concerning the wives in the kingdom (Esther 1:15–21). Esther could have been killed for coming into the king's chamber without permission.

Esther 5:2 says, "When the king saw Queen Esther standing in the court, that she found favor in his sight." Five times the Bible mentions how Esther received favor in the sight of the king. Esther had good looks going for her, and the Lord used this to get the king's attention and his favor.

We see this principle of favor at work also in the lives of Daniel and Peter. Daniel interpreted a king's dream and saved the wise men in Babylon (Dan. 2:24). The church interceded for Peter, and God spared his life from death, delivering him about twelve hours before he was scheduled to be beheaded (Acts 12:1–18).

Favor can bring a double blessing.

Job's blessing was lost by a battle but regained by divine favor. In fact, the increase after the battle came in the form of a "double portion" (Job 42:10). Elisha received a double portion of the anointing of Elijah (2 Kings 2). Elisha found favor because he stayed with the prophet until the very end. While many sons of the prophets viewed Elijah from afar, Elisha followed Elijah until the end, and the double portion blessing fell on him.

Favor can speed up your destiny.

You may have waited for years to see the promises of God come to pass in your life. But one act of God's supernatural favor can move you from obscurity to prominence. Esther saved the Hebrews because she stood before the king. Ruth married a wealthy businessman and became famous in Bethlehem because of one night of favor.

Joseph went from the pit to a prison to the palace because he had great favor. God revealed Joseph's future in a dream, but the dream got him in trouble with his family. He ended up in an Egyptian prison. Yet God used Joseph's ability to interpret dreams to reach Pharaoh. The gift that seemed to bring such trouble was instrumental seventeen years later in making Joseph second in command over all Egypt.

Billy Graham, in his early beginnings, preached a tent revival in Los Angeles, California. The owner of a large newspaper sent word to his writers to "PUFF GRAHAM." The newspaper wrote an article that was favorable toward Graham's revival and that eventually hit national news wires. Overnight Billy Graham was recognized as a powerful evangelist.

Sometimes what looks bad is turned about for our good when the favor of God is upon us. Oral Roberts embarked upon his evangelistic fame in 1948 during a tent revival in Oklahoma. One night a man fired a shot from a gun at Roberts, missing him by inches. The local newspaper account of the incident eventually spread across the nation. Within twenty-four hours the nation knew of a young man who prayed for the sick and got results. The revival went for nine weeks, and the name Oral Roberts became known from coast to coast. The favor of God can turn a curse into a blessing!

Favor can bring the right companion into your life.

A great example of this is found in the story of Ruth. Ruth had a lot working against her. She was a widow and a stranger in the land of Israel, and her ethnic background was Moabite. The Jews did not take kindly to Moabites. In fact, a curse was placed upon them in Deuteronomy, up to the tenth generation. Yet Ruth choose to make the break from her past, enter into a covenant with the Hebrew God, and allow God to direct her path.

When you have prayed for favor and direction, you need not chase some man or woman around trying to get his or her attention. The favor of God can act like a magnet and attract the right person into your life.

Favor can bring the miracle birth of a child.

Many barren women in the Bible conceived after a visitation from God. Yet one received a child and certainly wasn't expecting or asking for it! Mary was engaged to Joseph and was a pure virgin. When Gabriel appeared to her, the angel announced, "Do not be afraid, Mary, for you have found favor with God" (Luke 1:30).

Under the old covenant barrenness was considered a sign of the disfavor of God. This is why Hannah became bitter in her spirit and began travailing before God for a son (1 Sam. 1). Hannah's prayers were so intense that they moved the heart of God toward her. Instead of one son, she bore seven children (1 Sam. 2:5).

Favor can be obtained with God and with man.

God's Word speaks of favor with *God* and with *man*.

> Samuel grew in stature, and in favor both with the LORD and men.
> —1 SAMUEL 2:26

> And Jesus increased in wisdom and stature, and in favor with God and men.
> —LUKE 2:52

Why is it important to obtain favor with God and with man? Look how many men (and women) you must encounter in a twenty-four-hour period. Your boss, your coworkers, people you must meet with regarding contracts and business arrangements, meetings to arrange setting up conventions and appointments. Your entire life revolves around dealing with people. God uses "men" to "give into your bosom" (Luke 6:38, KJV). Therefore, favor with God and man is important.

Favor can help land you the deal. Favor can cause you to get the best price, bring the best contract your way, and open the door you need to see the works of your hand blessed!

The Bible is filled with promises of favor for the believer.

> For You, O LORD, will bless the righteous;
> With favor You will surround him as with a shield.
> —PSALM 5:12

For whoever finds me finds life,
And obtains favor from the Lord.

—Proverbs 8:35

Good understanding gains favor,
But the way of the unfaithful is hard.

—Proverbs 13:15

Fools mock at sin,
But among the upright there is favor.

—Proverbs 14:9

He who finds a wife finds a good thing,
And obtains favor from the Lord.

—Proverbs 18:22

A good name is to be chosen rather than great riches,
Loving favor rather than silver and gold.

—Proverbs 22:1

What Favor Is Not

It is just as important to understand what favor is not as it is to understand what favor is.

Favor does not involve good looks or physical attraction.

Isaiah prophesied about the Messiah and said, "There is no beauty that we should desire Him" (Isa. 53:2). If the image on the Shroud of Turin is the image of Jesus, then He was not a naturally handsome man in His facial features. He had a very strong, manly appearance, but His physical beauty was not central to His attraction. God's anointing was His attraction!

Your physical beauty, form, or appearance do not determine your level of favor with God.

Favor is not charisma or a polished personality.

If a person is involved in sales, it never hurts to dress well, use good grammar, and take additional classes to "brush up" on the latest techniques. Yet the favor of God can do more in one hour than four years of secular training.

In the secular world, individuals use their charm or personality to persuade people. While God can use your personality as a *plus*, real favor does not involve either. Favor is a supernatural action from God that enables Him to receive the glory when He works on your behalf. If it was our gift, ability, or personality, then we would accept the praise of men and think our personal gifts obtained the favor.

A young woman in Maryland is in real estate. She sells more homes and apartments than anyone in the area. In fact, coworkers ask her to train them in the *art of sales*. When she tells them her *secret* is tithing and giving and the favor of God, they look at her strangely!

Favor is not knowing the right person to *open the doors.*

While God uses people to open doors of opportunity for you and uses men to "give into your bosom" (Luke 6:38, KJV), favor does not involve knowing the right *connections*. If all our *connections* opened the doors for us, then how could God receive the glory for His blessing toward us? I am reminded of John's words about Christ in Revelation 3:7: "He...opens and no one shuts, and shuts and no one opens."

In more than thirty-five years of ministry I have never attempted to open doors for speaking engagements or revivals. We do not send out information packets attempting to get a church to book us for a crusade. I have always asked God to give us favor with pastors. This way we minister in churches where the pastor has a leading of the Lord to have us come.

When Peter was locked in the *inner ward* as a prisoner for the gospel, three iron gates blocked his freedom to the outside world. The jailer had the key, the governor had the authority, and the iron gates were impossible to penetrate. Peter didn't need a letter *from the president* to bring his release. God sent an invisible messenger, an angel, to touch the chains and release the man of God (Acts 12:4–11).

Favor does not involve the amount of money you have.

Some believe that the large financial gifts they give to charity equate to true spirituality. The Bible says the kingdom of God is not meat and drink, but "righteousness and peace and joy in the Holy Spirit" (Rom.

14:17). When you are dying with a terminal disease, money cannot cure you, but the favor and blessing of God can.

Favor does not involve your family background.

People often feel that if they are part of a racial minority, there is no chance of receiving favor. Ruth was a Moabitess, and Moabites were under a ten-generation curse according to the Law of Moses. Ruth was a widow and was very poor. She moved to Bethlehem to live among strangers. She had a lot *working against her.* All Ruth needed was a Boaz to help fulfill her destiny. Today Ruth would be considered a minority. Yet because she worked hard and was faithful, she seized the attention of Boaz, and together their lineage produced Jesus Christ!

Quit making excuses, and make things happen! Make the break from your past to move into your future. Too many people are talking about their past, their ancestors, and the hard time their descendants had, and they are not making a change today. We are not living in yesterday. Learn from the past, but don't live in it!

Favor does not involve your economic background.

People allow the lack of finances to determine their outcome in life. With favor, you can go into a desert with one hundred dollars, pray, and work hard, and in twenty years you can have a small town and own the entire area!

Think about the Jews who came out of the Holocaust. Many returned to Israel with nothing. Yet today there are Jewish Holocaust survivors who are millionaires. I am familiar with one Jewish family who are actually billionaires. If you could hear the stories of how God began to bless them after their greatest hour of suffering, you would be moved to tears. In our pursuit of the favor of God, let us remember that seeking God's righteousness is the foundation to favor. When we are in right standing with God in our relationship, we position ourselves for an encounter with His favor!

Favor doesn't exempt you from trouble.

People feel that if they are in God's will, they are exempt from problems. Others believe that if they have the favor of God, everything will always go right. This is not true. Sometimes, even with favor, we will experience troubles. The reason I know I am blessed is not because I am exempt from trouble but because I keep making it through the storms. My boat has been cracked and filled with water, but I have made it to the other side. Occasionally I get beat up by people, but I still keep running the race. I am blessed because I have survived terrible attacks and can still walk with victory. Having favor is not a ticket of exemption from physical or spiritual attacks. It is the assurance that God is with you and will see you through in spite of these attacks! Are you ready to trust God and move forward from where you are to where you need to be?

When things seem to fall apart and trouble surrounds you, do not believe the lie of Satan that God has forsaken you and His favor cannot be found! Favor does not exempt you from tribulation...but favor will enable you to always come out on the other side with the victory.

FAVOR NUGGETS

Here are some other *nuggets* I have discovered about favor.

You must be in *training* before you begin *reigning*!

Prior to David slaying Goliath, he "practiced" by slaying a bear and a lion, because David had the heart of a shepherd. When God desired a king to replace Saul, the Lord desired a king who would have a shepherd's heart and not just seek a prominent promotion among men. We train before we reign.

You can't go through *large* doors until you go through *small* doors.

Often we sense a direction and immediately seek a door of opportunity, when in reality we should be looking for places to *serve* instead of *lead*. Joshua served as Moses's minister for forty years before leading the younger generation into the Promised Land. Joseph served before being exalted to second in command, and Elisha poured water on the hands of Elijah before receiving the double portion of the Holy Spirit.

You won't be *blessed* past your last act of *obedience*.

A woman once came to an altar and said, "Do you have a word from the Lord for me?" Suddenly I did hear a word, which ended up stunning her. The word was: "Don't be seeking a new word when you haven't yet obeyed the word the Lord has already given you!" On another occasion another person said, "I need a word from God!" I said, "Go get your Bible, read it, and do what it says. That's the Word you need!"

Let me give you five important truths that can become a combination of keys to assist you in your favor walk.

Be a problem solver and not a problem maker. Once while interviewing an individual for employment, I said, "Always remember that you will be paid for the problems you will solve and not for the problems you will make." The more information you can gain concerning your skill or type of labor, the more valuable you become to your employee. If you were to move tomorrow and leave your workplace, could you be replaced immediately, or would they attempt to beg you to stay? Solutions are more important than opinions.

God created you to be someone's blessing and to be a problem solver, not a problem maker. Joseph had a solution to a coming crisis, and his plan made room for his exaltation.

Fulfill someone else's dream, and you will eventually fulfill yours. When Joseph was preparing grain for seven years of storage, he was unknowingly preparing to save his own brothers from death and famine. When you help fulfill someone else's dream, God will eventually help you to fulfill your dream. Ruth took care of her mother-in-law but eventually married the man of her dreams. Esther prepared six months for a beauty contest and risked her life to save her own people; however, as queen she defeated Haman and his plot of death. Joshua spent forty years as Moses's personal minister but was selected to replace the man of God when he died. After following Elijah, Elisha was the one who received the double-portion anointing. David cared for his father's sheep and was in training to one day be Israel's king.

There seems to be a spiritual principle that when you serve others first, God eventually exalts you.

Endure your testing before arriving at your destination. Just look at David. After killing Goliath, he married King Saul's daughter. In jealousy, Saul attempted on numerous occasions to assassinate David, chasing him through the Judean wilderness like a hunter seeking a prey. Eventually Saul gave David's wife to another man. David had to take his family to a special place, hiding them from Saul's soldiers. Prior to his ascension to the throne, he experienced his worst trial when an invading army burnt down the town where he and six hundred of his men were living, capturing the wives and children and spoiling all their goods. Ziklag would be David's lowest point prior to taking the hill of Zion and becoming king.

The prophecy doesn't lie when the promise appears to die. God told Moses to tell Pharaoh, "Let My people go" (Exod. 5:1). However, the king of Egypt hardened his heart—not once but ten times (Exod. 7:13)! I wonder if Moses ever thought he was wasting his time and should just return to his career as a shepherd for Jethro. When Abraham was seventy-five, he was told he would have a son, but when he was ninety-nine, Sarah was still barren. Sarah felt she was too old and even laughed when the Lord told her she would become pregnant (Gen. 18:12).

Some things that seem wrong are actually things that are right (circumstances, not sins). Let's go back to Joseph. He was cast into a pit—that doesn't seem right. Then he was sold to a traveling band of the sons of Ishmael, and this really doesn't seem right. As a teenager, he ended up a slave in another nation—not only does that not seem right, but it also doesn't seem fair. Why would God allow him to be accused of something he never did, be arrested and thrown into a jail, and practically forgotten? People today would be saying, "I just don't understand why God would allow such a good boy to have such difficulty in his life. This is not fair!"

It was about timing; a famine was coming, and God needed a man to save the sons of Jacob from starving to death in the land of Canaan.

Joseph had the ring of favor placed upon his hand, giving him authority over all of Egypt. But first he had to pass the test. Continuing to believe and holding on to your faith will eventually pay off.

TROUBLE DOES NOT ALTER FAVOR

One more major point should be made. Often when trouble strikes our lives, we assume that we have lost favor with God, or else the difficulty would have been restrained from manifesting. I have often said that real "blessing" is not an exemption from trouble, but blessing is the favor to continually survive from crisis to crisis and come out on the other side smiling. The path of favor says, "I will make it. I will walk this path of affliction and opposition, and in the end I will have survived and thrived in a crisis!"

Circumstances cannot alter God's blessing. Favor enables a believer, like Joseph, to interpret the dreams of others while in prison (Gen. 40), eventually leading to the deliverance of God's man from thirteen years of prison to sit second in command with Pharaoh after interpreting the king's dream (Gen. 41). Favor brought Ruth from the cursed nation of Moab into the arms of Boaz in Bethlehem. (See the Book of Ruth.) Favor caused Paul and Silas to sing in prison, locked in stocks and bonds, praising their way into a prison jail break (Acts 16). Trouble, disaster, and difficulty are not signs of the lack of favor; they are only signs that you are still alive and living on an earth that is not exempt from difficulty. Always remember, when it comes to favor, "If God is for us [you], who can be against us [you]?" (Rom. 8:31).

The Power of a Spoken Word

For the word of God is living and powerful, and
sharper than any two-edged sword, piercing
even to the division of soul and spirit, and
of joints and marrow, and is a discerner of
the thoughts and intents of the heart.

—HEBREWS 4:12

ALL WORLD RELIGIONS seek new converts. Muslims, Hindus, Buddhists, and Christians believe it is their duty to teach others about their religion. In many world religions, a person is not *converted* to the god or the belief of that religion by a simple prayer but over a process of time. Through intense study and understanding of the concepts and beliefs of that religion, the person progressively becomes a believer. True Christianity is the only world religion where a person becomes a Christian by *faith* in Christ through a simple prayer of repentance. For millions of Christians, this initial prayer came at the climax of a message preached from Scripture that, in most instances, lasted for about thirty to sixty minutes.

For a moment, consider the power of the gospel of Jesus Christ through the spoken Word. A sinner is a person who has no redemptive covenant or relationship with God. That person has no righteousness or spiritual right standing in his or her life and is living under an eternal death penalty, which was initiated at the fall of Adam (Rom. 5:12).

A SHARP TWO-EDGED SWORD

In North America the redemption process often begins with an invitation for a sinner to hear a minister speak in a local church. As an example, a sixty-year-old man who has never received Christ is invited to attend a church to hear a guest speaker preach a message on biblical prophecy. Sixty other people are sitting in the congregation. This unsaved man walks into a church where he has never been, sits among people he has never met, and listens to a speaker he does not know preach a sixty-minute message he has never heard from a Bible he has never read. When the message is concluded, a salvation invitation is given for those who desire a saving relationship through Jesus Christ. The man is moved with conviction, something he has never felt before, and walks to an altar where he has never stood. He allows the minister to lead him in a prayer he has never prayed before. Within *sixty seconds* the man's simple faith, prayer, and confession transform him for the rest of his life and for eternity. He can sense a heavy burden has been lifted from his heart. Tears stream down his face, and he hugs the man who invited him to the service. When he returns home, his wife says, "You look different. What happened to you tonight?" He responds, "I was saved!" Thus one sixty-year-old man sitting with sixty people hears a sixty-minute message, and in sixty seconds his life is transformed into a new creation (2 Cor. 5:17). This spiritual transformation is repeated thousands of times every day around the world, and it all begins with a spoken message from God's Word!

Paul described the Word of God as *quick* (Heb. 4:12, KJV), a word meaning "alive and powerful." The Greek word alludes to being energized and sharper than any two-edged sword. The Greek word for "two-edged" is *distomos*, a word used of rivers and roads that branch. It literally means, "two-mouthed." This can be interpreted as a sword with two blades, one on either side. Consider this: When God spoke the Word out of His mouth and revealed it to the prophets to pen in the Scriptures, the sword—God's Word—became sharp on one side of the blade. However, it only becomes sharp on the other side of the blade—double-edged—when you speak the Word of God out of your mouth!

THE POWER TO CHANGE THINGS

I was once asked for evidence that Jesus was alive and that what I was preaching was real. I replied, "The power of change."

The person wanted a further explanation. I continued, "A drug addict hears the gospel, repents, and is instantly delivered from drugs. A prostitute hears one gospel message, repents, and instantly loses the desire to sell her body. An alcoholic kneels at an altar, repents of his or her sins, and suddenly feels the chains of alcoholism snap by the power of God. The fact that a sixty-minute message and a sixty-second prayer can do this is proof that there is power in the gospel message and that Christ is alive and still changing hearts today!" In no other world religion does the message impact the hearer in such a short time. This is because the Word of God is "quick [alive] and powerful [energized]" (Heb. 4:12, KJV). The very life of God is released through the preaching and the speaking of the Word.

A FAITH LESSON FROM A CHILD

Our small 421 twin-engine plane was departing from Nashville, Tennessee, after I had hosted a live television airing on TBN that had gone around the world via satellite. It was nearly 10:00 p.m. central time, 11:00 p.m. eastern standard time. Although it was just a brief *hop* of thirty-five minutes to Chattanooga, Tennessee, the entire sky between Nashville and the airport was covered in a string of storms, like black pearls lined side by side on a necklace. Normally the pilot simply *punches* through the lower clouds and ascends up to eighteen thousand feet, above the average storm. Because this trip was brief, we would never climb above eight thousand feet. My entire family boarded the plane for the flight, which we would later nickname the *flight from hell.*

My wife, Pam, has no tolerance for any form of turbulence. She never rides roller coasters and gets motion sickness from riding in the backseat of an SUV over West Virginia mountains! As we climbed in altitude, the plane began to rock from left to right. Rain pelted the frame. Then, in the darkness, lightning began to dance through the sky, lighting up the sky like Fourth of July fireworks.

I didn't mind the rain or the bumps in the air, but I knew lightning was dangerous. There were five passengers on board, six counting the pilot, and I told the passengers—most who were my family—to pray. The circumstances appeared to worsen. The rain hit harder, and the wind tossed the plane like a boat tossed by waves in a storm. The lightning seemed to be getting closer. I could hear my wife saying, "Jesus, help us…Jesus, help us…" Again I said, "We need to pray." For a split second I thought, "We are in danger. This could get real nasty." However, the pilot (who is very non-risky, cautious, and would never take a risk) sat with his headphones on and his hands on the gears acting as though nothing was going on.

At the peak of my fear I began to ponder about Jesus sleeping in the boat during a major storm on the Sea of Galilee (Matt. 8:24). According to the Bible, the violent waves were tossing the ship and were about to rip apart the wooden frame of the boat. Inside the boat the sloshing water began covering the disciples' feet. Suddenly, panic set in, and Christ's chosen twelve began fearing this was their last boat trip and that their doom would soon be sealed at the bottom of the sea. Yet there in the back of the boat, sound asleep, was Christ. *He was so tired from ministering He was too tired to worry about a storm and a sinking ship.*

As I meditated on this biblical narrative, seated to my left, holding our little three-year-old girl, was my lovely wife, Pam. At that moment I saw my little sweetheart, Amanda, take her little hand and rub her mother's face. She said, "Mommy, don't be afraid…I am here!" Then she put her head on her momma's shoulder and went sound asleep. I thought, "Well, she's like Jesus in the storm, sleeping while the rest of us are worried. She is sleeping because she does not understand the danger of this lightning. One strike on this plane, and we will go see Jesus!"

I looked out the window of the plane as the white light cracked through the clouds, and I asked myself, "How could Jesus sleep in the midst of a violent storm? Why was He at such peace?" Then I turned my head to the cockpit, and our pilot was still calm and cool. I thought, "Perhaps he is taking Colon Powell's advice, who, when he was asked, 'What was the most important thing you learned in battle?,' responded: 'Never let the troops see you sweat!'"

When we landed safely in Chattanooga, I received the answer to both of my questions—"Why was the pilot so calm?" and "How could Jesus sleep during a storm?" We stepped off the plane, and Pam said, "That was terrible! It was dangerous! Did you see all that lightning? What if it had hit the plane?"

Kevin, the pilot, replied, "That really wasn't anything. Because we flew low, we were in the clouds the entire trip. The lightning was more than one hundred miles away and nowhere near us. But because the clouds carry the light, it made it appear it was much worse than it was. It may have been a level 2, which is nothing to be concerned about. I would have never taken the flight if I thought it would be any risk to any of us."

My wife said, "Thanks for telling us now!"

That's when I discovered the secret of sleeping in a storm. It is not being ignorant of the dangers of storms, but the secret is *knowing something that others don't.* The key is having divine revelation about your situation that others may not be aware of.

WHY YOU CAN'T CHANGE YOUR SITUATION

When you are in a serious bondage or crisis, you need a revelation to change your situation. Often the circumstances may outweigh your faith, and you can center more on the storm than on the One who calms the storm. The weapon that will bring you through is an *inner knowing* that cannot be altered by circumstances. This is why Jesus could sleep when the entire crew was fearful. He had told His disciples, "Let *us* go over unto the other side…" (Luke 8:22, KJV). When Jesus tells you that you are headed to the other side, then you will make it to the other side—despite the storm, despite the wind, despite the boat being filled with water. Nothing can take the boat down when you are sailing on the sea on a word from the Lord! The disciples on the boat forgot one word, and that word was *US!* Jesus did not say, "I will go over" but "Let US go over." The plural pronoun means the entire group. They simply forgot the promise that they would make it to the other side. The circumstances were more important in their sight than the promise of their future.

Don't You Care About My Storm?

More than nineteen hundred years later, the storm clouds still hover. Sudden and unexpected storms strike our vessels on the sea of destiny. We know where we should be going (to the other side), and we have a misconception that if the Lord has told us to go to the other side, that He has prepared the way and made the crooked path straight! We jump in the boat looking for a *joy ride* that turns into a ride from the *pits*. We react like the disciples, demanding, "Why didn't You warn me this was coming? What are You trying to do, kill me or something?"

If we had interviewed Peter during the storm, he may have said, "Serving God isn't supposed to be like this, is it?" In his mind he saw success! The massive crowds were filling the outdoor crusade, and he was a part of the inner circle of three men chosen above the others. He sat stunned beyond belief at the numerous miracles of healing. He had witnessed five thousand men, plus women and children, camping out for three days to enjoy the greatest teacher on earth and experience His anointing. What a team! What excitement! This was the life!

When he thought it couldn't get any better, Jesus pulled the greatest miracle yet! He took a few fish and loaves and fed the entire crusade audience. Peter was there! What a story for headline news. Image it! They would never have to pay for a meal again. When the disciples were hungry, Jesus could just pull out a sandwich and duplicate it.

The time came to close the meeting and send the people home. Jesus told the crusade team, "Let us go over unto the other side," and they got into a boat to cross the Sea of Galilee. In the process of obeying the words of Jesus, a potentially devastating storm hit the entire lake.

They went from success to possible defeat in less than eight hours. They moved from the mountain peak of heavenly places to the raging waves of possibly sinking. Only Jesus remembered what they had forgotten—He had said, "Let *us* go over unto *the other side*." They could have also slept through the storm if they had remembered that one thing.

Their main problem was that they *forgot His word*. His word was His promise. His word cannot be altered, neither can He lie. This is why Jesus could sleep and the disciples could not. In fact, the Gospel writer says it this way: "They considered not the miracle of the loaves: for their heart was hardened" (Mark 6:52, KJV). How could they forget such an amazing miracle in such a short time? It is not that difficult. We do it all of the time.

Folks will sit in a church service, hear an anointed message, and walk out the door saying, "That's it! That word is for me!" They drive home meditating on the Word. But when they open the door at home, perhaps an unsaved loved one begins cursing them for being late coming home. Or that afternoon the dog gets run over, and the youngest child falls down the step and breaks his wrist. Suddenly the Word is choked out with the "cares of this world" (Mark 4:19). The truth is choked by the thorns of circumstances. Circumstances cause us to forget the promises of God.

The disciples forgot eight simple words: "Let us go over to the other side." Jesus knew that when He said "Let us go over unto the other side" (Luke 8:22, KJV), *US* meant *ALL* of the disciples!

WHEN WE FORGET THE PROMISES

Three main problems arise when we forget the promises in God's Word. These three problems can birth mistakes that we must live with the rest of our lives. The perfect example is Abraham.

At age seventy-five Abraham was told he would have a son whose seed would produce a great nation. At that time Sarah was sixty-five years of age and was barren. Both prospective parents no doubt made the effort to conceive, but eleven years later, there were no children in the crib. Sarah saw herself getting older, and she assumed that this son must come through another woman. She offered her Egyptian handmaiden to Abraham for a second wife.

Twelve months later, Ishmael was born. This seemed like a simple solution to help God fulfill a promise. However, it was totally out of God's will. It would not be until fourteen years later that Isaac, the seed of promise, would be born.

Sarah was trying to help God out. Yet, according to the Scriptures, God was purposely waiting for Sarah to go through menopause.

> Now Abraham and Sarah were old, well advanced in age; and Sarah had passed the age of childbearing.
> —Genesis 18:11

God waited until it was physically impossible for Sarah to conceive. This made the birth of Isaac a greater miracle.

The lives of Abraham and Sarah demonstrate what happens when we fail to rely upon God's promises to us. Abraham was seventy-five years of age when God reveled to him that he would have a son who would form a mighty nation. Eleven years later, Abraham and Sarah were still childless. Sarah instructed Abraham to move to *Plan B*—having a child through her handmaiden. Her action reveals three things that happen when we forget the promises of God.

1. We try to make it happen.

After waiting eleven years to conceive a son, Sarah felt it was time to help make the promise a fact. In her eyes she could assist in fulfilling Abraham's desire for a son. And her plan would be simple. However, her plan caused a family feud that continues to this day in the Middle East between the seed of Ishmael and the seed of Isaac. God's promises are fulfilled in the flow of God's perfect timing.

2. We birth something in the flesh.

Isaac was a child of the Spirit, and Ishmael was a child of the flesh. When we step out of God's will, we birth things in our flesh. What is birthed in the flesh must be maintained in the flesh.

3. What we birth becomes a thorn to our blessing.

At age thirteen Ishmael mocked Isaac. Hagar's son was becoming a *thorn* to Sarah and Isaac. Sarah demanded that Ishmael be separated from Isaac. The flesh needs to be severed from the spirit.

Our flesh is our carnal nature. When we lose our tempers, become unforgiving, have hateful attitudes, and become jealous or complaining, we are operating in the fleshly nature.

WORDS ARE POWERFUL

We have seen the potential power of our words in this chapter. We saw the supernatural power that there is in the words of Christ—when they were spoken directly by Him to feed a hungry crowd of five thousand, or directed at an angry storm to calm a sea, or given to the man of God to promise the birth of a son, which would not be fulfilled for many years.

As children of God, His words dwell within our spirits to empower our lives also. They can change the darkest circumstances and calm our greatest storms. We can use His words to transform the lives of others through the power of His Spirit at work in our lives.

But we have also seen the negative power of our words when we forget the promise of God in His Word. We can step out of God's timing with our words. We can use our words to birth something in the flesh. And our words may even be the catalyst to our greatest *thorny* circumstances.

We need to place our focus on the powerful Word of God, remembering that His Word is:

> …profitable for doctrine, for reproof, for correction, for instruction in righteousness, that the man of God may be complete, thoroughly equipped for every good work.
> —2 TIMOTHY 3:16–17

And we need to heed the Word of God that says:

> Let no corrupt word proceed out of your mouth, but what is good for necessary edification, that it may impart grace to the hearers.
> —EPHESIANS 4:29

When considering the power of words, remember that wars have begun with words, marriages have been wrecked by hateful words, and the cemeteries in the nation are filled with individuals whose lives were taken prematurely by a bullet, shot from the hand of an angry person whose argument with their victim sent them over the edge and cost two lives: the future of the victim and the future of the manslayer who now serves life behind bars. Words birth ideas, images, and imaginations. Words live on beyond our brief earthly time span and will be repeated both to our delight and our dismay. Think before speaking, and remember that what has been said can never be recalled from the atmosphere. Perhaps this is why James said that our yes should be yes and our no should be no (James 5:12).

Using the Power of the Seed

But other seed fell on good ground and yielded a
crop that sprang up, increased and produced: some
thirtyfold, some sixty, and some a hundred.

—MARK 4:8

PRAYERS ARE PRAYED with the intention of being answered. However, in the story of Jacob's ladder, Jacob made a vow to give a tenth of all that God gave him back to God (Gen. 28:20–22). In this chapter we will examine the power and principles of giving and correct several misunderstandings that I believe have arisen that have hindered people from receiving breakthroughs.

In the history of the world, there has only been one six-day time frame when things that are produced from seeds actually began without a seed—during the original six days of Creation. The sun, moon, and stars were created fully operational without some alleged evolutionary process (Gen. 1:14–19). The green grass, fruit-bearing trees, and flowering plants were spoken into existence fully mature (vv. 11–13), and even Adam was formed from the dust as a fully grown man, without enduring the normal nine months in a womb and the birth process all other living humans would experience (Gen. 2:7).

Each living thing from the plant, animal, and human realms living on earth must reproduce through the seed process. Men carry a seed (sperm) in their loins, giving them the potential of creating another human. All animals must mate in order to procreate, and each fruit has its own seed, which reproduces "according to its kind" (Gen. 1:12). God said the "seed is in itself" (v. 11).

Take a simple apple. A well-developed *sweet, juicy* apple grown during a good harvest year has five compartments (called carpels) containing a number of seeds, depending on the variety of apple. If one apple contains ten seeds per apple, then those ten seeds, planted and guarded under the right conditions, can eventually grow ten different sweet, juicy apple trees, although it may take four to five years before you have an edible crop.[1] The number of apples growing on each tree depends upon the pollination, the condition of the soil, the amount of water, and growth conditions. Under proper conditions, one tree can produce two hundred to four hundred apples a year. The seeds from one apple tree can eventually produce thousands of apples, capable of producing thousands of trees! All from one good seed.[2] Thus the power of a natural seed!

This seed multiplication can be observed in succeeding generations in a family. Two people begin building their family, and in several generations there can be hundreds of family members. From a spiritual perspective, Jesus Christ initiated not just a new religion but a global spiritual movement. It all began when He appointed twelve other men to follow Him (Matt. 10:1–4). From a few disciples, the group grew, and just three short years later one hundred twenty individuals gathered in an upper room to wait for the Holy Spirit to come (Acts 1:15). Days later, the *Jesus seed family* saw three thousand people converted at the Feast of Pentecost (Acts 2:1–4, 41). Within days a second wave of conversions to Christ brought in an additional five thousand new believers (Acts 4:4). Within a few days, there were more than eighty-one hundred people identified with Christ! As the gospel spread throughout the Roman Empire, entire cities were moved to faith in the gospel, including Samaria, a city despised by the Jews (Acts 8:1–14). Nearly two thousand years after the Resurrection, there are an estimated 2.1 billion people who profess some form of Christianity.[3]

All life is in a seed. This concept is often taught when a minister is instructing individuals to give tithes and offerings. However, we need to take another look at the *seed* to discover some often-overlooked facts that Scripture reveals concerning the *real seed*.

THE SEED-GIVING CONCEPT

The concept of a "seed-faith offering" was first taught during the early days of the restoration movement, which was birthed in the latter 1940s, near the time Israel was restored as a nation in 1948. During this season of American church history, numerous evangelists were crisscrossing the nation, erecting large tent cathedrals, and conducting area-wide healing campaigns, often seeing crowds of ten to fifteen thousand each night! The cost for such an operation was enormous. Each night during the service, freewill offerings were received, which were applied to the expenses of the meeting and provided general support for the evangelistic ministry.

It was during the early days of these meetings when the concept called *seed faith* was taught. Many ministers were raised on farms, and they likened the money people were giving to a farmer planting seeds in the earth in expectation of a harvest when the crops were grown. It was pointed out that a farmer who refused to plant a seed in the field would never receive a harvest. Likewise, if a Christian refused to plant his seed, then how could he expect a harvest?

One verse that pointed out the seed-harvest principle was in Galatians 6:7, which reads: "Whatever a man sows, that he will also reap." The seed-faith concept says that if we sow money, we can expect some form of financial remuneration or blessing in return. The following scriptures were also taught to emphasize this concept:

If we have sown spiritual things for you, is it a great thing if we reap your material things?
—1 CORINTHIANS 9:11

But this I say: He who sows sparingly will also reap sparingly, and he who sows bountifully will also reap bountifully. So let each one give as he purposes in his heart, not grudgingly or of necessity; for God loves a cheerful giver.
—2 CORINTHIANS 9:6–7

Let him who is taught the word share in all good things with him who teaches. Do not be deceived, God is not mocked; for whatever a man sows, that he will also reap. For he who sows to his flesh will of the flesh reap corruption, but he who sows to the Spirit will of the Spirit reap everlasting life. And let us not grow weary while doing good, for in due season we shall reap if we do not lose heart.

—Galatians 6:6–9

Since the late 1940s, the seed-faith teaching of giving and receiving was taught widely, especially in the many full gospel circles. The natural purpose of planting any *seed* is to receive a *harvest*. For a believer, the harvest is twofold: spiritual and material needs met on earth and a future reward in heaven. Mark 10 alludes to these blessings:

So Jesus answered and said, "Assuredly, I say to you, there is no one who has left house or brothers or sisters or father or mother or wife or children or lands, for My sake and the gospel's, who shall not receive a hundredfold now in this time—houses and brothers and sisters and mothers and children and lands, with persecutions—and in the age to come, eternal life.

—Mark 10:29–30

Much is taught about earthly blessings. However, more understanding is needed to comprehend how heavenly rewards will be given. I have personally experienced the principle of receiving a heavenly reward for your financial giving. Years ago at a conference, my wife received a ministry offering to purchase a television camera. Those who gave in the offering planted a *seed* for ministry. We purchased the camera and began taping programs in Israel for television. Throughout America and the world, millions have viewed *Manna-fest,* and hundreds have received Christ. Here is how the *soul-seed principle* works. If one hundred people received Christ as a result of the programs, then these souls are the *spiritual fruit* (Phil. 4:17), or the spiritual *harvest* resulting from the broadcast. The eternal reward is that every person who planted a financial gift in the offering for the camera now has eternal fruit (souls) credited to his or her heavenly account! They will be rewarded for this act of obedience at the judgment seat of Christ (2 Cor. 5:10).

Paul taught that the reason for supporting his ministry was that spiritual fruit would be credited in heaven to those who helped him reach the lost:

> Not that I seek the gift, but I seek the fruit that abounds to your account.
> —PHILIPPIANS 4:17

The principle of *seed-faith offerings* is based on the understanding of the natural law of sowing and harvest. A good seed will always produce fruit if the proper conditions are met.

THE NATURAL, THEN THE SPIRITUAL

> However, the spiritual is not first, but the natural, and afterward the spiritual.
> —1 CORINTHIANS 15:46

It has been said that spiritual truths are reflected in the natural world. For example, the Bible says: "You must be born again" (John 3:7). The spiritual experience of being born again is similar to a person begin naturally born. The natural birth procedure is a threefold process:

- *Descent*—when the baby drops in the birth canal

- *Rotation*—when the baby turns in the birth canal

- *Crowning*—when the head of the baby is seen

When a person is *born again*, the same threefold process occurs in the spiritual realm:

- *Descent*—a person must humble himself before God.

- *Rotation*—this alludes to repenting or turning from your wicked ways.

- *Crowning*—this is when we come away from an altar a new creation.

The question has been asked, "Is the seed-faith principle a biblical principle?" The answer is yes, but the seed concept is *not just about money*. Everything we do in the kingdom of God can be understood as a *seed principle*. When we pray, we are *planting* our words before God in heaven, believing for an answer in the near future. When we worship, we *plant* the words of praise before God's heavenly throne, and moments later we experience the fruit of our praise by enjoying the tangible presence of God flowing through the atmosphere of our gatherings. As we witness to a person who does not have a redemptive covenant with God, our words are planting seeds of Scripture into his or her mind, believing the time will come when the Word of God will take root and bring forth the desired result of repentance and conversion to Christ. This was Paul's concept of believers coming into the fullness of the gospel.

I planted, Apollos watered, but God gave the increase.

—1 Corinthians 3:6

The entire kingdom of God, on earth, operates on the principle of planting and harvesting, thus the seedtime and harvest principle is a valid truth.

THE SEED—THE BIBLICAL DEFINITION

If all you have ever heard is that *money and giving are your seed*, you have only heard a small portion of a truth. The seed principle as found in Scripture is far more than a personal check or paper money. The Scripture indicates that a *seed* can actually be one of four different things.

1. The word *seed* can allude to your descendants who are not yet born.

Throughout the Old Testament when God spoke of the future children of the patriarchs prior to their birth, He called them *seed* years in advance of their physical arrival. God promised Abraham a son when he was seventy-five years of age, and twenty-five years later Isaac was born. Before Isaac's birth, God called the child Abraham's "seed" (Gen. 12:7, KJV; 17:7, 9, KJV).

In these and other Old Testament instances, the word *seed* alluded to the fact that the sperm of the man is considered seed. Therefore, all of Abraham's descendants were in his loins long before they were born (Gal. 3:16). Thus, all of Abraham's future descendants for generations to come are identified as the *seed of Abraham*.

2. The word *seed* can allude to a natural seed that produces a plant or tree.

At Creation, God spoke of the "herb yielding seed" and fruit that would produce "after his kind, whose seed is in itself" (Gen. 1:11, KJV). A second biblical meaning of the word *seed* alludes to a natural seed that produces after its own kind. An apple seed produces an apple tree, and a grain of corn produces a cornstalk. Wheat creates more wheat, and a fruit seed has potential to produce a fruitful tree of the same type.

3. The word *seed* is used when speaking about faith.

Jesus spoke of having faith "like a mustard seed" (Mark 4:31). A mustard seed is one of the smallest seeds in the world. In its early stage it can be as small as a grain of salt or pepper. Yet when it matures, it becomes a tree large enough for the birds to make nests in its branches. The story of the mustard seed illustrates that a person does not need a large amount of faith to receive from the Lord, but he can begin with a small seed that will grow into a mighty tree!

4. The word *seed* is used when alluding to the Word of God.

The fourth and premier example from the New Testament reveals that the seed is the Word of God. This example is found in the parable of the sower in Mark 4. In this reference a man called a *sower* is planting seeds in the ground. Jesus taught that the word He was preaching was the seed of the Word of God. Not all of the seed fell on good soil. Some of the seeds were devoured by the birds. Some terrain was too rocky to produce a harvest. In other locations, thorns and weeds grew and began choking the root, thus killing the wheat before it could mature. According to the parable, only about 25 percent (or one-fourth) of the seed actually brought forth fruit (results).

When the disciples asked for an interpretation to this parable, Jesus said:

> The sower sows the word. And these are the ones by the wayside where the word is sown. When they hear, Satan comes immediately and takes away the word that was sown in their hearts. These likewise are the ones sown on stony ground who, when they hear the word, immediately receive it with gladness; and they have no root in themselves, and so endure only for a time. Afterward, when tribulation or persecution arises for the word's sake, immediately they stumble. Now these are the ones sown among thorns; they are the ones who hear the word, and the cares of this world, the deceitfulness of riches, and the desires for other things entering in choke the word, and it becomes unfruitful. But these are the ones sown on good ground, those who hear the word, accept it, and bear fruit: some thirtyfold, some sixty, and some a hundred.
>
> —MARK 4:14–20

In this parable the soil is actually the *condition of the person's heart* after he or she hears and receives the seed of the Word. I have heard it said: "Plant your seed offering into the soil of this ministry and expect a harvest." Certainly it is all right to make this statement in light of the natural-spiritual sowing and reaping principle. But in a more literal understanding of this passage, the soil is *not the ministry* you are giving to; it is *the spiritual condition of your heart*. Look closely at the parable and see that the emphasis is not on the seed (as the seed itself holds the life) or the amount of seed, but upon the *condition of the ground* upon which the seed falls. If the ground (heart) is not properly prepared, there will be no fruit from the seed! Satan attacks the soil, not the seed (except when the birds [spirits] attempt to remove the truth that has been planted in a person's heart).

This significant parable reveals the four main conditions of the human heart that are encountered when the Word of God is preached, or when the seed of God's Word is planted into the minds of the audience:

The Ground	The Condition of the Heart	The Result to the Person
The wayside ground	The hardened heart	No spiritual life
The stony ground	The rootless heart	A superficial life
The thorny ground	The worldly heart	A strangled life
The fruitful ground	The righteous heart	A successful, fruitful life

If I *only* teach that the seed is your money and our ministry is the soil, then the implication is that the blessings that come to a person for his or her giving are based upon how successful our ministry is or on how *we* are using the money that was given. This concept cannot be completely accurate for several reasons. Some people have given offerings to ministries that ended up with leadership leading abusive lifestyles or perhaps misusing the funds. Yet, despite these negative actions, honest people who gave to the ministry testified of how God blessed them for giving. Other believers have given offerings to ministries that have been reaching masses in North America and overseas, and yet the givers have not personally experienced any major financial breakthroughs. This lack of breakthrough seems like a contradiction. One group gives and the receiver is abusive, while another gives and the receiver is honest. Yet the results from the *seed* vary.

The answer to this paradox may lie in the soil! Throughout my ministry I considered the work I was doing for God the *soil* that the seed (offerings) were being planted in to produce the harvest. The money is turned into ministry products, airtime, salaries for workers, and the printing of books and magazines, and in return, it brings results to those who are saved, blessed, or healed by God's Word.

Yet as I reread the parable of the sower in Mark's Gospel, I realized that the four conditions of soil were the *attitudes* and *conditions* of the hearts of those hearing the Word of God, and the amount of return (or harvest) from the seed (Word in their heart) was contingent upon the spiritual condition of the heart.

Some hear the Word, and the message *goes in one ear and comes out the other.* Others experience a powerful message from the Scripture and become offended at the teaching, thus what is being taught produces resentment instead of revival. In my own ministry I have seen people walk out of a service when they disagreed with a point in the message. Others became excited for a short period, and eventually worldly distractions and the cares of life overwhelm them to the point of choking the strength from their spiritual progress. Soon they are working overtime to pay bills, attend church very little, and seldom if ever support God's work through tithes or offerings. The fourth group hears, receives, and acts upon the Word in faith. These 25 percent (or one in four, according to the parable) are the believers who will receive a return on their spiritual investment, some thirty, some sixty, and some one hundred.

In the seed-money principle, emphasis is often on the *place* where the offering is planted. We are told to "recognize those who labor among you" (1 Thess. 5:12). It is certainly important not to waste God's money and to know to whom, to what, and to where you are giving; but in the parable, the condition of the heart (not the ministry) is where the seed will either die or grow. When a person has a hard, traditional calloused attitude toward the church, the pastor, the message, or the messenger, all the financial giving in the world won't bring that stubborn and hard-hearted person into any spiritual breakthrough until there is first repentance and humility. If the heart is soft, tender, and receptive, the person will enjoy the change the Word makes in his or her life and thus experience the joy of a future harvest. Just as it takes time for a seed to grow, you may not see the results immediately, but they will come.

How Much Seed?

In this parable the seed is the Word of God. The Bible contains many promises, prophecies, and instruction for our daily lives. When someone preaches the Holy Scriptures, the Word has the potential to produce faith, because the seed of the Word enters the ears of the listeners and drops into their spirits. If a person does not allow distractions, deceit, and discouragement to enter his or her heart, then the truth that person is hearing will bring forth numerous promises for which he or she is believing God. Believing with the heart will initiate and release the power within the seed to spring forth and bring new life.

The Bible teaches that God will work with us to confirm His Word (Mark 16:20). The Greek word for "confirm" or "confirming" means, "to firm up, to stabilize and to undergird." When we preach salvation, the Holy Spirit makes firm the message by leading people to Christ. When we minister on the Holy Spirit baptism, the Holy Spirit confirms (makes firm) the message by baptizing believers in the Holy Spirit. The same is true with the message of healing.

At the peak of his ministry, my father carried a great burden for people who were sick. Dad often prayed hours each day for people to receive their healing. I have witnessed him ministering on the subject of healing in order to build faith into the hearts of the listener. Following the message, Dad would offer prayer for the sick, believing God was able to bring healing. Many times people were either instantly or progressively healed. The Lord will work with us to confirm His Word. If we believe that it is God's will to bless and prosper us, then we can receive the benefits of the promises. But we cannot receive a promise that we are unaware of. *The seeds of ignorance produce a harvest of spiritual and natural poverty.* The right seed must be planted in our spirits in the good soil of a pure and honest heart before God.

The level of faith and commitment a believer has is linked to the amount of God's Word (seed) that has been planted in his or her spirit. Those with little knowledge in the Word are considered spiritual babes in Christ who are nourished by the milk (basics) of the Word, which alludes to the simplicity of the Scriptures (1 Cor. 3:1; 1 Pet. 2:2). Those who have spent much time maturing in Scripture are considered *meat eaters* and are stronger in the knowledge of the Lord (Heb. 5:14).

The true benefit of knowing and abiding in the seed of God's

Word will be witnessed in your life when you respond to life experiences on a daily basis based on the spiritual principles found in the new covenant. The good seed will bring forth good fruit, and the good fruit will result in a good and more abundant life.

The Principles of Harvest

*The harvest truly is great, but the laborers are
few; therefore pray the Lord of the harvest
to send out laborers into His harvest.*

—LUKE 10:2

A T TIMES I have heard television ministers encourage viewers to stretch their faith and plant the largest *seed offering* they have ever planted. Some have gone as far as to *prophesy* that every person who will obey their instructions will receive a great financial blessing within a designated time. There is nothing wrong with people giving a large offering *if they are impressed to do so by the Lord.* However, there is a problem, from a biblical perspective, when *everyone* is promised the same level of *return.*

For example, before his death a world-renowned, well-respected elderly minister met with some of the top charismatic ministers in America. In the private meeting, he began rebuking them for the manner in which they were overemphasizing money. He asked them if they believed that when they gave they would receive a hundredfold return in the form of money as a result of their giving. Several of the men said they not only believed it but also taught it. He then asked each minister to share with him any specific time that minister gave an offering and received an exact hundredfold return. The ministers were speechless for a moment. One man finally spoke up and said, "I have not seen my hundredfold return, but I'm still believing for it!"

The older seasoned minister made an important point. He said, "You cannot tell *everyone* who is giving in your offering that they will all receive a hundredfold return, because the Bible says, 'Some thirty, some sixty and some one hundred.' Not everyone will receive a hundredfold return."

I do personally believe in a hundredfold return because it is in the Scripture. Yet I also know that it is incorrect to *guarantee* everyone this level of increase, because there are several levels of increase mentioned in the parable. This guarantee of a certain blessing has caused those who have not received to become confused and disillusioned.

Then there is the issue of the true interpretation of Jesus's parable of the sower. Note that He alludes to the planting of the seed of *the Word* (not money) in Mark 4:20. In this parable the *harvest* does not allude to your *financial harvest* but to *spiritual results* such as people being saved, healed, or delivered by the preaching of the gospel. Other scriptures also mention the "harvest":

> Then He said to His disciples, "The harvest truly is plentiful, but the laborers are few. Therefore pray the Lord of the harvest to send out laborers into His harvest."
> —Matthew 9:37–38

> Let both grow together until the harvest, and at the time of harvest I will say to the reapers, "First gather together the tares and bind them in bundles to burn them, but gather the wheat into my barn."
> —Matthew 13:30

> Do you not say, "There are still four months and then comes the harvest"? Behold, I say to you, lift up your eyes and look at the fields, for they are already white for harvest!
> —John 4:35

> Therefore be patient, brethren, until the coming of the Lord. See how the farmer waits for the precious fruit of the earth, waiting patiently for it until it receives the early and latter rain.
> —James 5:7

> And another angel came out of the temple, crying with a loud voice to Him who sat on the cloud, "Thrust in Your sickle and reap, for the time has come for You to reap, for the harvest of the earth is ripe."
>
> —REVELATION 14:15

If we look at the references to the harvest in the New Testament, Christ's ultimate concern and passion was, and still is, the ingathering of eternal souls into the kingdom of God. In each of the above passages, the ingathering and harvest refers not to *natural* seed or *financial increase* but to winning people for the kingdom, those whose eternal souls are priceless! The purpose of the new covenant and the Word of God is to produce eternal fruit for the eternal kingdom of God. *All of our financial giving should be geared to bringing in spiritual results for the kingdom of God, and the earthly blessings that follow should be an enjoyable side benefit—but not our main or only motivation for giving.*

Too many times our prayers and even the *inspiration* for our giving are motivated more by our fleshy desires than our eternal spiritual results. More stuff, a bigger and better home, a new luxury car...! *Whatever happened to giving because you want an eternal reward in heaven?* After all, when you depart this life, surviving family members will get your house, drive your car, and sit at your dinner table spending what money you left behind. It is very sad when the only way people can be stirred to give an offering to a ministry or a church is when the speaker has spent sixty minutes promising believers what they will get *here* instead of what they will have *where they are going*.

Please understand that God does bless our giving here. We receive "good measure, pressed down, shaken together, and running over" (Luke 6:38). I am not minimizing the blessing that follows giving. However, I am grieved that the motive for giving has been corrupted and the reason for giving has been lost in all the stuff.

How Do We Receive
the Hundredfold Return?

All blessings are based upon the promises of the Word of God. Yet the Word of God must be spoken or preached to enter the hearts of the people. I have preached one message and seen more than a hundred people come to Christ in a single evangelistic service. On several occasions, after I preached on the Holy Spirit baptism, more than two hundred fifty people were baptized in the Holy Spirit in one service. My life has been consumed with studying, praying, and traveling to preach the good news since I was eighteen years of age.

Jesus gave a unique promise to a person who would forsake family to travel preaching the gospel. In an unusual passage He taught that the person who would forsake the security of home and family to obey Him would receive houses, lands, brothers, and sisters in this life, and eternal life in the world to come.

> So Jesus answered and said, "Assuredly, I say to you, there is no one who has left house or brothers or sisters or father or mother or wife or children or lands, for My sake and the gospel's, who shall not receive a hundredfold now in this time—houses and brothers and sisters and mothers and children and lands, with persecutions—and in the age to come, eternal life.
>
> —Mark 10:29–30

Just what does this passage allude to? How can I fully obey God and receive this *compounded blessing* of a hundredfold return in this life, with persecutions, and in the life to come, eternal life? Jesus mentioned receiving houses, lands, brothers, and sisters (notice He speaks in the plural and not the singular). I presently own one house. I have one natural brother and two natural sisters, and I only own one piece of property where our home sits. I only have one mother and father, yet Jesus spoke of receiving "mothers, sisters, and houses." So how can I receive houses and lands by obeying the Lord?

The following illustration may help interpret this unique promise. After more than thirty-five years of preaching I have personally met thousands of people who have become my *spiritual* family. Today

I could start out in Maryland and travel to Florida, stopping every twenty-five to fifty miles to eat and sleep in the home of one of our personal friends or ministry partners. More than sixty thousand people have been converted to Christ through our ministry. Therefore I am a *spiritual father* to thousands of brothers (men) and sisters (women) in the Lord who have been converted to Christ during more than thirty-five years of ministry. Because of their love for me, my wife, and our children, they would open their homes and allow us to spend the night, feed us, then send us on our journey. Therefore, we have hundreds of partners who are our "brothers, sisters, mothers, and fathers," and their homes would become our home.

Christ had personal friends like Mary, Martha, and Lazarus who owned a home where He would stop between His evangelistic crusades to eat and be refreshed (Luke 10:38–42). The apostle Paul traveled the world and was fed and housed by believers in the cities where he ministered (Phil. 2:25). In Mark 10, Christ was saying that His own covenant family or fellow believers would help provide for the needs of those who were in full-time ministry, so that the minister could concentrate entirely on the work of the ministry and not be consumed with the cares of life (2 Tim. 2:4). The minister's needs would be met as he (the minister) concentrated on meeting the needs of others.

PLANTING SEED
WITH NO ROOT

One situation seldom discussed is how *people are giving of their finances without having any root in the Word of God.* Some are being taught that giving money is the key to cure all ills in their lives and the only way they can experience financial prosperity.

A minister will be judged by his life and his message. When any man or woman stands before lower middle-class believers and begins to brag about expensive clothes and flash objects he or she owns worth thousands of dollars, and implies that if they give to him they too can receive such blessings, often simpleminded people are impressed and believe that if they can sacrifice enough, heaven will send gold rain and money will appear out of nowhere. Without a root in the Scriptures, people will accept words that have no biblical foundation.

There have been some men who have even offered the audience their *anointing* if the price is right. First, if they are anointed, it is not *their* anointing, but the anointing comes from the Holy Spirit. Second, Acts 8:17–22 states clearly that the gift and gifts of the Holy Spirit cannot be purchased with money. When Simon the sorcerer offered Peter money to purchase the gift so he could lay hands upon people to receive the Holy Spirit, Peter did not yell, "Wow—the wealth of the wicked is laid up for the righteous! Bring your offering, Brother Simon, and I will lay hands on you!" Peter locked his righteous eyes on this magician and yelled, "Your money perish with you," and told the town's occult leader that his heart was not right with God (Acts 8:20–23).

WHEN THE GIVING FAILS

Did the promise of God fail the person who gave, or was the motive for giving pure and based upon the Word? When someone gives without the inspiration and love behind the gift, then he or she cannot expect a return from what was planted, especially if the giving was more *hype* than *right*.

At times the giver actually gave to a *man* and not to *God*. The Lord blesses what is given if it is given with the right motive, a pure heart, and in obedience to the Word and the leading of the Holy Spirit. Here are some questions to ask:

- Am I giving to *get* and not to be a blessing to the kingdom of God?

- Am I giving to a *self-acclaimed prophet* and not to a God-ordained ministry?

- Am I giving with *unrighteousness* in my heart?

- Am I giving without having a true *covenant* with God?

228

I have actually heard people teach that giving a huge offering will *force the hand of God* into moving on their behalf. It is as though the person is saying, "I will do something so great that God will be forced to bless me." If this were true, how does one explain poor third-world countries where people have nothing to give yet attend meetings and see amazing healings and miracles occur through the prayer of faith?

God is not moved by the *amount* of our gift as much as by the amount of our *faith and obedience*. Christ is touched by the "feeling of our infirmities" (Heb. 4:15, KJV), but His blessings are released by faith (Heb. 11:6). If the *needs* of people were the motivating force for releasing God's power toward man, then God's power would be released in every nation of the world twenty-four hours a day, because the entire world is full of serious needs. God, however, is moved by our *faith* and not just our needs.

> But without faith it is impossible to please Him, for he who comes to God must believe that He is, and that He is a rewarder of those who diligently seek Him.
>
> —HEBREWS 11:6

RESULTS OF MISINFORMATION

It is easy for a believer who has no root in the Word to take a scriptural truth and apply it in an improper manner or, worse yet, to stretch the interpretation beyond its context. Often when the promised results do not come, a believer becomes despondent. Soon the enemy tells that person that "all that giving stuff" is not true and doesn't work. I have received numerous e-mails and letters over the years from people who sincerely believed the words of a "prophet" speaking in the name of the Lord who promised that if they released a large offering, they would receive a great miracle or financial breakthrough. People acted in good faith on the word of the *person,* and too many times nothing resulted. The key may be that they *acted on a word that was not from the Lord but was from the heart of the person speaking.* The *prophetic utterance* may have been from the spirit of the man and not from the Spirit of God.

SHOW ME THE CASH

Perhaps one of the most disturbing trends occurring from time to time involves the North American *money prophets*. There is a small group of ministers who claim to have a special anointing that few humans in the church are permitted to carry. They claim superior spiritual authority in what they declare with their mouths—claiming that their very words create healings, jobs, and money out of nowhere. Of course there is one small catch—you have to *pay them* a large seed donation to receive a personal prophecy from them.

They claim there are several *levels* of prophecy based, of course, upon the amount in your checkbook. One recognized "prophet" can't waste his anointing giving a "word" on a mere ten- or twenty-dollar offering. His "powerful personal prophecies" begin at a hundred dollars and go as high as five thousand dollars per prophecy, per night. The larger the check, the longer and more detailed the prophecy! Those investing five thousand dollars will be placed on a prophetic mailing list to receive a personal word each month—along with a postage-paid envelope to ensure the prophecies keep coming into your home. The amazing fact is that these *prophets for profit* are filling up large churches and raking in thousands of dollars each night from gullible souls who are so hungry to hear from God that they clean out their checkbooks, hoping it will gain the attention of the Lord and bring an unexpected financial blessing.

Let me be clear. In this case there is no difference between the Christians in a church paying for an alleged prophecy than paying a fortune-teller or a psychic for a *word*. Both are wrong! The idea that self-appointed and self-anointed money-seeking prophets would charge money to operate in some type of prophetic gift or word of knowledge not only goes against every precept of the gospel, but it also falls under the category of *merchandising the gospel*. Peter gave this warning:

> But there were also false prophets among the people, even as there will be false teachers among you, who will secretly bring in destructive heresies, even denying the Lord who bought them,

and bring on themselves swift destruction. And many will follow their destructive ways, because of whom the way of truth will be blasphemed. By covetousness they will exploit you with deceptive words; for a long time their judgment has not been idle, and their destruction does not slumber.

—2 Peter 2:1–3

The word *merchandise* means, to "travel as a peddler." Their method of deception is feigned words. The word *feigned* means, "artificial or fictitious." It alludes to making up a word from God that *is not* from God in order to sell someone on what is being taught or preached. This would include a prophecy out of their own spirits to encourage a person to give. Their motive is *covetousness.* The New Testament word *covetousness* means, "*To get an advantage or make a gain by defrauding.*" The emphasis in this passage is not upon meeting the needs of the person but upon how a person can be manipulated to *help out* the one making the claims—in this case how the alleged prophet can profit from his fictitious words. Untold damage is done when the Lord is not in the words being spoken.

The One-Dollar-Offering Check

A noted woman Bible teacher was ministering in a large midwestern city known for its strong charismatic churches. The crowds were large, yet the offerings were very small. She related to me that after counting the offerings each night, she noticed numerous checks made out for one dollar. After several services, she asked the pastor why so many were giving a check for one dollar. Was there an economic crisis in the area? Were many people out of work?

To her surprise the pastor responded by saying, "Most of the people giving a dollar are people who have moved here from other states. You see, they were watching television ministers preach on money and prosperity, telling them if they wanted financial blessings, they must plant large *seeds* to their ministries. Many of them gave most of what they had and, sadly, never saw a breakthrough. They finally decided to move to this city, hoping that by being near the *man of God,* they would receive a financial miracle. Eventually, they left those churches and have been attending here."

Once again it goes back to the motive. Since the *promises* were not working, the people moved, hoping to force the favor of God upon their actions. They did not move because they were led by the Holy Spirit. They did not pack up and head west because the church was going to be a great blessing to their family. They were chasing the hundredfold pot of gold at the end of the rainbow. Certainly if they were closer to the spout where the anointing was pouring out, they could close their umbrella and get drenched in the prosperity anointing. Once again we see the motive behind the madness. People want to be blessed and prosperous and are earnestly searching the road for a sign that says, "This way to your biblical wonderland." Too many times their sincerity is being manipulated by self-appointed and self-anointed prophets for profit.

IS YOUR LUST INVOLVED?

There are reasons given in Scripture as to why believers can pray or perform a certain act and still not receive a response from the Lord. James dealt with this when he wrote:

> You ask and do not receive, because you ask amiss, that you may spend it on your pleasures.
> —JAMES 4:3

Years ago in Virginia a man came forward who was injured in an accident. He told me he had a back injury and wanted me to pray that he could receive a severance package to assist his family's needs. I prayed, and in a short time he received a large amount of money. Months later he came to a revival and asked me to pray that the Lord would heal him. I said, "Didn't you get a huge sum of money?"

He said, "Yes, and now that I have the money, I want to be healed so I can do what I want to do."

I said, "OK, I will pray and believe God to heal you if you will give the money back! You would be deceiving the state if you took money saying you can't work when you could actually work!" Needless to say, he departed angry, and I never prayed for his healing. He was praying a prayer that was "amiss." The Greek word for "amiss" is a strong word that is translated in the English Bible as "worthless, diseased, miserable and sick." God is saying that when we pray for something to fulfill our own lust, it is a diseased and sick prayer that will not be heard!

Another man came forward for prayer. He believed he had married the wrong woman, and he knew he could not divorce her because she too was a Christian. He wanted God to *take* (literally kill) his wife to release him from his marriage so he could marry a woman he had met and was "spiritually attracted to." This is a fine example of spiritual stupidity and a lust-driven prayer request. He needed to learn to get along with his wife and to make the break from his spiritual soul tie.

I have met people who said, "I have given for years and have never seen a financial breakthrough." I have also met many, many more who have great testimonies of provision and increase because of their obedient and Spirit-led giving. Those who have never experienced the joy of increase must evaluate their motives, attitudes, and hearts to see if there are openings where the enemy has entered and is devouring their blessings.

THE BLESSING SIDE OF GIVING

When the church at Philippi gave an offering to assist Paul's ministry, Paul told them that God would "supply all [their] need according to His riches in glory by Christ Jesus" (Phil. 4:19). The believers in Philippi were giving offerings to Paul to assist his missionary efforts. Paul told them that fruit "abounds to your account" (v. 17). This fruit was the souls Paul would win on his journeys that would be accredited to the church at Philippi at the judgment seat of Christ (2 Cor. 5:10). This is God's cycle of blessing. As you plant into the soil of ministry, knowing the promise of the Word in your heart, God will honor your gift by producing spiritual fruit for your heavenly account. He also blesses you with increase to continue being a blessing. My wife and I have seen this principle not only with money but also with other items we have given.

Throughout our marriage the Lord has directed my wife or me to assist a personal friend in need. We have given away furniture from our house, a few vehicles, clothes, food, and other items of importance. In each case, within a few weeks or months we have received an unexpected blessing. We could relate the blessing back to an act of obedience. Not once have we ever given and said, "We are doing this to get something back." We remember the words of Jesus:

> And if you lend to those from whom you hope to receive back, what credit is that to you?
>
> —Luke 6:34

We gave to meet a need. Yet God in His mercy gave back to us because when we give, then men will give to our bosom.

> Give, and it will be given to you: good measure, pressed down, shaken together, and running over will be put into your bosom. For with the same measure that you use, it will be measured back to you.
>
> —Luke 6:38

We were able to release our *stuff* with confidence, because we have a strong root in the Word of God. Remember, the seed is the Word, and the amount of Word you know increases the amount of seed in your spirit. The condition of the soil is the condition of your heart and spirit. If you are in covenant with God, have a pure motive and a heart of righteousness (right standing) with God, you can expect the blessings to follow you and increase to come automatically.

Offering God Something He Doesn't Want

For I desire mercy and not sacrifice, and the
knowledge of God more than burnt offerings.

—HOSEA 6:6

T TIMES, SPIRITUAL principles are turned into spiritual formulas. We are told if we confess the right things, follow the
right instructions, and react in the proper manner in four
easy steps, then these actions guarantee any spiritual benefits we are
seeking. Spiritual rituals may appeal to the flesh, but they have little
impact on moving the blessing of God in your direction.

I believe too many Christians attempt to use spiritual *formulas* in
order to produce a desired result. An important biblical truth that
often turns into a *formula* is the biblical instructions related to tithing
and offerings.

To tithe means giving the tenth to God. Abraham was the first biblical tither, followed by his grandson Jacob (Gen. 14:20; 28:22). Later,
Moses established a pattern for the tithe, which consisted of grains,
fruits, meat offerings, and other items being brought to the tabernacle (and future temple) to provide for the Levites and the priesthood. Tithing also continued into the New Testament, as indicated
in Hebrews 7:8. In the early day of the Pentecostal movement, when
church members were farmers the finances came in at harvest time

when the farmers sold their produce. At times the faithful farmers would bring a tithe of eggs, bread, or other food to the church to provide food for the pastor and his family. In the southeastern mountains of Virginia, it was called a *pounding*. As God blessed the believers with jobs, they would then bring a tenth to God's house in appreciation for God's blessing them with work. The tithe assisted in the ministry salaries, church mortgages, church mission's projects, and other important functions. Offerings were received for special guest ministries, needs of the congregation, and so forth.

Under the old covenant, the Hebrew people were to bring certain animal sacrifices and present them to God at the temple. The daily routine at the temple eventually caused the sacred meaning of these offerings to be lost in the rituals. Eventually people presented blemished animals, which were blind, lame, or even diseased. The *worshipers* were keeping the best of their flocks for themselves and giving the worst as offerings to God. The Lord told the Hebrews that He would not receive their offerings because they were not following the commandments in the Torah.

> "You offer defiled food on My altar,
> But say, 'In what way have we defiled You?'
> By saying, 'The table of the Lord is contemptible.'
> And when you offer the blind as a sacrifice,
> Is it not evil?
> And when you offer the lame and sick,
> Is it not evil?
> Offer it then to your governor!
> Would he be pleased with you?
> Would he accept you favorably?"
> Says the Lord of hosts.
>
> —Malachi 1:7–8

Under the old covenant, if the offering was blind, lame, crippled, or sick, the priest might accept it, but God rejected it. The reason: These offerings were pointing to the day a Redeemer would come and offer Himself as a final sacrifice for man's sins. That Redeemer, Jesus Christ, was pure, perfect, and sinless. The animal sacrifices were a picture of the coming sacrifice and therefore must be perfect and spotless before God. When the Hebrews brought a blemished offering, what was accepted by men was rejected by God!

The same spiritual principle applies under the new covenant. Today we do not bring a blood offering in the form of an animal to church and lay it at the minister's feet. Instead we bring a tithe or an offering to the house of God and present it before God. When God looks at the offering, He is not judging the *amount* but looking at the *motive* and the *attitude* of the giver. Are you giving with a pure heart? Are your motives for giving to be a blessing to others and to the kingdom of God? If so, you will be blessed. But if a person's heart is filled with carnality and unrighteousness, then that person's gift (offering) may be received by the church, but it will not have the blessing of God!

THE CONDITION OF THE HEART

The first key to true prosperity begins with the spiritual condition of a person's heart. I am not speaking of that muscle in your chest that pumps blood through the physical body, but the inward thoughts of the soul and spirit (Heb. 4:12). There are some spiritual fakers in the body of Christ. They sing in the choir but behind the scenes are always starting small fires. One day out of the week they worship, and six days out of the week they live the life of a hypocrite. I call it *living like a devil but looking like a saint.* Some name the name of Christ but are filled with unforgiveness, bitterness, strife, jealousy, and the other works of the flesh (Gal. 5:19–21). If we attempt to perform spiritual acts with a darkened heart, then we *make void* both the promises and the spiritual blessings. If we attempt to offer to God praise that is from our lips and not from our hearts, it is a sacrifice that is not received by God. We are offering God something He doesn't want and will not receive.

During the past years of ministry I have heard many messages and mini-sermons on giving and receiving. Yet the one passage that is seldom taught is a warning Christ gave to those who would attempt to leave their gifts at the altar while they still had unforgiveness in their hearts:

> Therefore if you bring your gift to the altar, and there remember
> that your brother has something against you, leave your gift
> there before the altar, and go your way. First be reconciled to
> your brother, and then come and offer your gift.
>
> —MATTHEW 5:23–24

This scripture is clear. We must give our offerings with a clear conscience and a pure heart, or we will not experience the blessings that
follow obedience. This may be one reason why some long-standing
church members have given tithes and offerings for many years and
have never experienced a major financial harvest. They have given a
blemished offering, just as some did in the Old Testament. The people
were to bring the best lambs as a burnt offering at the temple. All sacrifices were to be without blemish (Exod. 12:5; Lev. 1:3; 4:28). Blemished
sacrifices were blemished offerings, and they hindered the blessing of
God from flowing down from heaven to the people.

Our bodies are the temple of the Holy Spirit, and the blemishes
are in our attitude, our thinking, and the words we speak. Bitter and
sweet water cannot come from the same fountain, and grapes and figs
cannot come off the same tree (James 3:11–12).

It is sad to admit, but I have encountered men and women in churches
who were *charter members* and prided themselves on how long they had
been Christians. Yet their attitude toward others was critical and their
words were cutting. Some were continually active in organizing small
group rebellions to rise up against those in spiritual authority, including
their pastor. They continued to give, sing in the choir, and serve on the
church board, yet their heart was dark and filled with unclean motives.
Do you think God will bless their giving and worship in spite of their
uncleanness of spirit? The answer is no! Yet the spiritual cancer silently
grows in a malignant body, while the head continues to receive offerings
and pronounces promises of prosperity to a spiritually sick congregation.
Their sacrifices have been filled with strife.

> Better is a dry morsel with quietness, than a house full of feasting
> with strife.
>
> —PROVERBS 17:1

This verse in Proverbs is clear. A dry, quiet church is far better than one where people are whooping and shouting above the strife and unforgiveness.

It is sad that in the church we engage in worship that may not be acceptable to God. Jesus said some people praised Him "with their lips, but their heart is far from Me" (Matt. 15:8). It may be possible that ministers accept offerings that are *blemished* with strife, bitterness, and unforgiveness. It is clear that God is more concerned with the *condition* of your heart than the *amount* of money you are giving.

Jesus made this clear in the parable of the unforgiving servant. One man owed the king fifty-two thousand dollars. He begged the king for mercy, and the good-hearted king forgave the debt. This forgiven servant went out and found a friend who owed him fifty-two dollars. He had the poor fellow arrested. The king heard about it, arrested the unforgiving servant, and placed him in prison to be beaten by the prison guards until he would submit to obedience.

Jesus warned, "So My heavenly Father also will do to you if each of you, from his heart, does not forgive his brother his trespasses" (Matt. 18:35). Jesus states that He will allow the "torturer" to move into your life if you walk in unforgiveness (v. 34)! This is exactly what occurred at the church at Corinth. A young man was committing fornication with his stepmother. Paul rebuked him and commanded that they "deliver such a one to Satan for the destruction of the flesh" (1 Cor. 5:5). Later Paul wrote to Timothy and told the young pastor to instruct those who are in opposition, "If God perhaps will grant them repentance, so that they may know the truth, and that they may come to their senses and escape the snare of the devil, having been taken captive by him to do his will" (2 Tim. 2:25–26).

Strife is a food that feeds evil spirits. King Saul became jealous of a teenage shepherd boy, David, who had decked a giant (1 Sam. 17). From that day forward, Saul "eyed David" and began to plan a setup for him to be killed by the Philistines (1 Sam. 18:9). Saul's secret strategies were soon made known, and the spirit world began to go into operation. Eventually Saul was "troubled" by an evil spirit. God permitted his mind to be turned over to a tormenting demon that finally drove the king to fall upon his own sword in battle!

I believe there are a large number of people who sit in church each week, tormented in their minds by spirits.

Unforgiveness opens a door to the devil. In the New Testament, Jesus revealed other dangers to our spiritual walk with God that result from unforgiveness:

1. If you do not forgive others, then the Lord does not accept your offerings (Matt. 5:23–24).

2. If you do not forgive others, then God will not forgive you (Mark 11:26).

3. If you do not forgive others, you can be turned over to a tormenting spirit (Matt. 18:34–35).

Consider this. If we walk in unforgiveness and God does not hear our prayers, then Satan is not obligated to obey our warfare. I can yell, "Satan, I rebuke you...I bind you...I come against you...I cast you down...," and the prayer is empty words. If God is under no covenant obligation to hear the prayers of an unforgiving person, then what makes us believe that Satan is under scriptural obligation to obey our commands to depart? In order for Satan to "flee from us," we are to "submit therefore to God and *resist* the devil" (James 4:7). Resisting the devil also means to resist the bitterness, strife, and unforgiveness he is attempting to send!

Jesus gave His twelve disciples power over all demons and diseases (Luke 10:19). Yet, in Mark 9, the disciples encountered a boy who was having an epileptic seizure, and the demon was so stubborn that it would not come out of the lad. Jesus came off the mountain, spoke the word, and the evil spirit exited the boy's body with great force. When the twelve disciples asked, "Why could we not cast it out?," Jesus answered, "Because of your unbelief" (Matt. 17:20).

But the root is more than just unbelief. Prior to this event the disciples had a heated argument concerning who was the greatest in the kingdom. Then they were rebuking others who were not in their inner circle for casting out devils. In short, there was a lot of strife among the disciples prior to this demonic encounter. At other times they cast out devils and were rejoicing (Luke 10:17). This time was different. Something had occurred to change their spirits, and the evil spirit was not listening to their rebukes.

After more than thirty-five years of full-time ministry, I am convinced that many ministers are defeating themselves through jealousy of other ministers. This *King Saul syndrome* has them bound in the palace, plotting how they can damage that young preacher across town who has received a fresh anointing. Saul was more concerned about the opinion of the people than the favor of God. He said to Samuel on one occasion, "Make me look good in the eyes of the people." This is what concerns me with the overemphasis of giving on Christian television. Some ministers pronounce great promises to the entire viewing audience, stating that the larger amounts given will move God closer and faster to their problem. What about poor people who can't afford a chicken for Thanksgiving, living in a nation with a limited income? Are these blessings stamped from heaven with, "North America only"? What about those who plant the *big seed* but tomorrow curse their wives, watch Internet pornography, and still claim the promises? We must understand that right standing with God (righteousness) is the breeding ground for God's favor. We must give with clean hands and a pure heart.

Have you ever heard the following statements?

- "Plant a seed and get a harvest."

- "It is not a seed until you release it out of your hand."

- "Your level of giving will produce the level of harvest."

- "The greater the seed, the greater the harvest."

The above statements are true if you are giving out of obedience with a pure heart and the right motive. If, however, you are giving an offering or a tithe with unforgiveness, strife, and bitterness toward

God or people, and are sowing with the wrong motive, you cannot expect a true *return* on your investment of giving. Jesus said it this way:

> Seek first the kingdom of God and His righteousness, and all these things shall be added to you.
>
> —MATTHEW 6:33

RIGHTEOUSNESS IS THE BREEDING GROUND FOR PROSPERITY

It is righteousness or your right standing with God that is the breeding ground for spiritual and natural prosperity. As we enter into a covenant relationship with the Lord Jesus, our sins are erased, and we enter into a right relationship with God. This right relationship (or covenant) is manifested through the righteousness of God. Righteousness is imputed to us when God declares us free from sin and releases us from the penalty of death. Another word that describes this action is *justification*. If a man is assumed guilty yet the judge declares him innocent, he has been justified.

Right standing with God is the breeding ground for all spiritual blessings. This right standing is not found in our righteousness or our personal struggle to be good or do better, but it is received inwardly when we understand who we are in Christ! Some Christians place the responsibility of righteousness only on the Lord and place no responsibility on their own personal conduct. I call this *sloppy agape*! God tells us to "cleanse ourselves from all filthiness of the flesh and spirit" (2 Cor. 7:1). Through His power we lay aside the weights and sins that so easily ensnare us (Heb. 12:1). God gives us the ability, but we take on the responsibility. True prosperity begins in the spirit when we receive Christ's nature through being born again. At that moment our names are written in heaven, and the promises of God become ours!

In the Old Testament blood offerings (sacrifices) were burnt on the altar for forgiveness. Today Christ has paid the final price for our redemption. Under the old covenant the people brought items to the temple to minister to the priests, who ministered continually in God's house. Today, the tithes and offerings are given to keep ministry going.

Important Principles for Opening Heaven's Gates

WE HAVE TAKEN a journey in this book to discover not only how to open the window of heaven but also how to walk in and under the favor of God. As you have seen and understood the significance of the gates of heaven, you have seen that there are important keys to obtaining God's favor and grace and to living under an "open heaven" where the blessings of God can flow into your life.

After more than thirty-five years of ministry, I have learned several great principles that will help you to stay in the flow of God's blessings to you through the open gates of heaven. Review these principles carefully, and ask God for wisdom so that you may pass along His truth to others as they encounter situations needing the blessing of God. These first seven principles have been the foundational principles of our ministry, and they can be used by you and others also.

1. Enter little doors before you enter large doors.

I have heard men preach and young people sing who can out preach and out sing most of the ministry personalities who appear on national Christian television. Often I have commented to Pam, "I wonder why they are not known on a national level." It seems for many, it takes years to develop a ministry gift that is recognized. I believe the answer has to do with private battles.

God raises up champions not among champions, but among sheep. Moses was a shepherd before he was a pastor of three million people. David killed bears and lions in private before he defeated Goliath. When men can win private battles, God allows them to win public battles.

Several years ago there was a great woman minister who was destined, I believe, to be one of the most outstanding ministers in the nation. I often wondered why she never received national recognition. After years of marriage, she fell into adultery, lost her husband, and, for several years, her ministry. What if she had been well known? The devastation within the body of Christ would have been great. God restrained her from becoming internationally known to avoid another tragedy in the body of Christ. In recent years there have been far too many public examples of Christian leaders who have failed to win their private battles, causing much spiritual upheaval in the body of Christ. Success can make or break a person. So God desires to build character in the minister before He builds the ministry.

Are you becoming weary, thinking, "God is never going to use me"? Do you wonder why your gift has not been noticed? Are you sitting around waiting for a big door to open, or are you willing to do little things that no one notices? Are you willing to clean up the church after a service? Will you clean the bathrooms and sweep the sidewalk? Do you love God's house? Do you love God's people? Can you feel their needs and their hurts? God opens big doors when we are ready. If the big door has not opened, it may be because you are not as ready as you think!

2. God uses people to give into your bosom.

We discussed earlier the spiritual principle that "men shall give into your bosom." The Bible says that Jesus found favor both with God and with man! God has always used men to bless men. The source is the Lord, but the method He uses to channel these blessings is men.

When a person is first called into the ministry, there are few churches that desire to use them. Since he or she has little ministry experience, ministers are hesitant to use a person whom they may not know. I used to say, "How can I get the experience if they never use me?" This is where total dependency upon God comes in. If I am called of God, then *God* will open the door, and He will speak to people to do it.

Early in our ministry we began having revivals that continued for several weeks. Soon word spread, and pastors were calling and requesting that I come to their church and lead a revival. Not all the revivals were effective, but God moved upon men to give us a door of utterance for ministry. God can give you favor at work or on the job. He can speak to men and women to help open the door.

3. Not all open doors are from God.

God gives a person a vision. In order to distract you, Satan often brings another vision. Anything with two visions is division. A God-called evangelist should never try to pastor, and a pastor should never try to evangelize. Each person has their gift and calling. Often a person will *prophesy* (or proph-a-lie) over another person and declare the will of God for him or her. Often people rely more on the words of a prophecy than they do on the instruction given by the Bible. I have met scores of people whose lives have been shattered and their families ruined because of a personal prophecy. A true personal word will agree with and confirm what the Lord has already shown you.

When pressure is on, some desire to escape by discovering God's will somewhere else. Therefore, when another apparent door is opened, some assume this is God's direction. Pastors change churches because there is contention in their congregation. They move only to discover the same problems are waiting for them at the new church. The reason—people are people, sheep are sheep, and sheep always leave dung in the field.

4. There is a *kingdom connection* looking for you.

God allows people to bless people. The Bible says, "Men shall give into your bosom" (Luke 6:38, KJV). Pastors open their churches and invite evangelists to speak. Thriving businesses are dependent upon customers. Someone, somewhere has an answer that you have been praying for. Out there somewhere is the person who holds the solution to your situation. God connects people—Elijah and Elisha, Paul and Timothy, Elisha and the widow woman. God connects people together. My friend Jentezen Franklin calls these persons *kingdom connections.*

In ages past God has used widows to feed hungry prophets (1 Kings 17). During Christ's earthly tenure, God used several women with wealthy husbands to help finance his ministry (Luke 8:1–3). Boaz was the miracle connection for two lonely widows who needed a financial and material breakthrough in their lives. There are thousands of Ruths in the church who are looking for a Boaz, and thousands of Boazes looking for Ruths. This is why you must be in the right place at the right time and connected with the right people at the right season.

5. The timing of God reveals the plan of God.

You must be at the right place at the right time for the plan of God to be revealed to you. Timing may be the greatest key to the fulfilling of God's purposes.

You may not be ready for the very things you are praying about. God has a perfect timing to launch your ministry and to bless your business and family. Our ministry has been through six buildings over the past fifteen years. We have grown from one room in a small apartment to a new 25,000-square-foot ministry center. Each time we ran out of room I would go out looking for another place. I would always become frustrated, unable to find what we needed. When I released my plans and turned them over to God, within a few days the unexpected always happened and we found the perfect place.

If Ruth and Naomi had not come to Bethlehem at *harvesttime,* they would have missed every blessing in the present and would not have fulfilled their destiny. If Ruth's destiny had not been fulfilled, God's perfect plan for Israel's future would have been interrupted.

6. Obedience releases the blessing.

Obedience is simply *doing the Word of God.* James said, "Faith without works is dead" (James 2:26). We would say, "Faith without corresponding action is dead." Your actions should correspond with what you believe.

Jesus often *required action* before He actually healed a person. He would say, "Go show yourself to the priest," or "Rise, take up your bed and walk," or "Stretch forth thy hand." When we act upon what we believe, it is visible evidence that we actually believe. When a group of men tore off a roof and lowered a paralyzed man into the living room of a house where Jesus ministered, the Bible says, "Jesus *saw* their faith" (Matt. 9:2, emphasis added). God can see your faith. He sees your faith when you act upon His Word. This is very true in relation to giving. When a minister receives tithes and offerings, what do you hear, and what is your reaction?

- "All he wants is my money."
- "I wish he would hurry up so we could get on with church."
- "All preachers do is beg for finances."
- "Now is my opportunity to sow my seed and reap a harvest."

Can you imagine a farmer looking at the cold, dark ground saying: "All that ground wants is my seed." "I'll just pass over this ground so I can get to my barn." "All people want from farmers is food."

If all you ever hear is *money* when the offerings are received, then you need to clean out your ears. It is all about *obedience*! Salvation comes through obedience; healing comes through obedience. In fact, *all* spiritual blessings come through obedience to God. If you are waiting for a giant door to open, think again. Little doors open first, then after you walk through them, there will be more open doors. Ruth had to listen to the words of Boaz and obey them in order to obtain the blessing.

7. A rhythm of blessing follows favor and obedience.

After years of faithfulness in your field of labor, there is a rhythm of blessing that you can encounter. Often you feel you are always planting seed or giving of yourself. Often the ultimate breakthrough seems impossible. Don't be discouraged. In the Bible, a Shunammite woman, after years of struggle, finally tapped into the rhythm of blessing. She and her husband prepared a chamber for the prophet Elisha to spend the night as he traveled from "revival to revival" (2 Kings 4:8–10). As a result, she received five major miracles in her life.

- Though she was barren, God have her a son (2 Kings 4:14–17).

- Her son died, but God raised him from the dead (2 Kings 4:20–37).

- She was warned of a seven-year famine and was protected from the devastation caused by the famine (2 Kings 8:1–2).

- She stood before the king seven years later to plead for her land, and the king returned her property back to her (2 Kings 8:5–6).

- She was given all the fruit of the field for a total of seven years (2 Kings 8:6).

I believe these blessings followed her because she prepared a place for the prophet of God. She "sought first the kingdom of God," and as a result, many "things were added unto her."

There will come a time, as you are obedient to all the Lord commands you to do, that you will begin to see small doors open and little breakthroughs occur. You must never criticize someone else's breakthrough or financial blessing because you don't know what they have had to sow in order to receive those blessings.

I have met people who were worth millions of dollars. Some of these people relate how badly others envy them and become critical of them. Yet when I hear their stories, I realize that those critical people are probably not willing to be as obedient as these people have been. Some of these blessed people started out with nothing. Some were living in their cars or in a small dilapidated house. But because of their obedience and their sacrificial giving, God gave them a breakthrough in their finances. Their gift to the church is the gift of giving. Remember, everyone starts in a corner. It may be a small church, a small ministry, a small business, or a small checking account, but as you draw close to your Boaz (Jesus), and as you obey Him, He sends great favor and blessing into your life.

IN CLOSING

The principles you have learned in this book will help you to open the gates of heaven. God has incredible blessings for His children, and as you follow the principles in this book, you will experience the flow of His blessings from heaven to you.

Here are some simple keys to keeping the windows of heaven open:

1. *Search yourself before you pray.* Pray a purity prayer as you begin, asking God to forgive you of any offenses and to enable you to keep the channel of blessing open in your life.

2. *Search the Scriptures.* Find a promise in God's Word that speaks to the specific need you are presenting to God. Lock into that promise with your faith, reminding God not only of His promise but also of the covenant He has established with you.

3. *Search the will of God.* It does little good to pray for something that is outside of the will of God. Remember God's Word that says: "Ye ask, and receive not, because ye ask amiss, that ye may consume it upon your lusts" (James 4:3, KJV).

4. *Search your own spirit.* Pray in the Spirit when you do not know what to pray for in your own heart. What are God's issues related to your request? How does He feel about this situation?

5. *Be spontaneous.* You don't have to pray in King James English! Let your prayer arise out of your spirit and heart—not from a piece of paper where you have listed your needs.

6. *Be specific.* I cannot overemphasize the importance of this key. When you are praying for your child, say, "Father, here is [name]. This is my child, who is [age] years of age. He needs [state specific need]." I often have people calling my ministry office to order a tape. Someone may say, "Please send me the tape on *mystery*." I have 250 tapes with the word *mystery* in them. What is the specific tape they want to order? Remember this practical principle, because it mirrors a great spiritual principle: the person who states the specific tape they are ordering will get his or her tape far quicker than the person who does not ask specifically!

7. *Be sincere.* Have a pure motive for your prayer. Do not come before God with a proud, boastful, or arrogant spirit.

8. *Be energetic.* "The effective, fervent prayer of a righteous man avails much" (James 5:16). Pray with energy and fire. Pray with the anointing of God.

9. *Be steadfast.* Pray without ceasing. Pray when you are driving to work, walking in the neighborhood, or taking a shower. Pray continually. Pray without wavering.

These simple keys will help you to keep the heavens open over your head. When you pray and don't feel anything happening, remember to thank God that He is hearing your prayer. He wants you to pray by faith.

Thank God for the answer to your prayer—no matter what that answer is. Thank Him even when you don't understand the answer. Remember that God knows and understands things that we will never understand until we reach heaven. We pray the Word and the will of God. He knows what He has in mind for our lives, and He may open His gates and pour out blessings that we will not fully understand until sometime down the road.

Begin today to follow the principles in this book, and you will experience an increase of the blessings of God in your life!

I have penned in this book numerous scriptural insights, keys, and practical examples that have been tested and proven and can be applied in every situation of life. As you learn and follow these truths, it can lead to a life of intimacy with God, confidence in your prayer life, and enjoying answers to your prayer. The blessings of favor will follow, which leads to a more abundant life in Christ.

JOURNALING SECTION

Use these pages to record what you are learning about how to interpret your dreams and visions.

NOTES

CHAPTER 1
THE MAN WHO SAW THE GATE OF HEAVEN

1. NASA.gov, "Image of the Day Gallery: Majestic Disk of Stars," http://www.nasa.gov/multimedia/imagegallery/image_feature_1867 .html (accessed October 10, 2011).

2. J. Berg, J. Tymoczko, and L. Stryer, *Biochemistry* (n.p.: W. H. Freeman and Company, 2002), referenced in Wikipedia.org, s.v. "DNA," http://en.wikipedia.org/wiki/DNA (accessed October 10, 2011).

3. Text for the Book of Jasher may be accessed on the Internet at Christian Classics Ethereal Library, http://www.ccel.org/a/ anonymous/jasher/1.htm (accessed October 10, 2011).

4. Joshua Trachtenberg, "Twelve Gems and Their Magical Qualities," *Jewish Heritage Online Magazine*, http://jhom.com/topics/ stones/gems.html (accessed October 10, 2011). Various sources are available online to show this link of the emerald stone to the tribe of Judah. Other sources link the emerald to other tribes or link the tribe of Judah to other stones.

5. Hebrews4Christians.com, "Ten Commandments: Torah and Mishrah on Aseret Hadiberot," http://www.hebrew4christians.com/ Scripture/Torah/Ten_Cmds/ten_cmds.html (accessed October 10, 2011).

6. This information was obtained during discussion with Wayne Penn, laser researcher and developer, who serves on the Board of Directors for the Voice of Evangelism.

CHAPTER 2
THE FIVE GATES OF THE HOLY SPIRIT

1. Meir Ben-Dov, *In the Shadow of the Temple* (New York: HarperCollins, 1985), 88.

2. *The Mishnah*, trans. Herbert Danby (New York: Oxford University Press, 1933), "The tractate Middot, Chapters 21–23, 28–29, composed c. 100 C.E.," http://homepages.luc.edu/~avande1/jerusalem/sources/middot.htm (accessed October 10, 2011).

3. Moshe Chaim Luzzatto, "Secrets of the Future Temple," Azamra.org, http://www.azamra.org/TempleSecrets/Mount.htm (accessed October 10, 2011).

4. Antonio L. Mitchell, "Biblical Meaning of Numbers," Christian Resources Today, www.christian-resources-today.com/biblical-meaning-of-numbers.html (accessed October 10, 2011).

5. TempleInstitute.org, "A Day in the Holy Temple," http://www.templeinstitute.org/day_in_life/24_shifts.htm (accessed October 11, 2011).

6. Studies are from W. E. Vine, *Vine's Expository Dictionary of New Testament Words* (Minneapolis, MN: Bethany House, 1984).

CHAPTER 3
PRAYER TYPES AND SECRETS

1. Nissan Mindel, "The Meaning of Prayer," Chabad.org, http://www.chabad.org/library/article_cdo/aid/682090/jewish/The-Meaning-of-Prayer.htm (accessed October 11, 2011).

2. Ibid.

3. For more information about the temple incense, you may want to order my teaching on "Temple Secrets" from my website, www.voe.org.

4. John Lightfoot, "Exercitations Upon the Evangelist St. Luke, Chapter 1," in *A Commentary on the New Testament From the*

Talmud and Hebraica, Philologos.org, http://philologos.org/__eb-jl/ luke01.htm (accessed October 11, 2011).

5. This information came from one of the main students at the Temple Institute in Jerusalem in 1989 when I was hosting a tour group.

6. The Temple Institute, "Incense," http://www.templeinstitute.org/ incense.htm (accessed October 11, 2011).

7. John A. Tvedtnes, "Temple Prayer in Ancient Times," Neal A. Maxwell Institute for Religious Scholarship, http://maxwellinstitute .byu.edu/publications/books/?bookid=21&chapid=105 (accessed October 11, 2011).

8. This information was obtained during a crusade in Kenya with Pastor Don Matheny.

CHAPTER 4
SEVEN SPIRITUAL LAWS FOR ANSWERED PRAYER

1. Vine, *Vine's Expository Dictionary of New Testament Words*, s.v. "*metron*."

2. Ibid., s.v. "wavering."

3. Rick Renner, *Sparkling Gems From the Greek* (Tulsa, OK: Teach All Nations, 2003). This book can be purchased from: Teach All Nations, P. O. Box 702040, Tulsa, OK 74170-2040.

4. Harold L. Wilmington, *Wilmington's Guide to the Bible* (Wheaton, IL: Tyndale House, 1981), 13.

5. Ibid., 14.

6. Ibid.

CHAPTER 5
WHO CLOSED THE HEAVENS OVER MY HEAD?

1. This information is from public and historical information about Oral Roberts following the death of his daughter.

Chapter 6
Praying Through the Battle of the Firstborn

1. Kristine Cassady, "What Was the Birthright?" Academy of Shem, General Topics post, Noahide Nations, http://noahidenations .com/education-and-training-/204-what-was-the-birthright (accessed October 13, 2011).

2. *Adam Clarke's Commentary*, electronic database, PCStudy Bible, copyright © 1996 by Biblesoft, s.v. "Exodus 1:16."

3. Flavius Josephus, Antiquities of the Jews, book 2, chapter 9, viewed at Sacred-Texts.com, http://www.sacred-texts.com/jud/ josephus/ant-2.htm (accessed October 13, 2011).

4. Ibid., book 15, viewed at Sacred-Texts.com, http://www.sacred -texts.com/jud/josephus/ant-15.htm (accessed October 13, 2011).

5. Barbara Kreiger, "Finding King Herod's Tomb," *Smithsonian*, August 2009, http://www.smithsonianmag.com/history-archaeology/ Finding-Herods-Tomb.html (accessed October 13, 2011).

Chapter 7
Miracle Prayers—Making the Impossible Possible

1. Vine, *Vine's Expository Dictionary of New Testament Words*, s.v. "*soteria*."

2. Renner, *Sparkling Gems From the Greek*, 73.

3. Vine, *Vine's Expository Dictionary of New Testament Words*, s.v. "*battologeo*."

4. Ibid., s.v. "*soudarion*."

Chapter 8
Praying in Whose Name—Jesus or Yeshua?

1. Perry Stone, *Mystery of the Priesthood and the Blood* (Cleveland, TN: Voice of Evangelism, n.d.), 124–125. Research for this was

compiled by Marcus Hand, former editor of the Church of God *Lighted Pathway.*

CHAPTER 9
WHAT TO DO WHEN YOU DON'T KNOW HOW TO PRAY

1. Justin Martyr, *Ante-Nicene Fathers*, vol. 1, as quoted in Early Christian Dictionary, "Gifts of the Holy Spirit," http://www .earlychristiandictionary.com/GiftsHolySpirit.html (accessed October 14, 2011).

2. Irenaeus, *Adversus Haereses* 5.6.1, as quoted in Early Church Texts, "Irenaeus on Humanity and the Image and Likeness of God—Latin and Greek Text With English Translation," http:// earlychurchtexts.com/public/image_and_likeness.htm (accessed October 14, 2011).

3. Novatian, "A Treatise of Novatian Concerning the Trinity," *Ante-Nicene Fathers*, vol. 5, as quoted in Sacred Texts, http://www .sacred-texts.com/chr/ecf/005/0050138.htm (accessed October 14, 2011).

4. Tertullian, *The Five Books Against Marcion*, book 1, chapter 8, Northwestern Theological Seminary library, http://www.ntslibrary .com/PDF%20Books/TERTULLIAN%20Five%20Books%20 Against%20Marcion.pdf (accessed October 14, 2011).

5. Robert Sungenis, "Speaking in Tongues, a Historical, Psychological, and Biblical Anaylsis," view at Love4theWord.org, http://love4theword.org/tongues.htm (accessed October 14, 2011).

6. John Greenfield, *When the Spirit Came* (Minneapolis, MN: Bethany, 1967), 15, 24, 60, as referenced in "The Moravians," http:// ultimatecore.net/Vision/ChurchHistory/THE%20MORAVIANS .htm (accessed October 14, 2011).

7. Michael Pollock Hamilton, *The Charismatic Movement* (Grand Rapids, MI: William B. Eerdmans Publishing Company, 1975), 75.

8. Edward Burrough, "Epistle to the Reader," in George Fox, *The Great Mystery of the Great Whore Unfolded, and Antichrist's Kingdom, The Works of George Fox*, vol. 3 (New York: Isaac T. Hopper, 1831), 13, viewed at Google Books, http://books.google.com/books?id=OUBUXRr-y-4C&printsec=frontcover#v=onepage&q&f=false (accessed October 14, 2011).

9. Edward Irving, "Facts Connected With Recent Manifestations of Spiritual Gifts," *Frasers Magazine*, January 1834, referenced in Webster's Online Dictionary, "Extended Definition: Glossolalia," http://www.websters-online-dictionary.org/definitions/glossolalia (accessed October 14, 2011).

10. Charles W. Conn, *Like a Mighty Army* (Cleveland, TN: Pathway Press, 1955).

11. For more information about dreams and visions, see my book *How to Interpret Dreams and Visions* (Lake Mary, FL: Charisma House, 2011).

Chapter 10
Twelve Significant and Effective Insights My Dad Taught Me About Prayer

1. Vine, *Vine's Expository Dictionary of New Testament Words*, s.v. "without ceasing."

2. Ibid., s.v. "amen."

3. Biblesoft's *New Exhaustive Strong's Numbers and Concordance With Expanded Greek-Hebrew Dictionary*, copyright © 1994, Biblesoft and International Bible Translators, Inc., s.v. "*halal*."

4. Renner, *Sparkling Gems From the Greek*, 569.

5. Vine, *Vine's Expository Dictionary of New Testament Words*, s.v. "*tupos*."

CHAPTER 11
THE POWER OF MEDITATING UPON THE LORD

1. Biblesoft's *New Exhaustive Strong's Numbers and Concordance With Expanded Greek-Hebrew Dictionary*, s.v. *"siyach"* and *"hagah."*

CHAPTER 12
RELEASING THE ANGEL OF BLESSING

1. Biblesoft's *New Exhaustive Strong's Numbers and Concordance With Expanded Greek-Hebrew Dictionary*, s.v. *"parakupto"* and *"eis."*

2. Cecil Roth, ed., *The Encyclopedia Judaica*, vol. 6 (New York: Coronet Books, Inc., 1994), 690.

3. Rabbi Daniel Yaakov Travis, *Days of Majesty* (New York: Feldheim Publishers, 2003).

4. Ibid.

CHAPTER 13
WHEN THE JOSEPH RING IS PLACED ON YOUR FINGER

1. Antique Jewelry University, "Signet Ring," http://www .langantiques.com/university/index.php/Signet_Ring (accessed October 18, 2011).

CHAPTER 15
USING THE POWER OF THE SEED

1. University of Illionis Extension, "Apples and More: Apple Facts," http://urbanext.illinois.edu/apples/facts.cfm (accessed October 20, 2011).

2. Ibid.

3. Adherents.com, "Major Religions of the World Ranked by Number of Adherents," http://www.adherents.com/Religions_By _Adherents.html (accessed October 20, 2011).